NEW DIMENSIONS IN PSYCHIATRY:
A WORLD VIEW

NEW DIMENSIONS
IN PSYCHIATRY:

A WORLD VIEW

Silvano Arieti, M.D. *and*
Gerard Chrzanowski, M.D.

A Wiley-Interscience Publication

JOHN WILEY & SONS   New York   •   London   •   Sydney   •   Toronto

Library of Congress Cataloging in Publication Data:

Arieti, Silvano.
　New dimensions in psychiatry: a world view
　Includes bibliographies.
　1. Psychiatry.　2. Psychotherapy.　I. Chrzanowski,
Gerard, joint author.　II. Title.　[DNLM: 1. Psychia-
try—Essays.　2. Psychotherapy—Essays.　WM100 A698w]

RC454.A68　　616.8′9　　74-16150
ISBN 0-471-03317-0

Printed in the United States of America

10 9 8 7 6 5 4 3 2 1

AUTHORS

Australia

G. Allen German M.B., Ch.B., D.P.M., F.R.C.P.E., F.R.C. Psych., Professor of Psychiatry, University of Western Australia

India

D. R. Doongaji Honorary Associate Psychiatrist and Honorary Associate Professor in Psychiatry, K. E. M. Hospital and Seth G. S. Medical College, Bombay

D. V. Jeste Honorary Assistant Psychiatrist and Honorary Assistant Professor in Psychiatry, K. E. M. Hospital and Seth G. S. Medical College, Bombay

N. S. Vahia Head, Psychiatric Department, Honorary Psychiatrist and Honorary Professor in Psychiatry, K. E. M. Hospital and Seth G. S. Medical College, Bombay

Israel

Pinchas Noy, M.D. Jerusalem

Italy

Aldo Giannini, M.D. Professor and Chairman, Department of Psychiatry, Medical School, Sassari

Guilia Del Carlo-Giannini, M.D. Chief, Department of Infantile Psychiatry, Luria

Germany

Hanscarl Leuner, M.D. Professor of Psychiatry, Visiting Professor, Yale University 1966, Director, Psychotherapeutic Division, Psychiatric Hospital, University of Goettingen, Goettingen

N. Matussek Psychiatrische Klinik der Universität München Neurochemisches Laboratorium, München

Hans Molinski Department of Obstetrics and Gynecology, Dusseldorf University, Dusseldorf

Anton Schelkopf Ph.D. Secretary for the Federation of International Psychoanalytic Societies

Great Britain

Desmond Kelly M.D., M.R.C.P., M.R.C. Psych., Consultant Psychiatrist, St. George's Hospital Medical School, Atkinson Morley's Hospital, London

Japan

Akihisa Kondo Psychiatrist, Tokyo

Soviet Union

I. L. Akopova Institute of Psychiatry, U.S.S.R. Academy of Medical Sciences, Moscow

L. I. Golovan Institute of Psychiatry, U.S.S.R. Academy of Medical Sciences, Moscow

I. A. Kozlova Institute of Psychiatry, U.S.S.R. Academy of Medical Sciences, Moscow

L. K. Lobova Institute of Psychiatry, U.S.S.R. Academy of Medical Sciences, Moscow

V. D. Moskalenko Institute of Psychiatry, U.S.S.R. Academy of Medical Sciences, Moscow

M. L. Rokhlina Institute of Psychiatry, U.S.S.R. Academy of Medical Sciences

G. M. Rudenko Institute of Psychiatry, U.S.S.R. Academy of Medical Sciences, Moscow

I. V. Shakhmatova-Pavlova Institute of Psychiatry, U.S.S.R. Academy of Medical Sciences, Moscow

V. L. Shenderova Institute of Psychiatry, U.S.S.R. Academy of Medical Sciences, Moscow

T. M. Siryachenko Institute of Psychiatry, U.S.S.R. Academy of Medical Sciences, Moscow

United States

Richard Abrams, M.D. Associate Professor of Psychiatry, Director, University Psychiatric Service, Department of Psychiatry and Behavioral Science, State University of New York at Stony Brook, Stony Brook, New York

Marc Aronson, B.A. Research Assistant, Department of Psychiatry, College of Physicians and Surgeons, Columbia University, New York, New York

A. A. Bridger, M.D. Instructor, Department of Psychiatry, College of Physicians and Surgeons, Columbia University, New York, New York

Henry Brill, M.D. Director, Pilgrim State Hospital, West Brentwood, New York; Clinical Professor of Psychiatry, Downstate Medical Center, Stony Brook, New York

Patricia Carrington, Ph.D. Lecturer, Department of Psychology, Princeton University, Princeton, New Jersey

Gerard Chrzanowski, M.D. Associate Professor of Clinical Psychiatry, New York Medical College; Training and Supervisory Analyst, William Alanson White Institute of Psychiatry, Psychoanalysis, and Psychology, New York, New York

Harmon S. Ephron, M.D. Clinical Professor of Psychiatry, New Jersey College of Medicine and Dentistry, Piscataway, New Jersey

Ronald R. Fieve, M.D. Chief of Psychiatric Research, Lithium Clinic and Metabolic Unit; Professor of Clinical Psychiatry, Columbia University, New York, New York

Joseph L. Fleiss, Ph.D. Associate Research Scientist, Biometrics Research Unit, New York State Department of Mental Hygiene, New York, New York

Viktor E. Frankl, M.D. Ph.D., Professor of Neurology and Psychiatry, University of Vienna Medical School; Professor of Logotherapy, United States International University at San Diego, San Diego, California

Otto F. Kernberg, M.D. Director, General Clinical Service, New York State Psychiatric Institute, Professor of Clinical Psychiatry, College of Physicians and Surgeons, Columbia University, New York, New York

Nathan S. Kline, M.D. Clinical Professor of Psychiatry, Columbia College of Physicians and Surgeons, New York, New York; Director of Research, Rockland State Hospital, Orangeburg, New York

Baron Shopsin, M.D. Clinical Associate Professor of Psychiatry, New York University School of Medicine; Chief, Unit for the Study and Treatment of Affective Disorders, New York University-Bellevue Hospital Center, New York, New York

Herbert Spiegel, M.D. Associate Clinical Professor, Department of Psychiatry, College of Physicians and Surgeons, Columbia, University, New York, New York

PREFACE

The present volume is not a usual textbook or a collection of papers on a single theme. It is a new venture that aims to supply psychiatrists and professionals working in related fields with important but not easily accessible information. Some very pertinent psychiatric knowledge may be hard to find because it is very new and not yet integrated in the standard textbooks of psychiatry; or it may be originated in foreign countries and written in languages not commonly known. It may have a daring or exotic quality, not easily accepted in the Western World.

Psychiatry has steadily expanded its horizons and has come to encircle a broad spectrum of disciplines. At the same time, psychiatric research and practice have reached out beyond narrow, national boundaries. There is a wealth of contributions to the field the world over that provide novel, unusual, and unfamiliar parameters. For most professionals it has become increasingly difficult to keep track of contributions not ordinarily or not quickly enough presented in the psychiatric mainstream. The conscientious clinician, who does not want to be caught by surprise by what has escaped his reach, the therapist who wishes to be up to date with the latest progress in the established forms of treatment, the researcher who seeks new dimensions, need an international medium that will fulfill these requirements. We hope to provide such a medium by initiating a new series of volumes, published at two-year intervals. This series follows one initiated by one of us and published by Basic Books under the title "The World Biennial of Psychiatry and Psychotherapy." This new series, of which the present volume is the first, has been envisioned and organized with broader scope and goals. There are two editors, and the editorial board has been expanded. In the present volume the United States is still the country with a larger representation, but the contributions of authors from abroad distinctly outnumber American contributors. Authors from nine countries have participated. The papers have been divided into four parts: the first dealing with the newest advances in the established somatic methods of treatment, the second with progress made in psychotherapy and hospital psychiatry, the third with new or not widely known forms of psychotherapy, and the fourth with clinical studies covering different areas of psychiatric knowledge. The different chapters will have different relevance for various readers, in accordance with their predominant interest. Hopefully there will be something relevant for any concerned worker in the large fields of mental health and human behavior.

SILVANO ARIETI, M.D.

GERARD CHRZANOWSKI, M.D.

December 1974
New York, New York

CONTENTS

CHAPTER ONE

NEW DEVELOPMENTS IN
MANIC-DEPRESSIVE ILLNESS

RONALD R. FIEVE, M.D.

NEW PERSPECTIVES ON AN OLD PROBLEM

Possibly the most exciting single development in psychiatry in recent decades, and certainly one of the most significant, is the spectacular success of lithium treatment in manic-depressive illness.

Most current double-blind controlled studies indicate that lithium is by far the most effective treatment for control of the acute manic phase in clear-cut bipolar manic-depressive illness, and for prophylaxis of subsequent episodes of both mania and depression.[1, 3, 28, 11, 35] Moreover several double-blind controlled studies have shown that some unipolar recurrent depressed patients may also have a significant prophylactic response to lithium.[1, 3, 28]

One of the most extensive programs of long-term interdisciplinary research on lithium therapy and prophylaxis is being conducted at the New York State Psychiatric Institute and Columbia Presbyterian Medical Center in New York City. These investigations have amassed evidence in years of research with more than a thousand patients. The findings, strongly supported by other studies, clearly define lithium as the drug of choice in the treatment and prevention not only of most manic-depressive disorders, but even of some forms of recurrent depression.

Indeed, on the basis of almost all studies in the recent literature, lithium can appropriately be called the first truly prophylactic agent available in psychiatry, since it not only calms manic states in 80 to 85% of patients, but also prevents recurrences of both mania and depression in most of them.[8]

Until recently, electroconvulsive therapy was still the most effective treatment for many patients with severe depressions. The advent of lithium therapy has in large measure obviated the use of electroshock, except for the acute assaultive manic patient or the suicidally depressed patient—and even in such patients, electroshock therapy is needed only for a brief period before the patient begins to respond to lithium.

These developments are radically and permanently altering the psychiatric approach to the treatment of manic-depressive illness. Many manic-depressives who would formerly have required hospitalization can now be treated successfully as outpatients.

Furthermore the effectiveness of lithium in manic depression has had a stimulating impact on genetic and biochemical research in affective disorders. As a result of such research, the outlook is bright for further new developments that may soon improve the diagnosis, treatment, and prognosis of these afflictions. Some of these developments, such as the emergence of genetic, biological, and biochemical criteria for improved classification and differential diagnosis of affective disorders, seem to be near at hand.

Though it is technically correct to hail the therapeutic and prophylactic effectiveness of lithium as a dramatic "breakthrough" of the 1970s, this concept obscures certain important facts about lithium: It is an ancient remedy long forgotten, not a new chemical compound or discovery. Its salts are inexpensive and widely available. They abound in rocks and soils and waters of the earth, and some ancient peoples valued the healing powers of certain mineral springs many centuries before lithium was associated with the physical and mental effects of these springs.

Available on the American market for treatment of mania only since 1970, this "new" drug was unwittingly prescribed for manic depression at least 1500 years ago. In the Greek and Roman tent hospitals of the fifth century, a physician named Aurelianus was prescribing treatment with alkaline water from mineral springs for manic insanity and melancholia, and for other physical and mental illnesses. Today some of these springs are known to contain large quantities of lithium.

The wonder, then, is not that lithium is today revolutionizing the treatment of manic depression. The wonder is that recognition of lithium's value for this purpose has taken so long to come and is spreading so slowly—at a leisurely pace of introduction that reflects the traditionally slow tempo of change in medical practice rather than the needs of the millions of manic-depressive patients whose lives could be changed by lithium therapy and prophylaxis.

For a clearer perspective of the current management of manic-depressive illness, and of the changes at hand and on the horizon, it is helpful to review some of the factors related both to the delayed recognition (or rediscovery) of lithium's therapeutic value, and to the urgent need that effective pharmacotherapy has created for improved classification and diagnosis.

The tardiness of the "discovery" of lithium is due in part to the paucity of our knowledge of the brain. Though we know much about the brain's anatomy and ultrastructure, our understanding of how it functions and dysfunctions is still primitive. Hallucinogenic and mood-changing drugs have been used since prehistory, and psychoactive agents have been used therapeutically since the 1950s; yet despite many hypothetical assumptions, we still cannot explain completely how or why any of these drugs work. The effectiveness of electroconvulsive shock, which has continued to be the best treatment for many patients with severe depressions, was almost a total mystery until recent biochemical research provided some clues to its action.

Evidence accumulating over many centuries has long pointed toward biochemical involvements in the pathophysiology of affective disorders. But among many physicians the belief persisted far into the twentieth century that chemistry could offer no significant help in the treatment of these disorders, including manic depression.

This belief reflects the fairly general lack of knowledge of practicing physicians about affective illness. Most physicians, including many psychiatrists, still do not understand the nature of manic-depressive illness, how to diagnose it, how to differentiate it from schizophrenia, how to treat it, and so on. And against this background ranging from simple ignorance to sophisticated confusion, many physicians simply deny the effectiveness of drug therapy and the validity of documentation supporting it, and decline to try to learn how to administer it correctly.

Historical and economic factors have also played an important role in retarding the use of lithium for manic depression.

Soon after lithium was identified in 1817, it was observed that lithium salts could dissolve urate deposits, and they became widely used for renal calculi, gout, and other physical diseases. Early in this century more effective remedies were found for those ailments, and lithium bromide came into brief use as an antiepileptic agent.

In the late 1940s lithium chloride became a popular salt substitute for patients on sodium-free diets. It was not yet known that lithium can be toxic to persons with heart or kidney disease; by the time this was discovered, four deaths and many serious but nonfatal poisonings caused lithium to be taken off the market in the United States. This was in 1949—the same year, by a strange coincidence, that Australian psychiatrist John Cade discovered the therapeutic effectiveness of lithium against mania.

Even though pharmacological research and extensive double-blind clinical studies in several countries confirmed Cade's findings, lithium remained in disrepute in America for another 20 years. Not until 1970 was it released by the United States Food and Drug Administration, and then specifically for the treatment of mania.[7]

Another important factor in the unhurried pace at which lithium is being brought to the attention of the medical community in America (and perhaps elsewhere) is purely economic. This factor is the indifference of the pharmaceutical industry, which cannot be expected to work up much enthusiasm for a simple, abundantly available salt that is nonpatentable and offers no proprietary benefits.

Notwithstanding all these factors that have been operating to confuse the picture of lithium's therapeutic value and to delay its acceptance in psychiatric practice, only 3 years after its release in the United States more than 30,000 manic-depressive patients are being treated with lithium, and many are being maintained prophylactically by regular administration, with monthly monitoring of lithium blood levels to prevent toxic effects.[8]

Yet this is only a minute fraction of the estimated number of people in the United States who could benefit from lithium therapy. Surveys have indicated that the estimated number of manic depressives and recurrent unipolar depressives in the United States alone is between 6 and 8 million.[25]

In terms of the well-documented 80 to 85% success of lithium therapy in such patients, this suggests that in America alone the lives of millions of people could be improved, in many cases greatly. On a worldwide scale, what an enormous gain this could mean in conservation of human energy and productivity, and in reduction of the vast social and economic cost of maintaining many large institutions that could be reduced in size or shut down completely!

Apart from the established clinical effectiveness of lithium in mania and of lithium and other drugs in depressions, another aspect of the use of these drugs is a radical improvement in the prospect for improved diagnosis, treatment, and prophylaxis of affective disorders.

Among the factors that are contributing significantly to the new perspectives on affective illnesses in general and on manic-depressive illness in particular, are the outgrowth of an improved system of classification of affective disorders; the emergence of genetic and biochemical criteria that may soon facilitate more accurate differential diagnosis and more reliable predictability of response to various therapeutic modalities; the discovery of X-linked genetic transmission of the predisposition for manic-depressive illness; enzyme and electrolyte studies that are providing new insights into neuronal mechanisms involved in affective disorders; and a new hypothesis of neuronal mechanisms that may not only help to explain the effectiveness of lithium, but also open new avenues of research into the understanding and treatment of mental illnesses.

CLASSIFICATION AND DIAGNOSIS

To appreciate the magnitude of the problem of classification and diagnosis of affective disorders, especially depressions, one must dwell for a moment on its purely statistical aspects.

According to a letter from the Biometry Branch of the National Institute of Mental Health (United States Department of Health, Education and Welfare), a recent survey found that 15% of American adults between 18 and 75 suffer significant depressive symptoms in any given year. On the basis of the 1970 population of 132,000,000 adults 18 or over, this gives an estimate of more than 19,000,000 Americans who are significantly depressed at some time during the year.[25] The letter continues:

> The only data we have available is patients under care in psychiatric facilities (including all inpatient and outpatient clinics). If we assume that the same proportion of depressives exists in the population as in the facilities, we can use the following breakdown: Approximately 19% are

manic, 10% psychotic depressions and 71% psychoneurotic depressive disorders—or roughly, in millions: manic, 3.8; psychotic, 1.9; psychoneurotic, 14.1.

Bipolar manic-depressive illness together with recurrent unipolar depression occur in about 2 to 4% of the general population, preponderantly in females. The risk period is between the ages of 16 and 70, with peak incidence between 20 and 40. This means that between 4 and 8 million people suffer recurrent bouts of mania and depression, or depression alone, just in the United States.[8, 9]

Ironically, the victims of manic depression include many of the most gifted members of society—scientists, statesmen, teachers, business leaders, writers, and artists—highly creative people whose great spurts of manic energy have enabled them to climb to the top of their fields, only to plunge intermittently into frequent suicidal depression.[8]

Classification Presents Problems

The availability of effective drugs for depressions and manias, and the differing patterns of response to these drugs have dramatized the heterogeneity of affective disorders and the importance of differential diagnosis as a prelude to successful pharmacotherapy.

But this presents clinicians with an acute problem. Now that family physicians as well as psychiatrists can treat many depressives with drugs, they are more than ever before confronted with the inadequacy of many currently used systems for the classification of affective disorders. With few exceptions, these classification systems are based entirely on clinical signs, symptoms, and history, unsupported by biological criteria. This is a shaky foundation for the differentiation of many of these disorders.

The absence of genetic and biochemical criteria is not a matter of choice, since reliable and clinically useful biological criteria are not yet available; but the developing emergence of such criteria is one of the prospects brightening the horizon of current research. For the present, however, the absence of these criteria for differential diagnosis imposes a great burden of sophisticated guesswork on the physician, and emphasizes the urgent need for a better classification system.

Most of the classification systems in current use tend toward a dichotomous separation of all depressive disorders into two major classifications—bipolar and unipolar. The former tends to be a fairly homogeneous grouping of depressions, while the latter tends to lump together all or most of the remaining depressions in a single heterogeneous and undifferentiated subgroup. Recent research has emphasized the subtlety of pathophysiological differences between these disorders—indicating that no matter how similar depressions may appear to be, they may nevertheless constitute many separate and distinct entities with highly different patterns of response to various forms of therapy. Even when these subtypes are further subdivided, in the absence of specific biological criteria to distinguish one from another, there remains a considerable risk of misdiagnosis, leading to incorrect management and therapy.

As Goodwin et al. wrote in a recent report:[13]

> The classification of depressions on the basis of clinical phenomenology alone has clearly been inadequate, confused, and arbitrary. The classification of patients on the basis of differential response to drugs, as well as the use of genetic and biological criteria, should allow for the development of a classification system for the affective illnesses that would be more meaningful in terms of etiology, treatment, and prognosis.

One example of confusion in the classification of affective disorders is the tendency to underdiagnose depression in favor of schizophrenia. According to Winokur, affective disorders are at least three times as frequent in the general population as schizophrenia, which occurs in 1%.[37] Until recently, American psychiatrists were increasingly labeling any acute psychotic episode as schizophrenia, and a diagnosis of manic-depressive illness was relatively uncommon. Over 30% of so-called schizophrenics in state mental hospitals were found to be either unipolar depressives or bipolar manic depressives, in a recent study by Zubin and his colleagues at the New York State Department of Mental Hygiene and the Maudsley Hospital in London.[38]

By contrast, European psychiatrists, especially in England, have tended to label what we call schizophrenia as primary affective disorder—either recurrent depression or manic depression. The difference is critically important today, since lithium carbonate is known to be effective in the treatment and prophylaxis of manic-depressive illness and possibly in recurrent depression, but not in schizophrenia. Thus a unipolar or bipolar depressive patient who is mislabeled schizophrenic not only is likely to be denied effective therapy, but also is in danger of receiving wrong treatment and of being relegated to a possibly detrimental regimen because of the poor prognosis usually associated with schizophrenia.

Some improvement has resulted in recent years from the practice of classifying primary affective disorders into unipolar and bipolar types. Although this classification system is relatively new, the rationale for the unipolar-bipolar division is supported by studies of clinical, familial, pharmacological, and biological factors in depression.

The term primary affective disorder, also of recent origin, was adopted to classify depressions without regard to presumptive etiology, symptomatology, or age of onset. A primary affective disorder is an affective illness that occurs in a patient who has no other specifically defined psychiatric illness predating the onset of the affective disorder. If on the other hand a depression occurs during the course of a severe or life-threatening medical illness or in association with the administration of psychoactive drugs, it is classified as a secondary affective disorder.

Patients with primary affective disorders are classified as unipolar if they experience depression only, and bipolar if they have depressions with mania or hypomania. Thus it is possible to have bipolar manic-depressive illness (which includes bipolar mania and bipolar depression), unipolar depression, or (rarely) unipolar mania.[9]

A history of one or more depressions and one or more manias provides a clue to the diagnosis of manic-depressive illness. The sad mood of bipolar depression is usually associated with lack of energy and a shift in physiological functioning—either weight loss or gain, anorexia or increased appetite, insomnia or hypersomnia, crying spells, and definite curtailment of social, sexual, and vocational activities. There may also be suicidal thoughts or attempts.

Bipolar manic episodes are characterized by elation, talkativeness, high-flown ideas, many projects going at once, bursts of energy, increased libido, reduced need for sleep, and frequent displays of poor judgment. Manic patients feel well and do not believe they need treatment. They may cherish their euphoria and resist or thwart therapy.

Laced through the contrasting moods of mania and depression are certain elements of the opposite pole. For example, in mania there may be either euphoria or irritability, which is often labile, with short bursts of depressive affect, insomnia, increased sexual drive, and greater physical and mental activity. In depression, while the overall mood is one of sadness, with psychomotor sluggishness, at times there is increased physical activity (agitated depression).

A patient with a history of periodic highs and lows can be diagnosed as bipolar manic-depressive, provided (1) there are intervals of relatively normal mood and function (which may last from weeks to years) between episodes of depression and mania; and (2) the illness does not run a deteriorating course, and the patient is able to resume his normal status and function fairly well between episodes. When no normal intervals occur between the periodic cycles of mania and depression, the diagnosis is circular manic-depressive illness.

Under unipolar depression may be included four previously labeled types of depressive illness: neurotic, involutional, reactive psychotic, and endogenous psychotic. Primary unipolar depression is heterogeneous and covers a wide range of syndromes, the common characteristic of which is absence of significant prior medical or other psychiatric illness, including mania.

In the depressed phase, bipolar and unipolar depressions are indistinguishable, and the patient's history (and if possible his family's history) is needed to make the differential diagnosis. In unipolar recurrent depressive illness, the more depressive episodes have occurred with no instance of mania, the more certain is the unipolar diagnosis.

The duration of periods of mania and depression varies in both the bipolar and unipolar illnesses. Episodes may last from several weeks to 6 or more months, with depression usually persisting 2 to 6 months and mania 1 to 3 months.

Bipolar patients may be further separated into four subcategories based on severity of illness and on type of treatment received for manic or depressive symptoms:[9] Bipolar I, Bipolar II, Bipolar Other, and Cyclothymic Personality.

Bipolar I patients are those who have been hospitalized for a manic episode or who have required medical management at home for severe manic behavior. They may also have been treated or hospitalized for depression.

Bipolar II patients are those bipolar patients who have been hospitalized for depression or have required medical management at home for depressive behavior. In these patients the severity of manic symptoms has never led to hospitalization, although they may have received outpatient treatment for their manic or hypomanic symptoms. The Bipolar II classification includes patients whose hypomanic episodes may coincide with treatment and recovery from depression; thus a patient is considered Bipolar II and not unipolar if clear hypomanic periods are induced by drug or electroconvulsive therapy for depression.

Bipolar Other patients have been treated for depression or hypomania but never hospitalized. Cyclothymic Personality describes patients with bipolar mood swings who have not sought help or been treated for either depression or hypomania.

A parallel subclassification of unipolar patients, based on Winokur's studies, includes Unipolar I, Unipolar II, Unipolar Other, and Depressive Personality.[9, 36]

The Unipolar I group includes patients with at least one hospitalization for depression, no personal history of hypomania, and no family history of mania or hypomania. Unipolar II patients have been hospitalized for depression and have a family history of mania or hypomania. Unipolar Other patients have sought help for depression or been treated but not hospitalized. Depressive Personality includes patients who have periods of depression but have not been specifically treated for affective illness.

Differential Diagnosis: Manic-Depressive Illness Versus Schizophrenia

As stated earlier, many hospital and private physicians are still mislabeling manic depression as schizophrenia. Such misdiagnosis, followed by inappropriate treatment, may have dire consequences.

The onset of schizophrenia is frequently in the teens and early 20s, whereas manic-depressive illness is likely to develop in the early and late 20s, and unipolar depression in the early or late 30s.

The schizophrenic patient tends to be less capable than most manic-depressives of normal functioning between episodes, and his illness generally continues its downhill course despite all efforts at treatment—unlike manic-depressives, who do not deteriorate mentally, and many of whom are now doing extremely well on lithium.

Acute schizophrenia is often indistinguishable from acute mania or depression. It is therefore extremely important for the physician to take a longitudinal history, and to interview the patient's relatives for a family history of mania, depression, suicide, or alcoholism.

The psychiatric history of both patient and family is the critical factor in making the differential diagnosis. To obtain an accurate psychiatric history of the patient's family, the "family study" method has been designed. It consists of interviewing as many close relatives of the patient as possible, with the question of who has ever been sick, and with what ailment. Such interviews usually yield a reasonably accurate picture of an individual patient and his family, and they also usually accentuate the strong familial aspect of affective disorders.

GENETIC FINDINGS AND FAMILY HISTORY STUDIES

It has recently been found that a dominant gene located on the X chromosome appears to be involved in the transmission of manic-depressive illness.

In several genetic linkage studies, the locus for manic-depressive illness appeared to be closely linked with the loci for protan and deutan color blindness and also with the locus for the Xga blood group.[12, 22, 30, 37]

It has long been clear that heredity plays a significant role in the etiology of many if not most primary affective disorders, but much remains to be learned about the genetic factors involved and their manifestations in the pathophysiological substrates underlying specific disorders.

One of the most consistent and easily reproducible findings in psychiatry, long noted by clinicians as well as researchers, is that affective disorders in a family are usually traceable over at least several generations. It is remarkable, therefore, how often a history of psychological illness in a patient's parents, siblings, or other relatives is overlooked or ignored not only by clinical psychiatrists and family physicians, but also by researchers.

Studies of morbid risk in large populations have shown the incidence of manic-depressive illness to be much higher in relatives of manic-depressive patients than in the general population. In first degree relatives of manic probands, moreover, depression is the most frequently found type of illness.[37]

Studies of twins have shown that, in monozygotic twins, if one has manic-depressive illness, the probability of the same illness in the other is 70 to 100%, but in dizygotic twins the probability is only 15 to 25%.[37]

Even though such observations show that heredity is a major factor in the pathogenesis of manic-depressive illness, the precise mode of transmission is still controversial. Over the past few years two major lines of evidence have accumulated. One supports the polygenic theory, which is favored by the findings of Slater et al.[34] and Perris.[26] The other line of evidence supports a hypothesis of single-gene X-linked transmission, which is compatible with the findings of Winokur et al.,[37] Reich et al.,[30] Mendlewicz et al.,[22] and Fieve et al.,[12] and with the known higher incidence of manic-depressive illness in female members of families.[37] Despite the fact that occasional manic-depressive fathers appear to have sons with manic-depressive illness, claims of father-son transmission of the illness are still rare, and it is possible that in some of these circumstances the presence of undetected affective illness on the mother's side exists.[12]

Recent support has been given to the X-linkage hypothesis by two recent studies in the Lithium Treatment and Research Clinic of the New York State Psychiatric Institute. Both studies involved the family history study method to evaluate the presence of psychopathology in the relatives of patients.[22, 12]

One of these studies focused on the Xga blood group, a dominant X-linked marker, in six informative families assorting for this genetic marker and for manic-depressive illness.[12] These were families of patients in a sample of over 80 carefully diagnosed bipolar manic-depressive patients consecutively admitted to the Lithium Clinic. Bipolar depression was diagnosed in patients and relatives if there was a clear history of manic behavior and of depressive episodes severe enough to require treatment or hospitalization or to disrupt daily activities for at least 3 weeks. Periodicity of illness, with symptom-free intervals, was another criterion for bipolar depression. Unipolar depression was diagnosed in patients who had never experienced mania or hypomania, but had had one or more depressive episodes requiring treatment or hospitalization.

The results of linkage analysis in this study were consistent with a measurable linkage relationship between the locus for manic-depressive illness and that for the Xga blood group.

The original study involved the same sample of 80 manic-depressive patients.[22] It focused on protan and deutan color blindness (recessive X-linked markers) in seven informative families assorting for these markers and for manic-depressive illness. This study confirmed the probability of close linkage between the locus of manic-depressive illness and the loci of both color blindness markers; for the deutan marker the linkage was slightly less close, but still significant.

The aggregate data from both studies showed that the transmission of manic-depressive illness fits the model of dominant inheritance and constitute significant evidence for dominant X-linked transmission of manic-depressive illness. This is not to say that all families necessarily transmit the disease in this way. But these studies appear to have delineated a subtype of manic-depressive illness that is transmitted on the X chromosome, in the same fashion as the Xga blood group, or protan and deutan color blindness.

It is also possible that the individual's internal or external environment may affect the outward expression of the bipolar genotype, and that within a family, unit bipolar and unipolar illness may be genetically related and may express the same genotype. Thus it may be that a patient who appears to have only recurrent depressions, with no known history of mania, should actually be considered manic-depressive if some member of his family also has had manias.

Some findings have suggested that another gene besides the X-linked one may have to be present before mania can manifest itself, since considerable alcoholism and other psychiatric illnesses are found on both sides of the families of bipolar probands. A second gene might therefore manifest itself in alcoholism, for example, or in a form of seemingly unipolar depression.[37]

If an extra genetic factor is indeed essential to the transmission of mania, the treatment of a depression-only patient from a family that has had a history of mania may differ from the treatment of another member who has had both manias and depressions. In such a case, the second gene might manifest itself in an altered response to treatment.

Winokur has also suggested that treatment modalities and pharmacological responses might well be evaluated in two groups of affectively ill relatives of a patient—those who have had both mania and depression, and those who have had only depression.[36]

The case for genetic transmission is also supported by studies showing differences in response to lithium maintenance therapy and course of illness between manic depressive patients with or without a family history of the illness.[21, 35, 20]

In a family study in the Lithium Clinic of the New York State Psychiatric Institute, data were obtained on all possible first and second degree relatives of 72 manic-depressive patients involved in a double-blind trial of lithium prophylaxis. The evidence of bipolar illness in the genetic background was far greater for lithium responders than for nonresponders. Thus response or nonresponse to lithium prophylaxis tended to reflect the presence or absence of manic-depressive illness in the families studied. Patients with a positive family history of bipolar illness also had an earlier age of onset, ran a more severe course of illness, showed more mania, and were more responsive to long-term lithium therapy than patients without a family history.[20]

The genetic findings that have been reviewed here underscore the need to correlate a patient's hereditary background with his response to lithium maintenance to predict the long-term prognosis.

POSSIBLE MECHANISMS OF ACTION

Alteration of Biogenic Amine Metabolism

In a recent review of studies of the actions of lithium in several physiological systems, Singer and Rotenberg find that it is a highly effective agent in the treatment of mania, but there is still no commonly accepted explanation of its therapeutic benefits.[33]

During the two decades since the discovery of biogenic amines in the brain, many studies of the mechanisms of psychoactive drugs have focused on their effects on the metabolism of these amines. Many recent investigations have endeavored to link the effectiveness of lithium in mania with alterations of amine metabolism in the central nervous system.

Studies of biogenic amines in depressed patients and in animals have supported the concept that drugs that affect mood alter the metabolism and neuronal activity of catecholamines (mainly norepinephrine and its precursor dopamine) and indoleamines (mainly serotonin) in the brain. (The term "biogenic amines" has been primarily associated with these compounds, which are also often referred to as monoamines because of their chemical structure.)

Findings from animal research have generally been corroborated in human studies by evidence of the effects of psychoactive drugs as well as by some direct measurement of monoamines and their metabolites in urine and other body fluids. Recent methodological advances have made possible direct measurement of monoamine transport and turnover and the activity of enzymes involved in human monoamine metabolism.

As outgrowth of these studies is the catecholamine hypothesis of affective disorders. This hypothesis is that depression may be associated with a deficiency of catecholamines, particularly norepinephrine, at critically important adrenergic receptor sites in the brain; and conversely, mania may be associated with increased levels of these monoamines. Although this hypothesis is regarded by its proponents as a reductionistic oversimiplification of complex biological states that involve many factors besides the catecholamines, it has been of considerable heuristic value and has served as a stimulus to research.[2, 31]

Recent investigations have suggested that catecholamines may be important determinants of the manic state. For example, the increased psychomotor activity of mania is accompanied by an abnormally high level of the urinary norepinephrine metabolite MHPG. Since from animal studies lithium is known to accelerate the presynaptic destruction of norepinephrine, inhibit the neuronal release of norepinephrine and serotonin, and increase the neuronal reuptake of norepinephrine, it may indeed reduce mania by altering neuronal amine metabolism, thereby affecting synaptic transmission and nerve excitation.

Even though the precise mechanisms by which lithium produces its therapeutic effects have yet to be defined, there is increasing evidence that these effects may result from alterations of ion transport or distribution (through incomplete ion substitution for other extracellular and intracellular cations), from inhibition of adenyl cyclase-mediated responses, or from more direct interference with neuronal amine metabolism.[33]

Schildkraut et al. examined the effects of lithium chloride on the metabolism of intracisternally administered H^3-norepinephrine in rat brain and found that lithium caused a shift in norepinephrine metabolism from O-methylation to deamination. This finding suggested that lithium may increase the intraneuronal inactivation of norepinephrine, thereby decreasing the amount available to adrenergic receptors. This mechanism is supported by studies in humans, which indicate that lithium, independent of a diagnosis of mania or depression, decreases urinary excretion of two catecholamine metabolites, normetanephrine and metanephrine.[32] The urinary level of these metabolites in humans may reflect the level of norepinephrine discharged extraneuronally and therefore available to receptors.

In a study of Corrodi et al., lithium appeared to accelerate the depletion of norepinephrine from noradrenergic neurons.[4] More recently, this group has shown that lithium itself does not affect brain amine levels.[5]

Notwithstanding the findings of these and other studies of the possible relation between the effectiveness of lithium and the metabolism of biogenic amines, it has not yet been determined conclusively whether the administration of lithium causes an actual or functional decrease in monoamines at the neuron in humans.

The Role of Enzymes

Much of the recent research on biogenic amine metabolism has focused on the role of certain enzymes, and on the changes that take place in the levels or activity of these enzymes in affective disorders or in response to psychoactive drugs.

For present purposes, it is possible to present only a brief indication of the nature of such research and the kind of findings it may lead to, especially in relation to lithium.

Among the enzymes that have been most studied are monoamine oxidase (MAO) and catechol-O-methyltransferase (COMT).[6, 23, 24]

Monoamine Oxidase. Oxidative deamination by monoamine oxidase (MAO) is part of the major degradative pathway for catecholamines and indoleamines. Indirect evidence derived from the use of MAO-inhibiting drugs has also indicated that mitochondrial MAO in neurons, platelets, and other cells has a major role in determining the level of free intracellular monamines available for release into the synaptic cleft in a physiologically active form. MAO may thus secondarily influence the rate of synthesis of these amines by an end-product feedback mechanism.

Because of these multiple effects on amine formation, storage, and degradation, MAO is a uniquely important controlling factor in the regulation of cellular monoamine metabolism.

In a recent study, Murphy and Weiss found that cellular MAO activity measured in blood platelets was significantly lower (45%) in depressed patients with a history of mania (bipolar) than in unipolar depressed patients and normal controls.[24]

They also found a higher level of MAO activity in platelets of older patients and in women, suggesting a possible relationship to the higher incidence of depression in older people and in women at all ages.

According to the catecholamine hypothesis, a lower level of MAO activity would probably be reflected in a correspondingly higher level of catecholamines at functionally important neuronal receptors. This would be consistent with three characteristics that distinguish the clinical course of bipolar patients. These characteristics are mood lability with a tendency toward mania, the induction of hypomania by L-dopa, and the antimanic, antidepressant, and prophylactic effects of lithium carbonate in reducing the frequency and severity of manic-depressive cycles.

Thus the correlation of altered levels of MAO activity in bipolar patients with other biological and psychological characteristics of these patients may be further evidence that bipolar patients constitute a distinctive and homogeneous subgroup of patients with affective disorders. This finding is in agreement with other evidence from genetic and family history studies.

These studies support the identification of bipolar patients as a separate group that appears to constitute about 10 to 15% of patients hospitalized for depression.

Lithium carbonate does not appear to act directly on MAO activity. It produces increased reuptake of monoamines in the brain and in platelets, along with other changes in monoamine metabolism that appear to be antagonistic to those produced by drugs that inhibit MAO. This could account at least in part for the effects of lithium in decreasing the frequency and severity of manic-depressive cycles in bipolar patients.

The effectiveness of lithium may be further elucidated by the findings of Murphy et al. in a previous study.[23] In nine bipolar manic-depressive patients, chronic lithium treatment caused a significant increase in uptake of monoamines by platelets. This and other effects of lithium on monoamines are all consistent with the overall effect of lithium in decreasing the level of free monoamines available for extraneuronal function in the synapse—thus possibly providing further evidence of a cellular basis for the observed antimanic effects of lithium.

Catechol-*O*-methyltransferase.   Catechol-*O*-methyltransferase (COMT) is another important enzyme in the metabolism of catecholamines. It is the principal enzyme in the metabolic deactivation of extraneuronal norepinephrine remaining in the synaptic cleft after nerve stimulation.

Studies by Dunner et al. have indicated that women with primary affective disorders, as a group, have reduced red cell COMT activity.[6] The same investigators have also found that COMT activity is significantly lower in unipolar women than in bipolar women. Both groups have significantly lower red-cell activity than normal controls, schizophrenics, and men with primary affective disorders or antisocial personality.

No satisfactory explanation has yet been found for the fact that the low levels of COMT in affective disorders seem to apply only to women, and are apparently unrelated to age, diet, degree of depression, drug effects, or any other known factors. COMT activity appears to be unaffected by various treatments, including lithium carbonate, tricyclic antidepressants, phenothiazines, and electroconvulsive therapy.

COMT activity has also been found to remain at the same level after recovery from an affective episode and does not appear to reflect the severity of affective illness. The stability of red-cell COMT levels suggests that this enzyme may reflect the underlying genetic predisposition of certain individuals to affective illness. These positive findings with COMT in affective disorders have not been confirmed by Perris.[27]

The foregoing references to studies of MAO and COMT are compatible with a growing body of literature supporting the bipolar and unipolar classification of patients with primary affective disorders.

Some of the findings summarized briefly here, while highly tentative, do indicate the potential value of further research into the interaction of biogenic amines, enzymes involved in their metabolism, and psychoactive drugs—and into the relation of all of these to affective disorders.

A New Hypothesis of Depression?

Mendels and Frazer[17, 18] reported open and double-blind controlled studies indicating that there might be a subgroup of depressed patients who have a significant clinical response to lithium carbonate.

In a study of the varying responses of depressed patients to lithium carbonate, Mendels and Frazer examined the distribution of lithium across the cell membrane.[18] They examined the lithium concentration in the erythrocyte (RBC) in 13 depressed male patients. The concentration was significantly higher in eight patients who responded to lithium than in five who did not respond. Moreover, clinical improvement was definitely associated with a higher RBC lithium concentration and a higher RBC lithium:plasma lithium ratio, while the dosage of lithium, duration of treatment, and plasma lithium concentration were the same for responders and nonresponders. This suggests that the transfer of lithium across the cell membrane differs between the two groups of patients. The difference in RBC lithium concentration between responders and nonresponders was significant after 7 days of treatment, suggesting that this measurement may provide a means of anticipating clinical response of depressed patients to lithium after that length of time.

A report on the complementary action of two drugs, lithium and rubidium, has suggested a new theory as a possible alternative to the catecholamine hypothesis.[15] This is the membrane-transport hypothesis, which implicates the neuronal membrane as the site of the primary defect in manic-depressive illness.

This hypothesis takes altered hormone levels into account, but suggests that the hormone changes are secondary to the genetic membrane defect. The duration of the action potential along the nerve fiber may reflect the primary defect(s) involved in mania and depression. The action potentials are controlled by the relative rates of flow of sodium and potassium ions through the neuronal membrane. When lithium is introduced, the potassium permeability is increased, and the nerve impulses are diminished, thereby reducing or correcting mania.

When rubidium is added, the duration of the action potentials is augmented, causing behavioral activation. This makes rubidium a potentially useful drug for treatment of depression. Its use as an antidepressant agent would complement the established antimanic effectiveness of lithium. An early report of its potential application as an antidepressant has been published.[10]

The new membrane-transport hypothesis is based on the following experimental and theoretical considerations.

In a study of monovalent ion metabolism in hospitalized depressed patients,[16] it was found that daily urinary excretion of endogenous rubidium varied unpredictably. However, the ratio of endogenous rubidium to potassium (Rb/K) was virtually constant. After treatment with a tricyclic antidepressant drug, no consistent changes occurred. When lithium was administered, however, the urinary Rb/K ratio immediately rose, and when lithium was withdrawn the ratio immediately fell.

In a study of the effect of lithium on transport of rubidium across membranes, it was found that rubidium moved into the cell faster when lithium was present.[15] Lithium increased the rate of movement of rubidium through the erythrocyte membrane in both directions. It is believed that the effect of lithium on rubidium membrane transport will soon be shown to be a consistent phenomenon.

Regarding a hypothesis of the mode of action of rubidium and lithium in the central nervous system, it has long been known that rubidium is qualitatively similar to potassium in a variety of biological systems. It is not unlikely that the effect of lithium on rubidium membrane transport will be generalized to include a similar effect on potassium transport across membranes. The membrane of immediate interest seems likely to be the axonal membrane, where the nerve action potential is generated.

Meltzer and Fieve[15] postulate that lithium acts neurophysiologically and therapeutically by foreshortening the normal neuronal action potential in the central nervous system, and rubidium acts neurophysiologically by extending the action potential. It is reasonable to suppose that the information content of an action potential is altered by the presence of rubidium or lithium, and that ultimately such changes should be reflected by changes in brain function—which would in turn result in alteration of such behavioral states as mania and depression.

It is hoped that the new membrane-transport hypothesis will stimulate a new surge of electrolyte research in manic-depressive illness.

ACCUMULATING SUPPORT FOR LITHIUM PROPHYLAXIS

The case for lithium prophylaxis in bipolar manic-depressive illness is gaining ground rapidly, with the support of impressive findings in a number of carefully designed double-blind controlled studies.[1, 3, 11, 28, 29, 35]

These studies have found the effectiveness of lithium prophylaxis in the manic stage of bipolar disorders to be dramatic and unequivocal. Its effectiveness in bipolar depressions has been little less remarkable.

In several studies,[1, 3, 29] lithium was also found to be an effective prophylactic in unipolar depressions. Here the evidence is less definitive, however, and in one of these studies[29] imipramine was found to be just as effective as lithium for prophylaxis in unipolar disorders.

In our study of patients attending the Lithium Treatment and Research Clinic at the New York State Psychiatric Institute (part of a lengthy lithium prophylaxis project currently in progress),[11, 35] a total of 52 patients were included. All were diagnosed as bipolar manic-depressives. All were symptom-free; none were being treated with antidepressants or tranquilizers, but 33 had been receiving lithium openly as a prophylactic. All were assigned on a 50–50 basis to lithium or placebo.

Of 25 lithium patients, 14 remained in remission for the full 25 to 28 months of the study, but only two of the 27 placebo patients remained in remission. Of the original 52 patients, 31 dropped out; 22 of these were from the placebo group, nine from the lithium group. Only three lithium patients dropped out because of an acute episode; the remaining lithium dropouts were for reasons unrelated to an affective episode.

Comparisons with placebo showed that lithium was strikingly prophylactic in its effects on the manic phase. For bipolar depression, lithium prophylaxis was clearly evident, though not so dramatic as in the case of mania.

These results give striking evidence for lithium prophylaxis for bipolar manic-depressive illness.

Strong evidence of lithium prophylaxis was previously provided in the study by Baastrup et al. (1970)[1] of 50 bipolar and 34 unipolar depressed patients, all of whom had been on open lithium treatment for at least a year. Matched pairs of patients were assigned at random to either lithium or placebo groups, and were followed closely for 5 months. During this period, 21 placebo patients experienced affective disorders, but *no lithium patients did.* Evidence for lithium prophylaxis was found both in (1) the prevention of manic and depressive episodes in bipolar manic-depressives, and (2) the prevention of depressive episodes in unipolar endogenous depressives.

Similarly, in the British collaborative double-blind study reported by Coppen et al. (1971),[3] 65 patients in four centers (both bipolar manic-depressives and unipolar recurrent depressives) were randomly assigned to either lithium or placebo for up to 112 weeks.

The results clearly demonstrated the benefits of lithium prophylaxis, as measured by reduction in number and severity of episodes and in amounts of antidepressant and antimanic medications when these were needed. As in the Baastrup study, lithium was found equally effective in preventing manic and depressive episodes in bipolar patients and depressive episodes in unipolar patients.

The recent study by Prien et al.[29] not only confirms the value of lithium prophylaxis in bipolar disorders, but also lends additional support to the possibility that lithium may be effective in preventing unipolar recurrent depression. However, in this study unipolar patients responded equally well to prophylaxis with lithium or imipramine—a comparison that had not been previously studied in prophylactic trials of lithium in unipolar depression. Both imipramine and lithium were significantly more effective than placebo in preventing unipolar depressive relapses.

Notwithstanding the impressive accumulation of demonstrations of lithium prophylaxis in manic-depressive illness, successful prophylaxis is not a universal finding, and a significant number of failures do occur. Recent studies have probed into possible factors that might explain and perhaps even predict such failures.

A review of failures reported in clinical trials shows that most of them are reported during the first year of maintenance therapy, and that successful prophylaxis becomes more demonstrable as lithium is given over longer periods of time.[6a, 11]

The demonstration of prophylaxis in clinical trials appears to depend on the presence of at least two variables: (1) a prior history of adherence to a maintenance regimen of lithium (usually in an outpatient clinic), and (2) a family history of mania. Failure appears to be related to the absence of either or both of these factors.

Both of these variables have been explored in detail in two special studies instituted as part of the long-range investigation still in progress in the Lithium Treatment and Research Clinic.

In one study, patients were evaluated in relation to whether they had previously been part of an "old" lithium treatment sample before entering the study, or were cases freshly admitted for this clinical trial, without previous lithium treatment. On this basis the sample of 52 patients was divided into 33 "old" and 19 "new" cases.

Among the "old" cases, within the first 6 months of the trial, lithium showed a clear-cut advantage over placebo in preventing "old" manic failures as well as "old" depressive failures. Among "new" cases, this demonstration took a little longer: Lithium was not significantly better than placebo in preventing manic relapses until 6 months had elapsed; in prevention of depressive relapses, the comparable period was 8 to 12 months.

These findings suggest that previously treated lithium patients who have managed to adhere to a lithium regimen are likely to be lithium responders. It is possible, moreover, that fresh bipolar cases randomly selected for clinical trials may not show a clear prophylactic advantage of lithium over placebo during their first year on the drug. This might explain why lithium failures tend to be reported more during the first year, since the above constitute statistical evidence that in some patients prophylaxis may require a year or more to become clearly established.

Another study conducted by the Lithium Clinic at the New York State Psychiatric Institute is focusing on genetic aspects of manic-depressive illness as related to long-term treatment response in its double-blind study of lithium prophylaxis. In this study 72 manic-depressive patients were randomly assigned to lithium carbonate or placebo in October 1969. Of these, 67% are lithium responders and 33% are long-term failures. As part of the genetic investigation, a family history study was undertaken on each patient admitted. The investigation is still in progress, and the latest report analyzes data only for the first 37 months, i.e., up to November 1972.

As mentioned earlier, in the discussion of recent genetic findings, an impressive correlation has been observed between response to lithium treatment of mania and a family history of manic-depressive illness. As might be expected, studies of lithium prophylaxis show a similar correlation. Striking differences have been found in the genetic background of lithium responders and failures. Responders to lithium prophylaxis are significantly associated with the presence of bipolar illness in their families, and nonresponders with its absence.

On the other hand, the isolation of a group of patients with affective disorders who do not respond to lithium prophylaxis raises a further possibility. This possibility is that there may be a subgroup of manic-depressive patients who do not respond to lithium, because they are genetically different from those who do respond.

In this respect, it has been noted that patients with a positive family history of bipolar illness run a more severe course of illness and experience more mania than patients with no family history.[20]

Genetic findings in bipolar manic-depressive illness and in many unipolar depressions underscore the need, *in each specific case*, to correlate lithium response with genetic background to predict a patient's long-term prognosis on lithium maintenance therapy.

REFERENCES

1. Baastrup, P. C., Poulsen, J. C., Schou, M., Thomsen, K., and Amidsen, A.: Prophylactic lithium: Double-blind discontinuation in manic-depressive and recurrent depressive disorders. *Lancet* II:326, August 1970.

2. Bunney, W. E., Jr. and Davis, J. M.: Norepinephrine in depressive reactions. *Arch. Gen. Psychiatr.* 13:483–492, 1965.

3. Coppen, A., Noguera, R., Bailey, J., Burns, B. H., Swani, M. S., Hare, E. H.,

Gardner, R., and Maggs, R.: Prophylactic lithium in affective disorders. *Lancet* II:275, 1971.

4. Corrodi, H., Fuxe, K., Hökfelt, T., and Schou, M.: The effect of lithium on cerebral monoamine neurons. *Psychopharmacologia (Berlin)* 11:345–353, 1967.

5. Corrodi, H., Fuxe, K., and Schou, M.: The effect of prolonged lithium administration on cerebral monoamine neurons in the rat. *Life Sci.* 8:643–651, 1969.

6. Dunner, D. L., Cohn, C. K., Gershon, E. S., and Goodwin, F. K.: Differential catechol-O-methyltransferase activity in unipolar and bipolar affective illness. *Arch. Gen. Psychiatr.* 25:348–353, 1971.

6a. Dunner, D. L. and Fieve, R. R.: Clinical factors in lithium carbonate prophylaxis failure. *Arch. Gen. Psychiatr.* 30:229–233, 1974.

7. Fieve, R. R.: Lithium in psychiatry. *Int. J. Psychiatr.* 9:375–412, 1970.

8. Fieve, R. R.: Clinical use of lithium in manic depression, recurrent depression, and the creative personality. Paper presented at the Symposium on Depression, 122nd Annual Convention of the American Medical Association, June 24, 1973.

9. Fieve, R. R. and Dunner, D. L.: Unipolar and bipolar affective states. In *World Textbook of Depression*, F. Flach, and S. Draghi, (Eds.), Wiley, New York, 1974 (in press).

10. Fieve, R. R., Meltzer, H., Dunner, D. L., Levitt, M., Mendlewicz, J., and Thomas, A.: Rubidium: Chemical, behavioral and metabolic studies in humans. *Am. J. Psychiatr.* 130:55–61, 1973.

11. Fieve, R. R. and Mendlewicz, J.: Lithium prophylaxis of bipolar manic-depressive illness. Presented at annual meeting of Collegium Internationale Neuro-Psychopharmacologicum (CINP), Copenhagen, August 1972, Avicenum-Czechoslovak Medical Press, Prague, Czechoslovakia, 1973. Abstract in *Psychopharm.* 26, 93, suppl. 1972.

12. Fieve, R. R., Mendlewicz, J., and Fleiss, J. L.: Manic-depressive illness: linkage studies with the Xg blood group. *Am. J. Psychiatr.* 130:12, 1355–1359, 1973.

13. Goodwin, F. K., Murphy, D. L., Dunner D. L., and Bunney, W. E., Jr.: Lithium response in unipolar versus bipolar depression. *Am. J. Psychiatr.* 129:44–47, 1972.

14. Hullen, R. P., McDonald, R., and Allsopp, M. N.: Prophylactic lithium in recurrent affective disorders. *Lancet* I:1044–1064, 1972.

15. Meltzer, H. L. and Fieve, R. R.: Some metabolic interactions of rubidium and lithium: a membrane transport hypothesis for mechanism of action in the CNS. Paper presented at the Annual Meeting of the American Psychiatric Association, May 7–11, 1973.

16. Meltzer, H. L., Lieberman, K. W., Shelley, E. M., Stallone, F., and Fieve, R. R.: Metabolism of naturally occurring Rb in the human: the constancy of urinary Rb/K. *Biochem. Med.* 7:218–225, April 1973.

17. Mendels, J.: Lithium and depression. In *The Lithium Ion*, S. Gershon, (Ed.), Plenum Press, New York (in press).

18. Mendels, J. and Frazer, A.: Intracellular lithium concentration and clinical response: Towards a membrane theory of depression. *J. Psychiatr. Res.* 10:9–17, 1973.

19. Mendelwicz, J., Fieve, R. R., Rainer, J. D., and Cataldo, M.: Affective disorder on paternal and maternal sides: Observations in bipolar (manic-depressive) patients with and without a family history. *Brit. J. Psychiatr.* 122:31–34, 1973.

20. Mendlewicz, J., Fieve, R. R., Rainer, J. D., and Fleiss, J. L.: Manic-depressive illness: A comparative study of patients with and without a family history. *Brit. J. Psychiatr.* 120:523–530, 1972.

21. Mendlewicz, J., Fieve, R. R., and Stallone, F.: Relationship between the effectiveness of lithium therapy and family history. *Am. J. Psychiatr.* **130**:1011–1013, 1973.

22. Mendlewicz, J., Fleiss, J. L., and Fieve, R. R.: Evidence for X-linkage in the transmission of manic-depressive illness. *JAMA* **222**:1624–1627, December 25, 1972.

23. Murphy, D. L., Colburn, R. W., Davis, J. M., and Bunney, W. E., Jr.: Stimulation by lithium of monoamine uptake in human platelets. *Life. Sci.* **8**: Part I, 1187–1193, 1969.

24. Murphy, D. L. and Weiss, R.: Reduced monoamine oxidase activity in blood platelets from bipolar depressed patients. *Am. J. Psychiatr.* **128**:11, May 1972.

25. National Institute of Mental Health (U. S. Department of Health, Education and Welfare): Personal communication from Biometry Branch, July 5, 1973.

26. Perris, C.: Abnormality on paternal and maternal sides: Observations in bipolar/manic-depressive and unipolar depressive psychosis. *Brit. J. Psychiatr.* **118**:207–10, 1971.

27. Perris, C.: Personal communication.

28a. Prien, R. F., Caffey, E. M., Jr., and Klett, C. J.: Prophylactic effect of lithium carbonate in manic-depressive illness. *Arch. Gen. Psychiatr.* **28**:337–341, 1973.

29b. Prien, R. F., Caffey, E. M., Jr., and Klett, C. J.: Lithium prophylaxis in affective disorders. *Sci. Proc. Am. Psychiatr. Assn.* **126**:55, 1973.

30. Reich, T., Clayton, P. J., and Winokur, G.: Family history studies: V. The genetics of mania. *Am. J. Psychiatr.* **125**:1358–1368, 1969.

31. Schildkraut, J. J.: The catecholamine hypothesis of affective disorders: a review of supporting evidence. *Am. J. Psychiatr.* **122**:509–522, 1965.

32. Greenspan, K., Schildkraut, J. J., Gordon, E. K., Baer, L., Aronoff, M., and Durell, J.: Catecholamine metabolism in affective disorders. III. MHPG and other catecholamine metabolites in patients treated with lithium carbonate. *J. Psychiatr. Res.* **7**:1, 1970.

33. Singer, I. and Rotenberg, D.: Mechanisms of lithium action. *N. Engl. J. Med.* **289**:254–260, August 2, 1973.

34. Slater, E., Maxwell, J., and Price, J. S.: Distribution of ancestral secondary cases in bipolar affective disorders. *Brit. J. Psychiat.* **118**:215–18, 1971.

35. Stallone, F., Shelley, E., Mendlewicz, J., and Fieve, R. R.: The use of lithium in affective disorders: III. A double-blind study of prophylaxis in bipolar illness. *Am. J. Psychiatr.* **130**:9, 1006–1010, 1973.

36. Winokur, G.: The types of affective disorders. *J. Nerv. Mental Dis.* **156**(2):82–96, 1973. 1973.

37. Winokur, G., Clayton, P. J., and Reich, T.: *Manic-Depressive Illness.* C. V. Mosby, St. Louis, 1969.

38. Zubin, J.: Cross-national study of diagnosis of the mental disorders: methodology and planning. *Am. J. Psychiatr.* **125**:10, Suppl. April, 1969.

CHAPTER TWO

WHAT'S NEW IN PSYCHOPHARMACOLOGY?

BARON SHOPSIN, M.D., AND NATHAN S. KLINE, M.D.

". . . though, broadly speaking, human beings are not unique in their responses to some given treatment, there is no doubt that they are likely to be variable, and sometimes extremely variable. Two or three observations may, therefore, give, merely through the customary play of chance, a favourable picture in the hands of one doctor, and an unfavourable picture in the hands of another. As a result, the medical journals become an arena for conflicting claims—each in itself, maybe, perfectly true of what the doctor saw but insufficient to bear the weight of the generalisation placed upon it."

Principles of Medical Statistics, 8th ed., Sir Austin Bradford Hill, Oxford University Press, New York, 1967, p. 6.

NEW AND EXPERIMENTAL DRUGS IN THE TREATMENT OF DEPRESSION AND MANIA

Some Comments Concerning Brain Monoamines in Affective Disorders

The current biological theories of mania and depression are united in postulating a role for brain monoamines in this group of disorders:[27, 53, 63, 143, 194] the catecholamines of importance include dopamine (DA) and norepinephrine (NE); serotonin (5-HT) is the putative indolamine involved (Figure 1). The catecholamine and indolamine theories of affective illness, simply stated, relate a functional deficit of brain neurotransmitter amines at specific central synapses in depression, and, conversely, a functional excess of these amines in mania. The indolamine hypothesis, in recent years, has been modified to include a deficit of indolamines in both mania and depression,[155] with a greater functional deficit of serotonin in depression. The monoamine hypotheses of affective illness largely germinated from retrospective observations concerning the biochemical activity of certain psychoactive drugs used in the treatment of mental patients. It is thus that imipramine, the prototype tricyclic antidepressant, increases brain norepinephrine, serotonin, and dopamine, whereas reserpine, on the other hand, depletes brain amines and is associated with depression in many individuals. Difficulty in interpreting these hypotheses has arisen on many counts, one of which has been the inability to pinpoint definitely the particular amine responsible for the clinical changes observed.[24, 53, 155, 194] Direct ways to study the function of a specific amine in mania or depresssion include the techniques known as "precursor loading (or the "precursor-load strategy"), which has been used successfully in studying certain metabolic diseases, and "synthesis inhibition." Amine precursors are generally used in the treatment of depression (where it is

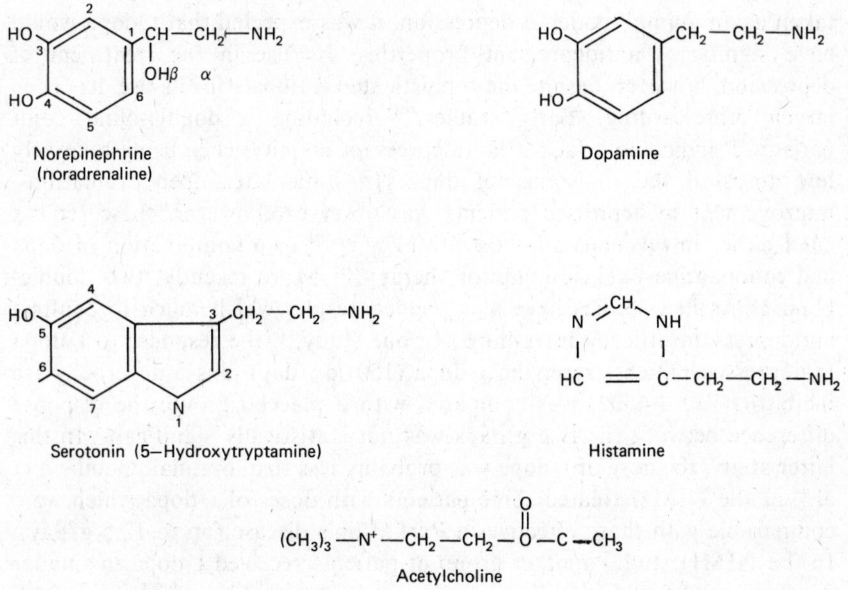

Norepinephrine
(noradrenaline)

Dopamine

Serotonin (5–Hydroxytryptamine)

Histamine

Acetylcholine

Figure 1.   Structure of biogenic amines.

believed that a functional deficit in amines exists), and synthesis inhibition is used as a stratagem for treating mania (where an excess in these amines is believed etiopathogenic).

The Psychopharmacology of Depression

Catecholamine Precursors.   Dopamine and norepinephrine do not readily cross the blood-brain barrier. Their immediate precursor, dihydroxyphen-ylalanine (DOPA), does enter the brain, where it is converted to dopamine, with little or no effect on norepinephrine levels.[29] L-Dopa is the active isomer. The effects of L-dopa on mood, thinking, and behavior, as observed in patients with Parkinson's disease, have been reviewed;[93] it is clear that mental side effects widely vary from individual to individual and that the drug does not uniformly produce a specific set of mental changes. Factors that may account for this variability include psychiatric morbidity and neurological state of the individual prior to L-dopa treatment. Individual variation in the enzymatic system for handling the L-dopa load may also account for the occurrence of mental symptoms.

The rationale for using L-*dopa in depression* is based on the established "precursor load" strategy. L-Dopa has been shown to reverse the reserpine-induced sedation in animals and man. Since reserpine sedation has been taken as an animal model of depression, it was expected that L-dopa would have significant antidepressant properties. Its use in the treatment of depression, however, despite the sophisticated rationale for its use, has been largely unrewarding. Early studies,[164] including a double-blind comparison,[135] indicated a lack of antidepressant activity when using relatively low doses of the DL-isomer of dopa. In some later open evaluations, improvement in depressed patients was observed; however, these reports cited either intravenous administration[115, 149, 166] or a combination of dopa and monoamine oxidase inhibitor therapy.[217] More recently, two double-blind controlled studies have also yielded results which failed to confirm antidepressant efficacy for L-dopa. In one study,[150] the response to L-dopa in depressed patients receiving L-dopa (150 mg/day) plus a decarboxylase inhibitor (RO 4-4602) was compared with a placebo group; the response difference between the two groups was not statistically significant. In this latter study, the dose of L-dopa was probably less than optimal. Goodwin et al.[95] at the NIMH treated some patients with doses of L-dopa which were comparable with those effective in Parkinson's disease (up to 12.5 g/day). In the NIMH study, another group of patients received L-dopa in smaller doses, up to 1.5 g/day, in combination with α-methyldopa hydrazine (MK 485), an inhibitor of peripheral dopa decarboxylase. Improvement was observed in only the patients whose depression was characterized by retardation; even here, results were highly equivocal. The degrees of clinical improvement in such patients were reported less than those subsequently obtained with imipramine. An important finding in this NIMH study includes the production of anger in patients who did now show any apparent antidepressant response, as well as the induction of manic behavior in bipolar manic-depressive subjects, that is, in those depressed individuals with a history of mania. Despite these findings, patients studied by Goodwin et al. responded to L-dopa with unequivocal elevations in the urinary excretion of dopamine as well as of different dopamine and norepinephrine metabolites. The predominantly negative antidepressant results reported across most studies suggest that amine depletion, as defined by the reserpine model, is not a sufficient explanation for the pathophysiology of depression in the majority of patients.[161] Brain dopamine is likely involved in regulating psychomotor function, and is only indirectly related to mood *per se* in man.

A small study has been conducted by Coppen et al.,[47] who concluded that *tyrosine* was not effective in treating depressed patients, although details of the trial are not given. Most investigators in the field have not regarded this amino acid as a potentially useful precursor of the catecholamines.

Serotonin Precursors. In contrast to the situation described for L-dopa, more enthusiastic claims have been made for the use of precursors of serotonin in depression. *Tryptophan*, the precursor of serotonin, has been shown in several controlled studies to possess antidepressant activity: some reports have indicated comparable efficacy with imipramine;[24, 52] other studies report that the effect of tryptophan is enhanced with the addition of a monoamine oxidase (MAO) inhibitor,[48, 88, 163] and that tryptophan, together with MAOI, is a more effective antidepressant than an MAOI alone.[88] Using the L- or DL-isomer of tryptophan in doses up to 18 g/day, these studies would suggest that it is the amines derived from tryptophan which are responsible for the antidepressant effects. Van Praag[171] has shown that the subgroup of depressed patients responding most favorably to tryptophan are those depressives showing abnormally low levels of 5-hydroxyindoleacetic acid (5-HIAA) in cerebrospinal fluid following probenecid administration. T_3 has been given along with L-tryptophan in depressed patients;[176] although there was a tendency for T_3 to enhance the L-tryptophan effect in women, it was not statistically significant. Enthusiasm for tryptophan as a treatment for depression reached its peak with the claim, from Coppen et al.,[49] that the amino acid was as effective as electroconvulsive therapy in the management of the depressed patient. Their study has been critically reviewed, and the deficiencies in the trial have been underlined.[40] A sequential controlled trial using matched patient pairs was carried out by Carroll et al.,[41] and indicates that L-tryptophan was clearly inferior to ECT as a treatment for severely depressed patients. Perhaps the most damaging evidence against the routine use of L-tryptophan as a treatment against depression comes from the NIMH group,[28] who reported the virtual absence of any clinical improvement in their depressed individuals treated with tryptophan, in spite of biochemical evidence suggesting that L-tryptophan was metabolized and did produce an increase in both serotonin levels and serotonin metabolites in peripheral tissues as well as in the central nervous system. Other studies would also suggest that tryptophan appears to be ineffective in treating depression.[22]

5-Hydroxytryptophan (5-HTP), a more immediate amine precursor of serotonin, has been used intravenously in at least five studies as a treatment for depression.[89, 136, 138, 164, 166] The overall impression from these studies,[40] including the only double-blind comparison,[138] is that 5-HTP does not have a powerful antidepressant action, nor does it appear to potentiate MAO inhibitors. The doses used, however, have been very low (50 mg) in comparison with those found effective in other conditions, such as manganese poisoning, in which 3 g/day of the DL-isomer of 5-HTP have been used.

The interpretation of clinical results with tryptophan and 5-HTP in depressive illness is complicated by several factors. Different clinical diagnostic criteria used in the selection of patients across the various studies may have led to differences in treatment outcome; depression is a heterogenous illness, and even depressed patients who appear clinically similar may differ with regard to biochemical pathophysiology. With specific reference to studies dealing with tryptophan, some investigators have used pyridoxine HCl or vitamin B_1 supplements with the tryptophan regimen. The role of pyridoxine in enhancing the tryptophan effect has not been clearly established.[41] Then too, pyridoxine may itself exert antidepressant effects.[229] Further investigations are required to determine further whether select clinical or biochemical subgroups of depressed patients may be responsive to treatment with tryptophan or 5-HTP.[171]

The Lithium Ion.   Lithium carbonate has been used investigationally in recent years in the acute depressive phase of manic-depressive disorder, where its efficacy in this illness remains uncertain. Recent evidence derived from controlled studies, although somewhat conflicting, tends to suggest that an antidepressant effect with lithium may occur in some patients. Fieve,[70] in comparing lithium and imipramine, concluded that any antidepressant effect of lithium was mild. Dyson and Mendels,[66] first in an open study and later in a controlled trial comparing lithium with desimipramine,[156] concluded that lithium showed marked antidepressant properties—equivalent to desimipramine—in the latter study. Mendels' group[66, 156] has indicated efficacy for unipolar patients; this has also been suggested in another investigation.[123] The NIMH group, headed by Goodwin,[94] has suggested that it may be the bipolar patient who appreciates a more favorable response to lithium carbonate. The use of lithium in acute depressive disorder is not approved by the Food and Drug Administration (FDA). It is, however, of theoretical importance that this ion may be effective in select cases of depression, since such an effect is difficult to reconcile with the catecholamine hypothesis of affective illness if one also considers that lithium is highly specific against mania and shows prophylactic efficacy against both recurrent mania and depression. It may well be that lithium affects the endogenous or core illness entity, rather than merely affecting the symptoms of an illness.

Phenothiazines.   Klein and Davis[134] indicate that several double-blind controlled studies (with comparisons against either placebo or imipramine) indicate efficacy for these compounds in depressions, even in depressions of a primary nature, unrelated to such secondary illnesses as schizophrenia or neuroses, for example. The accuracy of these studies has not been subjected to critical evaluation or adequate duplication. The use of phenothiazines as antidepressants is certainly not advocated; it is offered here because of its academic interest and theoretical importance, since the phenothiazines and antidepressants are usually considered by investigators to be psychobiological antagonists.

Combined Use of Reserpine-Imipramine. Since one of the undesirable side effects of rauwolfia treatment is said to be depression, it is interesting to note reports in which depressed patients pretreated with impramine or desmethylimipramine dramatically improve after 2 days of reserpine administration.[169] Amelioration of depression is followed by induction of a transient mania; this conspicuous stimulating effect resembles the sudden mood reversals that occur occasionally in cyclic manic-depressive disease. Some investigators do use this combination in cases of depression that are unresponsive or otherwise refractory to more conventional forms of drug therapy.[107]

Combined Use of Stimulants and Tricyclic Drugs. Although the procedure is not approved by the FDA, psychiatrists will often use the stimulants such as amphetamine or methylphenidate as a temporary adjunctive measure, while awaiting the more specific but delayed effects of the standard tricyclic/MAOI antidepressant compounds. The usefulness of such an approach has been questioned, since (1) there have been no data from controlled studies to support such use, and (2) many endogenous depressives will not show a response to lower doses of stimulant medications. However, some studies would suggest that there may be good indication for the combined use of these drugs, irrespective of any obtained stimulant effect. Studies have indicated that methylphenidate inhibits the metabolic degradation of tricyclic antidepressants,[165, 222] leading to enhanced blood levels of the latter. A more recent report[46] has indicated that methylphenidate added to a high-dose imipramine regimen to a depressed patient was accompanied by a marked increase in both imipramine and desmethylimipramine plasma levels when the patient received methylphenidate; this elevation in plasma levels was accompanied by marked clinical improvement. Methylphenidate withdrawal during continued imipramine treatment was accompanied by a reduction of plasma levels of imipramine and desmethylimipramine which corresponded to a rapid return to the patient's previous state of depression. This study would appear to confirm reports by Perel et al.[165] and Wharton et al.[222]

Combined Use of Tricyclic-Monoamine Oxidase (MAO) Inhibitors. Despite theoretical synergism between tricylic antidepressants and the MAO inhibitors in the treatment of depression, as outlined by biochemical research, reports of severe morbidity and mortality when these two types of drugs are used together have prompted the FDA and drug firms to warn against their concomitant use. Consequently, their combined use on any large scale and/or systematic basis in this country has never been undertaken. However, a more critical look at the reports in the literature indicates that the potential dangers are likely grossly overexaggerated, and that there is likely an overreaction on the part of the professional community in response to them. Schuckit et al.,[196] in a comprehensive review of available case reports on which concern with morbidity is based, was unable to uncover any convincing evidence that the antidepressant combination taken in therapeutic doses was responsible for the different illnesses reported. These investigators also carried out an informal review of 350 outpatients, recorded examinations of 50 inpatients, and a drug trial with 10 other patients, and were unable to show any drug-related morbidity. In their review of 50 inpatients receiving drug combinations, these authors indicated that these patients ranged in age from 15 to 76 years, with a mean of 52.4 years. Males and females were included, and 869 inpatient-days was given as the time on the tricyclic-MAO combination. Even if one will forget about any possible efficacy of such polypharmacy, a review of concomitant medical illnesses and other drugs used in these patients appears so outrageously incompatible that one might have predicted disaster. Concomitant medical illnesses included congestive heart failure, grand mal epilepsy, hypertension, and hyperparathyroidism, while concomitant drugs range from barbiturates to stimulants such as methylphenidate as well as other drugs including methysergide, guanethidine sulfate, warfarin sodium, methyldopa with hydrochlorthiazide, conjugated estrogens, phenylephrine hydrochloride, and various phenothiazine compounds. Certain patients received concomitant electroshock therapy as well. At no instance was the MAOI-tricyclic stopped because of developing medical illness or side effects in these cases.

A host of uncontrolled clinical reports from Great Britain would also indicate that, in certain individuals, combined therapy is both safe and highly effective in treating depression, especially in treating refractory patients.[59, 60, 81, 82, 182, 191, 192, 221] Kline and Shopsin have data to support this.[140]

Certainly, at this point the routine use of combined tricyclic-MAOI medication for depression cannot be advocated as a proven therapeutic tool. The important issue to underline here is that, aside from potential clinical efficacy, the drug combination does not appear to run a higher risk of morbidity than with either drug used alone. The combination should likely be used only in those refractory cases where single drugs have been used in high (therapeutic) doses for adequate treatment periods of 3 to 6 weeks. The important considerations for insuring safety include: (1) diagnostic accuracy (the drug combination should be used only in the "endogenous" or "autonomous" depressions); (2) exclusion of individuals who are poor medical risks and/or of those who are concomitantly taking other medications which may be incompatible; and (3) strict adherence to readily available dietary precautions (avoiding foods containing tyramine) which have been laid down by the pharmaceutical industry and the FDA. Large-scale studies evaluating efficacy and safety, carried out in double-blind controlled fashion, should be undertaken by clinical investigators to resolve these issues, because of the potential benefits to certain depressed patients who do not otherwise show response to conventional therapy with antidepressant medication.

Thyroid Hormones. Several reports have indicated that L-*triiodothyronine* (T_3) can be used to accelerate or enchance the therapeutic action of imipramine. [172, 173, 175-177, 226, 227] Men may respond more rapidly than women to imipramine. However, when T_3 is added to imipramine, women benefit enormously; T_3 has little benefit if any to the primary treatment with imipramine in men.[176] It is apparently not necessary to continue T_3 for longer than 14 days; the "enhanced effect" will be sustained on imipramine treatment alone. The degree of psychomotor retardation or agitation has no influence on the T_3 phenomenon. This tricyclic-T_3 interaction is apparently not limited to imipramine; in a double-blind study of outpatients, Wheatley[224] has shown that it pertains to amitriptyline, and Earle[67] showed in an open trial that it pertains to other tricyclic drugs as well, including the demethylated tricyclics. Reportedly,[176] T_3 can enhance the antidepressant effects of tryptophan in female patients, but this is not a statistically significant amelioration over tryptophan alone.

Thyroid-stimulating hormone (TSH), when combined with imipramine, has been shown to produce a more rapid recovery from depression than does imipramine alone.[174] It seems more potent than T_3 in potentiating imipramine, but dose differences prevent accurate comparison.

Extending their line of investigations, Prange et al.[178] reported that *thyrotropin-releasing hormone* (TRH) has an antidepression action. This finding has been duplicated,[125] although the results with TRH in depression observed by other investigators have been equivocal.[97, 203] The available reports await critical evaluation and duplication before its use in depression can be determined. Certainly, whatever the effects, the use of TRH as a treatment for depression is extremely limited. In the available studies, TRH has been given intravenously as a single bolus; the antidepressant effect, when seen, is short-acting and dissipates after a few hours. Repeated injections would be needed so that the depression is therefore not reversed, and the use of repeated injections to induce or maintain lasting remissions of depression has obviously not been assessed. Oral TRH may prove useful, inasmuch as there is suggestion that the hormone given by mouth has a prolonged action. However, caution must be exercised when considering the use of a hypothalamic hormone, inasmuch as the effects of prolonged use have not been assessed, nor can one readily justify continued adminis- tration of such a hormone in individuals who are both clinically and chemically euthyroid.

Despite attractive hypotheses and very alluring possibilities, the mechanisms by which the various thyroid hormones may either potentiate imipramine or act alone in the treatment of depression remain unknown. There is no evidence at this time to indicate that depressed people, as a population, have abnormal thyroid functioning compared with the non- depressed population, nor can available studies readily indicate that the patient populations employed had clinical or chemical evidence of thyroid pathology that may have accounted for their response to such hormones.

Hormones other than T_3, TSH, or TRH may interact with imipramine.[152]

Drugs That May Cause Mental Depression

There are many commonly used drugs which may cause serious mental depression, especially when taken for an extended period of time. Here, we would like to outline briefly some of the drugs capable of causing depression, and, by calling attention to this fact, urge that their use be at- tended with circumspect ambition and with awareness of their personal, fa- milial, and social consequences.

The Rauwolfia Alkaloids.   Various studies have reported serious incidence of depressive reactions which range from 2 to 18%[154] with prolonged use of reserpine and other rauwolfia alkaloids in the treatment of hypertension. While, in general, the severity of depression has been reported related to dosage and duration of treatment, it should be noted that even small doses, and for relatively limited periods of time, may be accompanied by severe, and sometimes suicidal, depression. The incidence of depression related to its use may be far greater than realized, inasmuch as individuals do not readily recognize or admit to depression, and reports in the literature likely reflect only a small percentage of actual cases. Inasmuch as severe, even in- tractable, depression can be a frequent side effect of reserpine treatment, and in light of the host of other commercially available effective antihypertensive agents, the risks of depression seem to outweigh the potential benefits of this compound.

Steroids: Estrogen and Progesterone Preparations.   The evaluation of estrogenic or progesteronic steroids (alone or in combination) in the production of mood disorder is frought with difficulty, inasmuch as there is a paucity of available clinical information, especially well-designed, controlled studies which might shed light on this subject.[154, 229] The relationship between depression and the ingestion of these steroids would seem to be far greater than meets the eye. Physicians often prescribe estrogenic preparations alone or in combination with progesterone empirically following surgical or spontaneous menopause; there is little in the way of hard-core data to indicate that these drugs prevent depression in such women or that they can relieve depression in a significant number of women in the immediate or postmenopausal states. Similar preparations in the form of oral contraceptives also appear capable of either precipitating or contributing to depressive states. The problem of insidious onset, inability to recognize depresssion, and the use of denial can prevent adequate appreciation of the incidence of mood decrement accompanying steroid ingestion. Although definitive studies will be needed to define more clearly the role played by the estrogenic-progesteronic steroid preparations in the production of depressed states, we would conclude that, unless there is an absolute indication for their use, the routine introduction of steroids should be avoided, and that particular consideration be paid to individuals with a history of recurrent affective disorder or neurotic depressions. Severe depressions, or even psychotic reactions, have been reported in patients with no previous psychiatric disorders who were taking corticosteroids or corticotropin for prolonged periods.

It has most recently been postulated[229] that "contraceptive" depression may, in some cases, be due to inhibition of the synthesis of biogenic amines in the central nervous system as the result of a functional pyridoxine deficiency caused by estrogen in the oral contraceptive. Vitamin B_6 is suggested as preventive or amelioratory for these depressions.

Other Drugs. The long- or short-term administration of amphetamine-type drugs, including dextroamphetamine and methylphenidate, can bring on depressions. This effect can manifest when a patient is "coming down" from a "high" (i.e., "crashing") or when the drug is discontinued after chronic use. One of the adverse effects of L-dopa includes depression. Drugs that act on the central nervous system or on autonomic ganglia may indirectly cause depression by adverse effects on sexual performance, although psychological factors are perhaps most critical in influencing sexual performance and desire. The commonly used agents that may reduce libido or inhibit erection or ejaculation are the major tranquilizers and the sympathetic blockers such as guanethidine and alcohol. Psychotomimetic drugs, especially LSD, may also cause severe depression.

There may be indication that marihuana can cause, contribute to, or precipitate depression in select individuals. It has been our experience, however anecdotal, that individuals who are prone to depression, whether having actually experienced recurrent acute episodes or having been otherwise "moody" or mildly depressed before the use of marihuana, are particularly prone to becoming depressed after using this drug. Marihuana may in fact dampen or otherwise inhibit the effects of conventional anti-depressant drugs, such as the tricyclic compounds, in depressed patients; clinical-biochemical studies should be designed to explore this possibility.

The Psychopharmacology of Mania

Inhibitors of Catecholamine and Serotonin Synthesis

METHYSERGIDE. Preliminary studies by Dewhurst,[64] Haskovec,[106] and Haskovec and Soucek[108, 109] indicated a marked, rapid-acting, antimanic effect for methysergide, an antiserotonin agent. This compound is obviously of tremendous tactical and theoretical interest, since several observations suggest that the metabolism of 5-hydroxytryptamine (serotonin) is disturbed in affective illness. In these reports, methysergide seemed to be quite specific in its effect on mood as well as on the manic phenomena accompanying it. This indicated to Dewhurst that the specificity of response suggested a use for methysergide as a diagnostic test in cases of undiagnosed excitement, since results would be evident within 48 hours. However, controlled cross-validation is lacking; in fact, Coppen et al.[50] have indicated that this compound exhibited no apparent therapeutic action in their patients with moderate to severe mania, and that, since it compared poorly to placebo effects, it may even be detrimental. McCabe, Reich, and Winokur[151] also reported on an open trial of methysergide in acute mania. Of the 12 patients in the study, only one responded during the 4- to 5-day trial. Several who did not respond were given a considerably longer trial than the usual 4 days, but they showed no change.

CINNANSERIN. Itil et al.[116] have indicated efficacy for a relatively new antiserotonin compound, called cinnanserin (2´-3-dimethylamino-prophylthiocinnamanilide hydrochloride), in the treatment of manic patients. These authors indicate that the drug seems to have a very potent and dramatic effect on manic patients, with a particularly noteworthy speed of effectiveness. This finding is in agreement with a report by Kane,[124] who also observed a rapid improvement in manic patients with cinnanserin treatment. In the study by Itil et al., cinnanserin was given to manic patients, in a fixed dose range of 800 mg, reached after a 2- to 5-week treatment period; this was followed by a 4-week placebo period before and after treatment. Treatment efficacy was measured by standard rating instruments. The most common physical side effects were hyperkinesia, stimulated behavior, and insomnia.

In another study by Itil et al.,[117] another antiserotonin and antihistamine compound was found effective in bipolar patients with manic episodes. The compound, called *homochlorocyclazine*, was given in a single-blind fashion to 10 manic patients, for a period of 2 to 33 days, in mean daily dosages of 120 to 300 mg. The results are highly preliminary and difficult to interpret at this point, but the investigators have indicated promising results.

In light of the negative studies following the early enthusiastic claims for methysergide in mania, it would be wise to await the results of further investigations currently underway before ascribing a definite role for cinnanserin and other antiserotonin/antihistamine compounds in the treatment of mania.

PARACHLOROPHENYLALANINE. Parachlorophenylalanine (PCPA) is a specific inhibitor of tryptophan hydroxylase, the rate-limiting enzyme in the conversion of tryptophan to serotonin. No specific antimanic effects were observed with PCPA in an NIMH study, in which the drug was used in doses of up to 4 g/day on a limited number of manic individuals.[170]

α-METHYL-PARA-TYROSINE. α-Methyl-para-tyrosine (α-MPT) has been demonstrated to be a potent and specific inhibitor of dopamine and norepinephrine synthesis, centrally as well as peripherally. The NIMH group[25, 28] has evaluated the effects of α-MPT in hospitalized patients for mania; although this compound was found to have some antimanic properties, it does not appear as effective as lithium in the small series carried out. Others find no antimanic properties for α-MPT.[205]

Precursor Loading. Wilson and Prange[228] have indicated, in a double-blind study of tryptophan versus chlorpromazine (CPZ) in 10 manic patients, that *tryptophan* has antimanic properties, and that l-tryptophan was superior to CPZ in most respects, though statistical significance in molecular rating items was apparently absent. However, there are few data concerning the actual clinical assessments; the fact that only 400 mg of CPZ was used per day for only a 2-week period makes the results of this study highly questionable. This departure from orthodox adherence to using synthesis inhibitors in the treatment of mania stems from current theory that serotonin is also lowered in mania, albeit to a lesser extent than in depression.[155]

Beta-Adrenergic Blockers. Another compound newly tried in the treatment for manic illness is *propranolol*, a beta-adrenergic blocking agent. Reporting on the rapid, distinct improvement with this drug in certain types of psychotic patients including manics, Atsmon et al.[14] indicated that an outstanding impression of treatment was the "complete return to normal within hours, recovery taking place from 12 to 48 hours after initial treatment." Nearly all patients received an initial dose of 600 to 800 mg daily of propranolol. The dosage was increased in some cases, and in one instance it reached 5800 mg. There was a clear-cut parallelism between the onset of amelioration of symptoms and lowering of pulse rate, followed by a lowering of blood pressure after 12 to 24 hours. The specific outcome in manic patients cannot be extracted from the overall results of treatment in psychotics. These results have not been duplicated by others in the United States.[162]

Physostigmine. Physostigmine is a reversible, centrally active acetylcholinesterase inhibitor. This drug has been given intravenously under experimental conditions to manic patients, and has been reported to antagonize or neutralize mania[119] as well as euphoric symptoms related to other illnesses.[120] In addition, it has been reported by these same authors to cause depression,[119] and has been shown to have opposite effects to those occurring in situations in which adrenergic activation occurs (e.g., amphetamine-induced euphoria and psychomotor stimulation).[120] For this reason, it was proposed that central cholinergic factors may play a role in the etiology of affective disorders, and specifically in the balance between central cholinergic and adrenergic neurotransmitter activity in specified brain areas which regulate affect, with depression being a disease of cholinergic dominance and mania being one of adrenergic dominance. However, other studies now completed seriously question the specificity of this drug in qualitatively altering the manic state.[42, 204] Further studies are needed to resolve this issue.

Dibenzazepines and Dibenzocycloheptenes. There have been several uncontrolled trials concerning the usefulness of both imipramine and amitriptyline in the treatment and prophylaxis of mania.

A therapeutic response to imipramine by a manic patient was first reported by Akimoto[2]; in a subsequent study of 20 manic patients by this same author, 13 patients showed complete remission or marked improvement with this drug.[3] Andersen and Kristiansen[6] and Kristjansen[142] have separately reported prompt, favorable therapeutic responses to imipramine by manic patients. Akimoto[2] also indicated that treatment with amitriptyline is effective in certain cases of mania. This suggestion was supported by Stromgren and Stromgren,[214] who indicated that amitriptyline also exhibited a prophylactic effect against manic as well as depressive relapses. There are no confirmatory reports based on systematically conducted clinical trials or specially designed controlled investigations in this area; in the absence of better documentation, the findings above can be considered only an experimental approach.

Despite the persistent investigational preoccupation with brain amines over the past decade, it may be said that clinical studies have not been able to reveal unequivocal, consistent, or unique physiological abnormalities in mania or depression which complement the pharmacologically derived monoamine theories. However, the general monoamine theories have been remarkably productive, leading to an impressive body of experimental and clinical data which have provided new insights into brain neurotransmitter activity and affective disorders only dimly suspected a decade ago.

The Lithium Ion. Lithium is now an established treatment for manic illness. Although its use in psychiatry has been documented since 1949,[30] its acceptance and commercial availability in the United States as a specific pharmacological approach to the treatment of mania is relatively recent. The readers of this volume are referred to several reviews which offer a broad, comprehensive account of the use of lithium in manic illness.[84, 86, 96, 201] We only summarize here the status of this ion in the treatment of manic phase, manic-depressive illness; a more comprehensive account would itself constitute a chapter.

The many open and controlled trials of lithium in mania show a remarkable degree of consistency in concluding that this ion has definite therapeutic properties in the great majority of manic patients. There are, however, some unresolved questions concerning the efficacy of lithium as a treatment for acute mania. What is the relative efficacy of lithium as compared with phenothiazines or haloperidol in the management of acute mania? What clinical or diagnostic features might be used to define the potential lithium responder? A critical review of the evidence makes it clear that definite "answers" to these two questions are not yet possible. Nevertheless, the bulk of the available evidence does suggest the following: (1) Lithium has a more specific/unique effect against "pure" mania than do the phenothiazines; lithium exerts its antimanic effects without the non-specific sedation and tranquilization seen with phenothiazines. (2) Lithium produces its antimanic effects more slowly than phenothiazines, particularly when the level of manic excitement and hyperactivity is intense; the mania begins to dissolve on lithium after a lag period of 4 to 10 days. (Studies indicate a mean of 7 to 8 days.) This lag period probably accounts for the reported advantage of chlorpromazine over lithium in the initial management of highly active manics. (3) As more schizo-affective features are included in the patient populations studied, the advantages of lithium diminish and the advantages of phenothiazines increase. (4) Most of the evidence suggests that lithium alone is the treatment of choice for those manic patients whose hyperactive behavior can be managed during the lag period before lithium begins to exert its effects; for those manic patients whose hyperactivity requires immediate control, chlorpromazine (or halo-peridol) plus lithium is generally the best approach.

For patients clearly in the schizo-affective group, phenothiazines (or haloperidol) are superior to lithium for treatment of the acute episode.

Prophylactic Maintenance Against Recurrent Depression and/or Mania

In recurrent affective illness, the logical treatment approach would clearly appear to be preventive (i.e., treatment should be addressed to preventing relapses) rather than to treating the acute episode when it recurs. Even in the absence of an absolute obliteration of symptom recurrence, maintenance therapy may modify the usual severity of a given episode, and increase the intervals between. It is thus that patients may, although feeling a definite decrement in mood, be able to work and function as usual and to avoid hospitalization and/or constant care in the home.

Lithium carbonate has been the only drug used in trials, some of them double-blind controlled comparisons, in which maintenance therapy for several years has been continued in efforts to guard against or to minimize recurrences of mania.[16, 17, 51, 180, 195] The results have proven highly effective; lithium will shortly be approved by the FDA as a prophylactic treatment against manic relapses. The question today is whether lithium is better than any other drug; further studies will have to be carried out in efforts to cla-rify the role of neuroleptics in staving off further manic episodes, including the use of haloperidol, chlorpromazine, and such.

Lithium carbonate has also proven highly effective against both bipolar and unipolar depressive occurrences.[16, 17, 51, 168, 180] Although the FDA has not approved lithium for use as a prophylactic treatment against unipolar depressions, controlled trials carried out in the United States as well as in several European countries strongly suggest that lithium is a highly ef-fective maintenance therapy against recurrent endogenous depression and is significantly superior to placebo.[17, 51] A recent double-blind controlled study[180] (the only such available) indicates that both lithium and imipramine were equally effective in staving off future relapses of acute depressions; both were significantly better than placebo.

Inasmuch as tricyclic drugs are established treatment modalities in acute endogenous depression, it is odd that so few studies have appeared in which attempts have been made to assess the possible benefits of continuing medication. In fact several reports in the literature indicate the utility of continuing tricyclic antidepressants as a maintenance treatment.[7, 102, 114, 126, 136] Some recent double-blind controlled comparisons indicate that con-tinuing therapy with tricyclic antidepressants is significantly better than placebo.[158, 159] and, in one study,[180] it was equal to lithium in staving off future acute episodes. Tricylcic medications may be continued at doses of 75 to 150 mg, either in divided daily doses or as a single h.s. dose.

Similar studies should be carried out to evaluate efficacy for MAOI maintenance against recurrent endogenous depression.

THE USE OF LITHIUM IN PSYCHIATRIC DISORDERS OTHER THAN MANIA

As early as the mid-1950s, Glessinger[90] and Gershon and Trautner[85] presented case reports suggesting that lithium might be useful in a broad spectrum of psychiatric disorders. The majority of claims for lithium in illnesses such as obsessive-compulsive neuroses, anxiety states, and a variety of schizophrenic subtypes have not been substantiated.[181] The only reasonably well-controlled published studies in which lithium has been shown to exhibit promising results are in the area of emotionally unstable character disorders. Open, more anecdotal studies dealing with the use of lithium in the control of aggression, in different childhood disorders, and in the management of premenstrual tension are sufficiently encouraging to justify more systematic research, both to find more effective therapy, and to increase our theoretical understanding of lithium in these disorders.

Rifkin et al.[183] have carried out a double-blind, controlled study of lithium in neurotic and personality disorders in which a clear or presumptive affective component was present. In their study using hospitalized patients diagnosed as having emotionally unstable character disorder (EUCD), lithium was compared with placebo, with lithium significantly better in two measures of moood fluctuation: global judgment and a rating of the daily range of mood. The fact that both lithium and chlorpromazine diminished the mood fluctuations of EUCD appears analogous to the relationship between the two drugs in manic-depressive and schizoaffective mania; both drugs are at times effective, but lithium appears to have fewer side effects and can be more specifically control the short-lived mood swings and components of disturbed, sociopathic behavior.

In a pilot study testing the usefulness of lithium in the control of violence and aggression, Tupin[216] has reported suggestive efficacy for this ion, and in another pilot study by Sheard[199] on the use of lithium in explosive personalities, encouraging results were reported. These investigations appear to have important implications in light of the growing social-political concern in the control of violence and aggression. Efficacy for lithium in the control of unmanageable antisocial behavior, as well as in cyclothymic personalities, has been alluded to in reports of previous years.

Because of its obvious affective component and inherent periodicity, it would seem logical to test lithium in the premenstrual syndrome. Separate open studies by Sletten and Gershon[208] and Fries,[77] however anecdotal, indicated promising results with lithium in premenstrual syndrome. Currently in the United States, at least two research centers are actively engaged in comparing lithium in double-blind fashion with other drugs more conventionally used in the treatment of premenstrual tension, such as hydrochlorthiazide. It should be stated that the use of hydrochlorthiazide in symptoms of premenstrual tension is largely empirical, inasmuch as there is a paucity of data to substantiate the routine use of such diuretics in this disorder.

The use of lithium in the treatment of abstinent alcoholics and its use in childhood and adolescent disorders are included elsewhere in this chapter.

THE PSYCHOPHARMACOLOGY OF SCHIZOPHRENIA

Psychopharmacology is now established as a necessary, if not always sufficient, part of any comprehensive treatment program for schizophrenia. Antipsychotic or neuroleptic drugs have had a significant impact on therapeutic practice in psychiatry, and have been accompanied by striking changes in the delivery of mental health care. There are many new drugs of the phenothiazine, thioxanthene, and butyrophenone classes which have been recently made available in the United States for general prescription as antipsychotic agents. Also many new investigational drugs of these and other classes of compounds are under investigation.

Drug Class: Phenothiazines (Figure 2)

Piperidine Subclass. *Mesoridazine* (Figure 3; Table 1) has recently been marketed in the United States. A host of studies have been carried out,[13, 23] some of them double-blind comparisons,[76, 105, 153, 209] from which definite antipsychotic efficacy has been shown in hospitalized schizophrenic patients. It has been shown equal in effectiveness to thioridazine, and shows similar side effects. The effectiveness of mesoridazine as compared with chlorpromazine has been demonstrated in long-term studies of psychiatric patients. The parenteral administration is accompanied by rapid onset of action,[13, 23, 105] which has prompted some investigators to suggest that the drug is valuable in the treatment of psychiatric emergencies. The rapid action is reportedly devoid of the usual sedative effect of other phenothiazines.

Piperacetazine has also become available for prescription use in the United States. Two recently published reports[122, 131] compare the effects of

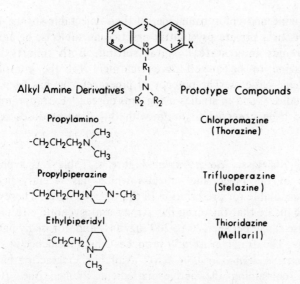

Alkyl Amine Derivatives

Prototype Compounds

Propylamino

$-CH_2CH_2CH_2N\overset{CH_3}{\underset{CH_3}{}}$

Chlorpromazine
(Thorazine)

Propylpiperazine

$-CH_2CH_2CH_2N\underset{}{\bigcirc}N-CH_3$

Trifluoperazine
(Stelazine)

Ethylpiperidyl

$-CH_2CH_2\underset{CH_3}{\bigcirc}$

Thioridazine
(Mellaril)

Figure 2.   Major prototype substituted phenothiazines.

Alkylpiperidyl Derivatives

R	X	Generic Name	Selected Trade Names
$(CH_2)_2\underset{CH_3}{\bigcirc}$	SCH₃	Thioridazine	Mellaril
$(CH_2)_2\underset{CH_3}{\bigcirc}$	SOCH	Mesoridazine	Serentil
$(CH_2)_3\bigcirc-CH_2CH_2OH$ 2-H 3-COCH₃		Piperacetazine	Quide

Figure 3.

piperacetazine and chlorpromazine, in their injectable forms, using either outpatients in a private psychiatric practice as subjects, or agitated acute schizophrenics in a state hospital setting. Both reports have found piperacetazine to be an effective treatment for the control of acute schizophrenic patients. The potency of piperacetazine has been reported in animal studies[141] and in studies using oral doses.[111] Extrapyramidal side effects have been observed to occur with this drug at doses of 50 to 100 mg/day.

Piperazine Subclass. *Butaperazine* Figure 4; Table 2 is a phenothiazine derivative of the piperazine subclass which has recently become commercially available for prescription in the United States. There is good evidence to indicate that this drug has strong antipsychotic effects with an effective dose range between 20 to 200 mg/day, and, for many patients, 40 to 50 mg/day. The drug consistently produces a high incidence of side effects.

Fluphenazine decanoate is a newly available, long-acting phenothiazine derivative containing the active ingredient fluphenazine. It resembles fluphenazine enanthate (previously marketed), in that both given intramuscularly can have an extended duration of effect. The basic effects of both the decanoate and enanthate are no different from fluphenazine hydrochloride, with the exception of duration of action. Fluphenazine has a high mg/mg potency compared with chlorpromazine; 1 to 2 mg is approximately equivalent to 100 mg of chlorpromazine.

The esterification of fluphenazine markedly prolongs the drug duration of effect, without unduly attenuating its beneficial action. The onset of

Propylpiperazine Derivatives

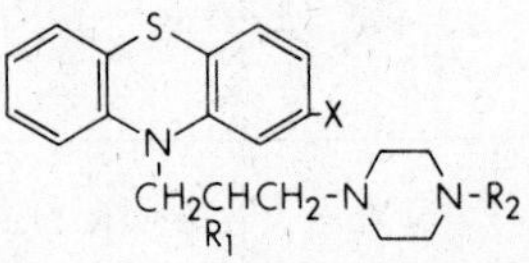

R₁	R₂	X	Generic Name	Selected Trade Names
H	CH_2CH_2OH	CF_3	Fluphenazine	Prolixin Permitil
H	CH_3	$CO(CH_2)_2CH_3$	Butaperazine	Repoise

Figure 4.

action generally appears between 24 and 72 hours after injection, and amelioration of symptoms can continue from 1 to 3 weeks or longer. The decanoate is said to last longer than the enanthate, but definitive proof is lacking. Both compounds can act for 1 or 3 days in some individuals, and in others up to several weeks, reflecting differential metabolic handling in patients. The long-acting, or depot, phenothiazines present the advantage, both in hospital and out of the hospital, or overcoming noncompliance, and, in the hard-to-manage inpatient, may eliminate the necessity for the daily use of IM injections. The most frequently reported adverse effects are extrapyramidal symptoms, and can be quite severe. These extrapyramidal symptoms can last up to several weeks following only one injection, and we recommend routine administration of concomitant antiparkinsonian medication with the decanoate (or enanthate). While the usual dosage of decanoate is 25 mg, administered every 2 to 4 weeks, some individuals will require up to 75 mg, on a much more frequent basis. Daily oral ingestion of antiparkinsonian drugs is frequently indicated following single injection.

Drug Class: Thioxanthenes (Figure 5)

In recent years, thiothixene has become available for prescription in the United States as a treatment for schizophrenia. Like chlorprothixene, its chemical structure, pharmacologic actions, and range of clinical effects are very similar to those of the phenothiazines. Some clinicians report that thiothixene has a greater sedative, hypnotic, and antidepressant effect than the phenothiazines; some suggest particular efficacy in schizoaffective individuals. These claims have not been entirely substantiated in the investigational literature. Some reports indicate that this drug can be highly effective for childhood schizophrenia, especially when there is evidence of brain damage (see p. 63).

Drug Class: Butyrophenones (Figure 6)

The butyrophenones represent a distinct class of antipsychotic drugs. Only *haloperidol* is available in the United States for general prescription as an antipsychotic agent; it is thought to be the fourth most commonly prescribed antipsychotic agent in the country. While most physicians are aware of its indications and dose range in psychiatry, we would like to call

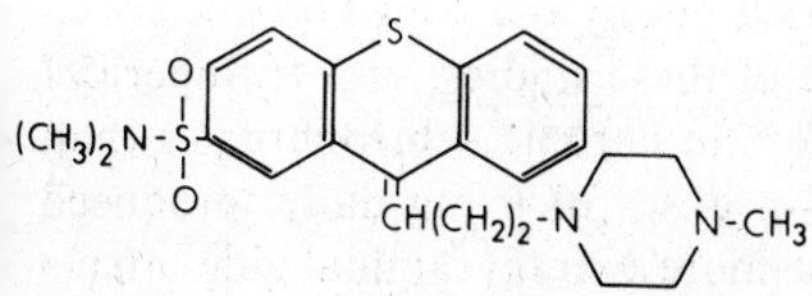

Figure 5.   Chemical structure of *thiothixene*.

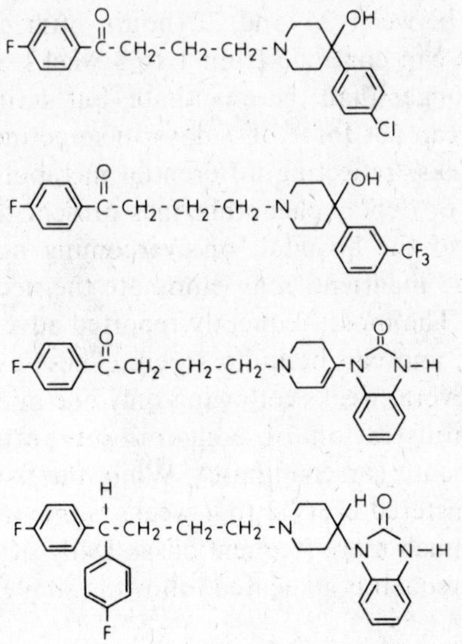

Figure 6.   Butyrophenones: Chemical structures.

attention to the fact that "low-dose" neuroleptics such as haloperiodol employed in large doses can be highly effective in patients not responding to
doses of 30 mg (FDA-approved maximum dosage), or in otherwise drug-
refractory patients. Doses of 60 to 100 mg are frequently cited throughout
the investigational literature; experience in this country indicates that these
doses can be not only effective, but safe as well. Extrapyramidal symptoms
are often seen to disappear with higher doses.[113] Other low-dose antipsychotic drugs, such as fluphenazine, have also been employed, in extraordinarily large doses, for treating otherwise refractory patients. In our clinical
experience, the usual starting dosage for acutely disturbed outpatients who
have a history of previous neuroleptic ingestion is in the range of 15 to 20
mg, as a general rule. Information for the discussion of the various
butyrophenones to follow is found in Refs. 65 and 121.

  Trifluperidol has been studied in a host of uncontrolled open trials, as
well as in double-blind, controlled studies both here and in other areas of
the world. Three of the more rigorous double-blind studies of trifluperidol
versus "prototype drugs" have been carried out by the New Orleans group
headed by Bishop and Gallant.[121] In one of these studies, oral trifluperidol
had significantly greater therapeutic effect in chronic schizophrenics than
did oral chlorpromazine. Trifluperidol, in doses of 6 mg daily, produced
much less hypertension and sedation but more extrapyramidal side effects

than did 1200 mg of chlorpromazine. In another study by this same group, trifluperidol had a greater and more rapid effect than trifluoperazine, and both drugs were clearly superior to phenobarbital in another group of chronic schizophrenics. Side effect liability of both drugs was similar. In a third double-blind study by this group, trifluperidol was compared with haloperidol as well as with chlorpromazine; 4 mg of trifluperidol, 16 mg of haloperidol, and 800 mg of chlorpromazine were used. Both butyrophenones were clearly superior to chlorpromazine on statistical analysis. In another double-blind study in the United States, oral trifluperidol in doses of 2 to 4 mg daily was rather similar to, albeit more effective than, haloperidol and significantly more effective than chlorpromazine at the end of one month of treatment. A host of other studies would appear to attest to the efficacy of trifluperidol. However, after showing promise in this country, trifluperidol was found to cause reduction in serum cholesterol levels and an increase in other sterols. In one study carried out in the United States by Hollister et al.,[112] trifluperidol was indeed found to increase serum cholesterol, but at very high doses of 12 to 15 mg daily, a level usually not given to schizophrenic patients and a range that is poorly tolerated.

Droperidol is another butyrophenone that has been shown promise in some clinical studies. In fact, droperidol has been selected as a neuroleptic of choice in anesthesiology, because of its high potency, short onset of action, and relatively short duration of its peak. Droperidol alone or in combination with fentanyl is currently marketed in the United States for use as a premedication in different surgical cases, and/or for relief of pain during surgical procedures. Droperidol has been subjected to clinical trials as an antipsychotic agent; in one uncontrolled as well as in one controlled comparison with haloperidol, droperidol was shown to have antipsychotic efficacy. In the controlled trial, it was equally effective as haloperidol. There are a host of reports indicating efficacy for droperidol in the European literature, all of which relate to open studies. Doses of droperidol are about the same as those for haloperidol; side effects are similar. Whether droperidol offers any advantage over haloperidol as an antipsychotic awaits further clarification.

As a general rule, substitution of the ketone in the butyrophenone skeleton leads to a loss of activity. Exceptions have, however, been provided by the discovery of 4-4-diphenyl-butyl-piperidine derivatives, of which *pimozide* (Figure 6) is the prototype. Pimozide is actually a derivative of benperidol, another butyrophenone derivative studied in clinical psychiatry. Although it is technically not a butyrophenone, pimozide is of interest in that some of its pharmacological effects are novel to existing neuroleptics. The drug is a specific blocker of post-synaptic dopaminergic synapses, and it is extremely long-acting. Clinical studies indicate that the drug has not been especially useful in curbing acute schizophrenic symptoms, but is highly effective for long-term maintenance treatment. It has been reported that increased socialization was associated with long-term treatment with this drug, which has significant implications as a primary goal in long-term rehabilitative programs. Like fluphenazine, the prolonged action of pimozide may simplify dosage schedules during maintenance therapy to every few days or weekly intervals. Certainly, if early reports continue to confirm such new properties, pimozide could be a valued addition to the treatment of chronic schizophrenic patients. However, at the present time, a conservative posture must be taken with regard to claims of specificity of action, until further documentation is forthcoming.

Drug Class: Benzoquinoline

Tetrabenazine is the prototype compound of the benzoquinoline series. These drugs are of interest to research psychopharmacologists, largely due to their common characteristics with reserpine, especially the capacity to deplete brain amines. It is not commercially available in the United States, but has been used investigationally, with some success, in the treatment of tardive dyskinesia.

Drug Class: Indolic Derivatives

The indolic derivatives are used investigationally now in the United States for drug treatment of schizophrenia. These include *molindone*, the most widely studied of this series; phenylpiperazines, of which *oxypertine* is the typical representative; and the *acridans*, chemically related to the phenothiazines.

Molindone (Figure 7) has been shown to have antipsychotic properties. In several open studies,[43, 112, 200] it has been reported that molindone is effective in chronic and new schizophrenic patients when used in doses of 10 to 300 mg/day. Side effects consist of drowziness, sedation, hypotension, and extrapyramidal symptoms. However, in a double-blind, placebo-controlled comparison,[44] antipsychotic efficacy was comparable to placebo and less effective than that of the standard drug, chlorpromazine, in hospitalized chronic schizophrenics. A possibility of an alerting effect was suggested, albeit tenuously held, by the authors.

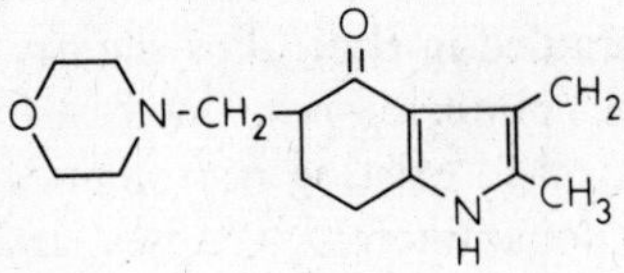

Figure 7.   Chemical structure of *molindone*.

Drug Class: Dibenzazepines

The introduction of new pharmaceutical agents is an exciting event, especially when such drugs are shown to be effective for a particular illness. In
the 20 or so years since the introduction of the rauwolfia alkaloids and
phenothiazines for psychotic psychiatric patients, the only new compounds
that have been introduced include the butyrophenones and the
thioxanthenes. In 1965, a new series of antipsychotic agents belonging to
the dibenzazepine series was introduced.[212] These drugs include *loxapine,
metiapine,* and *clozapine* (Figures 8 and 9). All of these drugs, which are
available only for investigational use in this country, have been shown to
have antipsychotic properties. Loxapine and metiapine are potent classic
neuroleptics; that is, they have antipsychotic properties and a tendency to
produce extrapyramidal side effects in man. Recently, however, the newest
member of this series, clozapine, was introduced clinically; contrary to
classical neuroleptics, this drug is claimed not to produce catalepsy in animals. Furthermore, it does not antagonize the effects of amphetamine or
apomorphine. All the studies carried out with clozapine to date have been
open trials. All of the studies have indicated antipsychotic efficacy; in two
reports, investigators indicated their impressions that clozapine was found
to have at least the same antipsychotic effect as leveomepromazine and
thioridazine.[8, 103] Clozapine can and does produce marked sedation.
*However, unlike classical neuroleptics, there are no extrapyramidal side ef-
fects reported in any of the reports.* These effects of clozapine formed the
basis of a suggestion by Stille and Hippius[213] that the concept of neuroleptic
drugs should be reevaluated; that is, that all neuroleptic drugs must have,
as a criterion, the ability to produce extrapyramidal side effects in man.

In a large-scale study by Angst et al.,[9] *clozapine* (Figure 8) was used in
doses usually ranging between 150 and 400 mg; some individuals received
a maximum dosage of 900 mg. Treatment lasted 30 days. Both manic
and schizophrenic individuals were treated, but, as in the case with many
European studies, the authors do not characterize the particular treatment
outcome in either population, saying only that it is a good antipsychotic
drug. Gross et al.[103] reported at the Seventh International Congress of the

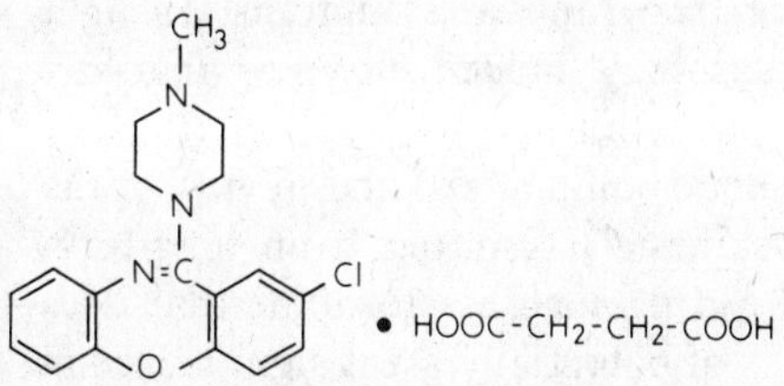

• HOOC-CH₂-CH₂-COOH

Figure 8.   Chemical structure of loxapine.

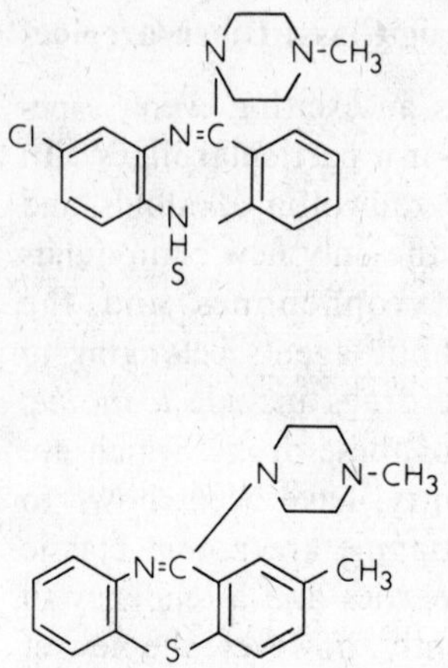

Figure 9.   Chemical structures of clozapine and metiapine.

CINP in Prague, in 1970, the results of a double-blind study of clozapine and thioridazine, in which the authors indicated that the drug was found to have at least the same antipsychotic effect as the reference compound, along with a marked tendency to produce sedation. As in the report by Angst et al., there were no extrapyramidal side effects. Kline and Blanda[139] report beneficial effects with clozapine in a private practice outpatient population. Many of the patients who responded favorably were maintained on daily doses of 100 to 200 mg/day. The authors formulated that the patients who responded best were unable to control inappropriate "acting out" behavior. Again, no extrapyramidal effects were recorded. In an open study[148] of 21 hospitalized patients with moderate to severe symptoms of acute schizophrenia, two-thirds of the patients showed moderate to marked improvement. Changes first occurred in the area of behavior, and it was behavioral changes that were most consistent in both groups. The study was divided into two parts. The first had eight patients, with a dose range of 50 mg p.o. t.i.d. to 100 mg p.o. t.i.d. The second part (13 patients) were given increasing doses from 25 mg t.i.d. to 300 mg p.o. t.i.d. Two of the patients in the second series were given up to 400 mg p.o. t.i.d. The greater efficacy was found in the second group, at the higher dose levels. Again, no patient showed any extrapyramidal symptoms. In light of the fact that antiparkinsonian drugs may induce enzymes that decrease effective blood-tissue levels of phenothiazine metabolites (thereby altering clinical response to such neuroleptic compounds) and in view of the now-recognized concern of tardive dyskinesia's resulting from long-term use of neuroleptics, the clinical use of a drug such as clozapine that does not produce extrapyramidal symptoms is of potentially great significance in the treatment armamentarium of psychotic states. Despite some very interesting hypotheses and sophisticated animal experiments,[5, 197, 213] the possible mechanisms that might dissociate clozapine from the classic neuroleptics as regards extrapyramidal symptoms remain unresolved at the time of writing.

Loxapine succinate is a tricyclic compound identified biochemically as 2-chlor-11 (4-methyl-1-piperazinyl) dibenz (*d,f*) oxazepine succinate (Figure 9). This compound has been found to exhibit antipsychotic efficacy for chronic schizophrenic patients in many uncontrolled clinical trials[130, 147, 160, 198] as well as in a controlled, double-blind comparison against trifluoperazine.[20] Some clinical studies have also indicated efficacy of this compound in acute schizophrenic patients.[62, 130, 160] However, in two studies, the antipsychotic effect of this drug in newly admitted acute hospitalized schizophrenics has left some unresolved questions. Gershon et al.[87] were not impressed by the antipsychotic effects of this drug in a noncontrolled trial. Shopsin et al.[202] compared loxapine succinate in a controlled, double-blind fashion with chlorpromazine in schizophrenic patients. The results of this latter study with hospitalized patients were not clear-cut; discrepancies in assessment methods preclude any definite statement regarding comparable drug efficacy in the psychiatric population. It can be stated that, despite the inelegance of the early uncontrolled clinical trials, and the critical assessment of other studies notwithstanding, the results of one collaborative study and of a controlled trial with a reference neuroleptic indicate that loxapine shows antipsychotic potency in chronic patients. With regard to the effects of loxapine in acute, newly admitted schizophrenics, however, the results are less clear-cut, and leave the question of drug efficacy in these patients an open one. Methodological problems in the study by Shopsin et al., specifically the fact that an adequate dose range of loxapine succinate may not have been employed, leaves the question unresolved.

Whereas early European trials either failed to report, or specifically reported no, extrapyramidal symptoms concomitant with loxapine treatment,[19, 61, 160, 198] a host of trials thereafter[20, 62, 87, 147, 219] indicate that extrapyramidal symptoms frequently accompany treatment with loxapine, the most conspicuous of which include akathesia, dystonia, tremor, and rigidity. Such side effects in fact appear more frequently with loxapine than with the phenothiazine compound chlorpromazine.

First in an uncontrolled trial[79] and then in a double-blind controlled comparison,[80] *metiapine* (Figure 8) was shown to be a highly active antipsychotic compound for the chronic schizophrenic patient. Superiority over trifluoperazine, the reference drug in the control study, was suggested by all standard NIMH efficacy measures employed. Having an allegedly low incidence of severe side effects, metiapine requires additional studies to determine comparable efficacy with available prototype drugs in acute schizophrenia and/or in subgroups of schizophrenics with particular target symptoms.

DRUG-INDUCED NEUROLOGICAL DISORDERS

Extrapyramidal symptoms (EPS) are known to be caused by the phenothiazine derivatives by the tricyclic antidepressants and by the butyrophenones.[92] Depending upon the dosage and duration of treatment, 21 to 79% of psychiatric patients receiving long-term phenothiazine therapy have been reported to develop these symptoms.[15, 104] In a report by the Boston Collaborative Drug Surveillance Program,[21] EPS occurred in 0.9% (i.e., 18 of 2049) of the medical inpatients taking one or more of the three classes of psychoactive drugs given above. The group found that the drugs most likely to produce these symptoms are the phenothiazine compounds; the highest rate among these phenothiazine users is seen in the trifluperazine-treated individuals, either alone or in combination with other drugs. The Boston group further suggested that the tendency for these drugs to produce EPS symptoms is enhanced in persons with systemic lupus erythematosus or in persons taking prednisone. Physicians prescribing these drugs should be aware of these frequent complications when considering a given treatment program.

Tardive dyskinesia has been described as a potentially irreversible neurological condition, not infrequently encountered in patients on prolonged neuroleptic therapy.[56] It is characterized by involuntary bucco-linguomasticatory movements, occasionally accompanied by choreiform movements of the extremities or trunk. A number of large-scale surveys of psychiatric groups have revealed the prevalence of this syndrome ranging from 3 to 30%.[74] The risk appears to be greater in elderly patients or in those with some underlying organic condition, especially in female patients. Tardive dyskinesia has caused special concern among psychiatrists because there is no known treatment; antiparkinsonian agents usually do not alleviate the symptoms. Then too, there is much concern because the dyskinetic movements may persist indefinitely after neuroleptic drugs have been stopped. In fact, one of the more interesting findings is a confirmation that the syndrome can be precipitated or aggravated by reducing or discontinuing the administration of phenothiathines.[57] Thus withdrawal of medication or pharmacological treatment each show inconsistency in remedying the situation. A variety of agents have been used in attempts to reverse the condition. Tardive dyskinesia has been linked to neuropathological lesions in the basal ganglia, and to an excess of dopaminergic activity in the same brain areas.[37, 110] Reports of marked short-term clinical efficacy have appeared for a dopamine-depleting drug, *tetrabenazene*,[91, 127] and for dopamine-blocking drugs, including *haloperidol*[127, 206] and *thiopropazate*.[26, 58, 207] These drugs are usually given over a 6- to 8-week period, with gradual dose incrementation. The successful management of this disorder with such drugs has supported the hypothesis that tardive dyskinesia may result from excessive dopaminergic activity in the brain. Other reports have indicated that *reserpine*[167, 193] or *isocarboxazide*[26] was effective in the symptomatic control of tardive dyskinesia. However, these latter trials were carried out over relatively short periods, and no satisfactory and long-term pharmacology for tardive dyskinesia has been found to date. *Amantadine*,[218] an antiviral agent with mild central nervous system stimulant properties, has also been suggested, but the findings from these investigations and the criteria on which they were based have been challenged.[55] The vitamin *pyridoxine*[54] has been tried, but also without success. *Levodopa*[133] has provided no help in tardive dyskinesia, nor has *methyldopa*,[128] a compound known to compete with levodopa *in vitro* and a commonly used antihypertensive, shown any clear effects in relieving tardive dyskinesia. A preliminary report by Prange et al.[179] with *tryptophan and lithium* has not been subject to critical evaluation or duplication. *Methylphenidate* has been used in a placebo-controlled study of 17 patients; the authors conclude that this stimulant is not effective in tardive dyskinesia.[69] Dalen[59] has used lithium carbonate.

Studies of drug treatments for tardive dyskinesia involve serious ethical issues, obviously. A group of investigators at Boston State Hospital[129] carried out a study to determine whether drugs they had previously shown to suppress dyskinetic movements (haloperidol, tetrabenazene) would be as effective over an 18-week period as they had been over an 8-week period. Their results indicate that the two treatments did not harm the patients, but unfortunately neither did they prove to be particularly useful in suppressing abnormal movements over an 18-week period. An initial suppression achieved for both drugs did not persist; even doubling the dosage in the latter phases of the study did not result in effective suppression.

At the present state of knowledge, no specific therapy for tardive dyskinesia can be recommended, although the withholding of all antipsychotic measures for prlonged periods or the use of such agents in the smallest amounts that will prevent major exacerbation of the patient's condition appears to be the wiser strategy. In point of fact, the FDA recommends[74] that the antipsychotic medication be withdrawn immediately if the syndrome appears. The ultimate utility of drugs such as clozapine, which is not accompanied by extrapyramidal symptoms, appears relevant in this regard.

ANTIANXIETY AGENTS

Clorazepate dipotassium is a new benzodiazepine derivative, known chemically as 7-chloro-2, 3-dihydro-2,2-dihydroxy-5-phenyl-1H-1,4-benzodiazepine-3-carboxilic acid dipotassium salt. Like other benzoidaizepines, this drug is an anxiolytic agent and is pharmacologically related to others in this group including chlordiazepoxide, diazepam, and oxazepam.

PROPRANOLOL

Propranolol is a β-adrenergic blocking agent which has made a significant contribution to pharmacotherapeutics, primarily in the field of cardiology. However, over the years, information is accumulating to indicate that the β-adrenergic blockers may also have psychopharmacologic significance.[100] They have proven useful in anxiety neuroses and phobic states and in a variety of functional cardiovascular disorders characterized by excessive β-adrenergic activity. In addition, propranolol seems to possess a distinct sedative, anticonvulsant, and muscle relaxant property, with effects at the level of the central nervous system. These latter properties are not well understood, and deserve careful study, since the β-adrenergic blockers seem to be potentially useful psychotropic drugs.

When administered in controlled trials in anxious outpatients, propranolol is as effective as chlordiazepoxide in alleviating the somatic manifestations of anxiety.[223] Propranolol has been shown more effective than placebo in this regard. Linken[145] has described cases of severe anxiety reactions following ingestion of LSD, unrelievable by diazepam and by phenothiazines, but effectively curtailed by propranolol. Another report described improvement of tension and depression in abstinent alcoholics.[39] The antianxiety efficacy of these drugs seems to be a peripheral, rather than central, effect.

However, a number of other investigations have led to the question of whether the psychotropic effects of propranolol and related drugs can be explained entirely by a peripheral β-blockade. Atsmon et al.[14] have indicated that short-term use of propranolol in schizophrenic and manic patients was followed by a marked decrease in psychotic behavior and anxiety and by amelioration of thought disorder, including subjective reduction of hallucinations. Symptoms recurred when propranolol was withdrawn. Other studies carried out in this country fail to confirm these findings, however.[162]

Propranolol has also been used in the treatment of essential tremor. A recent report by Schou et al.[132] in Denmark, indicates a potential use for propranolol in lithium-induced tremor. Since lithium-induced tremor shows spontaneous variations, and inasmuch as the authors do not offer specific data or any controls, these findings must be taken as tentative. Interestingly, these investigators indicate that tremor in patients who are treated concurrently with lithium and tricyclic antidepressants does not yield to propranolol.

Obviously, propranolol presents as a potentially useful psychotropic agent. However, its practical use in the conditions above elaborated must await very careful critical evaluation and duplication in further well-designed, controlled trials with larger populations. Reports of psychotic effects have frequently appeared in the literature[100, 211]; although there is no great incidence of such toxic morbidity in the literature, the investigational use of such agents as propranolol in psychiatric patients should be undertaken with circumspect ambition and used only in those centers which require careful collaboration with medical staff knowledgeable about the pharmacology and experienced in using β-adrenergic blockers.

THE USE OF PHARMACEUTICALS IN ALCOHOLISM

Drugs Used in the Prevention of Chronic, Periodic Alcoholism (or the "Abstinent Phase" of Chronic Alcoholics)

In an uncontrolled clinical study, *propranolol* was found to be selectively stress-relieving on the symptoms of alcoholics.[38] This effect was even more marked in a follow-up study by Carlsson.[39] Propranolol had no effect on dysphoric symptoms, but there was a great reduction in tension. The problems in methodology and study design in Carlsson's 1971 report, particularly the concomitant use of other psychoactive drugs and the lack of any data pertaining to symptom discrimination, really preclude drawing any conclusions about the efficacy of propranolol in abstinent alcohols. Several trials, including double-blind studies,[223] have indicated the anti-anxiety effect of propranolol, however.

In a study carried out by the Veterans Administration Hospital in Togus, Maine,[230] patients were randomized into a group receiving *lithium* and another group receiving identical-appearing placebo, during the abstinence phase of their illness following hospitalization for excessive drinking. Patients were selected who had a history of chronic alcoholism and nonpsychotic depression. The investigators chose one objective criterion of change in drinking habits: whether the patient had an episode of drinking that led to hospitalization for detoxification. They did not try to measure the amount or frequency of drinking, just the number of episodes which required hospitalization.

As expected, the patient population was unreliable. Of the 73 patients selected, 43 failed to complete the first follow-up period of 44 weeks. Of the remaining 30 who completed the 48 weeks of continuous treatment, 14 were from the placebo group and 16 from the lithium group. When the *readmission* rate of the two groups was compared, lithium appeared to modify the patients' drinking habits significantly. Of these patients readmitted for their drinking, the lithium group did not appear to repeat as frequently as did the control. Although both groups were less depressed at the end of one year, when compared with depression ratings at the beginning of the project, there was not a significant difference between groups when analyzed using analysis of covariance. This finding was in contrast to the original assumption of these investigators that lithium might control alcoholism by controlling depression.

The data suggest an exciting avenue for future research. It should be emphasized, however, that such studies need be undertaken with caution, since lithium and alcohol are not always compatible; there may be a risk of severe toxicity (including neurotoxic manifestations) when alcohol, especially in *large* quantities, is consumed under conditions of lithium ingestion.

Disulfiram is a drug which appears to decrease the rate at which certain drugs or alcohol are metabolized, and so many increase their blood levels and the possibility of clinical toxicity. It is thus that Antabuse has been marketed; available for prescription in the United States as an "enforced sobriety" medication, it is not likely that this aversive therapeutic approach to alcoholism has more than a brief effect on the drinking pattern of the chronic alcoholic. The literature regarding Antabuse is readily available.

Drugs Used in Nonepileptic Alcoholic Seizures and Impending Delirium Tremens

In another hospital study,[72] diphenylhydantoin with or without supplemental doses of diazepam has been found to be effective for preventive and treatment of nonepileptic alcoholic seizures and impending delirium tremens. The author does not use intravenously administered diphenylhydantoin, because of the risk of cardiac arrest, although he does indicate that this drug can be administered intramuscularly for early and prompt induction of the drug, followed by oral administration. Finer suggests that the use of diphenylhydantoin in nonepileptic alcoholic patients need not continue longer than a week, if the patient remains alcohol-abstinent.

Comment

Because of the widespread use of chlordiazepoxide hydrochloride in the treatment of acute alcoholism or in abstinent alcholics, we would like to call attention to the equally widespread habituation that accompanies its use today. An "abstinence syndrome" or "withdrawal" can occur, subsiding promptly with resumption of chlordiazepoxide therapy. Withdrawal symptoms resemble somewhat those which follow withdrawal of barbiturates, including restlessness, agitation, insomnia, tremulousness, and anorexia. Alcoholics have a tendency to abuse chlordiazepoxide in conjunction with alcohol, and may substitute their psychological dependence for alcohol with chlordiazepoxide in the manner so often observed in other addictions. Although Finer[71] indicates that the use of diazepam for the control of anxiety, tension, and the alcohol abstinence syndrome is much more desirable and is not accompanied by such abuse either during alcohol ingestion or in the abstinence phase ("Cessation of diazepam therapy is infrequently followed by pleading for resumption thereof"), our experience is at variance with this. We caution that diazepam habituation is at least as frequent as that to chlordiazepoxide in alcoholics, and that attention should be paid to the hazardous potential sequellae to alcohol intoxication, including comatose states, accidental injuries, aspiration of vomitus, pneumonia, neglect of other illnesses, and even death. The use of other psychoactive drugs more specific to the patient's underlying problem (e.g., phenothiazines for schizophrenics, and tricyclic antidepressants for depressions) appears to us to be conspicuously neglected in the specific treatment approach to this problem. The use of nonspecific, addicting drugs, such as diazepam, on a large-scale basis is cause for concern, and appears only to contribute or to replace one addiction for another.

Methadone in the Management of Heroin Addiction

The methadone maintenance treatment of heroin addicts is now offered to over 85,000 patients in some 500 hospitals and community programs in the United States.[154] Until March 15, 1973, methadone was still classified as an investigational new drug (IND) in this country. We will not deal with this drug at any length here. It should be emphasized, however, that methadone maintenance is not a complete and fully adequate treatment for narcotic addiction. Many programs, even with motivated persons and under careful supervision, have not been successful. Those programs making claims for its efficacy are part of a broad supportive orientation; the success rate as measured by a decreased incidence of sociopathy and resumption of employment/schooling is often very difficult to assess adequately. It is a difficult task to evaluate treatment outcome with any drug when such variables as psychotherapy, medical care, social-family services, supportive care, and sometimes financial care are uncontrolled.

Many psychopharmacologists are not at all enchanted with this form of treatment, holding that it, in fact, only replaces one form of addiction with another. The pharmacological activity of methadone and heroin, despite some differences, are very similar. Physical dependence on methadone does occur as a consequence of maintenance use. The most important contraindication to the use of methadone is the absence of physiological addiction to heroin; prescription of methadone for nonaddicts has resulted in death or primary methadone addiction. More than 100 fatalities have occurred in New York City alone from overdose of methadone. "Street" heroin in some communities is so heavily adulterated that many patients are addicted only in a psychological sense and show no symptoms on withdrawal. The possibility of long-term effects on the newborn from *in utero* exposure has not been adequately studied; such investigations are currently underway at the time of writing.

Methadone maintenance, like other social issues today, has assumed overwhelming importance in the community and in government. Society feels it is a panacea for getting addicts and other sociopaths off the streets (although nobody wants a mantenance program opening in his neighborhood); the government has poured large sums of money into methadone maintenance programs with less rigorous requirements for its safe and effective use then is usually demanded. Well-designed controlled studies are certainly lacking here. Suffice to say that better methods of treating heroin addiction should and are being sought.

NEW PSYCHOACTIVE DRUGS IN THE
TREATMENT OF CHILDREN AND ADOLESCENTS

If there are problems in evaluating chemotherapeutic agents for emotional conditions in adults, the dilemma is considerably magnified with regard to children. Psychiatrists have a fundamental difficulty agreeing on mere classification in childhood disorders; differences in opinion concerning the diagnosis of manic-depressive disorder in children or adolescents highlight the constitutional, clinical, and psychodynamic bewilderment often surrounding this problem. Similar symptoms may be caused by a variety of etiological factors; childhood schizophrenia may not represent a single homogenous entity, and autism may be the earliest expression of childhood schizophrenia. The concept of the "hyperactive child" underscores the therapeutic problems arising from complex diagnostic situations. It has become fashionable in recent years to perpetuate the simplistic idea that all hyperactive children simply require stimulant medication. The danger of this dictum is that it is oversimplistic. All too often, stimulants have been given as the only treatment for children who also required specific remediation for learning disabilities or more thorough psychiatric evaluation. Major or minor mental disorders in children are frequently associated with minimal brain dysfunction; it is therefore essential to consider such an eventuality, for example, in reaching a diagnosis. Overoptimistic claims of easy relief have led to equally unnecessary disappointment and scepticism. In addition to confusing the public, they have contributed to a recent fervor in the press over the thousands of school children who are supposedly receiving "mind-controlling drugs."

Experience has, nevertheless, shown that drug treatment, if carefully used, is often a valuable part of the total treatment of a disturbed child, and can make him or her more amenable to educational and other therapies, more manageable, and easier to live with in the community.

New Psychoactive Drugs in the Treatment of Hyperactive Children

Certainly, on the basis of present-day evidence, short trials of drugs are justified as symptomatic treatment and as an adjunct to remedial methods of education in the hyperkinetic and perceptually handicapped child; central nervous stimulants such as *methylphenidate* and *amphetamines* do remain the agents of choice. A recent report indicates that *imipramine hydrochloride*[144] has been successfully used in the treatment of hyperkinetic syndrome, where amphetamine or methylphenidate trials have been unrewarding. It was reported that imipramine has the advantage of having a long-lasting effect, so that a single 25-mg tablet 1 hour before bedtime may carry the patient through the entire day, thereby avoiding multiple doses during the day. Conners et al.[45] compared the efficacy, side effects, and safety of *magnesium pemoline* and dextroamphetamine with placebo. Magnesium pemoline is a central nervous system stimulant composed of pemoline and magnesium hydroxide which has been reported to have significant antifatigue and performance-enhancing properties in other studies with adults and children. The authors found significant improvement for both active drugs, and few differences between them. Side effects were similar, and laboratory data showed no toxic effects. The authors concluded that magnesium pemoline offers a good alternative for treatment of the syndrome of hyperactivity and minimal brain dysfunction. Interestingly, dextroamphetamine patients improved more immediately, with magnesium pemoline treatment being accompanied by fewer complaints of anorexic side effects. *Deanol* is thought to be converted to acetylcholine within neurons and to act as a central nervous system stimulant. The results of trials of deanol in 239 patients with behavior and learning disorders have been reviewed.[157] In doses of 10 to 1000 mg daily, administered for periods of 4 to 36 weeks, only two of six authors employed objective methods of evaluation, although the majority of studies included placebo controls and double-blind techniques. Three investigators reported improvement; an equal number of reports were negative. Side effects were minimal and infrequent.

Lithium carbonate has been used in the treatment of hyperactive children. In a study carried out by Greenhill et al. at the NIMH,[101] nine severely hyperactive children, unresponsive to drugs and psychotherapy, were placed on a 3-month modified double-blind trial of lithium carbonate alternating with dextroamphetamine or placebo. The results of this study indicate that, while lithium carbonate appears to be a safe drug for investigation in children, this ion is inadequate for treating hyperactive children unresponsive to stimulant medication. In another study[34] involving a controlled crossover between lithium and chlorpromazine in hyperactive severely disturbed young psychotic and nonpsychotic preschool-aged children, more symptoms diminished on chlorpromazine than on lithium. However, blind ratings indicated no statistically significant difference between the two drugs as well as an absence of any statistically significant change in behavior or psychopathology with either drug. The authors suggest that some of the observed effects by lithium on behavior warrant further studies to explore the effects of this ion in certain subdiagnostic categories with a cluster of symptoms, such as hyperactivity, aggressivity, and explosive affect. Gram and Rafaelson[99] also reported a decrease in hyperactivity, aggressiveness, stereotyped behavior, and psychotic speech in their controlled trial with lithium in psychotic children. Whitehead and Clark,[225] however, were unable to find any difference between lithium and placebo on hyperactivity in children.

Lithium Carbonate in Mood Disorders of Childhood and Adolescence

Annell in 1969[10, 11] reported very effective results against manic symptoms in young Swedish children treated with lithium carbonate. She also believes that maintenance lithium therapy is good in preventing recurrences of mania, and particularly successful in averting depressions. This author reports the clinical impression that lithium also yields good results in children whose illnesses are not basically mood disorders. An assessment of lithium's effect in these children is complicated by many issues. The dilemma of whether a diagnosis of mania (or depression) is ever applicable in young children is further complicated by the fact that many of the patients described by this author would be acknowledged by many clinicians as schizophrenic. Perhaps the most critical issue in questioning the validity of overall results is that, for Annell, lithium would appear useful in any child, regardless of presenting symptoms. She described favorable effects in children with periodic stupor, schizophrenia, and/or organic brain damage. Such broad applicability for any one drug deserves serious critical scrutiny. Frommer[78] also found lithium useful for emotionally disturbed children. Among them were children who showed behavior that, in an adult, would suggest hypomania. Lithium was also given a trial in other children who were described as periodically falling into moods marked by depressive features and temper outbursts of serious magnitude. Lithium therapy was considered successful in such cases. Other reports also suggest favorable results in children with affective disorder.

Rifkin et al.[183] have carried out a double-blind controlled study using lithium in a predominantly adolescent female inpatient hospital population, diagnosed as emotionally unstable character disorder (EUCD). These patients were defined as having maladaptive behavior patterns along with mood swings of hypomania and depression. Lithium was significantly better than placebo in dampening the affective-mood fluctuations, but did produce the undesirable side effects of sedation that chlorpromazine produces in such subjects.

Neuroleptics

The phenothiazine, *fluphenazine*, has been shown to be highly effective in prepuberal severely disturbed, schizophrenic, and autistic children.[68] Several investigators have found *thiothixene* to be a safe and effective therapeutic agent in psychotic children in doses from 1 to 40 mg/day, with a wide therapeutic margin.[31, 220] It is allegedly the combination of stimulating and antipsychotic properties which makes this drug superior to the phenothiazines in young children. *Trifluperidol*, one of the butyrophenones, was shown to have antipsychotic and stimulating qualities in preschool retarded schizophrenic and autistic children by Fish et al.[73] and Campbell et al.;[33] this drug was significantly more effective than chlorpromazine or trifluoperazine in the same subjects. *Molindone* was shown in a pilot study[32] to have stimulating as well as sedative therapeutic effects in a small number of schizophrenic and nonpsychotic children 3 to 5 years old, and may warrant further investigational attention here.

Of other drugs under investigation, *opipramol hydrochloride* has been reported to be a safe, well-tolerated, and effective psychotropic drug in a wide variety of emotional disturbances in childhood by Dr. John J. Stack of Dublin in a report to the Fourth Congress of the Union of European Pedopsychiatrists. There is little other information to confirm or to deny this report; in the absence of further investigational clarification, these findings must await duplication and critical evaluation.

L-Dopa maintenance treatment (over 6 months) to autistic children was accompanied by an observable decrease of blood serotonin concentrations in three of the four patients followed by Ritvo et al.[185] This was not accompanied by any significant clinical change, however. (Serotonin has been found to be elevated in blood and platelets of some autistic, schizophrenic, and retarded children, and/or to have an enhanced efflux from platelets of infantile autistics.[184]) Campbell et al.[36] at New York University Medical Center are currently investigating the effects of L-dopa in severely disturbed children (including schizophrenic and autistic).

Thyroid Hormone

A controlled study of *triiodothyronine* (T_3), a hormone with central nervous system effects and stimulating properties, was reported in detail and discussed by Campbell et al.[35] Blind ratings indicated statistically significant improvement in overall symptomatology for T_3 over dextroamphetamine; T_3 showed both antipsychotic and stimulating effects. The study, which suffers from several discrepancies in experimental design and methodology, did nevertheless suggest to the authors that T_3 is an agent of potential benefit in the treatment of childhood psychoses (schizophrenia and autism). Interestingly, in this study the children who improved had elevated baseline levels of serum thyroxin (T_4) levels as measured by column chromatography and "free" T_4.

Comments on Stimulant/Tricyclic Drugs in Children

Several reports have documented that, for hyperactive children, the initial period of stimulant drug use causes weight loss. Tolerance, however, develops to this drug-induced effect on weight. In children, after the phase of transient weight loss, it has generally been assumed, though never shown, that the continual use of a therapeutic dose of a stimulant drug has no lasting effect on normal growth. However, in a recent report of 29 hyperactive children receiving dextroamphetamine in doses of 10 to 15 mg/day, and methylphenidate in doses of 30 to 40 mg/day, suppression of weight gain was caused by these drugs.[188] Depression of growth and height varied in degree; however, children whose growth was depressed also had proportional depression of growth and height. Thirteen children who took stimulant drugs for 9 or more months showed a rebound weight gain when medication was abruptly stopped. Dextroamphetamine inhibition of weight gain was significantly greater than that observed with methylphenidate.

This report may be a cause for great concern, although it has apparently thus far been brushed aside.

The use of tricyclic antidepressants in the treatment of childhood enuresis is increasing, despite the fact that no specific mechanism of action in this regard has been uncovered. Inasmuch as overdose and poisoning are reportedly on the increase in children,[12] the possible benefits should be carefully weighed against the known and unknown potential for harm.

GERIATRIC PSYCHOPHARMACOLOGY

Recently, there has been considerable attention paid to the need for improvement in the mental and physical health care of elderly citizens.[4] There is precious little in the way of effective treatment, whether by pharmaceutical agents or by any other means, for mental problems resulting from organic changes due to old age. We would like here to focus on three treatment approaches, two of which are new and as yet experimental. The two new treatment modalities for improving, arresting, or otherwise ameliorating organic symptoms related to aging include the use of a drug called Gerovital, on the one hand, and on the other, the use of hyperbaric oxygen. A third approach, the use of dihydrogenated alkaloids of ergot (hydergine), is not new to medicine, and the drug has been on the market for years. However, recent information provided by Sandoz in Basel, Switzerland, using models for the quantification of dihydrogenated ergot effects on brain metabolism and function, may provide insights into the aging process, and has reopened the issues with regard to the use of hydergine.

Dihydrogenated Alkaloids of Ergot

It has been known for some time that the ergot alkaloids exert certain of their autonomic and circulatory effects by acting on the central nervous system. New findings indicate,[190] however, that the effect of hydergine on microcirculation of brain is a secondary effect depending on brain metabolism and activity. Sandoz presumes that a decrease of metabolism of brain tissue shown by the lactate and pyruvate-lactate ratio can be improved by hydergine. The improvement of metabolism by this drug also results in an increase of EEG energy. Furthermore, hydergine causes these changes under the influence of investational ischemia. Another explanation for the stimulative effect of hydergine on the central nervous system can be given by means of brain specific inhibition of phosphodiesterase. Correlating well with their explanation of the molecular pharmacological action of hydergine, there is an increase of protein metabolism of the brain by this drug on the thiopentone-inhibited brain metabolism. If these claims can be substantiated, the dihydrogenated alkaloids of ergot would have value in stimulating brain metabolic activity in older-aged people during long-term treatment. These very attractive findings, using very sophisticated means of exploring and quantifying brain metabolism and function, must be evaluated and considered against the rather equivocal effects resulting from years of hydergine use.

Gerovital (H_3)

Recently, Gerovital has exploded on the scene and has received considerable play by the lay press and other media. Gerovital is a procaine-based pharmaceutical compound that was first developed approximately 18 years ago by the Rumanian physician Dr. Anna Aslan, in Bucharest.[187] Since that time, Gerovital has been used by a large number of people in the European countries, with its proponents claiming that the drug is useful for treating various different, seemingly unrelated, areas of geriatric ailments, including depression, degenerative arthritis, hypertension, and certain coronary manifestations of aging. In Europe, such claims and arousal of public interest is not unusual; health spas of different sorts in mountain or sea resorts make similar claims for mineral water. Obviously, many of the claims are likely unfounded, and will not meet with replication in well-designed controlled studies. Now, in the United States, Rom-Amer is supporting several Phase I studies with this drug to determine efficacy in geriatric patients.

Double-blind clinical trials comparing the effects of Gerovital with procaine HCl on geriatric patients have demonstrated that Gerovital produced improvements on various physiological and psychological parameters that were statistically greater than improvement produced by plain procaine HCl.[1, 98, 146] It should be noted, however, that the results of other studies are not in agreement with these findings[83, 210]; improvements were attributed to a placebo action of Gerovital and to better care of the geriatric patients under study.

No clear-cut pharmacological explanation of its effects capable of fully satisfying the scientific community has ever been found. By uncovering evidence that Gerovital is a monoamine oxidase inhibitor, some insight into its mechanism of action, specifically with regard to effect on depression, is obviously forthcoming. Monoamine oxidase is an enzyme which increases with age.[186] Drugs belonging to the MAOI group exert a destructive or inhibiting effect on this enzyme, and thus might counteract effects it might have on the brain. In preliminary results of a trial carried out at New York

University Medical Center[189] with senile arteriosclerotic patients (ages 63 to 82) with features of depression, Gerovital H_3 was given intramuscularly to 10 patients three times per week for each of three weeks, in doses of 100 to 200 mg. Mild to moderate improvement was observed in six patients, in the form of mild euphoria, increased alertness, and a sense of well-being, with receding hypochondriacal complaints; in the remaining four no substantial changes in mental states were recorded at any stage. Of the seven patients who responded, only one maintained improvement beyond the active treatment period, the other five reverting to pretreatment levels of psychopathology. Orientation and memory impairment remained unaffected. The question of efficacy here remains open, inasmuch as some patients again improved one week after poststudy placebo medication was stopped. The study suggests that Gerovital H_3 may act as a mild short-lasting euphoriant.

At this point, clear presumptions of an effect of Gerovital against the aging process should be regarded with caution.

Oxygen

The role of cerebral oxygen metabolism in organic brain syndromes is well-recognized.

In an uncontrolled study, daily hypobaric (low-pressure) oxygen inhalation has been given to behaviorally distrubed geriatric patients at a nursing center.[75] Patients became more alert, less confused, less hostile, more cooperative, more sociable, and much more interested in the world around them. There were no untoward side effects. The scores for change in psychogeriatric and behavioral manifestations showed that almost 50% achieved ratings of "excellent" or "good." Jacobs et al.[118] in 1969 reported on hyperbaric oxygen in the treatment of cerebral arteriosclerosis; Barach in 1970[18] discussed the concept of ischemic hypoxia as a physiologic background for the use of oxygen inhalation in the treatment of senility. The NIMH has recently donated grants to centers in the United States having hyperbaric oxygen chambers. One such study is now underway at New York University Medical Center, where, with the use of a chamber at the Rusk Institute, geriatric patients will be accepted either on an inpatient or an outpatient basis for daily hyperbaric oxygen dives, in hopes of ameliorating organic emotional symptoms and behavioral disturbance.

MEGAVITAMIN AND ORTHOMOLECULAR
THERAPY IN PSYCHIATRY

A long-awaited report of the American Psychiatric Association (APA)
Task Force on Vitamin Therapy in Psychiatry was published in July
1973.[215] In a comprehensive review of available data since 1957, it would appear that megavitamin therapy is today a concept and term which is loosely
defined. Initially, the term dealt with the use of very large "massive" doses
of vitamin B_3 (nicotinic acid, or nicotinamide) for the treatment of
schizophrenia. Later, it included the use of nicotinamide adenine dinu-
cleotide (NAD), the co-enzyme derived from B_3. Over the years, it has
evolved to include ascorbic acid, pyridoxine (vitamin B_6), folic acid, vitamin
B_{12}, and other vitamins, minerals, hormones, special diets, drugs, and ECT.
It has also changed its name. The treatment is now called orthomolecular
treatment. The credibility of the megavitamin therapists is further
diminished by their consistent refusal over the past decade to perform controlled experiments and to report their results in a scientifically acceptable
fashion. They have instead relied upon anecdotal data which have been
broadly distributed in popular books, the lay press, and a journal published
by a society which they have organized. The Task Force found this posture
"deplorable."

The APA Task Force on Vitamin Therapy has concluded that the results
and claims of the advocates of megavitamin therapy for the treatment of
schizophrenia have not been confirmed by several groups of psychiatrists
and psychologists experienced in psychopharmacological research. Characteristic of these replicated studies is the reluctance to use ECT, which is so
commonly employed by megavitamin advocates. The double-blind studies
showed no therapeutic utility for this type of therapy. The most thorough-
going attempts at replication of the vitamin B_3 studies have been carried
out in the Canadian Mental Health Association collaborative studies.
These studies, involving several mental hospitals, large populations of
patients, and a diverse staff of psychiatrists, have been carried out under
the general supervision of Drs. Ban and Lehmann, from McGill University.
These workers selected from the general conclusions of the megavitamin
proponents several specific hypotheses which were directly testable. The
negative findings in these carefully controlled studies are clearly at variance
with the results claimed by the megavitamin proponents for the utility of
nicotinic acid or nicotinamide in the treatment of schizophrenia. Specifically, there is no support for claims of decreased time in hospital, a lowered
requirement for phenothiazines, and a quick response in acute
schizophrenics. On the other hand, they are entirely in agreement with the
studies of McGrath and Wittenborn et al. in showing no therapeutic utility.

Thus the claims of the megavitamin proponents made as far back as 1957 have not been confirmed, but rather found to be "useless and not without hazard."

REFERENCES

1. Abrams, A., Tobin, S. S., Gordon, P., Pechtel, C., and Hilkevitch, A.: The effects of a European procaine preparation in the aged population. I. Psychological effects. *J. Gerontol.* **20**:139–143, 1965.

2. Akimoto, H.: In Normothymics, "mood normalizers," M. Schou. *Brit. J. Psychiatr.* **109**:803, 1962.

3. Akimoto, H., Nakakuki, M., Honda, Y., Takahashi, Y., and Toyoda, J.: Clinical evaluation of the effect of central stimulants, MAO inhibitors, and imipramine in the treatment of affective disorders. *Proc. 3rd World Congress of Psychiatry* **2**:958, 1961.

4. American Psychiatric Association: Position statement on aging, official actions. *Am. J. Psychiatr.* **130**:950–951, 1973.

5. Anden, H.-E. and Stock, G.: Effect of clozapine on the turnover of dopamine in the corpus striatum and in the limbic system. *J. Pharm. Pharmac.* **25**:346–348, 1973.

6. Andersen, H. and Kristiansen, E. S.: Tofranil treatment of endogenous depression. *Acta Psychiatr. Scand.* **34**:387, 1959.

7. Angst, J., Dittrich, A., and Grof, P.: Course of endogenous affective psychoses and its modifications by prophylactic administration of imipramine and lithium. *Int. Pharmacopsychiatr.* **2**:1–11, 1969.

8. Angst, J., Jaenicke, U., Padrutt, A., and Scharfetter, C.: Ergebnisse eines dobbleblindversuches von HF 1854. *Pharmakopsychiatr.* **4**:192, 1971.

9. Angst, J., Bente, D., Berner, P., Heimann, H., Helmchen, H., and Hippius, H.: Das klinische wirkungsbild von clozapin (untersuchung mit dem AMP-system). In press, 1973.

10. Annell, A. L.: Manic-depressive illness in children and effect of treatment with lithium carbonate. *Acta Paedopsychiatr.* **36**:292–361, 1969.

11. Annell, A. L.: Lithium in the treatment of children and adolescents. *Acta Psychiatr. Scand.* **207** (suppl.):19–30, 1969.

12. Arena, J.: Dangers of tricyclic drugs in children. *Pediatrics* **51**:919–922, 1973.

13. Ast, H., Amin, M., Saxena, B. M., et al.: Mesoridazine in acute psychotic disturbances. *Curr. Ther. Res.* **9**:623–625, 1967.

14. Atsmon, A., Blum, E., Wijsenbeck, H., Maoz, B., Steiner, M., and Ziegelman, G.: The short-term effects of adrenergic-blocking agents in a small group of psychotic patients. *Psychiatr. Neurol. Neurochir.* **74**:251–285, 1971.

15. Ayd, F. J., Jr.: A survey of drug-induced extrapyramidal reactions. *JAMA* **175**:1054–1060, 1961.

16. Baastrup, P. C., and Schou, M.: Lithium as a prophylactic agent. Its effect against recurrent depressions and manic-depressive psychosis. *Arch. Gen. Psychiatr.* **16**:162–172, 1967.

17. Baastrup, P. C., Poulsen, J. C., Schou, M., Thomsen, K., and Amidsen, A.:

Prophylactic lithium: double blind discontinuation in manic-depressive and recurrent-depressive disorders. *Lancet* **2**:326–330, 1970.

18. Barach, A. L.: Oxygen inhalation in obliterative arterial disease, including its use in senility. *J. Am. Geriatrics Soc.* **18**:708–712, 1970.

19. Bente, D., Engelmeier, M. P., Heinrich, K., Hippius, H., and Schmitt, W.: Clinical investigations on a new group of tricyclic neuroleptic substances; substances with 7-membered heterocyclic central rings. Neuro-Psycho-Pharmacology, Proceedings of the 5th International Congress of the Collegium Internationale, Neuro-Psycho-Pharmacologicium, Wash., D.C., pp. 977–983, March 28–31, 1966.

20. Bishop, M. P. and Gallant, D. M.: Loxapine: a controlled evaluation in chronic schizophrenic patients. *Curr. Therap. Res.* **12**:594–597, 1970.

21. Boston Collaborative Drug Surveillance Program: Drug-induced extrapyramidal symptoms: a cooperative study. *JAMA* **224**:889–892, 1973.

22. Bowers, M. B., Jr.: Cerebrospinal fluid 5-hydroxyindoles and behavior after l-tryptophan and pyridoxine administration to psychiatric patients. *Neuropharmacology* **9**:599–604, 1970.

23. Brauzer, B. and Goldstein, B. J.: The differential response to parenteral chlorpromazine and mesoridazine in psychotic patients. *J. Clin. Pharmacol.* **10**:126–131, 1970.

24. Broadhurst, A. D.: L-tryptophan versys E.C.T. *Lancet* **1**:1392–1393, 1970.

25. Brodie, H. K. R., Murphy, D. L., Goodwin, F. K., and Bunney, W. E., Jr.: Catecholamines and mania: the effect of alpha-methyl-para-tyrosine on manic behavior and catecholamine metabolism. *Clin. Pharmacol. Ther.* **12**:219–224, 1970.

26. Bucci, I.: The dyskinesias: a new therapeutic approach. *Dis. Nerv. Syst.* **32**:324–328, 1971.

27. Bunney, W. E., Jr. and Davis, J. M.: Norepinephrine in depressive reactions. *Arch. Gen. Psychiatr.* **13**:483–494, 1965.

28. Bunney, W. E. Jr., Brodie, H. K. H., Murphy, D. L., and Goodwin, F. K.: Studies of alpha-methyl-para-tyrosine, L-dopa and L-tryptophan in depression and mania. *Am. J. Psychiatr.* **127**:872–881, 1971.

29. Butcher, L. L. and Engel, J.: Behavioral and biochemical effects of L-dopa after peripheral decarboxylase inhibition. *Brain Res.* **15**:233–242, 1969.

30. Cade, J. F. J.: Lithium salts in the treatment of psychiatric excitement. *Med. J. Australia* **2**:349–361, 1949.

31. Campbell, M., Fish, B., Shapiro, T., and Floyd, A., Jr.: Thiothixene in young disturbed children. A pilot study. *Arch. Gen. Psychiatr.* **23**:70–72, 1970.

32. Campbell, M., Fish, B., Shapiro, T., and Floyd, A., Jr.: Study of molindone in disturbed preschool children. *Curr. Ther. Res.* **13**:28–33, 1971.

33. Campbell, M., Fish, B., Shapiro, T., and Floyd, A., Jr.: Acute responses of schizophrenic children to a sedative and "stimulating" neuroleptic: a pharmacologic yardstick. *Curr. Ther. Res.* **14**:759–766, 1972.

34. Campbell, M., Fish, B., Korein, J., Shapiro, T., Collins, P., and Koh, C.: Lithium and chlorpromazine: a controlled crossover study of hyperactive severely disturbed young children. *J. Autism Childhood Schizophrenia* **2**:234–263, 1972.

35. Campbell, M., Fish, B., David, R., Shapiro, T., Collins, P., and Koh, C.: Response to triiodothyronine and dextroamphetamine: a study of preschool schizophrenic children. *J. Autism Childhood Schizophrenia* **2**:343–358, 1972.

36. Campbell, M.: Personal communication, 1973.

37. Carlsson, A.: Biochemical implications of dopa-induced action on the CNS. In L-*Dopa and Parkinsonism*, ed. A. Barbeau and F. H. McDowell (Eds.), F. A. Davis, 1970, pp. 205–212.

38. Carlsson, C.: Haemodynamic studies in alcoholics in the withdrawal phase. *Int. J. Clin. Pharmacol. Ther. Toxicol.* (suppl) 3:61–63, 1971.

39. Carlsson, C. and Johansson, T.: The psychological effects of propranolol in the abstinence phase of chronic alcoholics. *Brit. J. Psychiat.* 119:605–606, 1971.

40. Carroll, B. J.: Monoamine precursors in the treatment of depression. *J. Clinical Pharmacol. Ther.* 12:743–761, 1971.

41. Carroll, B. J., Mowbray, R. M., and Davies, B.: Sequential comparison of l-tryptophan with E.C.T. in severe depression. *Lancet* 1:967–969, 1970.

42. Carroll, B. J., Frazer, A., Schless, A., and Mendels, J.: Cholinergic reversal of manic symptoms. *Lancet* 1:427–428, 1973.

43. Claghorn, J. L.: Paychopharmacologic characteristics of an indole molindone. *Curr. Ther. Res.* 11:521–527, 1969.

44. Clark, M. L., Huber, W. K., Sakata, K., Fowles, D. C., and Serafetinides, E. A.: Molindone in chronic schizophrenia. *Clin. Pharmacol. Ther.* 11:680–688, 1970.

45. Conners, C. K., Taylor, E., Meo, G., Kurtz, M. A., and Fournier, M.: Magnesium pemoline and dextroamphetamine: A controlled study in children with minimal brain dysfunction. *Psychopharmacologia* 26:321–336, 1972.

46. Cooper, T. B. and Simpson, G. M.: Concomitant imipramine and methylphenidate administration: A case report. *Am. J. Psychiatr.* 130:721, 1973.

47. Coppen, A. J.: The chemical pathology of the affective disorders. In *The Scientific Basis of Medicine Annual Reviews,* Athlone Press, London, 1970, pp. 189–210.

48. Coppen, A., Shaw, D. M., and Farrell, J. P.: Potentiation of the anti-depressive effect of a monoamine oxidase inhibitor by tryptophan. *Lancet* 1:79–81, 1963.

49. Coppen, A., Shaw, D. M., Herzberg, B., and Maggs, R.: Tryptophan in the treatment of depression. *Lancet* 2:1178–1180, 1967.

50. Coppen, A., Prange, A. J., Whybrow, P. C., Noguera, R., and Paez, J. M.: Methysergide in mania. *Lancet* 2:338–340, 1969.

51. Coppen, A., Noguera, R., Bailey, J., Burns, B. H., Swami, M. S., Hare, E. H., Gardner, R., Maggs, R.: Prophylactic lithium in affective disorders. *Lancet* 2:275–279, 1971.

52. Coppen, A., Whybrow, P., Noguera, R., Maggs, R., and Prange, A. J., Jr.: The comparative antidepressant value of L-tryptophan and imipramine with and without attempted potentiation by liothyronine. *Arch. Gen. Psychiatr.* 26:234–241, 1972.

53. Coppen, A., Prange, A. J., Jr., Whybrow, P. C., and Noguera, R.: Abnormalities of indoleamines in affective disorders. *Arch. Gen. Psychiatr.,* 26:474–478, 1972.

54. Crane, G. E.: Failure of pyridoxine in tardive dyskinesia. *J. Neurol. Neurosurg. Psychiatr.* 33:511–512, 1970.

55. Crane, G. E.: More on amantadine in tardive dyskinesia. *N. Engl. J. Med.* 285:1150–1151, 1971.

56. Crane, G. E. and Paulson, G.: Involuntary movements in a sample of chronic mental patients and their relation to the treatment with neuroleptics. *Int. J. Neuropsychiatr.* 3:286–291, 1967.

58. Curran, J. P.: Management of tardive dyskinesia with thiopropazate. *Am. J. Psychiatr.* **130**:925–929, 1973.

59. Dalen, P. (1973): Lithium therapy in Huntington's chorea and tardive dyskinesia. *Lancet* **1**:107–108, 1973.

60. Dally, P.: *Chemotherapy of Psychiatric Disorders*, Plenum, New York, 1967.

61. Delay, J., Deniker, P., and Ginestet, D.: Unpublished material.

62. Denber, H. C. B.: Unpublished material.

63. Dewhurst, W. G.: New theory of cerebral amine function and its clinical application. *Nature* **218**:1130–1133, 1968.

64. Dewhurst, W. G.: Methysergide in mania. *Nature* **219**:506–507, 1968.

65. DiMascio, A. and Shader, R.: *Haloperidol and Related Butyrophenones, Pharmacological Agents*, Vol. 2., Academic Press, New York, 1967, pp. 199–248.

66. Dysen, W. and Mendels, J.: Lithium and depression. *Curr. Ther. Res.* **10**:601–608, 1968.

67. Earle, B. V.: Thyroid hormone and tricyclic antidepressants in resistant depressions. *Am. J. Psychiatr.* **126**:143, 1970.

68. Engfelhardt, D. M., Polizoes, P., and Margolis, R. A.: The drug treatment of childhood psychosis. In *Drugs, Development and Cerebral Function*, W. L. Smith, (Ed.) Charles C. Thomas, 1972.

69. Fann, W. E., Davis, J. M., and Wilson, I. C.: Methylphenidate in tadrive dyskinesia. *Am. J. Psychiatr.* **130**:922–924, 1973.

70. Fieve, R. R., Platman, S. R., and Plutchik, R. R.: The use of lithium in affective disorders. *Am. J. Psychiatr.* **125**:487–498, 1968.

71. Finer, M. J.: Habituation to chlordiazepoxide in an alcoholic population. *JAMA* **213**:1342, 1970.

72. Finer, M. J.: Diphenylhydantoin for treatment of alcohol withdrawal syndromes. *JAMA* **215**:119, 1971.

73. Fish, B., Campbell, M., Shapiro, T., and Floyd, A., Jr.: Comparison of trifluperidol, trifluoperazine and chlorpromazine in preschool schizophrenic children: the value of less sedative antipsychotic agents. *Curr. Ther. Res.* **11**:589–595, 1969.

74. Food and Drug Administration Drug Bulletin, May 1973.

75. Fraiberg, P. L.: Oxygen inhalation in the control of psychogeriatric symptoms in patients with long-term illness. *J. Am. Geriatrics Soc.* **21**:321–324, 1973.

76. Freeman, H., Oktem, M. R., and Oktem, N.: A double-blind comparison of the therapeutic efficacy of mesoridazine versus chlorpromazine. *Curr. Ther. Res.* **11**:263–270, 1969.

77. Fries, H.: Experience with lithium carbonate treatment at a psychiatric department in the period, 1964–1967. *Acta Psychiat. Scand. Suppl.* **207**:41, 1969.

78. Frommer, E.: Depressive illness in childhood. In *Recent Developments in Affective Disorders: A Symposium*, A. Coppen and A. Walk, (Eds.), British Journal Psychiatry Special Publication No. 2, 1968, pp. 117–136.

79. Gallant, D. M., Bishop, M. P., and Guerrero-Figueroa, R.: Metiapine: a new antipsychotic agent. *Curr. Ther. Res.* **12**:794–797, 1970.

80. Gallant, D. M., Bishop, M. D., and Guerrero-Figueroa, R.: Metiapine: a double blind evaluation in chronic schizophrenic patients. *Curr. Ther. Res.* **13**:734–736, 1971.

81. Gander, D. R.: Treatment of depressive illnesses with combined antidepressants. *Lancet* 1:107–109, 1965.

82. Gander, D. R.: The clinical value of monoamine oxidase inhibitors and tricyclic antidepressants in combination. In *Proceedings of the First International Symposium,* S. Garattini and M. W. G. Dulor, New York: Excerpta Medical Foundation, pp. 336–343.

83. Gericke, O. L., Lobb, L. G., and Pardoll, D. H.: An evaluation of procaine in geriatric patients in a mental hospital. *J. Clin. Exp. Psychopath.* 22:18, 1961.

84. Gershon, S.: Lithium. In *The American Handbook of Psychiatry,* Vol. VI, D. Hamburg, H. K. H., Brodie, and S. Arieti, (Eds.), Basic Books, New York in press.

85. Gershon, S. and Trautner, E. M.: The treatment of shock-dependency by pharmacological agents. *Med. J. Australia* 43:783, 1956.

86. Gershon, S. and Yuwiler, A.: Lithium ion: A specific psychopharmacological approach to the treatment of mania. *J. Neuropsychiatr.* 1:229–241, 1960.

87. Gershon, S., Hedimian, L. J., Burdock, E. I., and Kim, S. S.: Antipsychotic properties of loxapine succinate. *Curr. Ther. Res.* 12:280–285, 1970.

88. Glassman, A. H. and Platman, S. R.: Potentiation of a monoamine oxidase inhibitor by tryptophan. *J. Psychiatr. Res.* 7:83–88, 1969.

89. Glassman, A. and Jaffe, F.: Cited in *Indolamines and affective disorders,* A. Glassman, *Psychosom. Med.* 31:107–114, 1969.

90. Glessinger, G.: Evaluation of lithium in the treatment of psychotic excitement. *Med. J. Australia* 41:277–283, 1954.

91. Godwin-Austin, R. B. and Clark, T.: Persistent phenothiazine dyskinesia treated with tetrabenazine. *Brit. Med. J.* 3:25–26, 1971.

92. Goodwin, L. S. and Gilman, A.: *The Pharmacological Basis of Therapeutics,* Macmillan, New York, 1970, pp. 151–201.

93. Goodwin, F. K.: Behavioral effects of L-dopa in man. *Seminars Psychiatr.* 3:477–492, 1971.

94. Goodwin, F., Murphy, D., and Bunney, W.: Lithium. *Lancet* 2:212–213, 1969.

95. Goodwin, F. K., Murphy, D. L., Brodie, H. K. H., and Bunney, W. E., Jr.: L-dopa, catecholamines, and behavior: a clinical and biochemical study in depressed patients. *Biol. Psychiatr.* 2:341–366, 1970.

96. Goodwin, F. K. and Ebert, M. H.: Lithium in mania. In *Lithium: Its Role in Psychiatric Research and Treatment,* S. Gershon and B. Shopsin (Eds.), New York: Plenum Press, 1973, pp. 237–252.

97. Goodwin, F. K.: Data presented at the ACNP meeting, Puerto Rico, December, 1972.

98. Gordon, P., Fudema, J. J., Snider, G. L., Abrams, A., Tobin, S. S., and Kraus, J. D.: The effects of a European procaine preparation in an aged population. II. Physiological effects. *J. Gerontol.* 20:114–152, 1965.

99. Gram, L. F., and Rafaelsen, O. J.: Lithium of psychotic children. A controlled clinical trial. *Acta Psychiatr. Scand.,* in press, 1972.

100. Greenblatt, D. and Shader, R.: On the psychopharmacology of beta-adrenergic blockade. *Curr. Ther. Res.* 14:615–625, 1972.

101. Greenhill, L. and Reider, R. O.: Lithium carbonate in the treatment of hyperactive children. *Arch. Gen. Psychiatr.* 28:636–640, 1973.

102. Grof, P. and Vinar, O.: Maintenance and prophylactic imipramine doses in recurrent depressions. *Activ. Nerv. Sup. (Praha)* 8:383–385, 1966.

103. Gross, H., Hackl, H., and Kaltenbaeck, E.: Results of a double-blind study of clozapine and thioridazine. Presented at the VIIth Congress of the C.I.N.P., Prague, 1970.

104. Guttman, H., Lehman, H. E., and Ban, T. A.: A survey of extrapyramidal manifestations in patients attending an after-care clinic of a psychiatric hospital. *Laval. Med.* 41:449–455, 1970.

105. Hamid, T. A. and Wertz, W. J.: Mesoridazine vs. chlorpromazine in acute schizophrenia: a double-blind investigation. *Am. J. Psychiatr.* 130:689–692, 1973.

106. Haskovec, L.: Methysergide in mania. *Lancet* 2:902, 1969.

107. Haskovec, L. and Rysanek, I.: The action of reserpine in imipramine-resistant depressives. *Psychopharmacologia* 11:18–23, 1967.

108. Haskovec, L. and Soucek, I.: Trial of methysergide in mania. *Nature* 219:507–508, 1968.

109. Haskovec, L. and Soucek, I.: The action of methysergide in manic states. *Psychopharmacologia* 15:415–424, 1969.

110. Hippius, H. and Lange, J.: Zur problematik der spaten extrapyramidaten hyperkinsen nach langfristiger neuroleptischer therapie. *Arzheim Forsch.* 20:888–890, 1970.

111. Holden, J. M. C., Itil, T., Sanford, E., et al.: Paper read at the 7th International Congress of the Collegium Internationale Neuropsychopharmacologicum, Prague, August 18–22, 1970.

112. Hollister, L. E.: Some human pharmacological studies of three psychotropic drugs: thiothixene, molindone, and W-1867. *J. Clin. Pharmacol.* 8:95–101, 1968.

113. Hollister, L.: Treatment of chronic schizophrenia with butyrophenones. In *Butyrophenones in Psychiatry*, A. DiMascio and R. Shader (Eds.), New York: Raven Press, pp. 57–69, 1972.

114. Hordern, A., Burt, C. G., Gordon, W. F., and Holt, N. F.: Amitriptyline in depressive states: six-month treatment results. *Brit. J. Psychiatr.* 110:641–647, 1964.

115. Ingvarsson, V. C. G.: Orientierende klinische versuche zur wirkung des dioxyphenylalanine (L-dopa) bei endogener depression. *Arznei. Forsch.* 15:849–952, 1965.

116. Itil, T. M., Polvan, N., and Holden, J. M. C.: Clinical and EEG effects of cinanserin in schizophrenic and manic patients. *Dis. Nerv. Syst.* 32:193–200, 1971.

117. Itil, T. M., Polvan, N., Dincmen, K., and Sungarbey: Clinical effects of SA-97 (homochlorcyclazine) in manic patients, in press, 1973.

118. Jacobs, E. A., Winter, P. M., and Alvis, H. J.: Hyperoxygenation effect on cognitive functioning in the aged. *N. Engl. J. Med.* 281:753–756, 1969.

119. Janowsky, D. S., el-Yousef, M. K., Davis, J. M., and Sekerke, H. J.: Parasympathetic suppression of manic symptoms by physostigmine. *Arch. Gen. Psychiatr.* 28:542–547, 1973.

120. Janowsky, D., el-Yousef, M. K., Davis, J. M., and Sekerke, H. J.: A cholinergic-adrenergic hypothesis of mania and depression. *Lancet* 2:632–635, 1972.

121. Janssen, P. A. J.: Haloperidol and related butyrophenones. In *Psychopharmacological Agents*, Vol. 2, Academic Press, New York, 1967, pp. 199–248.

122. Johnson, A. C. and Kulkarni, A. S.: Pipe racetazine and chlorpromazine: a comparison. *Am. J. Psychiatr.* 130:603–605, 1973.

123. Johnson, G., Gershon, S., and Shopsin, B.: Antidepressant effect of lithium. *Comp. Psychiatr.*, in press.

124. Kane, F. J.: Treatment of mania with cinanserin, an antiserotonin agent. *Am. J. Psychiatr.* **126**:1020–1023, 1970.

125. Kastin, A. J., Ehrinsing, R. H., Schalch, D. S., and Anderson, M. S.: *Lancet* **2**:740–772, 1972.

126. Kay, D. W., Fahy, T., and Garside, R. F.: A seven-month double-blind trial of amitriptyline and diazepam in ECT-treated depressed patients. *Brit. J. Psychiatr.* **117**:667–671, 1970.

127. Kazamatsuri, H., Chien, C.-P., and Cole, J. O.: Treatment of tardive dyskinesia. II. Short-term efficacy of dopamine blocking agents, haloperidol, and thiopropazate. *Arch. Gen. Psychiatr.* **27**:100–103, 1972.

128. Kazamatsuri, H., Chien, C.-P., and Cole, J. O.: Treatment of tardive dyskinesia. III. Clinical efficacy of a dopamine-competing agent, methyl-dopa. *Arch. Gen. Psychiatr.* **27**:824–827, 1972.

129. Kazamatsuri, H., Chien, C.-P., and Cole, J. O.: Long-term treatment of tardive dyskinesia with haloperidol and tetrabenazine. *Am. J. Psychiatr.* **130**:479–483, 1973.

130. Kielholz et al: Unpublished material.

131. Kiev, A., Guclu, B., and Kulkarni, A. S.: Evaluation of piperacetazine (Quide) injection in acute schizophrenics. *Curr. Ther. Res.* **14**:376–380, 1972.

132. Kirk, L., Baastrup, P. C., and Schou, M.: Propranolol and lithium-induced tremor. *Lancet* **1**:839, 1972.

133. Klawans, H. L.: Levodopa in tardive dyskinesia. *J. Neurol. Sci.* **14**:189–192, 1971.

134. Klein, D. F. and Davis, J. M.: *Diagnosis and Drug Treatment of Psychiatric Disorders.* Williams and Wilkins, Baltimore, 1969.

135. Klerman, G. L., Schildkraut, J. J., Hasenbush, L. L., Greenblatt, M., and Friend, D. G.: Clinical experience with dihydroxyphenylalanine (DOPA) in depression. *J. Psychiatr. Res.* **1**:289–297, 1963.

136. Klerman, G. L. and Paykel, E. S.: Long-term drug therapy in affective disorders. *Int. Pharmacopsychiatry.* **5**:80–99, 1970.

137. Kline, N. S. and Sacks, W.: Relief of depression within one day using an MAO inhibitor and intravenous 5-HTP. *Am. J. Psychiatr.* **120**:274–275, 1963.

138. Kline, N. S., Sacks, W., and Simpson, G. M.: Further studies on one-day treatment of depression with 5-HTP. *Am. J. Psychiatr.* **121**:379–381, 1964.

139. Kline, N. S. and Blanda, J.: Clozapine, the first class of a new class of psychotropic drugs. In press, 1973.

140. Kline, N. S., and Shopsin, B.: Combined tricyclic-MAOI therapy in depressed patients. To be presented at the Congress of the C.I.N.P., July, 1974.

141. Knapp, D. L., Stone, G. C., Hambourger, W. E., et al.: Behavioral pharmacological studies of piperacetazine, a potent tranquilizing agent. *Arch. Int. Pharmacodyn. Ther.* **135**:152–166, 1962.

142. Kristjansen, P.: In Clinical observations of the side effects of haloperidol, B. Gerle, (Ed.) *Acta Psychiatr. Scand.* **40**:65, 1964.

143. Lapin, I. P. and Oxenkrug, G. F.: Intensification of the central serotoninergic processes as a possible determinant of the thymoleptic effect. *Lancet* **1**:132–136, 1969.

144. Levy, H. B.: Imipramine for the hyperkinetic syndrome. *JAMA* **225**:527, 1973.

145. Linken, A.: Propranolol for LSD-induced anxiety states. *Lancet* **2**:1039–1040, 1971.

146. MacFarlane, D. M.: A possible rationale for the use of Gerovital H_3 in geriatrics: Inhibition of monoamine oxidase. In press, 1973.

147. Maryland Journal of Clinical Pharmacology: Clinical Pharmacological Trial of Loxapine Succinate: A Cooperative Study of the Psychopharmacology Research Branch, National Institute of Mental Health, Bethesda. Md. J. Clin. Pharmacol. 10: no. 3, May–June, 1970.

148. Matz, R. and Gershon, S.: Personal communication, 1973.

149. Matussek, N., Pohlmeier, H., and Ruther, E.: Die wirkung von dopa auf gehemmte depressionen. Clin. Wochenschr. 44:727–728, 1966.

150. Matussek, N., Benkert, O., Schneider, K., Otten, H., and Poldmeier, H.: Wirkung eines decarboxylaschemmers (RO 4-4602) in kombination mit L-dopa auf gehemmte depressionen. Arzneim. Forsch. 20:934–937, 1970.

151. McCabe, M. S., Reich, T., and Winokur, G.: Methysergide as a treatment for mania. Am. J. Psychiatr. 127:354–356, 1970.

152. McClure, D. J. and Cleghorn, R. A.: Suppression studies in affective disorders, J. Can. Psychiatr. Ass. 13:477, 1968.

153. McIndoo, M. D.: A controlled study of mesoridazine: an effective treatment for schizophrenia. South. Med. J. 64:592–596, 1971.

154. Medical Letter on Drugs and Therapeutics: New Rochelle, N.Y.: Medical Letter, Inc., January 1973 issue.

155. Mendels, J., Fieve, A., Fitzgerand, R. G., Ramsey, T. A., and Stokes, J. W.: Biogenic amine metabolites in cerebrospinal fluid of depressed and manic patients. Science 175:1380–1382, 1972.

156. Mendels, J., Secunda, S., and Dyson, W.: A controlled study of the antidepressant effects of lithium carbonate. Arch. Gen. Psychiatr. 26:154–157, 1972.

157. Millichap, J. G. and Fowler, G. W.: Treatment of "minimal brain dysfunction" syndromes—Selection of drugs for children with hyperactivity and learning disabilities. Pediat. Clinics N. Am. 14:767–778, 1967.

158. Mindham, R. H. S., Howland, C., and Shepherd, M.: Continuation therapy with tricyclic antidepressants in depressive illness. Lancet 2:854–855, 1972.

159. Mindham, R. H. S., Howland, C., and Shepherd, M.: An evaluation of continuation therapy with tricyclic antidepressants in depressive illness. Psychol. Med. 3:5–17, 1973.

160. Muller, C. and Heimann, H.: Unpublished material.

161. Murphy, D. L., Goodwin, F. K., and Bunney, W. E., Jr.: A reevaluation of biogenic amines in manic and depressive states. Hospital Practice:85–92, 1972.

162. Orzack, M. H., Gardos, G., and Branconnier, R.: CNS effects of propranolol in man. Psychopharmacologia 29:299–306, 1973.

163. Pare, C. M. B.: Potentiation of monoamine oxidase inhibitors by tryptophan. Lancet 2:527–528, 1963.

164. Pare, C. M. B. and Sandler, M.: A clinical and biochemical study of a trial of iproniazid in the treatment of depression. J. Neurol. Neurosurg. Psychiatr. 22:247–251, 1959.

165. Perel, J. M., Black, N., Wharton, R. N., et al.: Inhibition of imipramine metabolism by methylphenidate. Fed. Proc. 28:418, 1969.

166. Persson, T. and Roos, B. E.: 5-Hydroxytryptophan for depression. Lancet 2:987–988, 1967.

167. Peters, H. A., Daley, R. F., and Sato, S.: Reserpine for tardive dyskinesia. *N. Engl. J. Med.* **286**:106, 1972.

168. Platman, S. R.: Comparison of lithium carbonate and imipramine; (in prevention of manic-depressive disease). *Dis. Nerv. Syst.* **31**:132-134, 1970.

169. Poldinger, W.: Combined administration of desiprimine and reserpine or tetrabenazine in depressed patients. *Psychopharmacologia* **4**:308-319, 1963.

170. Post, R. M., Kotin, J., and Goodwin, F. K.: Psychomotor activity and cerebrospinal fluid amine metabolites in affective illness. Presented at the Annual Meeting of the American Psychiatric Association, Dallas, Tex., 1972.

171. Praag, H. M. van, Korf, J., Dols, L. C. W., and Schut, T.: A pilot study of the predictive value of the probenecid test in application of 5-HT as antidepressant. *Psychopharmacologia* **25**:14-21, 1972.

172. Prange, A. J., Jr., Wilson, I. C., Rabon, A. M., and Lipton, M. A.: Enhancement of imipramine by T_3 in unselected depressed patients. *Excerpta Medica Int. Congr. Series,* no. 180, 532-535, 1968.

173. Prange, A. J., Jr., Wilson, I. C., Rabon, A. M., and Lipton, M. A.: Enhancement of imipramine antidepressant activity by thyroid hormone. *Am. J. Psychiat.* **126**:457-469, 1969.

174. Prange, A. J., Jr., Wilson, I. C., Knox, A., McClane, T. K., and Lipton, M. A.: Enhancement of imipramine by TSH: clinical and theoretical implications. *Am. J. Psychiatr.* **127**:109-117, 1970.

175. Prange, A. J., Jr., Wilson, I. C., Lipton, M. A., et al.: Use of a thyroid hormone to accelerate the action of imipramine. *Psychosomatics* **11**:442-443, 1970.

176. Prange, A. J., Jr., Coppen, A., Whybrow, P. C., Noguera, R., and Maggs, R.: L-tryptophan and imipramine in depression: Attempted potentiation by a thyroid hormone. In *Advances in Neuropsychopharmacology,* Proceedings of the VIIth Congress of C.I.N.P., Prague, Czechoslovakia, 1970, O. Vinar, Z. Votava, and D. B. Bradley, (Eds.), Amsterdam: North Holland, 1970.

177. Prange, A. J., Jr., Wilson, I. C., Knox, A. E., McClane, T. K., et al.: Thyroid-imipramine clinical and chemical interaction: evidence for a receptor deficit in depression. *J. Psychiat. Res.* **9**:187-205, 1972.

178. Prange, A. J., Jr., Wilson, I. C., Lars, P. P., Alltop, L. B., and Breese, G. R.: Effects of TRH in depression. *Lancet* **2**:999-1002, 1972.

179. Prange, A. J., Jr., Wilson, I. C., Morris, C. E., and Hall, C. D.: Preliminary experience with tryptophan and lithium in the treatment of tardive dyskinesia. *Psychopharmacol. Bull.* **9**:36, 1973.

180. Prien, R. F., Klett, C. J., and Caffey, E. M., Jr.: Lithium carbonate and imipramine in prevention of affective episodes. *Arch. Gen. Psychiatr.* **29**:420-425, 1973.

181. Quitkin, F., Rifkin, A., and Klein, D. F.: Lithium in other psychiatric disorders. In *Lithium: Its Role in Psychiatric Research and Treatment,* ed. S. Gershon and B. Shopsin, (Eds.), Plenum Press, New York, 1973, pp. 295-315.

182. Randell, J.: Combining the antidepressant drugs. *Brit. Med. J.* **1**:527, 1965.

183. Rifkin, A., Quitkin, F., Carillo, C., and Klein, D. F.: Lithium in emotionally unstable character disorder. *Arch. Gen. Psychiatr.* **27**:519-522, 1973.

184. Ritvo, E. R., Yuwiler, A., Geller, E., Ornitz, E. M., Saeger, K., and Plotkin, S.: Increased blood serotonin and platelets in early infantile autism. *Arch. Gen. Psychiatr.* **23**:566-572, 1970.

185. Ritvo, E. R., Yuwiler, A., Geller, E., Kales, A., Rashkis, S., Schicor, A., Plotkin, S., Axelrod, R., and Howard, C.: Effects of L-dopa in autism. *J. Autism Childhood Schizophrenia* 1:190–205, 1971.

186. Robinson, D. S., Davis, J. M., Nies, A., Colburn, R. W., Davis, J. N., Bourne, H. R., Bunney, W. E., Jr., Shaw, D. M., and Coppen, A. J.: Aging, monoamines, and monoamine oxidase levels. *Lancet* 1:290–295, 1972.

187. Rom-Amer Pharmaceuticals, Ltd.: *Annual Report*, 1972.

188. Safer, D., Allen, R., and Barr, E.: Depression of growth in hyperactive children on stimulant drugs. *N. Engl. J. Med.* 287:217–220, 1972.

189. Sakalis, G., Oh, D., Gershon, S., and Shopsin, B.: The use of Gerovital H-3 in depressed patients with senile dementis. *Curr. Ther. Res.,* in press, 1973.

190. Sandoz Pharmaceuticals: Experimental cerebral insufficiency: models for quantification of dihydrogenated ergot effects on brain metabolism and function. Presented at Sandoz Scientific Exhibit, Federation of American Societies for Experimental Biology, 57th Annual Meeting, Atlantic City, New Jersey, 1973.

191. Sargant, W.: In *World Psychiatric Association Symposium on Antidepressant Drugs: Studies of Anxiety,* M. H. Lader, (Ed.), Ashford, Kent Headley Brothers Ltd., pp. 1–6.

192. Sargant, W., Walter, C. J. S., and Wright, N.: New treatment of some chronic tension states. *Brit. Med. J.* 1:322–324, 1966.

193. Sato, S. Daley, R., and Peters, H.: Reserpine therapy of phenothiazine-induced dyskinesia. *Dis. Nerv. Syst.* 32:680–682, 1971.

194. Schildkraut, J. J.: The catecholamine hypothesis of affective disorders: a review of supporting evidence. *Am. J. Psychiatr.* 122:509–522, 1965.

195. Schou, M.: Prophylactic lithium maintenance treatment in recurrent endogenous affective disorders. In *Lithium: Its Role in Psychiatric Research and Treatment,* S. Gershon and B. Shopsin, Plenum Press, New York, 1973, pp. 269–294.

196. Schuckit, M., Robins, E., and Feighner, J.: Tricyclic antidepressants and MAO inhibitors: combination therapy in the treatment of depression. *Arch. Gen. Psychiatr.* 24:509–514, 1971.

197. Sedvall, G. and Nyback, H.: Effect of clozapine and some other antipsychotic agents on synthesis and turnover of dopamine formed from ^{14}C-tyrosine in mouse brain. In press, 1973.

198. Selbach, P., Hippius, H., Flugel, F., and Bente, D.: Unpublished material.

199. Sheard, M. H.: The effects of lithium on human aggression. *Nature* 230:113–116, 1971.

200. Shelton, J., Prusmack, J. J., and Hollister, L. E.: Molindone, a new type of antipsychotic drug. *J. Clin. Pharmacol.* 8:190–195, 1968.

201. Shopsin, B. and Gershon, S.: Chemotherapy of manic-depressive disorder. In *Brain Chemistry and Mental Disease,* B. Ho and W. McIsaac, (Eds.), Plenum Press, New York, pp. 319–377.

202. Shopsin, B., Pearson, E., Gershon, S., and Collins, P.: A controlled double-blind comparison between loxapine succinate and chlorpromazine in acute newly hospitalized schizophrenic patients. *Curr. Ther. Res.* 14:739–749, 1972.

203. Shopsin, B., Gershon, S., Shenkman, L., and Hollander, C. S.: Personal communication, 1973.

204. Shopsin, B., Janowsky, D., Davis, J., and Gershon, S.: Rebound phenomena in manic patients following physostigmine: Towards an understanding of the aminergic

mechanisms underlying affective disorders. Presented at the ACNP Meeting, Las Vegas, Nevada, December, 1973.

205. Shopsin, B. and Gershon, S.: Data presented at the American College of Psychopharmacology Meeting, Palm Springs, Calif., 1973.

206. Siegel, J. C. and Mones, R. J.: Modification of choreiform activity by haloperidol. *JAMA* **216**:675–676, 1971.

207. Singer, K.: Thiopropazate HCl in persistent dyskinesia. *Brit. Med. J.* **4**:22–25, 1971.

208. Sletten, I. W. and Gershon, S.: The premenstrual syndrome: a discussion of its pathophysiology and treatment with the lithium ion. *Comp. Psychiatr.* **7**:197–183, 1966.

209. Sletten, I. W., Altman, H., El-Toumi, A., et al.: A double-blind comparison of chlorpromazine and mesoridazine (TPS-23). *Clin. Med.* **77**:17–22, 1970.

210. Smigel, J. O., Piller, J., Murphy, C., Lowe, C., and Gibson, J.: H-3 (procaine hydrochloride) therapy in aging institutionalized patients: an interim report. *J. Am. Geriatric Soc.* **1**:785, 1960.

211. Stephen, S. A.: Unwanted effects of propranolol. *Am. J. Cardiol.* **18**:463–372, 1966.

212. Stille, G., Ackerman, H., Lauener, H., and Eichenberger, E.: The pharmacological properties of a potent neuroleptic compound from the dibenothiazepine group. *Int. J. Neuropharmacol.* **4**:375–383, 1965.

213. Stille, G. and Hippius, H.: Kritische stellungnahme zum begriff der neuroleptika an hand von pharmakologischen und klinischen befunden mit clozapin. *Pharmakopsychiatr.* **4**:182–195, 1971.

214. Stromgren, L. S. and Stromgren, E.: In Normythymics, "mood normalizers," M. Schou. *Brit. J. Psychiatr.* **109**:803, 1962.

215. Task Force: Report, Megavitamin and Orthomolecular Therapy in Psychiatry. *Am. Psychiatr. Assn.,* Library of Congress catalogue card no. 73-78890, 1973.

216. Tupin, J: Personal communication to F. Quitkin, A. Rifkin, and D. F. Klein,: Lithium and other psychiatric disorders. In *Lithium: Its Role in Psychiatric Research and Treatment,* S. Gershon and B. Shopsin, (Eds.), Plenum Press, New York, 1972, pp. 295–315.

217. Turner, W. J. and Merlis, S.: A clinical trial of pargyline and dopa in psychotic subjects. *Dis. Nerv. Syst.* **25**:538–541, 1964.

218. Vale, S. and Espejel, M. A.: Amantadine for dyskinesia tarda. *N. Engl. J. Med.* **284**:673, 1971.

219. Varga, E. and Simpson, G. M.: Loxapine succinate in the treatment of uncontrollable destructive behavior. *Curr. Therap. Res.* **13**:737–742, 1971.

220. Waizer, J., Polizos, P., Hoffman, S. P., Engelhardt, D. M., and Margolis, R. A.: A single-blind evaluation of thiothixene with outpatient schizophrenic children. *J. Autism Childhood Schizophrenia* **2**:378–384, 1972.

221. Watts, C. A. H.: Antidepressant drugs. *Brit. Med. J.* **1**:1114, 1964.

222. Wharton, R. N., Perel, J. M., Dayton, P. G., et al.: A potential clinical use formethylphenidate with tricyclic antidepressants. *Am. J. Psychiatr.* **127**:1619–1625, 1970.

223. Wheatley, D.: Comparative effects of chlordiazepoxide and propranolol in anxiety states. *Brit. J. Psychiatr.* **115**:1411–1412, 1969.

224. Wheatley, D.: Potentiation of amitriptyline by thyroid hormone. *Arch. Gen. Psychiat.* **26**:229–233, 1972.

225. Whitehead, P. L. and Clark, L. D.: Effect of lithium carbonate, placebo, and thiori-
      dazine on hyperactive children. *Am. J. Psychiatr.* **127**:824–825, 1970.

226. Whybrow, P. C., Coppen, A., Prange, A. J. Jr., Noguera, R., and Bailey, J. E.:
      Thyroid function and the response to liothyronine in depression. *Arch. Gen. Psychiatr.*
      26:242–245, 1972.

227. Wilson, I. C., Prange, A. J. Jr., McClane, T. K., Rabon, A. M., and Lipton, M. A.:
      Thyroid hormone enhancement of imipramine in nonretarded depressions. *N. Engl. J.
      Med.* **282**:1063–1067, 1970.

228. Wilson, I. C. and Prange, A. J., Jr.: Tryptophan in mania: theory of affective disorders.
      Psychopharmacologia (Suppl.)**26**:76, 1972.

229. Winston, F.: Oral contraceptives, pyridoxine, and depression. *Am. J. Psychiatr.*
      130:1217–1221, 1973.

230. Wren, J.: Lithium in the prevention of chronic (periodic) alcoholism. Presented at the
      VA-NIMH Collaborative Study Meeting, New Orleans, 1970.

DRUG REFERENCE

Generic Name	Brand	Company
Antipsychotic Agents		
Phenothiazines		
Acepromazine	Notensil, Plegicil	Clin-Byla
Acetophenazine	Tindal	Schering
Butaperazine	Repoise	Robins
Carphenazine	Proketazine	Wyeth
Chlorpromazine	Thorazine	Smith, Kline & French
Dixyrazine	Esucos	Union Chimiques Belge
Fluphenazine	Prolixin, Permitil	Squibb, White
Mepazine	Pacatal	Warner
Mesoridazine	Serentil	Sandoz
Methophenazine	Frenelon	Medimpex
Methotrimeprazine	Veractil, Levoprome, Nirvan	May & Baker, Lederle, United Drug
Methoxypromazine	Tentone	Lederle
Perphenazine	Trilafon	Schering
Pipamazine	Mornidine	Searle
Piperacetazine	Quide	Pitman-Moore
Prochlorperazine	Compazine	Smith, Kline & French
Promazine	Sparine	Wyeth
Promethazine	Phenergan	Wyeth
Propericiazine	Neuleptil	Rhone-Poulenc
Propiomazine	Largon	Wyeth
Prothipendyl	Timovan	Ayerst
Thiazinamium	Multergan	Rhone-Poulenc
Thiethylperazine	Torecan	Sandoz
Thiopropazate	Dartal	Searle
Thioproperazine	Majeptil	Rhone-Poulenc
Thioridazine	Mellaril	Sandoz
Trifluoperazine	Stelazine	Smith, Kline & French
Triflupromazine	Vesprin	Squibb
Butyrophenones		
Dehydrobenzperidol	Innovar	McNeil
Haloperidol	Serenace, Haldol	Searle, McNeil
Thioxanthenes		
Chlorprothixene	Taractan, Solatran	Roche, Warner
Clopenthixol	Sordinol	Ayerst
Thiothixene	Navane	Pfizer
Xanthiol	Daxid	Pfizer
Reserpines		
Deserpidine	Harmonyl	Abbott

DRUG REFERENCE

Generic Name	Brand	Company
Rescinnamine	Moderil	Pfizer
Reserpine	Serpasil and others	Ciba and others

Mood-Active Drugs

Tricyclics

Amitriptyline	Elavil	Merck
Desipramine	Pertofran, Norpramin	Geigy, Lakeside
Imipramine	Tofranil	Geigy
Nortriptyline	Aventyl	Lilly
Opipramol	Ensidon	Geigy
Protriptyline	Vivactil	Merck
Trimipramine	Surmontil	Rhone-Poulenc
Dioxiden	Sinervon	Pfizer
Lithium	Lithonate	Rowell
	Eskalith	Smith, Kline & French
	Cameolit	Camden Chemical Co.

MAO Inhibitors

Etryptamine	Monase (withdrawn)	Upjohn
Iproniazid	Marsilid (withdrawn)	Roche
Isocarboxazid	Marplan	Roche
Mebanazine	Actomol	Imperial Chemical Industry
Nialamide	Niamide	Pfizer
Pargyline	Eutonyl	Abbott
Phenelzine	Nardil	Warner
Pheniprazine	Catron (withdrawn)	Lakeside
Tranylcypromine	Parnate	Smith, Kline & French

Stimulants

Amphetamine	Benzedrine	Smith, Kline & French
Dextro-Amphetamine	Dexedrine	Smith, Kline & French
Deanol	Deaner	Riker
Methamphetamine	Amphedroxyn, Desoxyn	Lilly, Abbott
Methylphenidate	Ritalin	Ciba

Nonbarbiturate Minor Tranquilizers and Sedatives

Acetylcarbromal	Sedamyl	Riker
Azacyclonol	Frenquel	Merrell
Benactyzine	Suavitil	Merck, Sharp & Dohme
Benzquinamide	Quantril	Pfizer
Buclizine	Softran, Vibazine	Stuart, Pfizer
Captodiame	Suvren	Ayerst

DRUG REFERENCE

Generic Name	Brand	Company
Chlordiazepoxide	Librium	Roche
Chlormethazanone	Trancopal	Sterling-Winthrop
Diazepam	Valium	Roche
Ectylurea	Levanil	Upjohn
Emylcamate	Striatran	Merck
Hydroxyphenamate	Listica	Armour
Hydroxyzine	Vistaril, Atarax	Pfizer, Roerig
Mephenoxalone	Trepidone, Lenetran	Lederle, Lakeside
Meprobamate	Miltown, Equanil	Wallace, Wyeth
Oxanamide	Quiactin	Merrell
Oxazepam	Serax	Wyeth
Phenaglycodol	Ultran	Lilly
Tybamate	Solacen	Wallace
Clorazepute	Tranxene	Abbott

Nonbarbiturate Hypnotics

Ethchlorvynol	Placidyl	Abbott
Ethinamate	Valmid	Lilly
Glutethimide	Doriden	Ciba
Methaqualone	Quaalude	Rorer
Methylpentynol	Dormison	Schering
Methvorvlon	Noludar	Roche

CHAPTER THREE

WHAT'S NEW IN CONVULSIVE THERAPY?

RICHARD ABRAMS

Convulsive therapy is the oldest surviving somatic treatment in psychiatry, having antedated the introduction of psychosurgery by several years and witnessed the gradual demise of the older insulin coma therapy over the past decade. Convulsive therapy is widely used in the United States today[49], quite probably because of its unsurpassed clinical effectiveness in the treatment of patients with depressive illnesses. Antidepressant drugs were initially heralded as potential replacements for the unpopular "shock" treatments, but clinical experience and carefully controlled investigations[26, 51] have proven the older method most effective.

In recent years workers in convulsive therapy have attempted to reduce the undesirable side-effects of confusion and memory-loss by altering the method of seizure induction (unilateral ECT, anterior bifrontal ECT, flurothyl-induced seizures). Acceleration of the treatment course has been sought through increasing the frequency of treatment (multiple ECT), and even the older "regressive" ECT has been revived for the treatment of therapy-resistant patients. The prediction of the response to ECT in depressed patients has been studied, as well as the relation of induced EEG changes to that outcome. Finally, there have been theoretical attempts to understand, in part, the mode of action of convulsive therapy in chemical and neurophysiological terms.

UNILATERAL ECT

Friedman and Wilcox[24] were the first to alter the placement of treatment electrodes for ECT, which had previously been applied only bitemporally (bilateral ECT). They applied the electrodes to the left side of the head to induce grand mal seizures but did not describe the consequent therapeutic effect or memory changes. Goldman[25] was the first to specify placement of the treatment electrodes over the nondominant hemisphere to avoid the speech areas. He observed that seizures induced with this technique were therapeutically equal to those of bilateral ECT but yielded considerably less confusion. He was investigating a specialized direct-current treatment apparatus at the time and ascribed the reduced dysmnesia to the current waveform rather than the electrode placement. The first evaluation of unilateral ECT as such was by Thenon,[59] who used alternating current, nondominant hemisphere electrode placement, and reported reduced post-ECT confusion and amnesia as well as an accentuation of post-treatment slow wave EEG activity to the side of treatment electrode placement. He termed the method "monolateral" electroshock, but probably because his work appeared in an Argentine journal, it was ignored.

The present-day term unilateral ECT and its most frequent technique of application were introduced by Lancaster et al.[32] who reported a therapeutic equivalence for unilateral and bilateral ECT with markedly reduced memory-loss and confusion with the former method. Since their paper, over 20 studies of unilateral ECT have appeared, describing clinical effects, memory changes, and alterations in the EEG.

Clinical Findings

Most workers using objective criteria for evaluating treatment outcome in depressed patients have not reported significant differences between unilateral and bilateral ECT in depression-relieving potency. This is true for outcome criteria as diverse as psychiatrist-administered depression rating scales,[2, 16, 18, 20, 27, 43, 44, 57, 60] self-rating scales for depression,[18, 19, 23, 27, 43, 64] and the total number of ECT prescribed by a "blind" psychiatrist.[19, 20, 27, 57, 60, 64] Two exceptions to this overview are the report of Strain et al.[55] who found that patients receiving unilateral ECT required an extra treatment and stayed 2 days longer in hospital, and our own study described below.

In sharp contrast to the objective measures described above are the clinical impressions and general trends reported by the same authors. Thus it is asserted that bilateral ECT yields better and more complete improvement,[32] works faster and needs to be given less frequently than unilateral ECT,[16] yields greater reductions in depression scale scores,[27, 43] needs to be given less frequently,[19] requires fewer treatments,[20, 27, 57] yields more improvement,[23] works better in patients with severe endogenous depressions,[19] and causes a faster response.[57] Only one author has reported a trend for unilateral ECT to be more effective than bilateral ECT.[64]

Our own recent work is consonant with the many clinical impressions noted above.[5] We found bilateral ECT more effective than unilateral ECT in a study of 85 hospitalized depressed patients, and this finding remained true after the variability associated with the pretreatment severity of illness, age, sex, diagnosis, and concurrent drug therapy had been accounted for by multiple regression analyses. And, in a recently completed double-blind comparison of three methods of seizure induction,[11] we found that one bilateral ECT each treatment session was equal to two unilateral ECT in depression-relieving activity, suggesting a weaker effect of unilateral ECT. These findings are reflected in the widespread clinical practice of administering two unilateral ECT each treatment session to augment the therapeutic effect.

Memory Effects

Bilateral ECT has long been known to induce confusion and memory-loss which is dependent on the total number of seizures, their rate of administration, and the age of the patient. The memory disturbances include a retrograde amnesia, an anterograde amnesia, and impairment of short-term memory (retention) which, if severe, produces a Korsakoff-like amnestic confabulatory syndrome. Nondominant unilateral ECT is strikingly free from these memory alterations as observed in the earlier reports and confirmed in the more recent ones.[18, 19, 21, 23, 57] The absence of anterograde amnesia with unilateral ECT is especially noteworthy as its occurrence after bilateral ECT is responsible for the frequent complaint of patients receiving this treatment that they have no memory of their hospital stay or that it is "a complete blank." (Anterograde amnesia results from the faulty laying down of new information and is, therefore, permanent.) Unilateral ECT does not impair short-term memory and does not produce an amnestic-confabulatory syndrome regardless of the number of treatments or their rate of administration.

EEG Studies

Interseizure Records. Posttreatment slow-wave activity is a well-known sequel of bilateral ECT and is usually described as symmetrical, generalized, in the theta/delta range, and increasing with the number and frequency of induced seizures. Post-ECT slowing with unilateral ECT was observed by Thenon[59] to be accentuated over the side of treatment electrode placement and this was confirmed by subsequent workers.[44, 58, 63] In a comparison of unilateral and bilateral ECT in depressed patients we found marked differences for the visually-analyzed post-ECT distribution of slow activity.[3] EEG slowing after nondominant unilateral ECT was accentuated over the side of treatment electrode placement, whereas slowing after bilateral ECT was unexpectedly most pronounced over the *left* side of the head. A recent study by Small et al.[54] confirms this observation for bilateral ECT and also notes accentuation of slowing to the side of treatment electrode placement for both dominant and nondominant unilateral ECT.

To account for the asymmetrical post-ECT slowing after bilateral ECT we postulated an age-related increased sensitivity of the left hemisphere to noxious stimuli. In a subsequent study employing computer-analyzed EEG's,[61] we confirmed the lateralized EEG slowing observed visually and determined that the asymmetric response was age related, with the tendency for left-sided slowing to increase with age. We also examined the relation of the amount and distribution of the post-ECT slow-wave activity to the degree of clinical improvement as measured by changes in depression rating scale scores. We found no relation between any of the EEG measures and the response to ECT in the depressed patients studied.

EEG Seizure Patterns during ECT. Small et al.[53] reported a tendency for seizures with unilateral ECT to terminate in mixed alpha/beta activity. In a recent comparison of EEG seizure activity recorded during sessions of multiple unilateral and bilateral ECT[9] we confirmed this observation and demonstrated that "flat" post-seizure EEG patterns were more frequent after bilateral than after unilateral ECT. We also found seizures with unilateral ECT to be about 10 seconds shorter than those with bilateral ECT, and postulated that seizures with unilateral ECT were in some way "incomplete" and accounted, in part, for the reduced therapeutic effect of unilateral ECT.

MULTIPLE ECT

Attempts have been made to accelerate the treatment course of ECT by giving seizures daily rather than two or three times a week,[1] and by administering multiple seizures in a single treatment session.[14] In multiple ECT from three to eight seizures are given in a single session, spaced about two minutes apart. This method has been used with bilateral ECT[4, 13-15, 62] unilateral ECT,[2, 62] and anterior bifrontal ECT.[4] Clinical results with multiple ECT have been generally disappointing. To date, over 140 patients are reported to have received this method of ECT with only one mention of a dramatic clinical recovery after a single session.[4] An apparent acceleration of the treatment course is reported,[4, 15] but no controlled observations have been made.

On the other hand, there is a clearly increased risk of unwanted side-effects with multiple ECT. Strain and Bidder[56] treated a patient who developed prolonged status epilepticus during multiple ECT, followed by a transient Todd's paralysis. Abrams and Fink[4] reported two patients who developed prolonged postictal organic confusional states with disorientation, amnesia, and confabulation. This Korsakoff-like syndrome was accompanied by dominant EEG delta activity, and cleared in a week's time without sequel. Bridenbaugh et al.[15] had one patient who developed pulmonary aspiration and pneumonitis during the first session of multiple ECT, and they felt it necessary to institute routine intubation for all subsequent patients treated with this method. They also reported five episodes of supraventricular tachycardia requiring termination of treatment in two patients, an incidence for the 17 patients treated far in excess of that reported with conventional ECT.[49] The same authors treated a patient who developed status epilepticus during multiple ECT whose seizure was terminated after 62 minutes with intravenous diazepam. Their data on seizure duration are puzzling as they also report 15 other seizures lasting over 15 minutes. In our own studies of seizure duration during multiple ECT in 18 patients we observed no seizures lasting longer than 3 minutes. Finally, a prolonged period of postictal sleep and confusion has been observed with multiple ECT[4, 13] as well as the frequent occurrence of states of fearful apprehension and cognitive disorganization for as long as 8 to 10 hours posttreatment.[4]

Of theoretical interest is the observation that for most patients there was no dramatic increase in the post-ECT confusion and dysmnesia seen the day after multiple ECT. Formal studies were not done, but we observed a number of patients who received six bilateral ECT in a single treatment session yet showed scarcely more memory-loss the next day than if they had received one or two ECT. The observation has also been made that the therapeutic effects of multiple ECT may increase over the 24 to 72 hours following a single session.[4, 13] These observations suggest that both the amnesic and therapeutic effects of multiple ECT (and probably conventional ECT as well) require development over time and are not simply a function of the total number of seizures administered.[10]

To summarize, it has not been possible to administer a full therapeutic course of ECT in a single treatment session, and the possible acceleration of treatment provided by two or three sessions of multiple ECT must be weighed against the increased morbidity of this method.

ANTERIOR BIFRONTAL ECT

Our observation of a reduced therapeutic effect for unilateral ECT compared with bilateral ECT led to the hypothesis that bilateral cerebral stimulation might be critical for the fully developed therapeutic effects of ECT. We retained bilateral cerebral stimulation, at the same time avoiding the temporal lobes, by applying bilateral treatment electrodes as far forwards over the front of the head as was consistent with obtaining a grand mal seizure.[8]

Such anterior bifrontal ECT was effective in reducing depression scale scores after four and eight ECT but this clinical effect was less than that found for conventional bilateral ECT in a prior study of similar patients, using the same rating scale.[5] Memory alterations did not occur with anterior bifrontal ECT, an observation also made for nondominant unilateral ECT. We concluded that anterior bifrontal ECT was most similar to this latter method, and that the therapeutic advantage of conventional bilateral

ECT could not reside solely in the bilaterality of cerebral stimulation. We hypothesized that bilateral *temporal lobe* stimulation was required for the fully developed clinical effects of conventional bilateral ECT, and that such stimulation also produced the incidental, and causally unrelated, memory-loss and confusion seen with that method. (Anterior bifrontal ECT provided no therapeutic advantage over unilateral or bilateral ECT and we have not investigated the method further.)

CONVULSIVE THERAPY AND THE DIENCEPHALON

The results of the study above suggested a further evaluation of the possible anatomical locus of action for the clinical effects of ECT, and we undertook a double-blind, controlled study comparing the effects of three different treatment electrode placements for ECT in depressed patients[11]: two nondominant unilateral ECT each session; one nondominant followed by one dominant unilateral ECT each session; and a single unilateral ECT each session.

We found no difference in therapeutic effect among the three methods as measured by depression rating scale scores obtained before and after treatment. As two seizures each session with consecutive unilateral stimulation of both temporal lobes were not more effective than two seizures induced with stimulation over the nondominant hemisphere only, we concluded that bilaterality of temporal lobe stimulation alone could not be critical for the depression-relieving effects of conventional ECT. The possibility that *simultaneous* bitemporal stimulation is critical requires evaluation, but it seems more likely that direct diencephalic stimulation underlies the antidepressive effects of ECT.[17a] An investigation is now in progress which attempts to separate the effects of diencephalic stimulation and simultaneous bitemporal stimulation by varying the anatomical placement of the treatment electrodes.

REGRESSIVE ECT

Regressive ECT is a misnomer for a procedure which induces a temporary syndrome of amnesia, disorientation, confusion, incontinence, and reduced ability for self-care, by the administration of one or more bilateral ECT each day. The method was originally introduced for the treatment of neurotic patients and later used mainly in the treatment of those with "resistant" schizophrenia. The results with regressive ECT were not promising; objective methods of evaluation were rarely used, and the only reported controlled trial showed no beneficial effect of the treatment. Moreover, those who attributed therapeutic activity to the "regression" did not control for the number of seizures given, usually considerably in excess of a standard course of ECT.

Murillo and Exner[47] have recently revived regressive ECT in a study of its effectiveness in patients with "process" schizophrenia. The study lacks a control group of patients receiving ECT at the conventional frequency of treatment, and does not employ reliable measures of outcome or appropriate data analysis. The authors' conclusion that their patients on regressive ECT "apparently showed the greater gains" is not supported by the data. If future studies of regressive ECT are to be undertaken, they should include a control group of patients receiving an equal number of ECT given at the usual rate of three each week. Until the results of such a study demonstrate a therapeutic advantage for regressive ECT, the justification for its continued use remains obscure.

FLUROTHYL CONVULSIVE THERAPY (FCT)

The inhalant convulsant flurothyl (Indoklon) was introduced in the 1950s as an alternative method for administering convulsive therapy. Early studies of the therapeutic and side-effects of FCT revealed no significant differences from bilateral ECT. Recent studies have confirmed the therapeutic equivalence of FCT and ECT,[33, 52] but have indicated differences in the side-effects of confusion and amnesia for the two methods.

Small et al.[52] found more improvement in paired-associate learning with FCT than with ECT, and Laurell[33] found equal amounts of anterograde amnesia but significantly less retrograde amnesia with FCT. The immediate postconvulsive confusion observed during the initial 2 to 3 hours after treatment was greatest with FCT, a phenomenon clinically apparent even from casual recovery room observation. Laurell[33] attributes the increased posttreatment confusion to the longer seizure duration with FCT he recorded, a finding also reported by Small et al.[52] The reduced retrograde amnesia is attributed to the absence of electric current with FCT, as prior studies demonstrated that retrograde amnesia was primarily bound to the effects of the current, and only secondarily to the seizure itself.

These observations leave undefined the precise role of the convulsive seizure in the therapeutic action of FCT and ECT. Assertions that the seizure is the therapeutic agent are not supported by the observation that FCT and ECT are equally therapeutic but have different seizure durations. One important variable may be the pattern of EEG slow activity during the interseizure period. The left-sided accentuation of EEG slowing after bilateral ECT has already been commented on; the slowing after FCT, however, is symmetrical.[54]

At present there is no specific reason to choose FCT over ECT for any patient. As FCT is a bit more cumbersome to administer, it is not widely used. It is an acceptable alternative to some patients who do not want "electro" convulsive therapy, but who will agree to "inhalant" convulsive therapy.

PREDICTION OF RESPONSE TO ECT

Early clinical studies of the response of depressed patients to ECT showed recovery rates of 80 to 90% in patients diagnosed as having involutional melancholia or the depressed phase of manic-depressive illness.[30, 31] Later workers attempting to predict the response of depressed patients to ECT eschewed clinical diagnosis and employed instead a variety of separate clinical features which could be summed in a score and related to outcome.[17, 28, 29, 45, 46, 48] The predictive accuracy of these methods ranged from 76 to 90% with most workers reporting results closer to 76%. Three studies[17, 29, 46] provided methods for calculating a predictive index from a checklist of clinical and historical variables obtained prior to treatment. In our own recent work[7] we assessed the usefulness of these numerical indices and also tested the relation to outcome of 22 additional clinical variables not included in the indices.

We examined 76 hospitalized depressed patients prior to ECT and completed a depression rating scale, the three predictive indices, and recorded the 22 additional clinical and historical variables selected for their putative association with the response to ECT. None of the predictive indices nor any of the additional clinical and historical variables were related to improvement after 4 to 6 ECT as measured by reduction in the depression scale score or the global assessment of treatment outcome.

The methodological problems associated with attempts to predict outcome with ECT are described elsewhere,[6] but it seems likely that, as most severely depressed patients suffer from definable illnesses (e.g., manic-depressive illness, depressed phase) rather than simple accumulations of unrelated symptoms, the prognosis for ECT response is that of the disease entity rather than any individual or grouped "target" symptoms. The fact that a majority of hospitalized depressed patients will respond favorably to ECT is evidenced by the fact that the overall response for the entire sample of patients reported by Hobson[29] and Mendels[46] was about 60% regardless of the presence or absence of specific clinical features alone or grouped. And had ECT been reserved only for those patients with the diagnosis of endogenous depression, the response rate would have been 72%.[46]

CEREBRAL AMINES AND CONVULSIVE THERAPY

Altered levels of cerebral amines and their precursors and metabolites are reported in brain and cerebrospinal fluid of patients with affective disorders. The hindbrains of depressive suicides contain decreased levels of serotonin and its metabolite, 5HIAA, and low levels of 5HIAA are reported in the spinal fluid of some depressed patients. However, contradictory data exist, and the changes observed for manic patients, rather than reflecting an opposing process, are actually in the same direction.

There is no information yet available on the effects of ECT on human cerebral amine metabolism. Essman[22] has recently reviewed the literature and presented his own work on the central biochemical effects of electroconvulsive shock (ECS) in animals. With regard to alterations in biogenic amines, most studies show increased synthesis and turnover of indole and catechol amines in animals receiving ECS, and these observations are consistent with those observed in some depressed patients with or without antidepressant drug therapy.

We undertook a preliminary study of ECT-induced alterations of cerebral amine metabolism in depressed patients as reflected in pre- and post-ECT levels of 5HIAA and homovanillic acid (HVA) in the spinal fluid.[12] We studied endogenous depressed patients who were drug free for at least 1 week prior to ECT and throughout the study period. Spinal fluid samples were obtained before ECT and at varying intervals after treatment, and for varying numbers of treatments. Nine patients were studied, six of whom provided samples both before and after ECT (for three patients only post-ECT samples were obtained). Whenever possible, a depression rating scale was recorded on the same day as the spinal tap, and for six patients such depression scale scores were obtained before and after treatment.

We found a trend for the spinal fluid 5HIAA levels to increase several hours after ECT, to peak on the next day, and to decline gradually to baseline levels by 3 weeks posttreatment. However, none of the post-ECT values were significantly different from the pre-ECT value. No significant change in spinal fluid HVA levels were observed after ECT, nor was any trend noted. In 14 instances we obtained spinal fluid samples and a depression scale score on the same day in the same patient (six were pre-ECT, eight post-ECT). The product-moment correlations were not significant for either 5HIAA and depression score ($r = +0.04$), or HVA and depression score ($r = -0.16$). Nor were significant correlations obtained for the change in depression score after ECT and the changes in either 5HIAA or HVA.

These preliminary findings do not support the hypothesis of a specific relation between improvement with ECT in depressed patients and alterations in cerebral amines as reflected in the spinal fluid. However, the sample is small, and we measured only absolute levels of amine metabolites. It would be interesting to know the effects of ECT on the synthesis rates of serotonin and norepinephrine, as measured by the more accurate probenecid-induced accumulation of their metabolites in spinal fluid. Such studies are reported for patients receiving antidepressant drug therapy, and the amino acid tryptophan, and should be very informative in depressed patients who are receiving ECT.

REFERENCES

1. Abrams, R.: Daily administration of unilateral ECT. *Am. J. Psychiatr.* **124**:384, 1967.

2. Abrams, R. and deVito, R. A.: Clinical efficacy of unilateral ECT. *Dis. Nerv. Syst.* **30**:262, 1969.

3. Abrams, R., Volavka, J., Roubicek, J., Dornbush, R., and Fink, M.: Lateralized EEG changes after unilateral and bilateral electroconvulsive therapy. *Dis. Nerv. Syst. GWAN Suppl.* **31**:28, 1970.

4. Abrams, R. and Fink, M.: Clinical experiences with multiple electroconvulsive treatments. *Compr. Psychiatr.* **13**:115, 1972.

5. Abrams, R., Fink, M., Dornbush, R., Feldstein, S., Volavka, J., and Roubicek, J.: Unilateral and bilateral ECT: Effects on depression, memory, and the electroencephalogram. *Arch. Gen. Psychiatr.* **27**:88, 1972.

6. Abrams, R.: Recent clinical studies of ECT. *Semin. Psychiatr.* **4**:3, 1972.

7. Abrams, R., Feldstein, S., and Fink, M.: Prediction of clinical response to ECT. *Brit. J. Psychiatr.* **122**:457, 1973.

8. Abrams, R. and Taylor, M. A. T.: Anterior bifrontal ECT: A clinical trial. *Brit. J. Psychiatr.* **122**:587, 1973.

9. Abrams, R., Volavka, J., and Fink, M.: EEG seizure patterns during multiple unilateral and bilateral ECT. *Compr. Psychiatr.* **14**:25, 1973.

10. Abrams, R.: Multiple ECT: What have we learned? In *Psychobiology of Convulsive Therapy*, M. Fink, S. Kety, T. McGaugh, and T. Williams, (Eds.) V. H. Winston, 1973, pp. 79–84.

11. Abrams, R. and Taylor, M. A. T.: Electroconvulsive therapy and the diencephalon: a preliminary report, *Compr. Psychiatr.* **15**:233, 1974.

12. Abrams, R., Essman, W. B., Taylor, M. A. T., and Fink, M.: Cerebral amines and convulsive therapy, unpublished.

13. Bidder, G. T. and Strain, J. J.: Modifications of electroconvulsive therapy. *Compr. Psychiatr.* **11**:507, 1970.

14. Blachly, P. H. and Gowing, D.: Multiple monitored electroconvulsive treatment. *Compr. Psychiatr.* **7**:100, 1966.

15. Bridenbaugh, R. H., Drake, R. F., and O'Regan, T. J.: Multiple monitored electroconvulsive treatment of schizophrenia. *Compr. Psychiatr.* **13**:9, 1972.

16. Cannicott, S. M.: Unilateral electroconvulsive therapy. *Postgrad. Med. J.* **38**:451, 1962.

17. Carney, M. W. P., Roth, M., and Garside, R. F.: The diagnosis of depressive syndromes and the prediction of E.C.T. response. *Brit. J. Psychiatr.* **111**:659, 1965.

17a. Carney, M. W. P. and Sheffield, B. F.: Electroconvulsion therapy and the diencephalon. *Lancet* **1**:1505, 1973.

18. Costello, C. G., Belton, G. P., Abra, J. C., and Dunn, B. E.: The amnesic and therapeutic effects of bilateral and unilateral ECT. *Brit. J. Psychiatr.* **116**:69, 1970.

19. Cronin, D., Bodley, P., Potts, L., Mather, M. D., Gardner, R. K., and Tobin, J. C.: Unilateral and bilateral ECT: A study of memory disturbance and relief from depression. *J. Neurol. Neurosurg. Psychiatr.* **33**:705, 1970.

20. d'Elia: Unilateral electroconvulsive therapy. *Acta Psychiat. Scand. Suppl.* 215, 1970.

21. Dornbush, R., Abrams, R., and Fink, M.: Memory changes after unilateral and bilateral convulsive therapy (ECT). *Brit. J. Psychiatr.* **119**:75, 1971.

22. Essman, W. B.: Neurochemical changes in ECS and ECT. *Semin. Psychiatr.* **4**:67, 1972.

23. Fleminger, J. J., De L. Horne, D. J., Nair, N. P. V. and Nott, P. N.: Differential effects of unilateral and bilateral ECT. *Am. J. Psychiatr.* **127**:430, 1970.

24. Friedman, E. and Wilcox, P. H.: Electrostimulated convulsive doses in intact humans by means of unidirectional currents. *J. Nerv. Ment. Dis.* **96**:56, 1942.

25. Goldman, D.: Brief stimulus electric shock therapy. *J. Nerv. Ment. Dis.* **110**:36, 1949.

26. Greenblatt, M., Grosser, G. H. and Wechsler, H.: Differential response of hospitalized depressed patients to somatic therapy. *Am. J. Psychiatr.* **120**:935, 1964.

27. Halliday, A. M., Davison, K., Browne, M. W., and Kreeger, L. C.: A comparison of the effects on depression and memory of bilateral ECT and unilateral ECT to the dominant and non-dominant hemispheres. *Brit. J. Psychiatr.* **114**:997, 1968.

28. Hamilton, M. and White, J. M.: Factors related to the outcome of depression treated with E.C.T. *J. Ment. Sci.* **106**:1031, 1960.

29. Hobson, R. F.: Prognostic factors in electric convulsive therapy. *J. Neurol. Neurosurg. Psychiatr.* **16**:275, 1953.

30. Huston, P. E. and Locher, L. M.: Involutional psychosis, course when untreated and when treated with electric shock. *Arch. Neurol. Psychiatr.* **59**:385, 1948.

31. Huston, P. E. and Locher, L. M.: Manic-depressive psychosis, course when untreated and when treated with electric shock. *Arch. Neurol. Psychiatr.* **60**:37, 1948.

32. Lancaster, N. P., Steinert, R. R. and Frost, I.: Unilateral electroconvulsive therapy. *J. Ment. Sci.* **104**:221, 1958.

33. Laurell, B.: Fluothyl convulsive therapy. *Acta Psychiatr. Scand. Suppl.* 213, 1970.

43. Levy, R.: The clinical evaluation of unilateral electroconvulsive therapy. *Brit. J. Psychiatr.* **114**:459, 1968.

44. Martin, W. L., Ford, H. F., McDanald, E. C., Jr., and Towler, M. L.: Clinical evaluation of unilateral EST. *Am. J. Psychiatr.* **121**:1087, 1965.

45. Mendels, J.: Electroconvulsive therapy and depression: III. A method for prognosis. *Brit. J. Psychiatr.* **111**:687, 1965.

46. Mendels, J.: The prediction of response to electroconvulsive therapy. *Am. J. Psychiatr.* **124**:153, 1967.

47. Murillo, M. G. and Exner, J. E.: The effects of regressive ECT with process schizophrenics. *Am. J. Psychiatr.* **130**:269, 1973.

48. Nyström, S.: On relation between clinical factors and efficacy of E.C.T. in depression. *Acta Psychiatr. Scand. Suppl.* 181, 1964.

49. Pitts, F. N.: Medical aspects of ECT. *Semin. Psychiatr.* **4**:27, 1972.

50. Roberts, J. M.: Prognostic factors in the electroshock treatment of depressive states. I. Clinical features from history and examination. *J. Ment. Sci.* **105**:693, 1959.

51. Shepherd, M.: Clinical trial of the treatment of depressive illness. *Brit. Med. J.* **1**:881, 1965.

52. Small, J. G., Small, I. F., Sharpley, P., and Moore, D. F.: A double-blind comparative evaluation of flurothyl and ECT. *Arch. Gen. Psychiatr.* **19**:79, 1968.

53. Small, J. G., Small, I. F., and Perez, H. C.: Electroencephalographic (EEG) and neurophysiological studies of electrically induced seizures. *J. Nerv. Ment. Dis.* **150**:479, 1970.

54. Small, I. F., Small, J. G., Milstein, V. and Sharpley, P.: Interhemispheric relationships with somatic therapy. *Dis. Nerv. Syst.* **34**:170, 1973.

55. Strain, J. J., Brunschwig, L., Duffy, J. P., Agle, D. P., Rosenbaum, A. L., and Bidder, T. G.: Comparison of therapeutic effects and memory changes with bilateral and unilateral ECT. *Am. J. Psychiatr.* **125**:294, 1968.

56. Strain, J. J. and Bidder, T. G.: Transient cerebral complication associated with multiple monitored electroconvulsive therapy. *Compr. Psychiatr.* **32**:95, 1970.

57. Strömgren, L. S.: Unilateral versus bilateral electroconvulsive therapy. *Acta Psychiatr. Scand. Suppl.* 240, 1973.

58. Sutherland, E. M., Oliver, J. E. and Knight, D. R.: E. E. G., memory and confusion in dominant, non-dominant, and bi-temporal E.C.T. *Brit. J. Psychiatr.* **115**:1069, 1969.

59. Thenon, J.: Electrochoque monolateral. *Acta Neuropsyquiat. Argent.* **2**:292, 1956.

60. Valentine, M., Keddie, K. M. G., and Dunne, D.: A comparison of techniques in electro-convulsive therapy. *Brit. J. Psychiatr.* **114**:989, 1968.

61. Volavka, J., Feldstein, S., and Abrams, R., Dornbush, R., and Fink, M.: EEG and clinical change after bilateral and unilateral electro-convulsive therapy. *EEG Clin. Neurophysiol.* **32**:631, 1972.

62. White, R. K., Shea, J. J., and Jonas, M. A.: Multiple monitored electroconvulsive therapy. *Am. J. Psychiatr.* **125**:622, 1968.

63. Zamora, E. N. and Kaebling, R.: Memory and electroconvulsive therapy. *Am. J. Psychiatr.* **122**:546, 1965.

64. Zinkin, S. and Birtchnell, J.: Unilateral electroconvulsive therapy: Its effects on memory and its therapeutic efficacy. *Brit. J. Psychiatr.* **114**:973, 1968.

CHAPTER FOUR

REFLECTIONS ON RECENT CONTRIBUTIONS TO BIOCHEMISTRY AND PHARMACOTHERAPY OF AFFECTIVE DISORDERS

N. MATUSSEK, M.D.

Since antidepressant drugs were introduced at the end of the 1950s, interest in biological research of depression and the treatment thereof has increased immensely. Intense occupation with this subject implied that in solving a number of important problems, a great many new questions arose. It seems to become more and more difficult to comprehend biochemically affective diseases, since as a result of biochemical and pharmacotherapeutic research, further subgroups are formed.

In this chapter some of the problems that have recently appeared in the field of biochemistry and pharmacotherapy are discussed based on a critical analysis of recent findings.

As in other fields of research, depression research also depends on homogeneous test material for solving certain problems. Depression is known to arise from different causes. But a uniform classification of affective disorders has not yet been found, although numerous efforts have been made. A study which was recently carried out by Kendell with the aid of videotape between London, Paris, and Munich showed up the evident differences in diagnosis of several psychiatric diseases existing in the three European countries alone. Difference in diagnosis between Europe and the East of the United States is said to be even more marked (see Ref. 25, further papers and discussions to follow on this subject). As there is no conformity in criteria of diagnosis, it is not astonishing that even thorough and accurate studies produce contradictory results. Thus as long as a clear and uniform classification of affective disorders is not possible, it is necessary for biological psychiatry to specify each patient's psychological and somatic symptoms including important biographic dates and family anamnesis in a check list. In some countries, initial efforts have been made in this direction, the results of which are being integrated by WHO.[57] Then it will be possible to compare data of different laboratories better than is possible today, and thus perhaps to obtain a uniform biochemical classification of depression.

BIOGENIC AMINES

The two amine hypotheses still hold center stage in current research into the affective disorder. Everett and Toman[19] were the first to speculate on the possible importance of catecholamines in respect to affective disorders which were then formally elaborated in the 1960s by different groups.[9, 36, 59] The serotonin hypothesis was put forward in the work of Coppen et al.[16] Since there were both enthusiastic supporters and provocative reports, much of the basic research focused on basic mechanism of the biogenic amines and their interaction with various psychoactive drugs such as Reserpine and MAOI. Much of the work tended to support one or the other amine theories of depression. This work and the speculations derived therefrom have been copiously discussed and described, gaining a wide currency and familiarity. Therefore, I will not restate it in this context. Rather, I present some recent clinically oriented biochemical findings, reviewed with a critical eye.

Serotonin

In attempts to delineate the role of 5-hydroxytryptamin or serotonin (5-HT) in depression, its various metabolites have been measured in cerebrospinal fluid (CSF) of depressed patients. Although not uniformly substantiated, in a great number of patients low levels of 5-hydroxy indole-acetic acid (5-HIAA) have been found.[13, 49] Additionally, analyses of brains obtained at autopsy of depressed patients indicated decreased amounts of 5-HIAA and 5-HT[5, 46, 63]—a finding which supported the implication of the CSF studies. However, using rather sophisticated analyses Lloyd et al.[30] found 5-HT reduced in amount in only two raphé nuclei and no difference in 5-HIAA. The picture became cloudier when it was shown that low 5-HIAA concentration was found in mania as well.[15] Lower levels of 5-HT have been found in the brain of Parkinsonism patients at necropsy.[4] Therefore, and because of other studies which are not referred to at this place, it seems evident that lower 5-HT metabolism in brain is neither associated with a specific disease entity, nor can be uniformly related to the presence of depression, or an affective disorder at all. In a similar way, the finding of a lower concentration of free tryptophan in CSF and in plasma of depressed patients suggested a reduced 5-HT synthesis in brain. However, with treatment and after clinical improvement, although the free plasma tryptophan returned to normal, the 5-HIAA CSF level remained low even in the symptom-free period.[13, 15] Of great interest seems to be a preliminary finding of Coppen[14] stating that patients who do not respond to thymoleptic therapy are not showing an increase in free plasma tryptophan.

The apparent association of symptoms of affective disorder with a 5-HT deficit led various workers to use 5-HT precursors in an effort to increase functional 5-HT at receptor sites, hoping to achieve a somewhat "natural" antidepressant effect. Unfortunately such efforts with L-tryptophan[8, 11, 17] and (DL) 5-hydroxytryptophan (5-HTP)[49] have for the most part been negative or inconclusive. A very enthusiastic report by Sano[56] as to the therapeutic antidepressant efficacy of L-5-HTP, in part, encouraged our use of this agent in depression. However, our study failed to produce the same results, even when a peripheral decarboxylase inhibitor (Ro-4-46o2) was used in combination with L-5-HTP. We had expected at least to see some improvement in the sleep disturbance of our patients, since it has been shown that 5-HTP showed a sleep-inducing property in normal volunteers, but this was not the case.[39] Our observations may indicate that sleep mechanism in depression is, at least temporarily, somehow functionally different. Of itself, our study certainly does not rule out that some antidepressant effect can be obtained in certain depressed patients, either because of different methodologies or perhaps, most likely, the presence of a subgroup which may be responsive to this agent. Further studies will be necessary before it can be established that there is a meaningful correlation between low 5-HIAA levels in CSF and an improvement in depression after treatment with 5-HTP, as maintained by van Praag.[49]

Norepinephrine

Turning to the catecholamine hypothesis, what do the various reports of disturbances in norepinephrine (NE) metabolism in affective disorder indicate? First, it is probably more consistent to speak of a NE hypothesis, rather than a catecholamine hypothesis. Experience in Parkinsonism, which seems to be primarily associated with deficit brain dopamine, has shown that the dopamine level in such patients can be increased by L-Dopa with good therapeutic effects. Furthermore, a group of quite thorough, well-designed studies[21, 24, 35, 40, 66] have failed to establish a general antidepressant effect, despite evidence that the dopamine level within the central nervous system (CNS) is raised by administration of L-Dopa. Therefore, it clearly indicates that a dopamine deficiency of itself cannot account for depression. There are some results that tend to suggest certain associated symptoms seen in some depression may respond to L-Dopa, or that an occasional depressed patient will improve; but even in these cases, it is highly unlikely that the antidepressive effect depended only on an increased dopamine level; that is, its effect in these limited instances is probably due to changes induced in NE metabolism. To the extent that a catecholamine deficit is pertinent to depression at all, it seems that it can only be a NE deficit.

In the postmortem brain studies cited above,[5, 46] a decrease in NE was not found. But this indicates nothing regarding functional availability of NE or integrity of the receptor. As to autopsy analyses of human brains, it seems necessary for attention to be directed not only to the substrates and metabolites of the respective amine but also to the various enzymes, critical to its metabolism, as they occur in the specific brain areas. This seems to be of importance for both the NE and the 5-HT hypotheses. If determinations of the activities of the enzymes involved in biosynthesis and degradation are estimated, significant benefit can derive from such studies, as demonstrated by the important work of MAO activity cited later on. A great many earlier clinical studies in depression demonstrated apparent abnormalities in NE metabolism; indeed such findings became incorporated into and reinforced the NE hypothesis. Increasingly, it has become obvious that most of these deviations from normal dealt with peripheral events,[22, 62] or the degree to which they reflected central events could not be quantified. Regrettably, this state of affairs still exists to a not inconsiderable degree. Nonetheless, in an attempt to overcome some of these limitations, much attention currently has been focused on the O-methylated metabolite of NE, 3-methoxy-4-hydroxyphenylglycol (MHPG), since several workers have published evidence which they have interpreted to indicate MHPG may be the main CNS metabolite, and therefore, urinary excretion of this agent more directly reflected CNS NE metabolism.[34, 58] Recent studies with 6-hydroxy-dopamine support this assumption.[6, 32] But not all results are pointing in the same direction.[12] In studies from our laboratory with a new neuroleptic drug, Clozapine, a change in the level of CSF MHPG found in certain schizophrenic and manic patients was not reflected in urinary MHPG values,[1] which leads to the conclusion that further studies are necessary to establish the relationship between CNS catecholamine metabolism and urinary MHPG. However, be that as it may, the clinical results which have been obtained, especially by the groups of Maas and Schildkraut during the last years, are of great, maybe even decisive, importance to biochemical research of depression. Depressive patients show a lower urinary MHPG concentration, hypomanic patients an increased level. During antidepressant treatment, clinical improvement is associated with increasing MHPG excretion. Of special therapeutic, and potential nosological importance, are studies that have demonstrated that therapeutic response can be correlated with pretreatment MHPG levels in urine: imipramine response is better in those patients with low values as compared to those with normal; higher or normal values are associated with a better response to amitriptyline (see Refs. 33, 60, 61 for further references). Studies on CSF MHPG (see Ref. 64 for further references) did not show results being as clear as the urinary MHPG studies.

When one is concerned with relating the improvement achieved by any given treatment modality for depression to certain biochemical events, sleep deprivation therapy[47] is of especial value. Endogenously depressed patients improved for 1 or 2 days after sleep deprivation. Since the patients were studied longitudinally, one can relate biochemical changes to psychopathological state. In our study to date, of 14 patients treated, 50% showed significant improvement and 50% did not. Only the improved patients showed a significant increase in urinary NE and vanillylmandelic acid (VMA) on the day of improvement. Furthermore, certain other results, which are not discussed in detail here, indicate a significant increase in NE synthesis in the improved patients as contrasted to the unimproved.[38] Since the bulk of NE and VMA found in the urine derives mostly from the periphery, these results suggest that improvement is closely correlated to activation of peripheral sympathetic neurons, which has also been mentioned before by Schildkraut et al.[62] in an imipramine study. We expect to find a higher level of urinary MHPG in the improved group as compared to the unimproved, but thus far in the study this has not been established.

In studying the relationship between the catecholamines and depressive conditions, it is extremely important to keep in mind the motor activity of the patients, since it has been clearly demonstrated that catecholamine turnover is closely related to such activity. Recently Post et al.[48] demonstrated that elevations of CSF MHPG seemed to correlate with the motor activity of the patients. Yet Maas et al.[33] could not find a relation between motor activity and urinary MHPG excretion, but a correlation to NE output. In these studies, too, which have however been carried out under different conditions, there does not seem to be a correlation between CSF and urinary MHPG. Since we were concerned with the effect of the motor activity of our patients on their catecholamine metabolism, the said activity was measured with pedometers each day during the sleep deprivation study. But no significant correlation between NE excretion and motor activity was found in our patients.[31]

MONOAMINE OXIDASE

Of special interest in trying to elucidate the role of the amines are some interesting findings regarding the enzyme monoamine oxidase (MAO), since this is the main catabolic enzyme of NE and 5-HT. Among the several biological features reported to differ in bipolar and unipolar depression is that the former shows low platelet MAO activity while it is normal in unipolars.[43] MAO activity is higher in women that in men and has shown a marked increase with age in the human brain, platelets, and plasma. Additionally, 5-HIAA levels were similarly high, while NE levels were negatively correlated. This reciprocal correlation to MAO activity is indicative of a major role for MAO in the regulation of the cellular contents of the respective amines. Furthermore, it suggests that there may be a built-in tendency to affective disorder with increasing age and provides some reasonable basis for the commonplace clinical finding that most depressions occur in the middle to late life—not to mention a possible understanding of the irritability and dysphoric mood not uncommon in the elderly.[52, 53] There are findings suggestive of genetic and hormonal influences in the predisposition to and expression of affective disorder. A recent report which studies MAO activity of platelets and plasma in fraternal and identical twins found convincing evidence that the genetic factors influence such activities.[45] In this study, the authors cite that their interaction coupled with the extremely good evidence for a genetic basis in some affective disorders begin to point the way to a clearer understanding of how biological predisposition may express itself as a vulnerability to such disorder. However, a reduced MAO activity was found in platelets of schizophrenics as well.[44] In studies with schizophrenic twins, a reduced MAO activity was demonstrated to possibly be a genetic marker for vulnerability to schizophrenia, as the nonschizophrenic twin also showed a reduced MAO activity.[67] A similar study on depressed patients would be interesting. Would these findings lead us back to the "Einheitsspychose"?

GROWTH HORMONES

One of the most interesting developments of the past decade has been the elaboration of the relation between the amines and the hypothalamic-pituitary axis, in particular the role they play in facilitating and/or mediating the secretion of the various releasing factors and thereby the respective pituitary hormones. Apart from this somewhat theoretical frame work, attention focused on hypothalamic functions as it relates to amines; affect is indicated, since it has a well established role in emotion and in various basic drives (sexual, appetite, and sleep) and vegetative homeostasis (i.e., the autonomic function). Components of both these constellations, in addition to the core mood disorder, frequently form many of the symptoms and signs seen in affective disorder. Thus the altered sexual function, appetite, and such, may relate to aminergic changes which are reflected as well in mood changes and psychomotor activity.

One of the hormones in which we have been interested is human growth hormone (HGH), because its secretion is controlled by catecholaminergic, probably noradrenergic mechanism. A falling blood sugar is a potent stimulus for its release normally, but Sachar[55] et al. have shown that in some depressives this response is significantly reduced or virtually absent. Since the neuronal pathway is NE mediated and L-Dopa has been shown to release HGH in normals but to a much smaller degree in unipolar depressives, these observations suggest that this deficiency may be related to a functional inadequacy in NE.[55] In our sleep deprivation study mentioned before, besides the amine metabolism in some patients we measured HGH. It was found that depressives had a significantly lower basic level in the morning following the night of deprivation as compared to controls (in preparation).

It has been shown that there is normally a well defined, large rise in HGH nocturnally, generally in the early hours of sleep and generally associated with D wave sleep,[65] although there is some question about the specificity of the rise to this, or any specific stage of sleep. As a consequence we have a study in progress evaluating this function in depressives. Although the data are preliminary at this time and firm conclusions cannot yet be drawn, it seems as if at least some depressives do not show this response. Sachar[54] has in his excellent review mentioned similar unpublished observations by Hellmann. In this connection the most interesting findings of the groups of Prange and Lipton must be mentioned; they succeeded in improving the mood of depressive patients and healthy controls as well by thyreotrophic releasing hormone (TRH) application (see Ref. 29). Although no therapy for clinical use has been developed, the importance of hypothalamic pituitary adrenal axis for depression research has again been brought into focus.

PHARMACOKINETICS

In the course of the last few years, some data about pharmacokinetics of tricyclic thymoleptics have been obtained which might be of importance for clinical psychiatry as well. However, some of the results are contradictory. In the meantime the results of Åsberg et al.[3] have been confirmed by the same group.[27] These studies showed that patients having either a too low or a too high plasma level showed no therapeutic response when treated with nortriptyline (NT). Only patients with a mean plasma level responded well to NT treatment. These results could, however, not be confirmed by Davies.[18] There was no correlation between plasma level and therapeutic response found in the whole group. Only a linear correlation was shown by some of the patients.

It is of special interest to know whether a therapeutic response will be shown by changing the dose and thus changing plasma level as well. In some cases Davies[18] could demonstrate in a long-term treatment that patients showed a relapse following reduction of NT dose and an improvement following an increase of the dose in correlation to the plasma level. In the Scandinavian trial, too, of seven nonresponders to NT with high plasma levels, five responded to NT following dose-reduction.[26] With amitriptyline Braithwaite[6] et al. found a good linear correlation between plasma levels and therapeutic effect. In a study of Angst[2] with a new thymoleptic drug (Maprotilin = Ludiomil®) a linear correlation was found only if some patients were taken out of the study. When the same drug was applied in a 6-week treatment period with normal volunteers in a pharmacokinetic study, we did not find any significant correlation concerning plasma levels with regard to some psychophysiological tests and side effects.[41]

The conclusion drawn from the pharmacokinetic studies with thymoleptics is that a great number of patients show a correlation between plasma level and therapeutic response. One has to consider that the response to thymoleptics might also be dependent on the differing receptor sensitivity which might require either a higher or a lower plasma level or tissue level of thymoleptic drugs than the average. One has to consider furthermore that some of the depressive patients do not respond to thymoleptic drugs at all.[28]

LITHIUM

Probably the most important development in pharmacopsychiatry of the last decade has been the discovery of prophylaxis with lithium for both unipolar and bipolar depression by Schou and Baastrup. However, the mechanism of action of this treatment is still not yet completely clear. Antimanic efficacy is indicated by clinical and animal experiments, showing that an acute lithium application leads to a decrease of NE at the receptor sites. As it is known, especially from the studies on the switch process,[10] but also from others (see MHPG), that during hypomanic and manic phases probably more NE is available at the receptor sites, the antimanic effficacy of lithium can be explained by its influence to NE metabolism. As, however, depression is said to be connected with a NE deficit, the mechanism of action of lithium must be different, if it is applied chronically for prophylaxis. In animal experiments concerning NE metabolism in brain, lithium being applied chronically, we found interesting results which at the moment can be interpreted hypothetically in the following way. If lithium is applied chronically, NE is utilized more economically in noradrenergic neurones, probably caused by a displacement of electrolytes; that is, the neurones are able to maintain their functions with a lower NE amount.[37, 42] But these hypotheses must be further tested.

It is of interest in connection with the prophylactic effect of lithium that besides lithium, a chronical application of imipramine also has a prophylactic effect—however to unipolar depression only.[51] This effect has been confirmed by a study of the NIMH independently of the one cited above.

Only some of the various aspects of biological research of depression could be mentioned in this chapter. Essential relations between depression and sleep, cortisol, electrolytes, and so on have not been discussed. I think it to be of importance that, besides amine, acetylcholin should not be neglected in research of depression.[23] It will be necessary to get to know better the correlations between the various neurotransmitters, and to include them in clinical experiments. As emphasized above, plenty of questions are yet unanswered; many results are only preliminary ones, and we are just beginning to be able to classify biochemically some of the various forms of depression to find specific kinds and methods of treatment for each subgroup. One can hardly say today whether it will be possible before long to record biochemically the psychodynamic and sociological as well as the genetic compounds of depression. In any case the path to pursue will be hard and long, but it will be interesting and fascinating.

REFERENCES

1. Ackenheil, M., Hoffmann, G., Markianos, E., Nyström, I., and Rase, J.: Einfluß von Clozapin auf die MHPG-, HVS- und 5-HIES-Ausscheidung im Urin und Liquor cerebrospinalis. Arzneimittelforsch. 24:984–987, 1974.

2. Angst, J.: A double-blind study on plasma-levels of maprotilin and clinical response. In Classification and Prediction of Outcome of Depression, Schattauer-Verlag, Stuttgart, 1974.

3. Asberg, M., Cronholm, B., Sjöqvist, F., and Tuck, D.: Correlation of subjective side effects with plasma concentration of nortriptyline. Brit. Med. J. 3, 331, 1971.

4. Bernheimer, H., Birkmayer, W., and Hornykiewicz, O.: Zur Biochemie des Parkinson-Syndroms des Menschen. Klinische Wochenschrift 10:465–469, 1963.

5. Bourne, H. R., Bunney, W. E., Jr., Colburn, R. W., Davis, J. M., Davis, J. N., Shaw, D. M., and Coppen, A. J.: Noradrenaline, 5-hydroxytryptamine, and 5-hydroxyindoleacetic acid in hindbrains of suicidal patients. Lancet 2:805, 1968.

6. Braithwaite, R. A., Goulding, R., Theano, G., Bailey, J., and Coppen, A.: Clinical significance of plasma levels of tricyclic antidepressant drugs in the treatment of depression. Lancet 1:556–557, 1973.

7. Breese, G. R., Prange, A. J., Jr., Howard, J. L., Lipton, M. A., McKinney, W. T., Bowman, R. E., and Bushnell, P.: 3-Methoxy-4-hydroxy-phenylglycol excretion and behavioral changes in rat and monkey after central sympathectomy with 6-hydroxydopamine. Nature New Bio. 240:286–287, 1972.

8. Bunney, W. E., Jr., Brodie, H. K. H., Murphy, D. L., and Goodwin, F. K.: Studies of alpha-methyl-para-tyrosine, L-dopa, and L-trytophan in depression and mania. Am. J. Psychiatr. 127:872, 1971.

9. Bunney, W. E., Jr., and Davis, J. M.: Norepinephrine in depressive reactions. Arch. Gen. Psychiatr. 13:483, 1965.

10. Bunney, W. E., Jr., Murphy, D. L., Goodwin, F. K., and Borge, G. F.: The "switch process" in manic-depressive illness. Arch. Gen. Psychiatr. 27:295, 1972.

11. Carroll, B. J., Mowbray, R. M., and Davies, B.: Sequential comparison of L-tryptophan with E.C.T. in severe depression. Lancet 1:967, 1970.

12. Chase, T. N., Breese, G. R., Gordon, E. K., and Kopin, I. J.: Catecholamine metabolism in the dog: Comparison of intravenously and intraventricularly administered (^{14}C) dopamine and (^{3}H) norepinephrine. J. Neurochem. 18:135–140, 1971.

13. Coppen, A.: Biochemistry of therapy-resistant depressions. Pharmakopsychiat. **7**:85–87, 1974.

14. Coppen, A.: Personal communication.

15. Coppen, A., Prange, A. J., Whybrow, P. C., and Noguera, R.: Abnormalities of indolamines in affective disorders. *Arch. Gen. Psychiatr.* **26**:474, 1972.

16. Coppen A. and Shaw, D. M.: Biochemical aspects of affective disorders. *Pharmacopsychiatr. Neuro-Pharmacol.* **3**:36, 1970.

17. Coppen, A., Shaw, D. M., Herzberg, B., and Maggs, R.: Tryptophan in the treatment of depression. *Lancet* **2**:1178, 1967.

18. Davies, B.: Plasma level of nortriptyline and clinical response. In *Classification and Prediction of Outcome and Depression*, Schattauer-Verlag, Stuttgart, 1974.

19. Everett, G. M. and Toman, J. E. P.: Mode of action of rauwolfia alkaloids and motor activity. In *Biological Psychiatry*, Vol. 1, Grune & Stratton, New York/London, 1959, p. 75.

20. Goode, D. J., Dekirmenjian, H., Meltzer, H. Y., and Maas, J.: Relation of excercise to MHPG excretion in normal subjects. *Arch. Gen. Psychiatr.* **29**:391–396, 1973.

21. Goodwin, F. K., Brodie, H. K. H., Murphy, D. L., and Bunney, W. E., Jr.: Administration of a peripheral decarboxylase inhibitor with L-dopa to depressed patients. *Lancet* **1**:908, 1970.

22. Greenspan, K., Schildkraut, J. J., Gordon, E. K., Levy, B., and Durell, J.: Catecholamine metabolism in affective disorders. *Arch. Gen. Psychiatr.* **21**:710–716, 1969.

23. Janowsky, D. S., Yousef, M. K., and Davis, J. M.: A cholinergic-adrenergic hypothesis of mania and depression. *Lancet* **2**:632, 1972.

24. Klerman, G. L., Schildkraut, J. J., Hasenbush, L. L., Greenblatt, M., and Freind, D. G.: Clinical experience with dihydroxyphenylalanine (DOPA) in depression. *J. Psychiatr. Res.* **1**:289, 1963.

25. Kendell, R. E.: Differences in diagnosis concepts of affective disorders amongst european psychiatrists. In *Classification and Prediction of Outcome of Depression*, Schauttauer-Verlag, Stuttgart, 1974.

26. Kragh-Sørensen, P.: personal communication.

27. Kragh-Sørensen, P.: The relationship between plasma concentration and clinical effect of nortriptyline. In *Classification and Prediction of Outcome of Depression*, Schattauer-Verlag, Stuttgart, 1974.

28. Lehmann, H. E.: Therapy-resistant depressions—clinical classification. Pharmakopsychiat. **7**:156–163, 1974.

29. Lipton, M. A.: Effect of TRH in depressive patients and normal volunteers. *Symposium on 5-hydroxytryptamine and other Indolealkylamines in Brain*, Sardinia, 1973.

30. Lloyd, K. G., Hornykiewicz, O., and Farley, I.: Serotonin in raphe nuclei and suicide. *Symposium on 5-Hydroxy-tryptamine and Other Indolealkylamines in Brain*, Sardinia, 1973.

31. Loosen, P., Ackenheil, M., Athen, D., Beckmann, H., Benkert, O., Dittmer, Th., Hippius, H., Matussek, N., Rüther, E., and Scheller, M.: Schlafentzugsbehandlung endogener Depression. 2. Mitteilung: Vergleich psychopathologischer und biochemischer Parameter; submitted for publication.

32. Maas, J. W., Dekirmenjian, H., Garver, H., Redmond, D. E., Jr., and Landis, H. D.: Catecholamine metabolite excretion following intraventricular injection of 60H-dopamine. *Brain Res.* **41**:507–511, 1972.

33. Maas, J. W., Dekirmenjian, H., and Jones, F.: The indentification of depressed patients who have a disorder of norepinephrine metabolism and/or disposition. In *Frontiers in Catecholamine Research—Third International Catecholamine Symposium*, Pergamon, New York, 1973.

34. Maas, J. W., Fawcett, J., and Dekirmenjian, H.: 3-Methoxy-4-hydroxy-phenylglycol (MHPG) excretion in depressive states. *Arch. Gen. Psychiatr.* **19**:129, 1968.

35. Malitz, S. and Kanzler, M.: L-dopa in depression. In *L-Dopa and Behavior*, Raven Press, New York, 1972.

36. Matussek, N.: Neurobiologie und Depression. *Med. Mschr.* **20**:109, 1966.

37. Matussek, N.: Clinical and animal experiments concerning the function of brain catecholamines. *Int. Pharmacopsychiat.* **6**:170–186, 1971.

38. Matussek, N., Ackenheil, M., Athen, D., Benkert, O., Dittmer, Th., Hippius, H., Loosen, P., Rüther, E., and Scheller, M.: Catecholamine metabolism under sleep deprivation therapy of improved and not improved depressed patients. Pharmakopsychiat. **7**:108–114, 1974.

39. Matussek, N., Angst, J., Benkert, O., Gmür, M., Papousek, M., Rüther, E., and Woggon, B.: The effect of L-5-hydroxy-tryptophan alone and in combination with a decarboxylase inhibitor (Ro 4-4602) in depressive patients. In *Frontiers in Catecholamine Research—Third International Catecholamine Symposium*, Pergamon, New York, 1973.

40. Matussek, N., Benkert, O., Schneider, K., Otten, H., and Pohlmeier, H.: Wirkung eines Decarboxylasehemmers (Ro 4-4602) in Kombination mit -dopa auf gehemmte Depressionen. *Arzneimittelforsch.* **20**:934, 1970.

41. Matussek, N. and Aarons, M.: Wirkung akuter und chronischer Applikation von Maprotilin und ihre Beziehung zum Plasmaspiegel bei gesunden Versuchspersonen; submitted for publication.

42. Müller, S. and Matussek, N.: Studies on the biochemical mode of action; submitted for publication.

43. Murphy, D. L. and Weiss, R.: Reduced monoamine oxidase activity in blood platelets from bipolar depressed patients. *Am. J. Psychiatr.* **128**:1351–1357, 1972.

44. Murphy, D. L. and Wyatt, R. J.: Reduced monoamine oxidase activity in blood platelets from schizophrenic patients. *Nature* **238**:225–226, 1972.

45. Nies, A., Robinson, D. S., Lamborn, K. R., and Lampert, R. P.: Genetic control of platelet and plasma monoamine oxidase activity. *Arch. Gen. Psychiatr.* **28**:834–838, 1973.

46. Pare, C. M. B., Yeung, D. P. H., Price, K., and Stacey, R. S.: 5-Hydroxytryptamine, noradrenaline, and dopamine in brainstem, hypothalamus, and caudate nucleus of controls and of patients committing suicide by coal-gas poisoning. *Lancet* **2**:133, 1969.

47. Pflug, B. and Tölle, R.: Therapie endogener Depressionen durch Schlafentzug; praktische und theoretische Konsequenzen. *Der Nervenarzt* **42**:117, 1971.

48. Post, R. M., Kotin, J., Goodwin, F. K., and Gordon, E. K.: Psychomotor activity and cerebrospinal fluid metabolites in affective illness. *Am. J. Psychiatr.* **1**:67–72, 1973.

49. van Praag, H. M.: Biochemical and pharmacological aspects of therapy-resistant depressions, Pharmakopsychiat. **7**:88–97, 1974.

50. van Praag, H. M., Korf, J., and Schut, D.: Cerebral monoamines and depression. *Arch. Gen. Psychiatr.* **28**:827–831, 1973.

51. Prien, R. F.: Prophylactic treatment of recurrent affective disorders: Observations from a multi-hospital collaborative study. In *Classification and Prediction of Outcome of Depression*, Schattauer-Verlag, Stuttgart, 1974.

52. Robinson, D. S., Davis, J. M., Nies, A., Ravaris, C. L., and Sylvester, D.: Relation of sex and aging to monoamine oxidase activity of human brain, plasma, and platelets. *Arch. Gen. Psychiatr.* **24**:536–539, 1971.

53. Robinson, D. S., Davis, J. M., Nies, A., Colburn, R. W., Davis, J. N., Bourne, H. R., Bunney, W. E., Shaw, D. M. and Coppen, A.: Ageing, monoamines, and monoamine oxidase levels. *Lancet* **1**:290–291, 1972.

54. Sachar, E. J.: Endocrine factors in psychopathological states. In *Biological Psychiatry*, Wiley, New York, 1973.

55. Sachar, E. J., Frantz, E. G., Altman, N., and Sassin, J.: Growth Hormone and Prolactin in Unipolar and Bipolar Depressed Patients: Responses to Hypoglycemia and L-Dopa. *Am. J. Psychiatr.* **130**:1362–1366, 1973.

56. Sano, I.: L-5-Hydroxytryptophan (L-5-HTP)-therapie bei endogener Depression. *Münch. Med. Wschr.* **114**:1713, 1972.

57. Sartorius, personal communication.

58. Schanberg, S. M., Schildkraut, J. J., Breese, G. R., and Kopin, I. J.: Metabolism of normetanephrine-H^3 in rat brain-identification of conjugated 3-methyoxy-4-hydroxyphenylglycol as major metabolite. *Biochem. Pharmacol.* **17**:247–254, 1968.

59. Schildkraut, J. J.: The catecholamine hypothesis of affective disorders: A review of supporting evidence. *Am. J. Psychiatr.* **122**:509, 1965.

60. Schildkraut, J. J.: Biochemical criteria for classifying depressive disorders and predicting responses to pharmacotherapy. Pharmakopsychiat. **7**:98–107, 1974.

61. Schildkraut, J. J.: Catecholamine metabolism and affective disorders: Studies of MHPG excretion. In *Frontiers in Catecholamine Research—Third International Catecholamine* Symposium, Pergamon, New York, 1973.

62. Schildkraut, J. J., Green, R., Gordon, E. K., and Durell, J.: Normetanephrine excretion and affective state in depressed patients treated with imipramine. *Am. J. Psychiatr.* **123**:690–700, 1966.

63. Shaw, D. M., Camps, F. E., and Eccleston, E. G.: 5-Hydroxytryptamine in the hindbrain of depressive suicides. *Brit. J. Psychiatr.* **113**:1407, 1967.

64. Shopsin, B., Wilk, S., Gershon, S., Davis, K., and Suhl, M.: Cerebrospinal fluid MHPG: An assessment of norepinephrine metabolism in affective disorders. *Arch. Gen. Psychiatr.* **28**:230–233, 1973.

65. Takahashi, Y., Kipnis, D. M., and Daughday, W. H.: Growth hormone secretion during sleep. *J. Clin. Invest.* **47**:2079, 1968.

66. Turner, W. J. and Merlis, S.: A clinical trial of pargyline and DOPA in psychotic subjects. *Dis. Nerv. Syst.* **25**:538, 1964.

67. Wyatt, R. J., Murphy, D. L., Belmaker, R., Cohen, S. Domelly, C. H., and Pollin, W.: Reduced monoamine oxidase activity in platelets: A possible genetic marker for vulnerability to schizophrenia. *Science* **179**:916, 1973.

CHAPTER FIVE

WHAT'S NEW IN PSYCHOSURGERY

DESMOND KELLY, M.D.

T hree new trends in psychosurgery have taken place over the past few years. Two are scientific, and one is a change of attitude. Psychosurgery has advanced both because of a better understanding of the underlying physiology of the brain and because of the introduction of new techniques, particularly that of stereotaxis, which enables small lesions to be made with a high degree of accuracy.

During the past 4 years there has been increased interest in psychosurgery, with several symposia and reviews of the subject.[32, 34, 52, 82, 83,90] At the same time, there has been a considerable amount of opposition to psychosurgery in the United States.[9]

At the outset a very clear distinction should be made between psychosurgery to relieve intolerable emotional suffering as seen in patients with severe intractable depression, anxiety states, obsessional neurosis and schizophrenia, and operations designed to alleviate violent behaviour usually associated with epilepsy. Much of the emotion generated by the subject of psychosurgery was stimulated by fears that pathologically aggressive prisoners would be operated on, more for the benefit of society than for the individual, and that psychosurgery would become a common type of treatment for violence: "the implications of the use of permanent behaviour modification via psychosurgery for political and social reasons is ominous indeed."[98]

Surgery for violent destructive behaviour is in its infancy; it is less firmly established than other forms of surgery for mental illness; the results are less predictable, and it is likely to remain controversial. It should be recalled that affective disorders in general carry a 15% risk of death from suicide. In a recent study, 25% of patients referred for leucotomy had made a determined attempt on their lives before the operation.[44]

Although psychosurgery is a highly emotive subject, it is better to evaluate the facts carefully, scientifically, and objectively rather than to condemn it out of hand. Psychosurgery will, in any case, only be applicable to a tiny minority of patients whose suffering is extreme, and it will only be employed until better forms of treatment become available to relieve the enormous burden which these patients and their families have to bear.

The interest shown in psychosurgery can be charted historically by the numbers of publications on the subject. Between 1936 and 1941, the library of the Royal Society of Medicine listed less than 12 publications a year on psychosurgery;[88] during the next decade this number increased to approximately 300 a year in 1951 and then decreased to the former level during the 1960s.

The First International Congress on psychosurgery was held in Lisbon in 1949, but it was 21 years before the Second International Congress[34] took place in Copenhagen in 1970. At the conclusion of that Conference, it seemed appropriate that another meeting should be held to bring into clinical focus some of the recent advances in the basic sciences which contribute insight into brain mechanisms. This was the stimulus for the Third World Congress which took place only 2 years later in Cambridge, England. In the introduction to the monograph which records the proceedings of the Cambridge Conference,[52] the editors conclude the following:

> Psychosurgery is not, and must not become, a method for manipulation of the mind. Its only aim is to relieve individual, intractable suffering. It should be applied only when conventional psychiatric methods have not given sufficient help . . . .If psychosurgery is used wisely, it aims at, and can succeed in, relieving the patient from pathological suffering of the mind and restoring his ability to enjoy and suffer as normal human beings do [Laitinen and Livingston, Helsinki and Toronto, January 8, 1973].

During the last decade a great deal of research has been carried out in the field of neurophysiology and a major impetus to the development of more refined surgical techniques has been a better understanding of the limbic system.

LIMBIC SYSTEM

The rationale behind the various operations for different psychiatric syndromes can be better understood when they are seen in the context of the limbic system and its different connections and functions. Broca described "the great limbic lobe" which surrounds the brain stem and comprises most of the primitive cortex in mammals. The limbic system is thus the phylogenetically old rim of cortical tissue which encircles the inner part of the hemispheres of the brain. This primitive old mammalian brain is monitored and modulated by the new mammalian brain (neopallium), a higher order control, which exerts a major influence through the frontal lobes. Most psychosurgical procedures have been concerned with operations on frontolimbic connections, specific limbic pathways, or subcortical cell stations (Figure 1).

Limbic Circuits

In 1937 Papez wrote his important paper entitled "A Proposed Mechanism of Emotion."[79] In it he postulated that the anatomical basis of emotions was based in the hypothalamus, anterior thalamic nuclei, cingulate gyrus, hippocampus, and their interconnections. He considered that this system

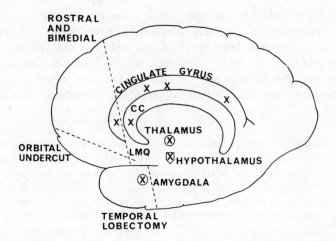

Figure 1.   Target sites for operations on frontolimbic pathways; limbic circuits and subcortical cell stations (indicated by crosses). Emotional responses or autonomic changes have been obtained from all these sites (X) except posterior cingulate and dorsomedial thalamus. Fronto-limbic pathways are divided by rostral and bimedial leucotomy with the approximate planes of section shown. In stereotactic tractotomy the posterior 2 cm of the orbital undercutting incision is the target site. This overlaps the lower medial quadrant target site (LMQ) of limbic, rostral, and bimedial leucotomy.

constituted "a harmonious mechanism which may elaborate the functions of central emotion, as well as participate in emotional expression."

The Papez Circuit.   This circuit passes from the septum, via the cingulum bundle in the cingulate gyrus, to hippocampus; and via fornix to mamillary body; via mamillothalamic tract to anterior thalamus, and finally via anterior thalamic radiation to cingulum bundle (Figure 2).

In 1948 Yakovlev expanded the Papez concept to include other structures in the limbic system, that is, orbitofrontal cortex, insular and anterior temporal areas, together with their connections with the amygdala and the dorsomedial nucleus of thalamus.[101]

The Basolateral Limbic Circuit.   This circuit goes from orbitofrontal and insular cortex to the anterior temporal region via the uncinate faciculus, to amygdala, to dorsomedial nucleus of thalamus, and back to orbitofrontal cortex via thalamofrontal radiation (Figure 3).[57, 58] These authors consider that the anatomical relationship of this circuit to the brain stem, thalamus, and neocortex are distinct from the Papez circuit. It is thought that the processes occuring in the amygdala might be reflected in the orbital cortex

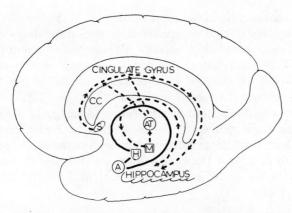

Figure 2. The papez circuit (broken line) passes via the cingulum bundle, in the cingulate gyrus, from septum (S) to hippocampus, and via fornix to mammillary body (M), via mammillothalamic tract to anterior thalamus (AT), via anterior thalamic radiations to cingulum bundle. The defence reaction circuit (solid line) passes from hypothalamus (H) via stria terminalis to amygdala, and via amygdalo-fugal pathway to hypothalamus. (From Kelly, D., Richardson, A., and Mitchell-Heggs, N. *Brit. J. Psychiatr.* 123:133–140, 1973).

of the frontal lobes.[36] The unicinate fasciculus forms a two-way connection between the frontal and temporal cortices and it contains fibers originating in the amygdala.

The Defence Reaction Circuit. The circuit passes from hypothalamus via stria terminalis to amygdala and via the amygdalofugal pathway back to hypothalamus (Figure 2). This circuit is so named because with gradual

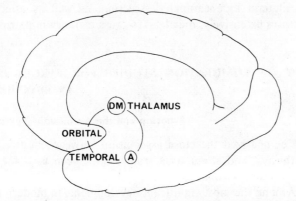

Figure 3. The basolateral circuit passes from orbitofrontal cortex and insular cortex to the anterior temporal region via the uncinate faciculus, to amygdala (*A*), to dorsomedial nucleus of thalamus, and to orbitofrontal cortex via thalamofrontal radiation.

increase in the intensity of electrical stimulation of the hypothalamus in the conscious cat, the animal progresses from rest to looking alert, then becomes agitated, and finally attacks in response to auditory or visual stimuli.[1] This behavioural pattern is accompanied by changes in respiration, and an increase in heart rate and muscle blood flow, presumably to prepare the animal for either "fight" or "flight." The defence reaction can also be obtained by stimulation of amygdala, stria terminalis, and amygdalofugal pathway.[29] Professor Hess in Zurich carried out the classic work on the defence reaction in animals in the early 1940s, and it is interesting to recall that Hess and Moniz, who first introduced leucotomy, shared the Nobel Prize in physiology and medicine in 1950 for their pioneering studies.

Memory and the Limbic System

The Papez circuit should be thought of as consisting of two functional parts, one concerned with emotion and temperament and one with memory, since the effects of ablation operations on the two parts are quite different.[97] It has been postulated that the anterior parts of the limbic system are concerned with emotion and social behaviour, and it is these parts from which autonomic responses have mainly been elicited[25]. Lesions have been made in the anterior cingulate region in patients suffering from anxiety, depression, and obsessional neurosis without detectable effects on memory or the loss of finer emotional feelings, blunting of affect or diminution of creativity.[42] Other structures in the Papez circuit such as hippocampus, fornix, mamillary bodies, and mamillothalamic tract are apparently concerned with recent and long-term memory.[97] Necrotizing encephalitis leading to bilateral hippocampal destruction, as well as affecting other limbic structures extensively, may lead to gross memory impairment.[24]

THE VALUE OF STIMULATION STUDIES FOR TARGET LOCATION IN PSYCHOSURGERY

Emotion and the Autonomic Nervous System

Livingston[56] emphasized the close association between emotional and autonomic pathways, and stimulation studies have been used for target location prior to lesion formation in limbic circuits or frontolimbic pathways (Figure 1). Among the most significant developments in modern neurology, has been the gradual recognition of the existence of vast areas in the forebrain subserving autonomic function and forming the structural background, not only of emotional expression, but also of affective behaviour in the broadest sense.[25]

It is common knowledge that the cardiovascular system can be profoundly affected by emotion. Respiration too can be modified by voluntary control, and in this way ideas and feelings can affect speech. Changes in respiration may accompany different emotions associated with laughing, weeping, and sighing.[17] The connection between parts of the limbic system and emotional behaviour is an indication of some cortical control of the autonomic system, which used to be considered as being activated solely by the hypothalamus. Now many investigators look upon the limbic system as the *primary autonomic centre* of the forebrain, and it is also known that stimulation or ablation of *nonlimbic* cortex does *not* produce changes in respiratory or circulatory responses.[25]

The Papez Circuit. Changes in respiration have been found on stimulation of parts of the Papez circuit from which emotional expression has also been elicited,[17, 41, 69] for example, anterior cingulate gyrus (Figure 1). Meyer et al. stimulated target sites in the anterior cingulate gyrus prior to lesion making and obtained responses in 65 of the 75 patients operated upon.[69] In each instance when no effect was observed the entire stimulating apparatus was rechecked to ensure optimal function. Changes were listed under (*a*) altered speech (55%), (*b*) temporal lobe symptoms or altered state of consciousness (60%), (*c*) affective responses (31%) (intense fear 17%, pleasure 12%, agitation 9%), (*d*) specific sensory motor responses (34%), and (*e*) other responses (23%). In only 13% were no responses obtained.

Stimulation of the cingulum under local anaesthesia, prior to lesion-making, resulted in a dramatic increase in the original symptoms of three patients studied by D. E. Richardson: "one patient became markedly depressed, another developed increase in headaches, which was one of her psychosomatic complaints, and the other developed compulsive thinking."[85]

Stimulation of the cingulum bundle has also been carried out in two patients with psychomotor epilepsy, prior to cingulotomy, as a means of studying the emotional circuit and its effects upon normal functions and altered behaviour.[18] Stimulation was associated with autonomic changes, an increase in blood pressure, marked respiratory slowing, and even periods of respiratory arrest of 30 to 40 seconds duration, but no perceptible changes in heart rate took place. The patients sometimes swallowed, yawned, or complained of feelings of hunger. Auditory and taste hallucinations occurred, agitation was sometimes seen, and motor responses were also elicited. The results lead the investigators to believe that this area of the cingulum, as part of the limbic system, is one of the higher centres controlling emotional and autonomic responses and, particularly, the exteriorization of acts and performances: "thus it is able to regulate behaviour through its influence over the temporal lobe, hypothalamus, thalamus, frontal lobe and other structures of the limbic system."[18]

As discussed later, the anterior cingulate gyrus is now a major target area for psychosurgery. Even under general anaesthesia electrical stimulation of the anterior cingulate gyrus can elicit autonomic responses (Figure 4), that is, below and just anterior to the genu of the corpus callosum and up to 3 cm posterior to the anterior tip of the lateral ventricle[41] at points marked by crosses (Figure 1). This has been used for target location of limbic pathways before lesion making in limbic leucotomy.[44] To enhance the accuracy of placement within limbic circuits, if autonomic responses are not found, the target is moved a few millimeters.[84]

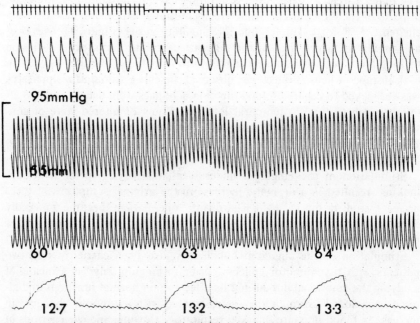

Figure 4. Polygraph recording during stimulation of the anterior cingulate gyrus with 10 V under general anaesthesia showing the following autonomic changes:

    Channel 1.   *Time* (seconds), line depressed during stimulation.
    Channel 2.   *Respiration* with decrease in amplitude.
    Channel 3.   *Blood pressure* with increase in systolic and diastolic pressures.
    Channel 4.   *Heart rate* increase with very slight increase in *finger pulse* amplitude after stimulation.
    Channel 5.   Forearm blood flow (ml/100 ml/min) is increased.

Finger pulse amplitude reflects changes in skin blood flow while forearm blood flow reflects predominantly changes in muscle. (From Kelly, D. Postgrad. Med. J. 49:825, 1973.)

Basolateral Circuit. Autonomic reactions have been produced by electrical stimulation of the posterior orbital gyrus, temporal lobe, anterior insular, and anterior hippocampus, and it is considered that these structures are reciprocally connected.[25] Stimulation of the orbital part of the frontal lobe prior to leucotomy resulted in changes in respiration and blood pressure and was sometimes accompanied by intense emotion.[60] Autonomic responses can be obtained from Area 13, and Livingston et al.[59] obtained respiratory and vascular responses from a continuous zone of cortex extending from the anterior cingulate gyrus to the posterior orbital surface in the monkey.

The amygdala is common to the basolateral and defence reaction circuits and is discussed under the latter.

The Defence Reaction Circuit

ANIMAL STUDIES. Stimulation of the hypothalmic "defence area" always produces an immediate and full defence reaction, and, provided the electrode is positioned correctly, all the behavioral and autonomic components appear rapidly. This is never so when stimulating the amygdala when the full expression of the response usually takes 20 to 40 seconds.[102] In freely moving animals, radio-stimulation through implanted electrodes shows that the lateral hypothalamus is a very important limbic structure for excitation and integration of autonomic somatomotor and endocrine effects seen in aggressive behaviour.[36]

Stimulation of the amygdala in the tame cat will produce "flight" or "defence" behavior depending upon the location of the electrode tip. "Flight" or "fear" is elicited from the rostral and lateral area, while "defence" is elicited from a zone localized further caudally and medially.[99] The frequency of hissing, growling, or striking in the cat does not rely only on stimulation of the amygdala, *but also on the previous experience of that cat.*

PATIENT STUDIES

Hypothalamatomy. Electrical stimulation of the rostral hypothalamus in conscious patients has caused anxiety with tachycardia and peripheral autonomic effects.[27]

Sano et al.[89] have stimulated the posteromedial hypothalamus and made lesions at sites where *the most marked signs of sympathetic discharge* were obtained (rise in blood pressure, tachycardia, pupillary dilatation). If the patient was in the waking state, he reported that he was obsessed by "extreme horror." This point Sano called the ergotropic triangle, and bilateral lesions produced "marked calming effects" in 95% of his patients suffering from violent, aggressive, or restless behavior (vide infra).

Electrical stimulation of the ergotropic triangle was also associated with a rise in plasma nonesterified fatty acids and growth hormone.

Amygdalotomy. Hitchcock and Cairns[35] use emotional responses for target location in conscious patients undergoing amygdalotomy. Stimulation of the *amygdala* has elicited a range of aggressive responses from "I feel I could get up and bite you" to uncontrolled swearing and physically destructive behavior.[35] No pleasurable emotional feelings were identified by these workers in any of their patients during stimulation or coagulation of the amygdala. Following amygdalotomy hormonal changes were reported.

Some of the most valuable stimulation studies of the amygdala have been in patients with psychomotor epilepsy and phobias. Anxiety, aggression, and excitement were observed from medical amygdaloid stimulation in 50% of cases studied by Kim and Umbach.[47] Visceromotor responses were obtained in 66%, reduced vigilance and vertigo in 30%, and seizure provocation in 30%. In *aggressive* patients *aggressiveness was increased* during stimulation, while in *nonviolent* patients *no aggressive reaction* was observed. The authors consider the following:

> . . . the amygdaloid complex seems not to be specific for anxiety alone or aggression alone, and shows no specificity of the subnuclei for these emotional states. The amygdala is rather considered to be involved in all these emotional states, probably by means of its modulating function.

The amygdaloid complex in man shows evidence of at least three functionally different areas, medial, basolateral, and probably central.[46] Seizure improvement occurs after both basolateral and medial amygdalotomy. Visceromotor effects are not so pronounced as those produced by stimulation of the hypothalamus.[47]

The plasma cortisol was found by Kim and Umbach[47] to be increased markedly after stimulation, but fell slightly postoperatively.

LIMBIC CORE

The three limbic circuits, *the Papez, basolateral*, and *defence reaction* circuits, are closely related to what may be described as the "limbic core." This is a highly differentiated subcortical apparatus known to be centrally involved in the regulation of endocrine and visceral-effector mechanisms, and Nauta speculates that its functional patterns express themselves in mood and behavioral motivations.[75] The "limbic core" is what he calls the septohypothalamomesencephalic continuum, which receives downward discharge from limbic structures, especially hippocampus and amygdala, medial forebrain bundle and stria terminalis, and projects to these structures by two main pathways (Figure 5).

The septohypothalamomesencephalic continuum is interconnected by distinct intrinsic circuitary,[73] into which lead afferent systems from the amygdala and hippocampus as well as from the spinal cord and brain stem, and from which emerge channels to the hypophysial complex and visceral motor systems.

FRONTOLIMBIC CONNECTIONS

Brodman estimated that the prefrontal area of the cat's brain constitutes only 3.4% of the whole, compared with 16.9% in the chimpanzee, and 29% in man. The prefrontal area (neopallium) in contrast to the

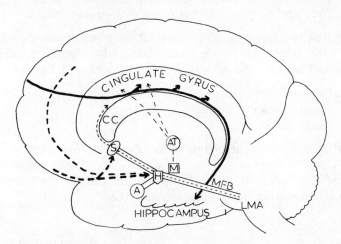

Figure 5. "Limbic core" and connections. The medial forebrain bundle (MFB) runs from the limbic midbrain area (LMA) to mammillary body (M) and hypothalamus (H) where one branch turns laterally to amygdala (A) and the other medially to septum (S). This system constitutes the septohypothalamic-mesencephalic continuum (SHMC) of Nauta and may be considered as the central "limbic core." It projects to the following:

(a) Anterior thalamic nucleus (AT) and cingulate gyrus, via mammillothalamic tract.

(b) Cingulate gyrus via medial forebrain bundle which contains serotonin fibres (interrupted line) which pass round the corpus callosum (CC).

The frontal lobe projections to the 'limbic core'

(1) From orbitofrontal cortex to   (i)   septum.
                                      (ii) lateral hypothalamus.

(2) From dorsal frontal convexity to lateral and dorsal hypothalamus.

(3) From dorsal frontal convexity via cingulate gyrus to hippocampus.

(From Kelly, D. Postgrad. Med. J. 49:825, 1973.)

phylogenetically old cortex (limbic lobe) has undergone extensive development in the evolution of man.[65] The prefrontal cortex lies at the top of the limbic system structures which are directly concerned with the organization of emotional and visceral behavior.[25]

There are four main projections from the frontal lobe to the "limbic core," two from the dorsal convexity and two from the orbitofrontal cortex (Figure 5).[74] (1) From the *dorsal convexity* the 'northern' pathway goes to anterior cingulate gyrus and into the Papez circuit. (2) The "southern" pathway goes to hypothalamus. From the *orbital* surface of the frontal lobe fibres go to (3) septum and (4) lateral hypothalamus.

From this it can be seen that there is a concentration of frontolimbic connections in three main areas (Figure 1 and 5):

1. The lower medial quadrant of the frontal lobe.
2. The fiber tracts overlying the posterior orbital cortex.
3. The cingulate gyrus which contains the cingulum bundle.

The first two target zones converge at their posterior end and overlap one another (Figure 1). For the relief of intractable depression, anxiety, and obsessional neurosis, the main areas operated on are as follows:

1. The lower medial quadrant of the frontal lobe.
2. The orbitofrontal region.
3. The cingulate region.

For severely abnormal aggressive behavior operations have been carried out on various parts of the defence reaction circuit. The limbic system is extremely complicated and only well-defined circuits and connections, which have a bearing on psychosurgery have been considered.

CLINICAL STUDIES

It is not possible to classify the various psychosurgical procedures satisfactorily, but they are discussed under the following sections:

Operations on Frontolimbic Connections

Standard Lobotomy. This operation has been almost completely superseded by modified operations and fell into disuse in Great Britain during the mid-1950s because of the unwanted effects on the personality. It had been introduced when much less was known about frontolimbic connections, and the adverse effects were due to unnecessary encroachment on the neopallium. The standard operation was made through lateral burr holes in the temporal region, and a blunt instrument was swept in the coronal plane dividing as much white matter as possible. Frontal lobe damage could result in intellectual impairment, lack of self-control, euphoria, increased irritability, and aggressive outbursts.

The results in some cases of schizophrenia were impressive in the pre-phenothiazine era, as in that chronic and incapacitating disease some unwanted effects were then acceptable. Tooth and Newton[95] reported on 10, 000 patients operated on by mainly the standard technique (84%), between 1942 and 1954. Sixtyfour percent were suffering from schizophrenia, and, of the total, 47% were able to be discharged from hospital, with considerable improvement in 36% of men and 44% of women. Freeman[22] reviewed the effects of lobotomy in schizophrenia and concluded that it was more successful in early cases and that in chronic schizophrenia it has limited value.

Few if any, psychiatrists would now advocate early operation for schizophrenia as Freeman suggested, since the phenothiazines, especially the intramuscular depot preparations, have altered the course of the disease to a considerable extent. It should be recalled too, that two retrospective studies on patients, many of whom had schizophrenia, failed to show that the improvement following standard lobotomy is superior to that of a control group.[62, 86] In contrast, in another study, 55% of chronic schizophrenics improved following lobotomy compared with only 3% of controls.*

Modified Leucotomy. *Lower medial quadrant leucotomy* was introduced to minimize the unwanted effects, while retaining the therapeutic benefit of the original standard operation. It had been demonstrated in 1949 that the severity of personality change varied directly with the number of segments of the frontal lobe involved.[64] The target is the lower medial quadrant of the frontal lobes, through either a lateral approach,[37-39, 80] or a superior approach, as in rostral leucotomy.[63] These operations have been firmly established and employed in many parts of the world—in England rostral leucotomy[63] and lower medial quadrant;[39, 97] in America,[8, 37] Australia,[80] West Germany,[77] and Denmark[11] lower medial quadrant leucotomy. The operation divides frontolimbic connections and also afferent and efferent fibres between the orbital cortex and the thalamus.[37]

A RECENT UNCONTROLLED STUDY.[45] The results of these operations were assessed recently (modified prefrontal, Jackson,[39] N = 48; rostral,[63] N = 23) and, if differences in diagnostic groups were taken into account, there was little difference between the two operations, the initial improvement in both being approximately 70%. Patients suffering from depression and anxiety had an initial (6-week) improvement of 80%, while in obsessional neurosis 20%, and schizophrenia 50% improved initially.

* *Am. J. Psychiat.* **108**:10, 1951.

After an 18-month follow-up the patients with anxiety states were found to have shown some deterioration and now only 55% were rated as improved. The depressives tended to maintain their early improvement, while of the patients with obsessional neurosis, 50% were improved at follow-up. Physiological measurements and psychometric determinations were made before and after operation, at 6 weeks and 18 months. There was a significant decrease on the Taylor Scale of Manifest Anxiety, and Neuroticism (Maudsley Personality Inventory) also decreased, but although there was a decrease on the Beck Depression Scale 6 weeks postoperatively, surprisingly this was not significant. There was also a decrease in physiological arousal postoperatively, as measured by heart rate, forearm (muscle) blood flow, and blood pressure, under both rest and stress conditions.

One of the main problems with this type of operation, however, is that the target site forms the base of a triangle with its apex at the burr hole. This means that some unnecessary damage is done between burr hole and target site, while another problem is that the lesion may be misplaced. Evans[19] reports two such cases where the patients failed to respond, and in both the thalamofrontal radiation in the lower medial quadrant had not been severed and both patients subsequently died from suicide. Evans considered that the blind approach was not an ideal surgical method.

Adverse personality change had been shown by Meyer and Beck[68] to be particularly associated with lesions which damaged the dorsolateral and lateral white matter and especially the cortex. With lower medial quadrant lesions correctly placed the risk of adverse personality change is not great.

Parker et al.[80] suggest that in Australia leucotomy has been avoided because of the reputation in previous years of older operations: "It seems likely that many patients are allowed to suffer for unduly long periods—sometimes for the remainder of their lives—because of ignorance or prejudice."

Bimedial leucotomy is the third firmly established modified leucotomy and has been carried out at The Maudsley Hospital for the past 20 years. The operation is performed through a superior frontal approach and white matter cut for a width of about 2 cm subjacent to grey matter medially and inferiorly. The incision skirts the front of the lateral ventricles and divides the thalamofrontal radiation.[81, 90] It was found that in 40% of patients bimedial leucotomy had been a decisive event after a prolonged period of mental illness, but that it proved harmful in 8% of patients[81]. Undesirable leucotomy effects occurred in permanent form in 59% of cases which was much higher than with lower medial quadrant operations.[45] Depression, especially when it recurred in a pure and psychotic fashion, had the best prognosis with this operation, but young neurotics without depressive admixtures responded disappointingly.

In Canada bimedial leucotomy is generally performed with a McKenzie leucotome.[21] Good results have been reported in anxiety states, with 76% improvement, and in depression, but the results in obsessional neurosis are not as satisfactory.[4]

CONTROLLED STUDIES. The only two retrospective controlled studies of modified leucotomy (bimedial) to be carried out in Great Britain were conducted at The Maudsley Hospital. They showed that patients suffering from severe agoraphobia[67] and obsessional neurosis[94] improved significantly more than controls.

Orbital Undercutting. This procedure divides many frontolimbic connections, affects the basolateral limbic circuit, and at the posterior end, the target site overlaps the lower medial quadrant target area (Figure 1). Knight[48] introduced a restricted orbital undercut extending for 6 cm posteriorly in the subcortical white matter above the orbital cortex (area 13). Later, by stereotaxis, radioactive yttrium seeds were placed in the posterior 2 cm of his orbital undercutting incision,[49, 50] and the posterior aspect of the lesion is in the presubstantia innominata.[16, 76] The results of stereotactic tractotomy are good in depression and anxiety, but less satisfactory in nuclear obsessional neurosis:[10, 93] "there does seem, however, to be a relatively small group of cases characterised by pure obsessional symptoms, without depression, of early age of onset which has a bad prognosis."[51]

In Canada, Hetherington[28] uses a McKenzie leucotomy to produce an orbital undercut while in Japan, Hirose[30, 31] uses an orbitoventromedial undercutting procedure for a variety of psychiatric patients, of whom the majority are schizophrenics, but affective disorders give the best results, and some neurotic disorders also do well. Hirose does not extend his lesions as far posteriorly as Knight, and does not undercut area 13, the lesion extending only 4 cm posterior from frontal tips. His lesion was found to affect both the uncinate fasciculus and dorsomedial nucleus in two post-mortem specimens, and he concludes that both orbitothalamic and orbitotemporal connections are affected.

Operations on the Papez Circuit

Anterior Cingulate. The anterior cingulate region is the chief target area for operations on the Papez circuit. Lewin[55] in England has recently reviewed selective operations and advocates "open" operation, which is also favoured by Gaches, Le Beau and Choppy[23] in France, and Bailey et al.[3] in Australia. Lewin's "open" cingulectomy entails the bilateral removal of 4 cms of cingulate gyrus extending into the white matter for up to 1 cm.[55] Stereotactic techniques are being used increasingly, however,[6, 12-14, 44, 69, 77, 84, 85] because much smaller lesions can be placed with a high degree of accuracy.

The general concensus is that operations in this area are particularly beneficial in obsessional neurosis,[23, 42, 44, 55] but patients with anxiety and depression may also benefit to a considerable extent.[6, 44, 69] Anterior cingulate lesions have also been used for treating severe behaviour disorders[70] and intractable pain.[78] Patients with schizophrenia have also benefited, but the results in alcoholics are less satisfactory.[69] Anterior ventral cingulotomy has been employed by Laitinen and Vilkki[53] for schizophrenic patients with marked anxiety, and these workers found an immediate anxiolytic effect during operations under local anaesthesia. More recently they have placed lesions in the genu of the corpus callosum with even better results.[54]

Unwanted effects from cingulate operations are rare if stereotactic techniques are used, but with "open" operation severe complications have been reported.[3, 11]

Posterior Cingulectomy.   Open operation on the posterior cingulate region has been used by Turner[96, 97] for "chronic resentful aggressiveness," but much less is known about the effects of lesions at this site than those in the anterior cingulate region. The side-effects of posterior cingulectomy have included paraesthesia in one or both limbs.[97]

Operations on the Defence Reaction Circuit

Lesions have been made in various parts of this circuit for the treatment, generally, of seriously aggressive or destructive behaviour, usually associated with epilepsy. The lesions have been placed in (1) hypothalamus, (2) amygdala, and (3) stria terminalis.

Hypothalamotomy.   Stereotactic lesions have been made in the postero-medial hypothalamus by Sano[89] in Japan and hypothalamotomy has been used alone or in combination with other lesions by a number of other workers in India,[5] Czechoslavakia,[71] Germany,[77] and America.[47] The operation has produced "marked calming effects" when lesions are placed in the region from which arise the most marked signs of sympathetic discharge: this Sano designates as the "ergotropic triangle."[89] It is reported that the calming effects in patients with violent, aggressive, and restless behavior occurred in 95% of cases. Kim and Umbach[47] also found that posteromedial hypothalamotomy produces a "sedative effect," but that, as with amygdalotomy, periodic terror and sudden outbursts of great violence cannot be sufficiently influenced at this level. The lesion must be very accurately placed and limited to a small area to avoid hypokinesia or lack of bladder control.

Amygdalotomy. This operation has been performed by a number of workers usually with similar indications to those of hypothalamotomy and Narabayashi[72] in Japan has operated on a large series of cases. Favourable results have been reported, with a decrease in the number of epileptic attacks and in maladaptive behavior.[5, 33, 35, 47, 66, 92]

Bilateral amygdalotomy for pathological aggression would appear to be safer than hypothalamotomy, more effective than standard leucotomy,[91] and does not produce any of the major defects of the Kluver Bucy syndrome that would result from bilateral temporal lobectomy.[66] After coagulation of the amygdaloid complex, elevation of mood, increased appetite and weight gain, and sexual libido have been observed.[47] Seizure improvement of over 80% was found in 70% of cases after uni- or bilateral amygdalotomy and phobias and aggressive behavior were markedly reduced.[47] In cases with marked aggression and severe periods of violent behaviour the results of some studies have not been very satisfactory.[35, 47]

Stria Terminalis. This structure links the hypothalamus and amygdala and is considered by Burzaco[15] to be an optional target in "sedative surgery." He found that small stereotactic lesions in the fundus region can suppress violent aggressive behavior in selected patients. This operation may be chosen after unsuccessful amygdalotomy or hypothalamotomy, or in cases of temporal lobe epilepsy where the focus is bilateral.[15]

Operations on the Basolateral Circuit

Temporal Lobectomy and Lobotomy. Operations on the temporal lobe have been performed for patients with personality disorders associated with epilepsy and aggressive outbursts of "uncontrollable rage usually of a particular kind ushered in by experiences of sudden fear, panic or stark terror." Fear is abolished if ictal, but anxiety is generally not helped.[97] The site of operation is at or just behind the uncus of the hippocampus and in or just behind the amygdaloid nucleus.

Temporal lobectomy, although an effective way of relieving some patients with disabling temporal lobe seizures, has disadvantages such as the removal of sizeable amounts of brain tissue, including a segment of brain not involved in the disease. Temporal lobectomy is applicable only to patients with focal disease, largely confined to nondominant lobe or to anterior 5 to 6 cm of dominant lobe.[66]

Unilateral temporal lobectomy is used by Falconer[20] for drug resistant epilepsy, and if due to mesial temporal sclerosis, 50% of patients became seizure free, compared with 33% if epilepsy was due to hamartomas, scars or infarcts, nonspecific lesions, or cortical dysplasia.

Amygdalotomy. See under operations on defence reaction circuit.

Thalamotomy. This has been carried out on 30 patients with "hyperresponsive syndrome," and good results have been claimed by Andy and Jurko.[2] The three major components of the syndrome are (a) aggression, (b) hyperkinesia, and (c) "pathoaffect." The optimum lesion site for good results appears to be in the area of center medianum and intralaminar nuclei. Orthner et al.[77] aim not to destroy the whole dorso-medial nucleus, but only to interrupt its connections with the frontal lobe within the internal medullary lamina: "Thus we form a barrier between the medial and lateral thalamic areas."

Obsessional neurosis has been treated successfully by unilateral or bilateral stereotactic coagulation of the rostral intralaminar and medial-thalamic nuclei. Bilateral operations were, however, associated with a considerable risk of adverse effects such as severe amnesia and psychomotor akinesia.[26] The risk of this operation for patients with obsessional neurosis seems to be unacceptably high, when operations on the anterior cingulate gyrus appear to be much safer.

Operation on Two Target Sites

Limbic Leucotomy. This operation[43, 84] is designed to interrupt some connections in the Papez circuit (anterior cingulate region) and in the lower medial quadrant of the frontal lobe. Small lower medial quadrant lesions alone were not sufficient to bring about the desired improvement, and as the operation evolved, it became apparent that the addition of cingulate lesions gave good results with a modest overall lesion size. Electrical stimulation of cingulate and lower medial quadrant target zones is performed at the time of operation to locate limbic pathways; thereby, it was postulated, increasing the accuracy of the operation. If physiological changes (Figure 4) are not elicited, the site may be moved a few millimeters. Three 8-mm diameter lesions are made in the lower medial quadrant, and two pairs of lesions interrupt the cingulate pathways (Figures 6 and 7).

Particularly good results have been obtained in *nuclear* obsessional neurosis, and the results in anxiety states and depression are also satisfactory.[42, 44] Psychometric scores of anxiety, neuroticism (Figure 8), and

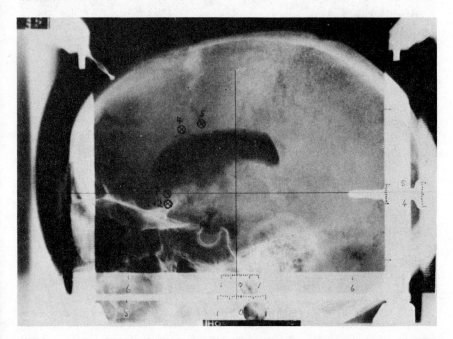

Figure 6. Lateral x-ray of the skull showing air in the lateral ventricles (dark shadow), and the stereotactic frame in place. The lower medial quadrant target sites (1, 2, and 3) and cingulate sites (4 and 5) of Limbric Leucotomy are shown. (From Kelly, D. Psychiat. Neurol. Neurochir. Amst. 76:353, 1973.)

obsessions (Figure 9) were all significantly reduced at 17 months follow-up. The mean depression scores were also significantly reduced (Figure 8 and 9), and this result was superior to that reported in a previous study of "freehand" lower medial quadrant operations.[45] Emotional blunting, disinhibition, postoperative epilepsy, and excessive weight gain were not encountered, and intelligence was unaffected by the operation, and in fact the mean Wechsler Adult Intelligence Scale increased significantly. (For case histories, see Kelly and Mitchell-Heggs[42]).

Combined Lesions

D. E. Richardson[85] in New Orleans has also used a combination of cingulate and lower medial quadrant lesions placed stereotactically in 12 patients with "excellent results" in 10 patients. He recommends operation for obsessive-compulsive states, manic-depressive states, and disabling psychosomatic symptoms that have not responded to the usual psychiatric treatments.

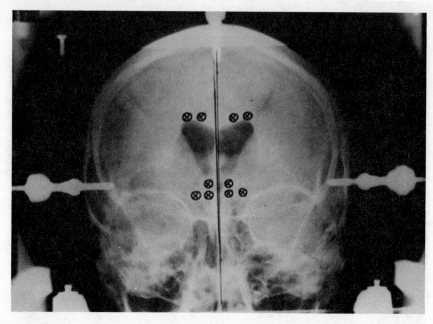

Figure 7. AP view of the skull with air in the lateral ventricles (dark shadow). The three lower medial quadrant target sites form a triangle, while the cingulate sites of Limbric Leucotomy are above the roof of the lateral ventricles. (From Kelly, D. Psychiat. Neurol. Neurochir. Amst. 76:353, 1973.)

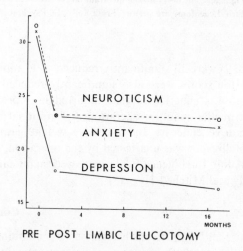

Figure 8. Psychometric scores pre- and postlimbic leucotomy.

Neuroticism   (Maudsley Personality Inventory)
Anxiety   (Taylor Scale of Manifest Anxiety)
Depression   (Beck Depression Scale)
N = 29

(From Kelly, D. and Mitchell-Heggs, N. Postgrad. Med. J. 49:865, 1973.)

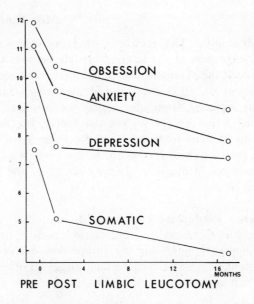

Figure 9. Psychometric scores pre and postlimbic leucotomy. On Middlesex Hospital questionnaire (phobic and hysterical scores not shown); $N = 29$. (From Kelly, D. and Mitchell-Heggs, N. Postgrad. Med. J. 49:865, 1973.)

Brown[14] uses multiple limbic lesions for hard-core schizophrenia and sociopathic aggression (cingulo-innominoamygdalotomy) and he advocates early surgery in schizophrenia.

Kim and Umbach[47] use combinations of targets for various syndromes, and claim the following results in:

(a) Aggression   (medial amygdala and posteromedial hypothalamus) 60% improvement

(b) Intractable Pain   (posteroventral thalamus—subthalamus and dorsomedial thalamus) 80% improvement

(c) Anxiety states   (medial amygdala and intralaminar nucleus) 75% improvement

(d) Obsessive-compulsive neurosis   (intralaminar nucleus and dorsomedial thalamus) 65% improvement

Vaernet and Madsen[100] use amygdala and substantia innominata (basofrontal tractotomy) lesions for psychotic patients with aggressive-destructive tendencies.

Miscellaneous Operations

Anterior Capsulotomy. The prefrontal-thalamic pathway is funnelled through the anterior part of the internal capsule between the head of the caudate nucleus and the putamem. Bilateral anterior capsulotomy has been found by Bingley et al.,[7] to be successful in alleviating symptoms in about 70% of patients suffering from obsessional neurosis and anxiety states. After the second lesion on the second side, some, but not all, patients reported a feeling of relief from anxiety and tension. In addition, in some cases after the production of the second lesion there was mild confusion and slight disturbance of memory.[7] Lopez-Ibor Alino and Burzaco[61] have also used this target site.

Sexual Disorders. Paedophilic homosexuality and other sexual disorders have been treated in Germany by stereotactic lesions in the ventromedial nucleus of the hypothalamus,[87] but the author does not know if any psychosurgical procedures have been carried out on sexual offenders in Britain or America. Such operations would probably engender a great deal of publicity.

FUTURE TRENDS

Operative Technique

The introduction of stereotactic techniques has been a major advance, and in future it is probable that "freehand" methods will be used less frequently in psychosurgery, because of the added risk of the lesion being misplaced and the greater damage between the surface and target site that inevitably occurs. Rostral leucotomy, which was probably the most common type of modified lower medial quadrant leucotomy used in Great Britain, has now largely been replaced at this hospital by limbic leucotomy, although bi-medial leucotomy retains its popularity elsewhere. Inevitably, a very small amount of damage occurs between burr hole and target site if a thin stimulating or coagulating probe is introduced, but in comparison with older techniques, this is negligible. Stimulation of the target area to identify limbic pathways may be used more frequently in the future, because if much smaller lesions are made, they must be placed with great accuracy. Individual anatomical variability can be taken into account by stimulation procedures.

Psychiatric Evaluation

Diagnosis. For ease of comparison between different series of patients, it would be helpful if the International Classification of Diseases (ICD) could be adopted for diagnostic purposes—it has a Glossary of Mental Disorders* which has been approved after much thought by an international committee. The diagnoses are coded numerically and this has advantages if data from different centers is subsequently pooled.

Symptom ratings. Overall clinical improvement rates are too crude a method of evaluation to be of comparative value to investigators working in other centers. Symptom rating, by the use of psychometric questionnaires, is far more valuable and informative because most patients who have failed to respond to all other therapies have an extremely complicated psychopathology by the time psychosurgery is contemplated. Certain operations appear to have advantages for particular symptoms, for example, lower medial quadrant and orbital undercutting (stereotactic tractotomy) for depression, and cingulate lesions for obsessional symptoms. Key symptoms such as depression, anxiety, and obsessions can be accurately quantified, although psychotic symptomatology is still very difficult to measure. Preoperative scores would indicate to other workers the degree of *severity* of particular symptoms, and postoperative scores can show the *degree of change* and the time course of that change (Figure 8 and 9). The extent to which individual symptoms improve may indicate future refinements of operative technique.

Controlled Trials. There is considerable body of opinion in favor of a controlled trial of psychosurgery, and a working party of the Royal College of Psychiatrists has been set up to examine this question. This is a necessary scientific step, although the selection of an adequate control group has been the problem in the past.

SURGICAL AND PSYCHIATRIC COOPERATION. Psychosurgery is a highly specialized form of treatment and calls for the closest co-operation between neurosurgeons, psychiatrists, and psychologists. If sophisticated methods of psychiatric rehabilitation and evaluation of the results of surgery are to be employed, it is probable that facilities will only be available in a few centers. If these are in teaching hospitals where medical students, psychologists, nurses, and psychiatric residents are in training, fear of abuse will not be a problem.

ETHICAL CONSIDERATIONS. Psychosurgery will always be an emotive subject. The results of amygdalotomy and hypothalamotomy in children from Japan and India are impressive, but this is a particularly delicate subject. Surgery as treatment for sexual offenders has been carried out in Germany and raises difficult ethical issues. Prisoners and sexual offenders, children,

---

* Studies on medical and population subjects No. 22 Her Majesty's Stationery Office, 1968, London.

and those patients detained in hospital against their wishes are not able to give their free consent to operation in the same way that voluntary patients can, and this has to be recognised. These ethical issues will need to be resolved, and the International Society of Psychiatric Surgery has formed an ethical committee to examine these problems.

CONCLUSIONS

There have been considerable advances in psychosurgery during the past 5 years. Present operations should be judged on their merits, and a blanket condemnation of psychosurgery is not justified. The results of mitral valvotomy of 20 years ago were associated with a considerable mortality and morbidity when surgeons were performing the operation by putting a finger through the mitral valve. Those operations are irrelevant to a debate about the present state of mitral valvotomy.

A clear distinction should be made between operations for severe mental illnesses with a potential mortality from suicide, and operations to alter violent behaviour, often in patients suffering from epilepsy. The result of the latter are less firmly established and are more controversial. Those who advocate psychosurgery should concentrate on scientific methods of evaluation of the results, so that different operative procedures can be compared with one another, and, as Kalinowsky[40] suggests, the number of different procedures advocated can be reduced. Psychosurgery has the capacity to alleviate great suffering when every other method of treatment has failed. This can now be done without altering the patient's personality. Great caution, however, should be exercised in its use because it is always a major procedure, and it is to be hoped that one day it will no longer be necessary.

REFERENCES

1. Abrahams, V. C., Hilton, S. M., and Zbrozyna, A.: Active muscle vasodilatation produced by stimulation of the brain stem: Its significance in the defence reaction. *J. Physiol. (London)* **154**:491, 1960.

2. Andy, O. J. and Jurko, M. F.: Thalamotomy for hyperresponsive syndrome. Lesions in the centermedianum and Intralaminar nuclei. In *Psychosurgery*, p. 127, see Ref. 34.

3. Bailey, H. R., Dowling, J. L., Swanton, C. H., and Davies, E.: Studies in depression 1. Cingulo-tractotomy in the treatment of severe affective illness. *Med. J. Aust.* **1**:8, 1971.

4. Baker, E. F. W., Young, M. P., Gauld, D. M., and Fleming, J. F. R.: A new look at bimedial prefrontal leukotomy. *Can. Med. Assoc. J.* **102**:37, 1970.

5. Balasubramaniam, V., Ramanujam, P. B., Kanaka, T. S., and Ramamurthi, B.: Stereotaxic surgery for behavior disorders. In *Psychosurgery*, p. 156, see Ref. 34.

6. Ballantine, H. T., Cassidy, W. L., Brodeur, J., and Giriunas, I.: Frontal cingulotomy for mood disturbance. In *Psychosurgery*, p. 221, see Ref. 34.

7. Bingley, T., Leksell, L., Meyerson, B. A., and Rylander, G.: Stereotactic anterior capsulotomy in anxiety and obsessive-compulsive states. In *Surgical Approaches in Psychiatry*, p. 159, See Ref. 52.

8. Boyd, H. R.: Psychosurgical treatment of neurosis. *Rocky Mountain Med. J.* **68**:25, 1971.

9. Breggin, P. R.: Lobotomies: An alert. *Am. J. Psychiatr.* **129**:97, 1972.

10. Bridges, P. K. and Goktepe, E. O.: A review of patients with obsessional symptoms treated by psychosurgery. In *Surgical Approaches in Psychiatry*, p. 96, see Ref. 52.

11. Broager, B. and Olesen, K.: Psychosurgery in 63 cases of open cingulectomy and 14 cases of bifrontal prehypothalamic cryolesion. In *Psychosurgery*, p. 253, see Ref. 34.

12. Brown, H. M. and Lighthill, J. A.: Selective anterior cingulotomy: A psychosurgical evaluation. *J. Neuros.* **29**:513, 1968.

13. Brown, H. M.: Double lesions of the limbic system in schizophrenia and psychopathy. In *Psychosurgery*, p. 195, see Ref. 34.

14. Brown, H. M.: Further experience with multiple limbic targets for schizophrenia and aggression. In *Surgical Approaches in Psychiatry*, p. 189, see Ref. 52.

15. Burzaco, J. A.: Fundus striae terminalis, an optimal target in sedative stereotactic surgery. In *Surgical Approaches in Psychiatry*, p. 135, see Ref. 52.

16. Corsellis, J. A. N. and Jack, A. B.: Neuropathological observations on yttrium implants and on undercutting in the orbitofrontal areas of the brain. In *Surgical Approaches in Psychiatry*, p. 90, see Ref. 52.

17. Delgado, J. M. R.: Report on respiratory centers of frontal lobes. *Res. Publ. Assoc. Res. Nerv. Mental Dis.* **27**:433, 1948.

18. Escobedo, F., Fernandez-Guardiola, A., and Solis, G.: Chronic stimulation of the cingulum in humans with behaviour disorders. In *Surgical Approaches in Psychiatry*, p.-65, see Ref. 52.

19. Evans, P.: Failed leucotomy with misplaced cuts: a clinico-anatonical study of two cases. *Brit. J. Psychiat.* **118**:165, 1971.

20. Falconer, M. A.: Pathological substrates in temporal lobe epilepsy with psychosis. In *Surgical Approaches in Psychiatry*, p. 121, see Ref. 52.

21. Fleming, J. F. R. and Baker, E. F. W.: Bimedial prefrontal leukotomy. In *Psychosurgery*, p. 322, see Ref. 34.

22. Freeman, W.: Frontal lobotomy in early schizophrenia. Long follow-up in 415 cases. *Brit. J. Psychiatr.* **119**:621, 1971.

23. Gaches, J., Le Beau, J., and Choppy, M.: Psychosurgery in severe obsessive syndromes. In *Psychosurgery*, p. 230, see Ref. 34.

24. Gascon, G. G. and Gilles, F.: Limbic dementia. *J. Neurol. Neurosurg. Psychiatr.:* **36**:421, 1973.

25. Girgis, M.: The orbital surface of the frontal lobe of the brain and mental disorders. *Acta Psychiatr. Scandinavica Suppl., 222*, 1971.

26. Hassler, R. and Dieckmann, G.: Relief of obsessive-compulsive disorders, phobias and tics by stereotactic coagulation of the rostral intralaminar and medial thalamic nuclei. In *Surgical Approaches in Psychiatry*, p. 206, see Ref. 52.

27. Heath, R. G. and Mickle, W. A.: Evaluation of seven years experience with depth elec-

trode studies in human patients. In *Electrical Studies on the Unanaesthetized Brain*, Ramsey and O'Doherty, (Eds.), New York.

28. Hetherington, R. F., Haden, P. and Craig, W. J.: Neurosurgery in affective disorder: Criteria for selection of patients. In *Psychosurgery*, p. 332, see Ref. 34.

29. Hilton, S. M. and Zbrozyna, A. W.: Amygdaloid region for defence reactions and its efferent pathway to the brain stem. *J. Physiol. (London)* 165: 160, 1963.

30. Hirose, S.: The case selection of mental disorder for orbitoventromedial undercutting. In *Psychosurgery*, p. 291, see Ref. 34.

31. Hirose, S.: Long-term evaluation of orbito-ventromedial undercutting in 'atypical' schizophrenic patients. In *Surgical Approaches in Psychiatry*, p. 196, see Ref. 52.

32. Hitchcock, E.: Psychosurgery today. *Ann. Clin. Res.* 3:187, 1971.

33. Hitchcock, E., Ashcroft, G. W., Cairns, V. M., and Murray, L. G.: Preoperative and postoperative assessment and management of psychosurgical patients. In *Psychosurgery*, p. 164, see Ref. 34.

34. Hitchcock, E., Laitinen, L., and Vaernet, K. (Eds.): *Psychosurgery, Proceedings of the Second International Conference on Psychosurgery*. Charles C. Thomas, Springfield, Illinois, 1972.

35. Hitchcock, E. and Cairns, V.: Amygdalotomy. *Postgrad. Med. J.* 49:894, 1973.

36. Hofstatter, L. and Girgis, M.: Depth electrode investigations of the limbic system with radio-stimulation, electrolytic lesions and histochemical techniques. In *Surgical Approaches in Psychiatry*, p. 224, see Ref. 52.

37. Holden, J. M., Itil, T. M., and Hofstatter, L.: Prefrontal lobotomy: Stepping-stone or pitfall? *Am. J. Psychiatr.* 127:591, 1970.

38. Holden, J. M., Paterson, D. B., Hofstatter, L. and Olson, G.: Applications of the inferomedial lobotomy operation in psychiatric illness. In *Psychosurgery*, p. 346, see Ref. 34.

39. Jackson, H.: Leucotomy—A recent development. *J. Ment. Sci.* 100:62, 1954.

40. Kalinowsky, L. B.: Questions from the psychiatrist to the neurosurgeon regarding psychosurgical methods. In *Psychosurgery*, p. 421, see Ref. 34.

41. Kelly, D.: Physiological changes during operations on the limbic system in man. *Cond. Reflex* 7:127, 1972.

42. Kelly, D. and Mitchell-Heggs, N.: Stereotactic limbic leucotomy: A follow-up study of 30 patients. *Postgrad. Med. J.* 49:865, 1973.

43. Kelly, D., Richardson, A., and Mitchell-Heggs, N.: Stereotactic limbic leucotomy: Neurophysiological aspects and operative technique. *Brit. J. Psychiatr.* 123:133, 1973.

44. Kelly, D., Richardson, A., Mitchell-Heggs, N., Greenup, J., Chen, C., and Hafner, R. J.: Stereotactic limbic leucotomy: A preliminary report on 40 patients. *Brit. J. Psychiatr.* 123:141, 1973.

45. Kelly, D., Walter, C. J. S., Mitchell-Heggs, N., and Sargant, W.: Modified leucotomy assessed clinically, physiologically and psychogically at six weeks and eighteen months. *Brit. J. Psychiatr.* 120:19, 1972.

46. Kim, Y. K.: Effects of basolateral amygdalotomy. In *Special Topics in Stereotaxis*, Umbach, (Ed.), Stuttgart, Hippokrates, Verlag, 1971.

47. Kim, Y. K. and Umbach, W.: Combined stereotactic lesions for treatment of behaviour disorders and severe pain. In *Surgical Approaches in Psychiatry*, p. 182, see Ref. 52.

48. Knight, G. C. and Tredgold, R. F.: Orbital leucotomy—A review of 52 cases. *Lancet* 1:981, 1955.

49. Knight, G.: The orbital cortex as an object in the surgical treatment of mental illness. *Brit. J. Surg.* **51**:114, 1964.

50. Knight, G.: Bifrontal stereotaxic tractotomy in the substantia innominata: An experience of 450 cases. In *Psychosurgery,* p. 267, see Ref. 34.

51. Knight, G.: Further observations from an experience of 660 cases of stereotactic tractotomy. *Postgrad. Med. J.* **49**:845, 1973.

52. Laitinen, L. V. and Livingston, K. E.: *Surgical Approaches in Psychiatry. Proceedings of the Third International Congress of Psychosurgery,* Medical and Technical Publishing Company Ltd., Lancaster, 1973.

53. Laitinen, L. V. and Vilkki, J.: Stereotaxic ventral anterior cingulotomy in some psychological disorders. In *Psychosurgery,* p. 242, see Ref. 34.

54. Laitinen, L. V. and Vilkki, J.: Observations on the transcallosal emotional connections. In *Surgical Approaches in Psychiatry,* p. 74, see Ref. 52.

55. Lewin, W.: Selective leucotomy: A review. In *Surgical Approaches in Psychiatry,* p. 69, see Ref. 52.

56. Livingston, K. E.: Cingulate cortex isolation for the treatment of psychoses and psychoneuroses. *Res. Publ. Assoc. Res. Nervous Ment. Dis.* **31**:374, 1953.

57. Livingston, K. E.: The frontal lobes revisited: The case for a second look. *Arch. Neurol.* **20**:90, 1969.

58. Livingston, K. E. and Escobar, A.: The continuing evolution of the limbic system concept. In *Psychosurgery,* p. 25, see Ref. 34.

59. Livingston, R. B., Chapman, W. P., Livingston, K. E., and Kraintz, L.: Stimulation of the orbital surface of man prior to frontal lobotomy. *Res. Publ. Assoc. Res. Nervous Ment. Dis.* **27**:421, 1948.

60. Livingston, R. B., Fulton, J. F., Delgado, J. M. R., Sachs, F. Jr., Brendler, S. J. and Davis, G. D.: Stimulation and regional ablation of orbital surface of frontal lobe. *Res. Publ. Assoc. Res. Nervous Ment. Dis.* **27**:405, 1948.

61. López-Ibor Alino, J. J. and Burzaco, J.: Stereotaxic anterior limb capsulotomy in selected psychiatric patients. In *Psychosurgery,* p. 391, see Ref. 34.

62. McKenzie, K. G. and Kaczanowski, G.: Prefrontal leukotomy: A 5 year controlled study. *Can. Med. Assoc. J.* **91**:1193, 1964.

63. McKissock, W.: Discussion on psychosurgery. *Proc. Royal Soc. Med.* **52**:206, 1959.

64. McLardy, T. and Meyer, A.: Anatomical correlates of improvement after leucotomy. *J. Ment. Sci.* **91**:411, 1949.

65. MacLean, P. D.: The triune brain, emotion and scientific bias. In *The Neurosciences: Second Study Program,* Schmitt, (Ed.), The Rockefeller University Press, New York, 1970, p. 336.

66. Mark, V. H., Sweet, W. H., and Ervin, F. R.: The effect of amygdalotomy on violent behavior in patients with temporal lobe epilepsy. In *Psychosurgery,* p. 139, see Ref. 34.

67. Marks, I. M., Birley, J. L. T., and Gelder, M. G.: Modified leucotomy in severe agoraphobia: A controlled serial inquiry. *Brit. J. Psychiatr.* **112**:757, 1966.

68. Meyer, A. and Beck, E.: *Prefrontal Leucotomy and Related Operations,* Oliver and Boyd, Edinburgh, 1954.

69. Meyer, G., McElhaney, M., Martin, W., and McGraw, C. P.: Stereotactic cingulotomy with results of acute stimulation and serial psychological testing. In *Surgical Approaches in Psychiatry,* p. 39, see Ref. 52.

70. Mingrino, S. and Schergna, E.: Stereotaxic anterior cingulotomy in the treatment of severe behavior disorders. In *Psychosurgery*, p. 258, see Ref. 34.

71. Nadvornik, P., Pogady, J., and Sramka, M.: The results of stereotactic treatment of the aggressive syndrome. In *Surgical Approaches in Psychiatry*, p. 125, see Ref. 52.

72. Narabayashi, H. and Shima, F.: Which is the better amygdala target, the medial or lateral nuclei? In *Surgical Approaches in Psychiatry*, p. 129, see Ref. 52.

73. Nauta, W. J. H.: Hippocampal projections and related neural pathways to the midbrain in the cat. *Brain* **81**:319, 1958.

74. Nauta, W. J. H.: The problem of the frontal lobe: A reinterpretation. *J. Psychiatr. Res.* **8**:167, 1971.

75. Nauta, W. J. H.: Connections of the frontal lobe with the limbic system. In *Surgical Approaches in Psychiatry*, p. 303, see Ref. 52.

76. Newcombe, R. L.: Anatomical placement of lesions in the ventromedial segment of the frontal lobe. In *Surgical Approaches in Psychiatry*, p. 83, see Ref. 52.

77. Orthner, H., Müller, D., and Roeder, F.: Stereotaxic psychosurgery: Techniques and results since 1955. In *Psychosurgery*, p. 377, see Ref. 34.

78. Ortiz, A.: The role of the limbic lobe in central pain mechanisms, an hypothesis relating to the gate control theory of pain. In *Surgical Approaches in Psychiatry*, p. 59, see Ref. 52.

79. Papez, J. W.: A proposed mechanism of emotion. *Arch. Neurol. Psychiatr.* **38**:725, 1937.

80. Parker, G., Gye, R., and Kiloh, L. G.: An appraisal of modified pre-frontal leucotomy, *Med. J. Aust.* **2**:935, 1972.

81. Post, F., Linford, Rees, W., and Schurr, P. H.: An evaluation of bimedial leucotomy. *Brit. J. Psychiatr.* **114**:1223, 1968.

82. *Postgraduate Medical Journal, Symposium on Psychosurgery,* **49**:823, 1973.

83. *Psychiatria Neurologia Neurochirurgia (Amsterdam),* Symposium on Development in Psychosurgery **76**, No. 5:319, 1973.

84. Richardson, A.: Stereotactic limbic leucotomy: Surgical technique. *Postgrad. Med. J.* **49**:860, 1973.

85. Richardson, D. E.: Stereotaxic cingulumotomy and pre-frontal lobotomy in mental disease. *South. Med. J.* **65**:1221, 1972.

86. Robin, A. A.: A controlled study of the effects of leucotomy. *J. Neurol. Neurosurg. Psychiatr.* **21**:262, 1958.

87. Roeder, F., Orthner, H., and Müller, D.: The stereotaxic treatment of pedophilic homosexuality and other sexual deviations. In *Psychosurgery*, p. 87, see Ref. 34.

88. Rylander, G.: The renaissance of psychosurgery. In *Surgical Approaches in Psychiatry*, p. 3, see Ref. 52.

89. Sano, K., Sekino, H., and Mayanagi, Y.: Results of stimulation and destruction of the posterior hypothalamus in cases with violent, aggressive or restless behaviors. In *Psychosurgery*, p. 57, see Ref. 34.

90. Schurr, P.: Psychosurgery. *Brit. J. Hosp. Med.* **10**:53, 1973.

91. Siegfried, J., and Ben-Shmuel, A.: Neurosurgical treatment of aggressivity: stereotaxic amygdalotomy versus leukotomy. In *Psychosurgery,* p. 214, see Ref. 34.

92. Siegfried, J. and Ben-Shmuel, A.: Long term assessment of stereotactic amygdaltomy for aggressive behaviour. In *Surgical Approaches in Psychiatry,* p. 138, see Ref. 52.

93. Strom-Olsen, R. and Carlisle, S.: Bi-frontal stereotactic tractotomy: A follow-up study of its effects on 210 patients. *Brit. J. Psychiatr.* **118**:141, 1971.

94. Tan, E., Marks, I. M., and Marset, P.: Bimedial leucotomy in obsessive-compulsive neurosis: A controlled serial enquiry. *Brit. J. Psychiatr.* **118**:155, 1971.

95. Tooth, E. L. and Newton, M. P., *Leucotomy in England and Wales 1942-1954*, H. M.S.O., London, 1961.

96. Turner, E.: Operations for aggression. Bilateral temporal lobotomy and posterior cingulectomy. In *Psychosurgery*, p. 204, see Ref. 34.

97. Turner, E.: Custom psychosurgery. *Postgrad. Med. J.* **49**:834, 1973.

98. Ukena, T. E. and Nichols, T. R.: Psychosurgery. *Lancet* **2**:434, 1972.

99. Ursin, H.: Limbic control of emotional behavior. In *Psychosurgery,* p. 34, see Ref. 34.

100. Vaernet, K. and Madsen, A.: Lesions in the amygdala and the substantia innominata in aggressive psychotic patients. In *Psychosurgery*, p. 187, see Ref. 34.

101. Yakovlev, P. I.: Motility, behavior and the brain: Stereodynamic organization and neural co-ordinates of behavior. *J. Nerv. Ment. Dis.* **107**:313, 1948.

102. Zbrozyna, A. W.: The organization of the defence reaction elicited from amygdala and its connections. In *The Neurobiology of the Amygdala* Eleftheriou, (Ed.), Plenum Press, New York, 1972, p. 597.

PART TWO

ADVANCES IN PSYCHOTHERAPY
AND HOSPITAL PSYCHIATRY

RECENT ADVANCES IN CONCEPTS AND TREATMENT OF
BORDERLINE CASES

NEW VIEWS ON THE PSYCHOTHERAPY OF COMPENSATION
NEUROSIS: A CLINICAL STUDY

THE ROLE OF IMAGERY IN PSYCHOTHERAPY

MODERN HOSPITAL MILIEU TREATMENT OF SCHIZOPHRENIA

INSTITUTIONAL PSYCHIATRY

CHAPTER SIX

RECENT ADVANCES IN THE CONCEPTS AND TREATMENT OF BORDERLINE PATIENTS

GERARD CHRZANOWSKI, M.D.

In view of the widespread occurrence of borderline states, it is noteworthy that the borderline spectrum has no diagnostic representation in standard psychiatric nomenclature. There is usually an element of vagueness involved when and where reference to borderline manifestations is made in psychiatric textbooks.

DEFINITION OF BORDERLINE SYNDROME

At present, borderline states are still by and large hybrid concepts without a particular psychiatric mooring. Most commonly, these conditions are classed with the schizophrenic reactions and are usually considered to be early, latent, transient, or ambulatory forms of schizophrenia. In recent years, greater emphasis has been placed on the relatively specific psychopathology of borderline states compared to conceptualizations of either a continuum ranging from neurosis to psychosis and vice versa or to a halfway station between moderate and severe mental illness.

Generally speaking, traditional psychiatry has turned its back to borderline states and relegated them largely to the group of unrewarding psychiatric patients. Psychiatric residents are usually taught that borderline patients require supportive treatment and are not suitable for so called insight therapy. This attitude is in sharp contrast to a group of avantguarde psychoanalytic investigators who have taken a renewed interest in borderline conditions without being plagued by excessive therapeutic pessimism (Otto Kernberg, Arlene Wolberg, Roy Grinker, Peter Giovacchini and others). Their work is discussed in some detail later on in this text.

At this point, I wish to stress that borderline conditions, character disorders, and narcissistic states are phenomena known to every practioner in the field. They constitute a significant percentage of referrals for psychotherapy and psychoanalysis. Borderline states are encountered in private office work, in supervisory activities, as well in every clinical and hospital setting.

There is evidence that we see today more borderline states than we used to. On the one hand, the spectrum of analytic office practice has expanded to include ambulatory schizophrenic patients and a variety of people who previously would have been rejected for intensive therapy. On the other hand, there is a paucity of bona fide analytic patients as every new candidate will testify, particularly when it comes to finding a suitable patient for analytic supervision. Be that as it may, borderline conditions are seen on a large scale, and their number may be increasing.

In my discussion of the clinical phenomena referred to as borderline states, I emphasize their relatively stable personality organization, as well as their more or less enduring boundaries. It is my contention that borderline conditions have an identity of their own which transcends both neurosis and psychosis. Borderline states are considered to be conditions sui generis. They do not fit into the realm of neurosis or psychosis, nor are they a way station between the polar opposites of mental disorder. It is my task to illustrate their characteristic patterns in a genetic, interpersonal, and therapeutic frame of reference.

In conventional, psychiatric terms, the borderline states are classified as schizoid personalities, latent schizophrenic reactions, and chronic, undifferentiated schizophrenia. The differential diagnosis centers around asocial and inadequate personalities, narcissistic states, character disorders as well as transitional states, psychotic adaptations, and pseudoneurotic schizophrenia. All of these conditions may be combined with obsessional, depressive, hysterical, paranoid, and every other clinical manifestation known to man.

On a descriptive level, borderline states have a common denominator in three attitudinal aspects:

1. There is an inhibition to display overt anger and aggression.
2. There is a tendency to maintain a measure of social distance.
3. There is a penchant toward intense transference phenomena.

THE VICISSITUDES OF TRANSFERENCE

It is specifically the vicissitudes of transferential aspects which take on a character of their own in borderline conditions. My reference here is to the often abrupt changes in emotional attitudes which forcefully come to the fore in the therapeutic work with borderline patients.

I have concerned myself with one aspect of this phenomenon in a paper called "Symptom Choice in Schizophrenic Manifestations."[4] In that connection, I coined the term instantaneous transference which refers to the acting out of intimacy with a total stranger. I described it as a pathognomonic symptom in certain schizophrenic conditions.

The appreciation of powerful transferential experiences with schizoid and schizophrenic patients has slowly become a focus of attention in recent years. It is a well-known fact that Freud drew a line of demarcation between the transference and the narcissistic neurosis. He stated (1915) that schizoid patients suffer from a narcissistic neurosis and cannot form a stable transference. It was Freud's point of view that the narcissistic person is incapable of investing himself wholeheartedly in the therapeutic process.

Today, there is no longer doubt that borderline patients manifest highly intense transference reactions. The main question is as to whether the particular quality of the borderline transference is therapeutically useful. In this connection, it is worth mentioning that the concept of excessive transference rather than a lack of it was first observed and discussed by Sullivan. He found in this work with schizoid and schizophrenic patients that they tended to be enveloped in a transference jam, that is, a flooding of powerful emotional experiences ranging from primitive types of affection to primitive types of hatred without having any words at their disposal to express their feelings.

Sullivan[18] postulated the occurrence of an interpersonal experience, referred to as anxiety, which is inculcated early in life. Once this anxiety is acquired, it triggers off a host of defensive maneuvers which he called security operations. The result is an insulating of emotional impulses by an overlay of apathy, disinterest, or withdrawal. In essence, Sullivan concluded that we observe in schizoid individuals an emotional storm of such intensity that the person tends to screen it out or make distance from it by a layer of overt indifference.

This insight or definition of Sullivan's was far ahead of his time, and even today, the full impact of his observation is not sufficiently appreciated by many people in the field. I address myself to this point later in connection with a comparison between Sullivan's interpersonal frame of reference and that of the classical analyst Otto F. Kernberg.

At this moment, it will suffice to make only the most fleeting reference to the numerous other authors who have made significant contributions to the understanding of borderline states; to mention just a few: Frieda Fromm-Reichmann, Margaret Mahler, Masud R. Khan, Harry Guntrip, Donald Winnicott, and Harold Searles.[9, 13, 17] The reader is referred to the excellent review of the literature on this subject in Arlene Wolberg's book, The Borderline Patient.[20]

Generally speaking, there are two major trends to be found among the above-mentioned contributors. Some are of the opinion that we are dealing with a basic adaptational deficiency connected to constitutional factors, while others emphasize predominantly early traumatic experiences.

For instance, Masud Khan believes that the modern family is not functioning as an integrated unit. There is an absence of a close emotional network of emotions. Hence he claims that "the intimacy between mother and child has taken on a more intense proportion and dynamism." In other words, he conceptualizes an emotional vacuum in the family system which intensifies the emotional charge between mother and child.

Harold Searles and Margaret Mahler, each in his own way, conceive of a pathological, symbiotic mode of mother–child relatedness. This highly charged pattern appears in a therapeutic symbiosis which must be worked through to bring about eventual individuation.

On the other hand, Roy Grinker et al.[8] focus their attention primarily on the kind of family pathology which gives rise to borderline disorders. They describe a marital relationship which Sullivan referred to as hostile integration; that is, marital partners relate to each other's weaknesses while undermining their respective strengths. Another characteristic is the parents' neurotic need to keep the children tied to the family and thus prevent their autonomy and individuation. This situation is further complicated by the parental denial of problems and their emotional ambivalence. The authors postulate a list of 10 characteristic attitudes of borderline patient parents without offering any concrete evidence of its pathognomonic impact on the genesis of borderline states. One would not wish parents with the above-mentioned problems on most children. This does not mean, however, that once we find parents with such neurotic difficulties, we can predict with any measure of certainty that the offspring will manifest borderline symptoms.

There is a great deal more to be found in the literature on this and related topics. Much emphasis today is placed on the quality of communicative channels within the nuclear family, on selective, empathic inattention, and a host of developmental miscarriages.

A COMPARISON BETWEEN A CLASSICAL AND INTERPERSONAL CONCEPTUALIZATION

In this paper, I wish to address myself initially to a relatively narrow frame of reference by highlighting the contributions of Otto Kernberg and his reflections from an interpersonal point of view. In this connection, I offer first a comparative study on this subject by sketching Kernberg's[10-12] concept side-by-side the formulations of Harry Stack Sullivan.[18] Kernberg concerns himself with the early internalization of object relations. He postulates a dual phenomenon on the level of ego-organization. To him, in borderline patients, there are (1) the essential primitive ego-defense of splitting or dissociation, and (2) the more advanced phenomenon of repression which takes the place of splitting. Kernberg assumes that is is the pathological fixation at the level of splitting which interferes with normal ego and superego development. In essence, Kernberg postulates that borderline patients demonstrate a morbid fixation at the lower level of ego organization whereby splitting, fragmentation, and dissociation prevail.

This concept is not incompatible with Sullivan's point of view. Sullivan holds that the formation of I, Me, My Body is fragmented depending on the degree of anxiety in the early mother–child relationship. Untroubled, or Good Me, emerges as a result of a relatively conflict-free field of cooperation between mother and child. By contrast, Bad Me, or the split-off Not Me aspect of the personality, comes into being when the integrating activities take place under the impact of severe anxiety. As far as it goes, Kernberg and Sullivan see eye-to-eye in regard to the phenomenon of splitting, except that Sullivan adds the dimension of anxiety as an interpersonal, dynamic ingredient.

As I see it, the classical scheme outlined by Kernberg about splitting refers predominantly to an inherent organizational ego-defect. In my opinion, the morbid fixation concept of Kernberg's lacks a dynamic quality and makes inadequate allowance for phenomena of the rest of the personality.

Sullivan, on the other hand, makes an effort to relate the pathology to particular unfortunate human transactions. There is mother and child on the one side, and mother and her interpersonal situation on the other side. In the presence of disturbed interpersonal relations, a warping of development takes place through the intervention of the self-system or antianxiety system which permits a certain personality development in spite of the destructive impact of anxiety. It means that the ego-defect as described by Kernberg is viewed by Sullivan as an interpersonal artefact, that is, a miscarriage of the tenderness principle in regard to the early mother–child relationship.

Kernberg prefers the concept of borderline personality organization to the term borderline states. He defines this conceptualization as a rather specific, quite stable pathological personality organization rather than transitory states. Compare this notion to Sullivan's formulation of schizoid and schizophrenic manifestations as valid, but varied styles of life (i.e., part of a common human repertory).

Both investigators conceive of the clinical syndrome as a relatively fixed entity. To Sullivan, a schizoid style of life is always a schizoid style of life—before, during, and after successful analytic treatment. It is what it is within the overall scope of human existence. The borderline condition does not constitute pathology per se, nor can it be seen as a norm. What we observe is an individually acquired adaptation to a particular interpersonal situation which prevailed during the developmental phases.

In contrast, Kernberg thinks more in terms of morbidity, pathology, or sickness. Kernberg feels that in borderline states, the transference psychosis prevails over the transference neurosis. Sullivan considers the intense transference to be a manifestation of emotional flooding with the inability to find a meaningful verbal channnel to put nonverbal experiences into communicable language. Furthermore, Sullivan's concept of transference jam involves a powerful mixture both of primitive love and of primitive hatred in the absence of expressive, integrating verbal tools. On the other hand, Kernberg stresses the negative aspects of the transference as a key factor. I discuss the significance of this concept for therapeutic considerations at a later point.

In the meantime, there is another aspect which deserves mention. Kernberg is of the opinion that clinically speaking, it does not matter whether the borderline pathology came about as a result of infantile frustration, maternal aggression, constitutional defects, or what have you. He is convinced that in one way or another, the end result is always a paranoid distortion of the early parental images. The result is a distorted view of the mother as an evil person by means of oral- and anal-sadistic impulses. In addition, there is a contamination of the father image and eventually both parents are seen united as "the enemy." The result is a later conceptualization of all sexual relationships as dangerous and aggression laden. There is a flight from oral rage into genital strivings which are contaminated by pregenital aggression.

A key problem of borderline patients, according to Kernberg, is their transference psychosis or acute transferential regression. This is viewed as a defense against primitive, negative transference reactions, that is, the projective paranoid identification (as described by Melanie Klein).

Kernberg considers this projective distortion to be one of the key problems in the working with borderline patients. He offers a clinical illustration of a patient who is suddenly struck by the thought that she experiences the analyst and her own mother as merging into one person because they really are identical. This phenomenon is considered by him to be a manifestation of transference psychosis.

In this connection, Kernberg emphasizes the basic intactness of reality-functioning in borderline patients, except within the sphere of the transference regression. To Kernberg the ego weakness of borderline patients is not to be explained mainly with the notion of a frail ego barrier which is easily flooded and broken through. His conceptualization of ego weakness is in the reduction of the conflict-free ego sphere, that is, lack of anxiety tolerance, lack of impulse control, and inadequate sublimatory channels.

Let us compare these formulations to interpersonal concepts. Here the so-called pathology is neither in the mother nor in the infant. It is locked into the interplay, or transaction, between mother and child. They are unable "to put it together" as far as working as a team is concerned, because of the intervention of anxiety.

Next, the infant does not wind up with a paranoid distortion of the early parental images. There is a major distinction made between the experiential concept of the "I and my mother" transaction on the one hand, and the actual mother on the other hand. Distressing other-child experiences become cognitively coded as Bad Me and Not Me phenomena.

In this frame of reference, it is assumed that the security operations were existential necessities connected with survival. The excesses of negative and positive transference are viewed as primitive emotions of a preverbal phase and the transference jam as a particular form of wordless intensity. Aggression and pregenital sexuality are viewed as later developmental disturbances rather than a deflection from oral rage. Finally, the patient's "Eureka" experience in regard to the fusion of mother and analyst is placed in the parataxic mode of cognition rather than viewed as a prototaxic phenomenon. It may indicate a relational short circuit based on an actual symbiotic transaction. In other words, analyst and mother may have merged because of a genuine miscarriage of the therapeutic relationship. The parataxic mode of cognition involves the world of people, distorted as this world may be. By contrast, the prototaxic mode comes closer to Kernberg's formulation of primitive ego splitting.

We must also appreciate here that Kernberg presents a sophisticated view of ego weakness. He is more concerned with a restriction of the conflict-free ego sphere than with the notion of a basically debilitated ego. Nevertheless, his concept of ego weakness does have a constitutional flavor.

THERAPEUTIC CONSIDERATIONS

I now discuss therapeutic considerations in working with borderline patients. It is not possible here to offer a detailed outline with clinical illustrations. This is best done in an on-going discussion course or seminar. At this point, I offer a brief summary of Kernberg's approach and compare it to my own technical considerations.

Kernberg refers to particular problems which a therapist has to cope with in working with borderline patients. He warns of trouble spots in the following areas:

1. In *ego weakness*, he points to the pitfall of splitting idealization, projection, denial, and omnipotence. In addition, there are a lack of anxiety control, problems with impulse control, and sublimatory channels.

2. An anticipation of a *transference psychosis* is combined with a powerful impulse to act out instinctual needs within the transferential situation. There is also a tendency to compromise formation as well as an identity confusion (Erikson's concept).

3. Kernberg speaks of an excessive development of pregenital and especially oral aggression leading to premature oedipal strivings.

At the end of the considerations, Kernberg arrives at the significant conclusion that supportive treatment of borderline patients is doomed to failure, since it aims to reinforce the defensive organization. It precludes the formation of a working alliance and shores up the pathological defenses in view of the negative transference. In my judgment, Kernberg's work is most valuable for this statement alone if for no other reason.

Next we come to Kernberg's therapeutic approach which centers on the following technical recommendations. There are seven points which I want to mention here as a basis for my discussion. They are as follows:

1. Systematic elaboration of the manifest and latent transference.

2. Confrontation with, and interpretation of, the particular pathognomonic defensive operations.

3. Structuring of the therapeutic alliance, setting limits in regard to the treatment situation and in regard to nonverbal aggression.

4. Utilization of environmental structures (hospitals etc.) Outside helper (Paul Federn).

5. Illustration of morbid, defensive operations via transference and life experiences.

6. Fostering of positive transference aspects as a means of strenghtening the therapeutic alliance.

7. Encouragement of more mature genital development in favor of pregenital aggression.

These points are all well-taken. It is in the next category that I disagree with Kernberg and view the therapeutic situation with borderline patients in a different light.

Kernberg claims that his technique with borderline patients differs from classical psychoanalysis in that a complete transference neurosis is not permitted to develop, nor is the transference resolved through interpretation alone. He admits to some supportive aspects in his approach, and states that in view of reality clarification, direct suggestions, and implicit advice giving are difficult to avoid. He goes on to say that the therapist should remain as neutral as possible.

CONCEPTUAL AND THERAPEUTIC MODIFICATIONS

It is particularly in regard to the last-mentioned point concerning neutrality that I differ significantly with Kernberg's recommendation. The reason for it is that central in my therapeutic model is the assumption that favorable change in a therapeutic alliance is based on the nature of the on-going patient–analyst relationship. The sensitivity to nuances in the Me-You transaction is highly pronounced in borderline patients. Accordingly, I consider Kernberg's recommendation that the therapist should remain as neutral as possible to be ill-advised.

This is not to encourage the compulsive encounter-prescription of misguided openness and physicality. I am firmly opposed to the notion of offering troubled people love and joy as an inducement for dropping their defenses. Many therapeutic ventures have sadly miscarried because negative transferential attitudes were insufficiently stressed or altogether denied. It leads to an acting out of the transference instead of working it through. There can be no question in my mind that setting limits is a basic therapeutic requirement. Furthermore, I appreciate the fact that reality encounters are often the rule and not the exception. In this connection, we also need to consider the obvious truism that every transference has seeds of ambivalence. Accordingly, we need not be unduly concerned with purely positive or negative transference manifestations.

In addition, I am puzzled by Kernberg's statement that he truncates the development of a complete transference neurosis in borderline patients and does not rely on an interpretative resolution of the transference alone. In my clinical work, I have not seen evidence that interpretation alone, regardless of how skillful, has the power to resolve a transference. As a matter of fact, I doubt that a significant aspect of transference can be fully settled as long as a patient is still in therapy. Furthermore, I am not persuaded of the necessity to regress any patient by means of a full-blown transference neurosis. As far as I know, analysis proceeds in the presence of transference as a gift, as well as a necessary evil. In the long run, it is the reality of the therapeutic relationship which turns the tide in a favorable direction if all goes well.

To get back to Kernberg once more, he believes that "opening one's life experiences, values, interests and emotions to the patient is of very little if any help." I believe that the opposite may frequently be true as long as the patient is not on any level an outlet for the analyst's needs. Harold Searles has creatively used personal fantasies in dealing with very troubled patients, and resisted the temptation to enter into a symbiotic cul de sac with concomitant impoverishment of the analyst's fantasy.[17]

In my own work, I have found a judicious sharing of personal experiences with patients to be a vital aspect of the therapeutic relationship. For instance, a patient brought in a dream in which I (his analyst) insisted that my meals be served to me at rigidly specified hours. It turned out that one of my alledged mealtimes coincided with one of the patient's analytic hours. In my response to the dream, I suggested that the patient sees me as a person who wants what he wants when he wants it, and who will not let anything stand in his way. Furthermore, I would not be expected to be a good listener while being fixated on my mealtime which at least once a week comes during the patient's analytic time.

It was interesting to find out that the patient had one parent to whom this pattern applied. It was equally interesting to acknowledge that at one time in my own life, I had experienced considerable anxiety when I was unable to eat at a particular time. In other words, the patient brought something from his own background into the therapeutic situation while also picking up a foible of the therapist. The important task then was to bring the two impressions into one mutually meaningful frame of reference. Let us also look at the other side of the coin. Here, the patient compulsively faults the therapist and weakens or dilutes the therapeutic alliance. There is evidence of a persistent negative transference which usually eludes the patient's attention. Under such circumstances, it proves helpful to confront the patient forcefully with his Dr. Jeckyl and Mr. Hyde image of the "good" and "bad" analyst which greatly obscures an acquaintance with the analyst as a person in his own right.

There are numerous other instances where opening one's own life experiences and emotions to the patient may be mutually a highly rewarding experience. Needless to say, that the primary focus in stepping out of the "neutral corner" is always in the direction of where the patient is in his particular life situation at that moment. It calls for genuine tact, sensitivity and a central awareness of the therapeutic alliance. Sullivan's conceptualization of the participant observer, as meaningful as it is, has certain limitations in the person-to-person encounter between patient and therapist. It focuses predominantly on the activating process of observation as the primary therapeutic tool while neglecting the sensitive monitoring of the analyst's emotional reactions as a sine qua non in the ongoing, evolving relationship. In my judgment, Sullivan's participant observer has a tendency toward splitting and reflects a potential borderline symptom in its own right.

At this point, it may be in order to offer a word of caution in this respect. Opening up to the patient should not be confused with the establishment of a narcissistic folie à deux. Borderline patients have a great penchant for bringing to the fore remnants of the analyst's narcissistic personality formation.[14] This is potentially dangerous territory in working with borderline patients. On the one hand, we may find transference cures and related flights from conflict. On the other hand, we may encounter a hostile, therapeutic integration leading to a nonproductive marathon procedure. In the first instance, patient and therapist tend to engage in a pseudorelationship of alledged mutual admiration and with careful avoidance of the patient's problems and the therapist's defensiveness. In the other situation, the therapist becomes an insatiable superego who obliges with compulsive fault-finding of the patient. The patient, under such circumstances, is cast in the role of the eternal sinner who cannot ever be redeemed. Neither party can let go in such an unfortunate "no exit" situation and both feel condemned to suffer each other until judgement day.

On the other hand, I have not found a transference psychosis to be the rule or to constitute a monumental problem in working with borderline patients. The difficulty has often been on my part an unwitting withdrawal from maintaining distinctly personal contact. In the past, I have permitted myself occasionally to be shut out by some patient without catching on to it and bringing my experience to their attention. From time to time, my mind would go blank when a patient walled himself off excessively. I then needed to find ways and means to stay alert while maintaining contact with the patient. At times, I found it difficult to let my mind wander independently rather than be overly attuned to the patient's lack of productivity. There needs to be a measure of healthy resistance on the part of the analyst against entering too far into ego-alien ideation lest the phenomenon of somnolent detachment takes over.

Finally, I would like to mention some random personal observations I have made in working with a variety of borderline patients. There is a common denominator of a general problem which is much more pronounced in these people. Most of them experience a distinct inability to be attuned to their own needs. The pursuit of simple satisfactions is often markedly impaired. There is frequently even a major limitation in the freedom to wish for things, for happenings, for occurrences, and such. I have encountered an embarrassed smile or an outright blank when I have invited such people to tell me what they desire. It is as if there were an underlying depressive pessimism which does not give license to such frivolities. Fantasies tend to be dereistic (away from reality) and not designed to lead to satisfactory experiences. Anyhow, it is my contention that borderline patients more often than not have profound difficulty in keeping in touch with their legitimate needs and desires (the old Marlene Dietrich song, "If I had a wish, it would embarrass me since I am not certain whether I should wish for good or for bad times.")

A major purpose of this paper has been the attempt to delineate the borderline syndrome as a condition sui generis. This point of view is in keeping with the conceptualization of borderline patients by R. Grinker, O. Kernberg, and A. Wolberg.[8, 10-12, 20] The difference lies largely in the dynamic formulation of the borderline phenomenon and the resulting clinical considerations.

In my judgment, all the authors above have overemphasized the element of anger and aggression as important as it is. There may be merit in looking at the anger–aggression inhibition in a different light. Generally speaking, borderline patients seem to be once removed from the immediacy of all relational emotions. I believe that a measure of awareness pertaining to frustration anger compared to primarily hostile anger is a prerequisite for making meaningful contact with another person. The same holds true in regard to nonmanipulative, nonhurtful, self-assertive aggression contrasted to power-oriented aggression with obvious destructive concomitants. In other words, I believe that the anger-aggression complex in the borderline patient is part of a larger problem connected with a phobic attitude toward intimacy and uncomplicated closeness. This is closely related to the distance-making operations which account for the isolating tendencies found in borderline patients. Here again, it probably is the negation of legitimate needs which fosters the above-mentioned phenomena. Finally, we may consider the intense underground emotions of the borderline patient to be an expression of major emotional inhibitory forces.

The discussion above emphasizes the clinical justification for making the diagnosis of a borderline patient on the basis of a particular phenomenological triad:

1.   Distinct inhibitions in the awareness and expression of anger-aggression feelings.
2.   A strong propensity for social distancing.
3.   A particular intensity of submerged, transferential emotions.

It is strongly suggested that the group of borderline syndromes be explored and dealt with outside traditional lines of neurotic or schizophrenic disturbances.

In closing, I wish to point briefly to some other considerations about borderline states. In the beginning, I suggested that there is evidence of a proliferation of borderline states judged on the basis of a cursory personal survey pertaining to patients seen privately, in clinics, and in supervision. It is my contention that a number of variables are tributary to this apparent increase.

There is evidence that society has a particular way of sanctioning borderline manifestations, that is, the societal attitude toward affectional expressions. There tends to be a polarization of emotions. On the one hand, it is "in good taste" to play it cool, to keep one's feelings well controlled, and to show predominantly the prescribed gestures in regard to love and hate. On the other hand, there is an acceptable tendency of acting-out closeness through transferential mirrors in the form of make-believe openness and artificial intimacy. The result is often an encouragement of play-acting and role-playing at the expense of personal relatedness.

There are several points that I have not covered in my discussion. One point is the necessity for safeguards in dealing with borderline patients who have strong antisocial and outright dangerous tendencies. In this situation, we are always faced with the potential risk of unwittingly reinforcing destructive character defenses. Another point is concerned with family dynamics, with the significance of primary and secondary process, with the concept of insight, and such. These topics transcend the boundaries of this paper.

At this point, I only wish to say one final word about what is different in working with borderline patients compared to working with other people. There is no inherent difference in my work with borderline patients compared to others as far as any specific set of technical maneuvers is concerned. I do not wear a different therapeutic hat in such situations. The primary difference lies in the repertory of my personality which is brought into play in dealing with borderline patients. The intensity of the transference, the powerful negative slant of it, the rigidly repressed aggression, and the nature of the fantasy life all combine in evoking feelings, and attitudes in me which are not centrally touched upon in working with others.

There is no room in my concept for the notion of a neutral corner from which we therapeutically manipulate the patient's borderline manifestations. As therapists, we are always in the midst of the therapeutic transactions.

There are numerous other details which I could mention here if it were not for the limitations of space. Instead, I summarize my major therapeutic considerations without repeating what has been stated already.

1.   Therapists working with borderline patients need to acquire an intimate know-how and a particular skill in that respect. They should be experienced clinicians who hopefully have been exposed to supervisory contact with experts in this field.

2.   I have serious doubt that therapists can help patients much beyond the level of their own unresolved difficulties. Accordingly, therapists working with borderline patients are expected to have worked through remnants of their own narcissism, their own aggression, and their own fantasy life to the point where they are not burdened by undue interference of their self-system activity.

3.   Therapists working with borderline patients should be able to set mutually meaningful therapeutic goals.

I believe that once the above-named conditions are met, we may find that it is the emergence of our basically human faculties, independently from our security operations, which provide a far reaching therapeutic commodity.

REFERENCES

1. Arieti, Silvano.: *Interpretation of Schizophrenia*, Brunner, New York, 1955.

2. Boyer, L. Bryce and Giovacchini, P. L.: *Psychoanalytic Treatment of Characterological and Schizophrenic Disorders*, Science House, New York, 1967.

3. Chrzanowski, Gerard.: Implications of interpersonal theory. In *Interpersonal Explorations in Psychoanalysis*, E. Witenberg, (Ed.), Basic Books, New York, 1970.

4. Chrzanowski, Gerard.: Symptom choice in schizophrenic manifestations. *Contemp. Psychoanal.* **4**(1):1967.

5. Chrzanowski, Gerard.: Treatment of asocial attitudes in ambulatory schizophrenic patients. In *Schizophrenia in Psychoanalytic Office Practice*, Rifkin, (Ed.), Grune and Stratton, New York, 1957.

6. Giovacchini, Peter L.: With special reference to the borderline state. *IJPP* **2**(1): February 1973.

7. Giovacchini, Peter L.: *Tactics and Techniques in Psychoanalytic Therapy*, Science House, New York, 1972.

8. Grinker, R., Werble, B., and Dyre, R. C.: *The Borderline Syndrome*, Basic Books, New York, 1968.

9. Guntrip, H.: *Schizoid Phenomena, Object Relations and the Self*, Hogarth Press, London, 1968.

10. Kernberg, Otto F.: Borderline personality organization. *J. Am. Psychoanal. Assoc.* **15**:641–685, 1967.

11. Kernberg, Otto F.: Structural derivatives of object relationships. *Int. J. Psychoanal.* **47**:236–253, 1966.

12. Kernberg, Otto F.: Treatment of borderline patients. In *Tactics and Techniques in Psychoanalytic Therapy*, Giovacchini, (Ed.), Science House, New York, 1972, pp. 254–290.

13. Khan, M. M. R.: Clinical aspects of the schizoid personality. *Int. J. Psychoanal.* **41**:430–437, 1960.

14. Kohut, H.: *The Analysis of the Self*, International University Press, 1971.

15. Rosner, S.: Problems of working-through with borderline patients. *Psychotherapy* **6**(1):1969.

16. Schmideberg, M.: The borderline patient. In *American Handbook of Psychiatry*, Vol. 1, S. Arieti, (Ed.), Basic Books, New York, 1959, Chap. 21.

17. Searles, Harold F.: Some aspects of unconscious fantasy. *IJPP*:**2**(1): February 1973.

18. Sullivan, Harry S.: *The Interpersonal Theory of Psychiatry*, Norton, New York, 1955.

19. Sullivan, Harry S.: Psychiatric training as a pre-requisite to psychoanalytic practice. In *Schizophrenia as a Human Process*, Sullivan, Norton, New York, 1962.

20. Wolberg, Arlene R.: *The Borderline Patient*, Intercontinental Medical Book Corp., New York, 1973.

CHAPTER SEVEN

NEW VIEWS ON THE PSYCHOTHERAPY OF COMPENSATION NEUROSIS: A CLINICAL STUDY

PINCHAS NOY, M.D.

Compensation Neurosis is commonly regarded as one of the most persistent psychiatric disorders, and is extremely resistant to any psychotherapeutic intervention. Most psychiatrists, frustrated by their various attempts to treat such cases, tend to declare such patients "untreatable." A "gentlemen's agreement" has gradually formed to exclude this topic from any psychiatric consideration, a state reflected by the existent discrepancy between the time and the energy invested by psychiatrists in clinical work with such patients, and the few, generally laconic, lines devoted to the subject in most textbooks.

The syndrom of compensation neurosis (CN) develops in patients who have experienced a physical or emotional trauma, acute or continuous, real or imaginary, and is therefore classified as one of the "posttraumatic" syndroms. In one of the phases following the trauma, the patient may become convinced that some person, institution, or agency is responsible for his suffering, and must therefore compensate him, whether with money, treatment, or some form of aid, or merely by readiness to admit responsibility by expressing regret or consolation. The patient gradually becomes involved in a stubborn, unyielding struggle against those he blames, whether they are real or imaginary. The struggle is then often complicated by law suits and legal court proceedings. Concomitantly with this struggle, an exacerbation of all symptoms and complaints usually occurs. It seems as if the patient somehow senses that he must persist in and nurture his illness and sufferings, which serve as his main argument in blaming those who are to compensate him. He is therefore unwilling to relinquish his illness until his claims are recognized. Psychiatrists take it for granted that because the patient, at this phase, "has no motivation for change," any attempt at psychotherapy and rehabilitation must be deferred until the legal proceedings are settled. However, since legal responsibility in such cases is very often obscure, the law suits usually take months or even years, so that the illness meanwhile becomes so chronic that no therapeutic intervention can be effective.

In reconsidering the problem of CN, we have to admit that several doubts should be expressed regarding our approach to this illness. After all, why should this illness be so refractory to any kind of psychological treatment, especially in these days when we are beginning to cope psychotherapeutically with personality disorders and psychosis? The accepted argument, that the dominant involvement of a secondary gain makes this illness so resistant to any therapeutic intervention, also does not make too much sense, since we know that hardly any neurotic state exists in which some secondary gain is not involved, whether it takes the form of expectation of love, dependency, recognition, or release from adult responsibility. The fact that some psychiatrists tend to regard monetary expectation as a more "real" motivation than expectation of love, dependency, and such, seems to reflect more their own bias and values than approved clinical evidence.

My interest in the problem of CN was aroused by the fact that I could not comprehend why therapy in such cases should be so much more difficult than in any other neurosis complicated by secondary gain. It may be assumed that if all approaches failed, then something must be wrong in our understanding of the psychopathology and dynamic background of this disorder. In other words, the failure of the psychotherapeutic approach today stems perhaps from our heading in the wrong direction.

A study of several cases convinced me repeatedly that the stubborn struggle for compensation dominating the clinical picture was never the real issue but only a displacement of another struggle, which was always, or at least in the cases I studied, a part of the long-term conflict between the patient and some other significant person in his family. Thus even the "secondary gain" is not that of money or of some other material compensation, but the gain of something within the family—status, love, dependency, and so on. To develop my argument, let me present three cases, each of which adds another angle toward understanding the problem.

CASE 1. A married man in his thirties, a father of two children, working in an academic profession, who has been suffering from a so-called discus hernia for the past several years. Over the last years he has periodically suffered "attacks," complaining of a terrible backache which confined him to bed each time for several weeks. During one of these attacks he was also treated surgically, but with no positive results. The orthopedic surgeon admitted that the roentgenologic indication was not clear and that the operation was performed mainly because of the patient's insistence.

The patient is a hard-working, responsible man, and a good father to his family. When he was "ill" and confined to bed, his wife attended him faithfully and with love, and she, his friends, and co-workers accepted him as being physically ill without ever blaming him for his illness. During the last months he enjoyed almost complete health with hardly any complaints, when a friend convinced his wife that considering her husband's illness they should be eligible to receive a tax exempt car. (In Israel there is a very high sales tax on cars, but people who can prove physical disability that restricts their movement are able to get a car without paying the taxes, the car being regarded as a "vital instrument." Such an exemption would mean buying a car at a third of its regular price.)

Upon hearing the suggestion from his wife, he at first rejected it claiming that "nobody will believe that I can't walk because of a backache." His wife, however, did not relent. At first she pressed him with arguments such as "You know how much I've always wanted a car, and we'll never be able to afford one at the regular price," or "I know of many people who have managed to get a tax exempt car with less of a disability than yours." As time went on she became more cynical and aggressive with such statements as "You are the only fool I know of who doesn't know how to take advantage of his illness," and so on, until finally she began to attack him directly saying: "At home you are a cripple, but outside you are a hero," or "If you give the medical committee the same play as you give me at home they'll automatically grant you a license for two cars," and so on.

The fellow finally gave in and began taking the formal steps in applying for such a car license, including medical certificates, committees, and such. At the same time his physical situation worsened from day to day, until he could hardly walk or stand straight. He was finally referred to a psychiatrist by the medical committee, who was greatly perplexed by the large discrepancy between his subjective complaints and the physical findings.

In a number of conjoint sessions with the couple the dynamic situation became quite clear. For years the couple had maintained a good dynamic equilibrium, where the husband could periodically "take a rest" from his adult responsibilities by legitimately regressing, under the pretense of his illness, to a semichildish position to get his wife's care, sympathy, and attention. Now, however, since his wife had turned against him, he could no longer continue the "game" which allowed him to regress periodically without losing face. His obstinate struggle for the license, which brought him from one medical committee to another and finally even to court, was in reality a struggle to restore the former family status.

In this case, a short family treatment aimed at bringing both partners to a confrontation with their problems was sufficient to halt the process of CN, and the husband's physical status gradually improved. Part of the therapeutic success, truthfully, must be granted to the orthopedic surgeon who called the wife in for a conversation and bluntly told her: "Leave your husband alone and forget your crazy idea about the car."

CASE 2.   A man in his fifties, a farmer, who came to Israel 10 years ago with his family from Yemen. He was referred to a psychiatrist after complaining for 2 years of "terrible pains in the upper abdomen," which began after he had received a kick in his belly in the course of a fight with one of his neighbors. Because of his persistent complaints, he was hospitalized several times, and even a laparatomy was performed without any findings. He filed suit against his neighbor, claiming that he was responsible for all his suffering, and he also asked for Social Security compensation. These steps brought him to court repeatedly. Except for a subcutaneous haematoma shortly after the trauma, no meaningful physical findings were ever found. None of the medical treatments he underwent had any effect on him, including phenothiazine or antidepressant drugs. During the psychiatric interview, the following story emerged.

In Yemen he had been a kind of scholar and teacher. After coming to Israel he had become a farmer but had great difficulties in adapting to his new occupation. Although he held the position of an authoritative father, as is the custom in oriental families, he depended heavily on his elder son, especially in his work on the farm. When the son enlisted in the army to serve his regular term, the father was certain that after his discharge the son would return to live on the farm. During the army service the son indeed devoted much of his vacations in working on the farm, but following his discharge he decided, to his father's despair, to leave his father's house and to take a farm of his own in the same village. The father tried hard to persuade his son to return home, promising to help him in building a new house for him and his future wife adjacent to his own house, but the son refused. This was the situation when one Saturday, before prayers had begun in the Synagogue, the patient discovered that one of the neighbors had occupied the seat usually reserved for his son, who for some reason was late that morning. While asking the neighbor to clear the seat a quarrel developed, and in the course of it the neighbor kicked him in the belly—on Saturday, in the Synagogue, before the entire community. What shame!

Naturally, after such a trauma, while the father was "seriously wounded," the son had to postpone his plans for independence and had to return home temporarily to help his father on the farm until he would recover—which never happened. With his abdominal pains the father was as if saying to his son: "Look what happened to me while defending your rights, and how can you leave me in such a condition?" By perpetuating the illness the father tried to restore the situation prior to his son's leaving, while by his claim for compensation, he hoped to receive the recognition that his suffering and weakness actually originated in the traumatic event inflicted by his neighbor.

With the aid of the community social worker, a family treatment plan was started, which included first his elder son, and then his wife and other children. The family problems were worked out, and the younger brothers were encouraged to fill the elder's son's place and to share in the responsibility of the farm while allowing the father to keep at least a part of his authority. These changes being affected, the father was gradually able to give up his symptoms and his claims for compensation.

CASE 3.   A man in his forties, married, and the father of six children, a blue collar nonprofessional worker at a large factory. While loading a truck with some other workers, a heavy case slipped and fell on his back. He was hospitalized with a suspected lumbar discus hernia. Because the diagnosis was not confirmed, he was sent home and was ordered to remain in bed and rest for a couple of weeks. His condition, however, did not improve, and for months he continued to complain of backaches, headaches, dizziness, weakness, and impotence. Even though he had received a certain sum of money as compensation, he demanded quite a larger sum, claiming permanent partial loss of his working capacity. As usually happens in such cases, the case was taken from court to court, each side bringing their own physicians to testify—these claiming that the organic findings do not explain the pains, and the others blaming the symptoms on the physical findings. In the psychiatric examination, to which he was referred by the medical committee of the "Social Security Agency," the following picture emerged.

A man of limited intelligence, he was striving hard to fulfill his duties as an authoritative father in an oriental family, working long hours to provide for his family's needs and his children's education. He was basically a weak person with strong, but latent, dependency needs. His wife, who seemed to be more intelligent than he, was a rather dominating and aggressive woman who managed to keep a facade of a passive and obedient housewife. The trauma inflicted on the husband and his consequent stay at home as a sick man dependent on his wife brought about an acute 180° shift in their interpersonal relationship. The husband became the weak, passive, and dependent party under the care of his wife who came to dominate him. What really happened was that the dyadic relationship which was latent prior to the trauma became manifest; that is, the facade of the authoritative-father-oriented family broke down to reveal the underlying state of a weak, passive husband dependent on his assertive, domineering wife.

In reaction to this shift in roles, the patient began a desperate struggle to regain his masculine status, a struggle which took place on two fronts—one, against his wife, who used every device at her disposal to maintain his present dependent situation, and the other, against his own strong regressive tendencies.

From a conversation with the social worker, who tried in vain to rehabilitate the patient, it became clear that the wife, under a facade of overconcern for her husband's physical condition, actually enfeebled her husband's sincere attempts to go back to work. Practically every time the husband went to work, the wife appeared after several hours full of concern, asking him whether he "really feels well" or is he only "trying to conceal his pain," and so always succeeded to take him back home to her care. With a few caresses she practically undermined all his authority vis-a-vis their children, urging him every time he asserted his authority over one of them to "leave it, the excitement may harm you!"

Feeling that all his attempts to cope with the problem inside the family circle were doomed to failure, the patient chose the tactics of externalization, that is, to displace the intrafamilial conflict onto his relationship with his place of work. The issue of compensation gradually became, for him and his wife, an almost magical proof of his masculine prowess. It was as if they had reached a silent agreement that only the success of getting the monetary compensation claimed would prove his return to being "a man." It was, of course, decided that the wife also had to be included in the treatment program, and in many conjoint sessions their interpersonal problems were exposed and worked out. Albeit the history of nearly a year of the *husband's* resistance to any therapeutic intervention, it soon became clear in the psychotherapeutic sessions that it was the *wife* who was the hard nut to crack. It was thus necessary to support the conjoint treatment with many individual sessions with the wife alone. Only after her deep problems concerning her relation the opposite sex were dealt with, a gradual change in her *husband's* position took place. Finally the husband returned to work while getting only a small percentage of the compensations he so persistently fought for.

These three cases may allow us to arrive at some general conclusions regarding the problem of CN as a whole. The reader may, of course, doubt the validity of any generalizations made on the basis of only three cases, especially since no attempt is made to prove these cases to be statistically representative of a larger clinical population of CN. In my opinion, however, the problem of validity can scarcely be approached statistically in any clinical study, which by its very nature is based mostly on the subjective impressions of the therapist involved. The only test of validity meaningful in such studies is the experienced reader's response: If, while reading a case presentation, he feels it to be resonant with his own clinical experience and reminiscent of several of his own cases, then the author is on the right track and his findings are therefore valid. If, on the other hand, the cases presented bear no meaning for the reader, then any derived generalization will remain irrelevant for him, even if supported by the best statistical methods. With this reservation in mind, allow me to make the following generalizations.

1. The three representative cases reported here prove that the interpersonal struggle for compensation characterizing CN always represents another existing interpersonal problem, which always seems to be an intrafamilial one.

To demonstrate this viewpoint, the first case is the most apparent one. In this case both partners were aware of the husband's use of his illness as a means of getting some sort of benefit, using it in the service of his wife as a kind of sacrifice for her sake. Such clear-cut cases are rather rare. Most cases are more similar to the second and third cases presented above, where the partners involved are relatively unaware of the underlying problem represented by the symptoms. In each of these two cases, it was as if both partners had agreed to regard the claim for compensation as the "real issue" and to use it as a convenient defense to keep the underlying problems between them latent. Sometimes, in such cases, it is only a thorough inquiry into the dynamic status of the whole family that will reveal the underlying problems. Since the struggle for compensation is only a symptom of something else, such an inquiry will therefore always be required, for no psychiatric intervention can achieve sufficient results if it is only directed at the symptom and not at the real underlying problem.

2. The kernel of the underlying intrafamilial conflict usually lies in the patient's relationship with one of his nearest relatives—a spouse, son, daughter, brother, sister, or one of the parents. The relation between the patient and this "key figure" is a typical one. The key figure is usually superior to the patient, whether in intelligence, experience, personal integrity, or aggressiveness, while the patient is in some way dependent on him. This dependency may be manifest or, as in the three cases presented above, hidden under a facade consisting of an inverse relationship where the patient seems to hold the "upper hand." It seems to me that most cases of CN are of such a dual relationship, where prior to the trauma the patient's dependency needs and regressive trends were satisfied only at a latent level. Such a bilevel relationship, by its very nature, may act as a constant source of tension between the partners involved, thus being a predisposition to possible disequilibrium in the future.

3. The original trauma leading to CN, or any other precipitating factor actually or symbolically related to this trauma, has its decisive influence by undermining the existing dynamic equilibrium between the two partners. The resulting change differs in each case, depending on the prior dynamic relationship. In the first case, it endangered the husband's regressive dependency satisfaction, while the wife became openly aggressive and "castrative" toward her husband. In the third case, the husband lost his authoritative masculine facade as a result of the trauma, and in the second case, both the father's authoritative facade and his dependency needs vis-a-vis his son were endangered. In all three cases, however, the resulting change did

not create some new relationship but only uncovered some prior, hitherto latent, situation. In most cases what happens is that the latent dominance of the "key figure" suddenly becomes manifest. This change is best demonstrated in the third case presented, where it expressed itself in a 180° inversion of the previous relationship existent between the couple.

4. The symptom of impotence present in the third case deserves some special discussion. While studying the problem of psychogenic impotence some years ago, I was impressed by the high incidence of the combination between impotence and CN. I learned from the Social Security people that they had also noted for quite some time this strange and frequent connection between CN and impotence, but they had never been able to find any explanation for the occurrence of this phenomenon in the psychiatric literature.

In studying several cases of impotence I got the clinical impression that in many of these cases an apparent inversion of the male–female roles occurred prior to the onset of impotence, especially where the symptom began after several years of normal sexual activity. Such a change is usually a part of a radical change in the family roles, where the husband, for some reason, loses his masculine status and the wife becomes dominant. The third case, where the husband complained of impotence following his trauma, is a very good example of this psychopathology. Impotence proved to be a consequence of the change in roles between the two partners, and the symptom disappeared in the course of treatment when the husband regained his masculine status within his family. I would suggest, therefore, that whenever CN and impotence are connected, it is best to explore the existing family dynamics for a role inversion between the patient and his spouse, a phenomenon which may also explain the dynamics of CN.

5. The last issue to be noted is the psychotherapeutic approach to CN. It is clear, from the discussion above, that prior to any psychotherapeutic intervention a thorough diagnosis must be made to locate the underlying intrafamilial conflict and to identify the "key figure" involved. In most cases, a family psychotherapeutic program has to be chosen to deal with the underlying conflict. Such therapy, if it is to be successful, must always include the "key figure," and often also other members of the family as well, depending on their relative involvement in the conflict. From our experience it appears that the therapy of the "key figure" is sometimes the more decisive and also has to be supported by individual psychotherapy. To achieve good results, a thorough working through of the problem has to be done with all the family members involved. In many cases, the insight gained will not by itself guarantee change, and the collaboration of a social worker will be required to aid the family in the application of the newly gained knowledge in its readjustment and actual change.

CHAPTER EIGHT

THE ROLE OF IMAGERY
IN PSYCHOTHERAPY

HANSCARL LEUNER, M.D.

I magery and visual fantasy have sporadically been examined in the early years of psychoanalysis.[8, 11-13, 41] Even Freud mentioned in 1923 in "The Ego and the Id" the close relation of "thinking in pictures" and unconscious processes.[9]* Apart from some poorly structured advice, the findings of Silberer, Jung, and Kretschmer were not followed up by systematic techniques for psychotherapy on the basis of imagery until 1945, when Desoille published his first book on "Rêve éveillée dirigé."[6] His technique originated from the Jungian and the Pawlowian concepts.

In spite of the astonishing impact that imagery had for the behavioral therapies such as the method of Wolpe, in the field of traditional psychoanalysis, only a mild stimulus was felt to approach the realm of imagery and daydreaming as an instrumental basis for theoretical and practical psychotherapy. Especially systematic examination on imagery has hardly been carried out within the frame of reference to psychoanalysis. The aspect of the mechanism of substitution, considering fantasies and daydreaming as irrealistic, was long dominant in psychoanalytic thinking. Daydreaming seemed to conflict with the necessity to confront the patient with reality. The prospective aspects of daydreaming and its relevant content of private intimacy have long been neglected.[10]

In 1948 I started a long-range experimental study of the efficacy of imagery in psychotherapy. My first publication in 1954 presented a new psychodynamic method useful for both diagnosis and for checking on the progress of therapy.[21] The method was "Experimentelles katathymes Bilderleben" (EkB), which means experimentally induced catathymic imagery.[21, 22] The term "catathymic imagery" refers to inner visions which occur in accordance with and are related to affects and emotions. It was coined by Ernst Maier, a co-worker of the late Eugen Bleuler. In the following years, I developed a clearly defined system of practical psychotherapy which is known in Germany as "Symboldrama."[21-36] The method was first made known in the United States by Swartley. His article[43] stressed the diagnostic use of the method, which he called Initiated Symbol Projection (ISP). Focusing more attention on the therapeutic aspect, R. Krojanker published an article on symbolic drama.[15] This paper presents a brief, general survey of the method with special reference to the various therapeutic tools that are used for intensive, analytically oriented psychotherapy.

On the basis of broad clinical experience, psychoanalytic training, and research done by my group and other interested therapists over the past 18

---

* ". . . it is possible for thought-processes to become conscious through a reversion to visual resides (and) in many people, this seems to be a favorite method. . . . Thinking in pictures . . . approximates more closely to unconscious processes than does thinking in words, and it is unquestionably older than the latter both ontogenetically and phylogenetically."

years, I was able to produce a sensitive instrument for psychotherapy which can provide the psychodynamic material needed for a genuine depth psychotherapy. This therapy is able to relieve acute neurotic disturbances in a short time.[17, 33, 38] Chronic cases can be treated in substantially less time than is usually needed for psychoanalysis. Cases with a history of as long as 15 years have been treated successfully.[26] The favorable results obtained with this method have persisted for follow-up periods of more than 6 years. The average treatment took 40 hours[2, 17], and the range was from 1 to 160 hours. The method is designed for step-by-step application so that even students in training can obtain good results when supervised.[30] Despite its broad applicability and efficacy in a variety of disorders, I have found that it should not be used in treating psychotics and addicts.

METHOD

The technique for applying the method of Guided Affective Imagery (GAI) is simple. The patient lies down on a couch. Outer stimuli are reduced as much as possible. The room should be quiet and the lights dimmed. The patient is then asked to relax. It may be advisable to offer some verbal suggestions to deepen the relaxation. Treatment then starts with the first standard motif, the meadow. The patient is asked to imagine a meadow—any meadow that comes to mind. No further comment is given. Everything is left as open and as unstructured as possible so that the patient can develop his own image of a meadow with its associated emotional quality. The therapist gently persists in asking the patient to give detailed descriptions of his imagery and of the feelings associated with it. The therapist is, so to speak, always the companion of the patient in his world of imagery.

How does GAI use the process of projection for therapeutic purposes? The vague suggestion offered by the therapist, for example, of a meadow, serves as a kernel or core around which the patient's fantasy production will crystallize. Subsequently, the patient's well-developed imagery of a meadow will also serve as the stage or screen onto which other actions will be projected.

It is essential to understand that when the patient is in this state of induced relaxation, the mind is functioning differently from situations of alert consciousness. During GAI, the patient's state of consciousness is similar to that which occurs in meditative states. It is often surprising to hear him excitedly describe vivid colors and detailed forms which are experienced as parts of a totally new world. The patient paradoxically seems to be living in this fantasy, while constantly being aware of the presence of the therapist. It is this experience of a "quasi-reality," with its concomitant feelings and associated affects that occur within a state of altered consciousness that we call catathymic imagery. This enhancement of emotions is the most important component of the therapeutic process. By no means is it to be explained simply in terms of abreaction.

TOOLS

Let me now consider the various specific therapeutic tools used in GAI:

1. Ten standard imaginary situations or symbolic themes are suggested by the therapist as starting points for the patient's daydream.[30]
2. Five general methods for evoking and interpreting imagery, namely:

    a. The training method.[30]
    b. The diagnostic method (ISP).[43]
    c. The method of associated imagery.[28]
    d. The symboldramatic method.[24]

Six specific techniques for guiding and managing the course of the ongoing symboldramatic events:

    (1) Inner psychic pacemaker.
    (2) Confrontation.
    (3) Feeding.
    (4) Reconciliation.
    (5) Exhausting and killing.
    (6) Magic fluids.

    e. The psychoanalytic method.

These methods overlap each other and are often used in conjunction with one another.

The Ten Standard Imaginary Situations

There are different kinds of standard situations. Some are structured simply while others have a very definite structure. The latter has themes which are designed to explore a special behavioral area, for example, sexuality. An example of a rather unstructured motif is the meadow. Nearly every acute problem can be projected into this image. There are other themes that only evoke deeply repressed dynamic material. This spectrum can be broadened to provide more information about specific dynamic patterns.[25] The various themes that comprise the 10 standard situations follow. The first three comprise the basic "training method" which is discussed in more detail later.

1. For every session, the starting point is a meadow. The symbolic meaning of the meadow is manifold. It may represent a fresh start, or it may be a screen onto which one's present mood, and most pressing problems are readily projected. It can also stand for the Garden of Eden; and, in this case, it may have deep connections to fundamental emotionality such as the nature of one's mother–child relationship.

2. Climbing a mountain and describing the view of the landscape is the second theme. To facilitate the manifestation of the second standard situation, the mountain, the patient is asked to look for a pathway on the meadow. The therapist suggests that, as he follows the path, it will lead him to a forest in the foothills of a mountain. The patient is then asked to traverse the forest, to climb the mountain, and to describe the view from the top. This symbolic situation is relevant to the patient's feelings about his ability to master his life situation and to succeed in his chosen career. It may also evoke any repressed wishes for extraordinary achievement and fame. In this connection, Kornadt[18] has shown that the altitude of one's imagined mountain is proportional to one's level of aspiration.

In terms of psychoanalysis, the mountain can also be seen as a phallic symbol. As such, it would then be related to the image of the introjected father. In that case, problems of competition are also evoked by the mountain theme. Here is an example:

A patient with a long-standing obsessive-compulsive neurosis visualized an extremely high mountain, of 24,000 feet. He saw himself standing on top of the mountain, surrounded by ice and snow. He was lonely and he was unable to climb down. This patient was a physicist who had often daydreamed about being an eminent genius like Einstein.

When the patient imagines himself as having reached the top of the mountain, he is asked to describe exactly what he can see. This procedure can be used to check on the progress of therapy. For example, at the beginning of therapy, the patient may find that his view is blocked by very high mountains or by a deep forest. In contrast, by the end of the therapy, patients tend to transform the view into a pleasant landscape with streams, hills, villages, towns, or cities. They may see themselves standing on top of the mountain, watching the traffic on the roads, or observing productive human activities in the countryside.

3. The third standard situation is to follow a brook upstream to its source or down to the ocean. After returning to the meadow from his trip up the mountain, or perhaps during the following session, the patient is asked to look around the meadow and find a brook. After describing it, he may decide for himself whether he prefers first to follow the flowing water downstream to the ocean or to take the way uphill to find the source of the brook.

The brook is supposed to symbolize the flow of psychic energy and the potential for emotional development. With neurotic patients, the imagined brook never flows down to the ocean without obvious signs of obstructions. The stream may get lost in a great hole in the ground, may be dammed by a wall, or may simply peter out. These various signs can be interpreted as signs of resistance. If the patient can be helped to focus clearly on them, unpleasant but useful feelings may be aroused. These feelings may then lead to a deeper insight into his inability to enjoy life and to develop his talents.

The meaning of a spring is well known from fairy tales and from mythology. Cool water pouring forth from the earth can be refreshing to the weary traveler. In a similar fashion, patients benefit by imagining drinking their imaginary waters and bathing in them during their daydreams. They may also benefit from rubbing the imaginary waters on those parts of their bodies which are subject to pains or other troubles, for example, the heart region in the case of a cardiac neurosis, or the forehead in the case of migraine. After imagining damming up the water, the patient may go on to see himself bathing in it for as long as he wishes. Psychoanalytically speaking, this imaginary symbolic visit to the spring can be seen as a symbol of a return to the archaic mother–child relationship. It may have both oral and uterine aspects. The intentional use of this kind of imagery for therapy can be considered an instance of an induced "regression in the service of the ego."

If the patient can be brought to an intense emotional experience of a good and refreshing spring, this will provide him with noticeable benefits. There will be a sense of relief from the pressure of his symptoms and a change of mood for the better. This therapeutic principle which is at work in this symbolic situation is called the principle of the magic fluide.[24] It belongs to the aforementioned group of techniques which are used in the management of GAI.

4. The next starting image is that of a house which is explored as a symbol of the person. It may appear spontaneously during the imagined walks through the countryside, or the therapist may suggest that the patient see a house near the meadow. Freud considered the house to be a symbol of one's personality. The patient can project all his fears and wishes about himself onto it. For example, if he visualizes a castle, he may demonstrate that he has very ambitious and grandiose expectations from life. On the other hand, if only a small hut can be visualized, this may indicate a serious lack of self-esteem. Dynamically important parts of the house are explored after the patient has stepped in: the storage of food in the kitchen and refrigerator, the toilet facilities, the sleeping quarters with special regard to the presence of double or single beds, the contents of the closets. Often a

young female patient may find her own clothes stored in close proximity to her father's. Of further interest are both the cellar and the attic because they often contain reminders of one's childhood such as toys or family albums. These may lead back to significant childhood events. This is illustrated by the following case:

A twenty-four-year-old woman was treated for severe psychogenic headaches. In the cellar of her imaginary house she found an old trunk. When asked to open it, she saw an old black coat and beneath it were the two old pairs of pants. She soon realized that she had owned a coat like this when she was fourteen and that the two pairs of pants belonged to her father and her grandfather. In fact, she had had a close relationship with her grandfather after her parents were divorced. This spontaneous imaginary juxtaposition of her clothes with those of her father and her grandfather were used to elucidate and resolve an oedipal problem.

These four standard situations, the meadow, the mountain, the brook, and the house, together with the tasks that are given to the patient, are the "elementary approach" (Unterstufe) of this method. Repetitive training in GAI using these images enables the therapist-trainee to practice the simpler form of therapy from the very beginning.

5. The fifth standard task is to visualize a close relative. The appearance of a closely related person may be suggested to the patient while he imagines himself in the meadow. The patient is asked to watch this relative from a distance, to describe his behavior, and to note especially his attitude toward the patient when the person approaches him. Closely related persons such as father or mother may appear. One may also imagine one's boss, spouse, siblings, or other significant figures.

A father may arrive angrily and shout at the patient; another person may ignore the existence of the patient; and in another case, the father may address the patient with a friendly "Hi!". These are all helpful indices of the quality of the patient's emotional relationships. The patient's father and mother may also be concealed in symbolic figures, such as an elephant and a cow. These figures to avoid the resistances which naturally would arise if the patient were questioned directly about his parents. In the case of a female patient in her late fifties, the imaginary elephant stomped toward the patient as she was lying on the grass, then put a big foot on her breast. The patient reacted with anxiety and shortness of breath; and to calm her, the therapist reassured her of his presence. he insisted that the patient should put up with the uncomfortable situation and see it through. This daydream symbolized a traumatic event from her thirteenth year. Once, when she appeared to be asleep, her father touched her breast and commented on her attractively developing body to her mother.

6. The patient may be asked to visualize situations apt to evoke pat-

terns of sexual feelings and behavior. To a female patient, I offer the following situation: She is to imagine that she has taken a long walk by herself in the countryside or, perhaps, that her car broke down on a lonely road far from home. In either event, another car comes along, stops next to her, and the driver offers her a lift.

There are innumerable possibilities: (a) *No* car comes at all; (b) A little boy arrives, driving a toy automobile; (c) The car is driven by a woman; (d) The car stops, but as the patient steps into it, it vanishes into thin air; (e) The driver of the car seems sexually inclined; he drives the car into a forest and the woman becomes frightened.

For male patients, I borrow the convenient symbol of a rosebush from a poem by Goethe, "Sah ein Knab' ein Roeslein stehn." The standard situation is the suggestion that the patient will see a rosebush in a corner of the meadow. I then ask him to describe the rosebush.

It is important to note whether the rosebush is big or small, whether the roses are "those sweet, nice, tiny, white flowers," as one young man put it, or whether they are deep red, full-sized blossoms. The essential test consists in having the patient pick one of the roses to bring it home and put it in a vase on his desk. The first young man of whom I spoke refused to pick the rose at all. He protested that it was too nice and sweet to be picked. An older man picked his rose so hastily that he got pricked by the thorns.

7.   The seventh standard motif is a lion. It can be aroused simply in response to the therapist's suggestion to visualize a lion. It may be seen in narrow cage, in the jungle, or on a desert.

The lion is a useful test for showing the patient how he deals with his aggressive tendencies. To do this, I ask him to visualize a person whom he dislikes very much. Then, to imagine that this person and the lion are brought face to face. He is to watch and describe the lion's behavior.

There was a salesman who, although physically sound, had a cardiac neurosis and various vegetative disturbances. These symptoms came on after a disliked customer had struck him lightly on the stomach. A year later, he was still unable to work. When I tried to get the lion to confront my patient's adversary, the animal reacted like a shy dog. It became smaller and smaller and it lay down at the feet of the patient. By the end of the therapy, the situation was quite different. Now the lion was ready to attack the adversary and swallow him without resistance from the patient. He had developed a much stronger feeling for his own rights and no longer felt like an underdog. Therapy took 25 hours, and there were no recurrences of symptoms during a 6-year follow-up period.

8.   The eighth standard motif is the manifestation in fantasy of a person who represents the patient's ego ideal. This can be achieved by asking the patient to quickly say a name of a person of his own sex and then to imagine a person who could be the bearer of this name. He then usually vi-

sualizes a person he would like to be. This is helpful for working through the problem of identity.

9. Certain imaginary situations facilitate the appearance of symbolic figures representing deeply repressed material, such as looking into a dark forest from the meadow, and for deeper-rooting material, looking into the dark opening of a cave. A witch, a giant, or other such fear-evoking creatures, usually of the same sex as the patient, may come out. These images symbolize introjects with their neurotic and associated affects.

For this standard situation, the patient should imagine taking a concealed position at a respectful distance from the forest or cave. When the creature approaches, the patient is to watch it carefully and to describe it. These two situations readily evoke symbolically important figures. Coming out of the dark depths of the forest, which symbolizes the unconscious, the figures are generally spontaneous manifestations of deeply repressed, sometimes archaic, instinctual material.

10. In the tenth standard situation, the patient is asked to imagine a swamp in a corner of the meadow. The therapist suggests that a figure will arise out of its murky waters. This may be a frog, a fish, a snake, or a human figure. This symbol is the manifestation of deeply repressed and sometimes archaic instinctual material concerning the sexual drive and its derivates.[22] These symbolic figures may be affect-laden animals which, in terms of Jung's theory, could be interpreted as archetypes. Because the patient may be intensely frightened by this image, the therapist must be experienced in the use and control of these situations. He must know how to protect the patient from too violent an upsurge of anxiety. In this case he may use either of two techniques, namely symbol confrontation or feeding, which are described later.

It should be borne in mind that noxious after-reactions may also occur if this technique is not handled carefully. The simplest way to deal with these symbolic figures as they develop and emerge from the patient's imaginary forest or the swamp is just to let them come out. The woods and the earth are excellent symbols of the unconscious, and, therefore, the act of bringing up these figures to the surface is equivalent to bringing them into consciousness.

Although I have learned a great deal about symbolism from the Jungian school, I do not see any reason to employ its rather "mystical" theory as long as there is an adequate theoretical framework which is more down to earth. My experience converges with the findings of Boss[4] who believes that these archaic affect-laden symbols can be explained in terms of the induction of a deep regression with marked intensification of emotional experiences from early childhood. This position is fostered by GAI expériences in which archaic symbols such as snakes and fish show constant transformation along the lines of phylogenetic development during the therapeutic process. At the end of the chain of transformation and as its result, there often appears a figure of a closely related person such as the patient's father or mother.[22]

Five General Methods for Guiding Affective Imagery

To deal effectively with these symbols, I employ the previously mentioned five general methods. All of these different methods can be combined as the situation and the case may require.

The First Three Images and Their Use Together as the Training Method. This technique is especially useful for those patients who are unable to release their imaginations to create freely a sequence of pictorial associations. In the majority of cases, such patients are either naive and uneducated or are overintellectualized persons with little awareness of their own emotions. In these cases it is the procedure to let the patient practice visualizing and describing the first four themes: the meadow, the mountain, the brook and the house. This repetitive procedure, using the least provocative symbols, trains both the patient and the inexperienced therapist. It requires no special skill or understanding of symbolism on the part of the therapist. A certain degree of empathy and sensitivity is of course necessary. Using the elementary approach can serve as a first step to introduce our method both to the patient and to the trainee.

The Diagnostic Method: Initiated Symbol Projection (ISP). The 10 standard themes can also serve as screens for psychodiagnostic purposes. Under these circumstances, they take the place of the pictures of a projective test such as the Thematic Apperception Test (TAT). For example, the first theme, a meadow, is vague enough to permit all kinds of variations. Everybody can create his own very personal kind of meadow. Later, the patient can be asked for a detailed description of his meadow. He may even paint a picture or draw a map of it.

The strictly diagnostic procedure, the ISP technique, is carried out like a projective test and is different from the therapeutic procedure as far as its goals and the nature of the responses evoked are concerned. All relevant standard situations are explored one after the other in a short time. ISP may take from one to three sessions. The following points are checked.

1.   The qualities of the different motifs such as the meadow, the mountain, the rosebush, the house.

2. The factors that inhibit progress on the given tasks such as accompanying the brook or climbing the mountain.

3. Registering incompatible situation; for instance, in the landscape two seasons may occur at the same time, or the refrigerator in the house may contain no food.

4. The nature of the emerging symbolic figures and their behavior. The latter can be tested by having the patient approach the figures and describe his feelings.

It should be clearly pointed out that the diagnostic method (ISP) is different from the therapeutic procedure. For diagnostic purposes, one tries to get a wealth of imaginative content. To accomplish this, it is generally necessary to guide the patient quickly through a variety of imaginary situations. This speed tends to prevent the development of intense feelings in response to any of the several diagnostic images. By contrast, when directing therapy, one seeks the underlying and deeper emotions that only manifest themselves gradually and in connection with a slower pace of imagery. Because this takes time, the therapist errs if he rushes the patient from one imaginary situation to another.

When GAI is used for therapeutic purposes, the diagnostic approach is naturally always involved. The therapist is continuously "reading" and interpreting the symbolic contents of the GAI experiences to connect them provisionally with the known life history and the dynamics of the patient.

One of the most fascinating points of GAI is that the therapist gets a survey of the main dynamics and subconscious problems of his patient within a short time. This is due to the clarity of GAI symbolism and its self-explanatory character. By having a patient redream a nightdream, one can use GAI to check on the meaning of the dream symbols.

One phenomenon which occurs during the course of GAI is especially useful diagnostically. I have called it "mobile projection." When a suggestion or an interpretation by the therapist is relevant to the meaning of the patient's imagery, it is followed by a sudden transformation of the picture. This apparently occurs because of the sensitivity of GAI imagery to every small change in emotions, whether conscious or not. For instance, if the therapist leaves the room momentarily during the course of a GAI session, the current state of the transference is likely to be reflected in a change in the patient's imagery. These "microdiagnostic" manifestations reflect the course of even the smallest details of the therapeutic process. In this way, GAI can be used as a check on the likely influence of any therapeutic procedure or spontaneous influence on the patient's psyche before he shows any behavioral change. The effects of long-term therapy, whether

GAI, psychoanalysis, counseling, or any other technique, will be manifested in transformations in the landscape of the meadow, in changes in the view from the top of the mountain, and in changes in the ways in which the other themes are structured in the patient's imagery.[22, 24, 25] In view of the stability of neurotic patterns, the results of these informal experiments with this phenomenon appear to be highly significant.

Again, a sharp distinction must be drawn between the therapeutic application of GAI and the use of the method for diagnosis (ISP). When the purpose of evoking imagery is diagnostic, one foregoes the possibility of helping the patient to develop intense emotional reactions to his own imagery. If a diagnostic ISP is carried out at the slower tempo that is more suited to the therapeutic purpose, the subject to be diagnosed may build up resistances to his own imagery, and these resistances may subsequently impede the course of GAI therapy. Therefore, for practical purposes, it is generally better to dispense with a full-scale diagnostic ISP before initiating GAI therapy. And during the course of therapy, it is advisable to limit one's diagnostic probing and to rely on the patient's spontaneously produced imagery. To put it in a nutshell, it is wise not to mix up ISP with the therapeutic technique of GAI.

The Third Method: Associated Imagery. The most spontaneous procedure of all is the use of associated imagery.[28] The well-known process of free association in psychoanalytic technique is applied to the patient's imagery, and the patient is encouraged to allow the free and spontaneous development of a series of pictures. They may occur with or without symbolic figures. In this case, one does not channel the patient's productions even if it is apparent that his imagery is becoming increasingly frightening. Nor does one sidestep deeply painful contents such as anxiety dreams. All one does is to help the patient see his daydream through to the bitter end. This vividly developed' imagery happens only in those patients who are good at fantasy production or who have had long experience in GAI. Then one very often finds "self-interpretation" of the symbolic image. This sometimes happens while the patient is experiencing a deep and spontaneous age-regression in which he relives an early childhood experience. Sometimes these experiences lead the patient back as far as the first year of life.

Barolin[1] has investigated the value of age-regression in therapy. It had previously been observed only in deep hypnotic states[7, 30] or during long-term analytic treatment. Those who have worked with GAI have learned how to extend the time scale of associative imagery. I do it by encouraging the patient to link the symbolic GAI experiences with both past events and with the here-and-now of his current life situation. The common denominator which links these various images from different periods of the patient's life is the shared feeling-tone. I ask the patient what he is feeling when he is in a particular imaginary situation, and I expect him to learn how to sharpen his awareness of the feelings that are arising from within himself. I may, for example, ask him about the atmosphere surrounding an unusual situation in the meadow, on top of the mountain, in the explored house, or elsewhere. When the patient finds himself facing a symbolically significant figure, one should be especially alert in asking him about the message in its eyes or the feeling that emerges from its whole facial expression. The bridge between the etiologic background and the present neurotic pattern is found in the answer to the question as to where the patient has previously experienced a similar feeling, seen a similar emotional expression of the eyes, or seen a facial expression like the one in his daydream. The verbal description of all the details of his picture and of the concomitant feeling-tone of his GAI experience clarifies preconscious GAI contents and raises them to the threshold of consciousness. By repeatedly focusing on the problem in question, an insight may occur as a sudden "Aha!" experience. I try then to relate the patient's GAI productions to the here-and-now by asking him in what way the emotional quality of this experience is similar to any experiences in his daily life and if it reminds him of his attitude toward any person or of his feelings about any specific life situation. This approach may develop insights into neurotic character structure and may uncover resistances to treatment.

To effect this kind of progress, the therapist must have both experience and psychoanalytic training. In both dependent and defensive patients, the neurotic character defenses should be analyzed by this technique as early as possible. This is the easiest way to work through resistances. It can be as important, or even more so, as the analysis of transference in classical psychoanalytic procedure.

Here is an example that illustrates how this new technique can be used:

During the workshop on GAI, a colleague offered to be a subject. Instead of developing the desired catathymic imagery, he visualized an event that had occurred on his trip to the meeting. He had stopped to visit a former female patient who had suffered from anorexia nervosa. Her faith in him had always touched him deeply. While daydreaming under relaxation, he reexperienced his meeting with her. I then told him to describe the expression in the girl's eyes. He big eyes seemed to look at him imploringly. They indicated that she was seeking his help and was full of trust in him. He was then asked whether he had ever before seen eyes with a similar expression. After a short pause, he said that he now remembered the epileptic fits that his mother used to have when he was a small boy. After she awoke from a seizure, she used to look at him, and her eyes expressed the same feelings that he now saw in the eyes of the girl. In this way, this man discovered a deep motive for his decision to become a physician.

The Symboldramatic Method: The Six Techniques for Guiding and Managing Imagery. Symboldrama is the general term originally applied to the standard therapeutic method of GAI. In this section, several specialized techniques used in symboldramatic psychotherapy are described.[24]

Experience has shown that the less the therapist guides the patient, that is, the fewer suggestions he gives and the less active he is, the better the therapy. Therefore, the techniques of management discussed in this section are only used when specifically indicated. The symboldramatic approach includes six techniques of management. They have proved highly effective for treatment. Moreover, in special cases, they are very useful for compensating an acute neurotic reaction. These different tools are the (a) inner psychic pacemaker, (b) confrontation, (c) feeding, (d) reconciliation, (e) exhausting and killing, (f) and magic fluids.

INNER PSYCHIC PACEMAKER. The patient should be given as much responsibility as possible for the direction and development of his own treatment. There appears to be a spontaneous inner pacemaker whose influence over the treatment process can be invoked by the GAI method. This is accomplished by asking the patient to let himself be guided by one of his own benign symbolic figures. For example, a horse, an elephant, a camel, or another animal may be mounted by the patient. One can then wait for the animal to guide the patient. Similarly, the patient may have manifested in his GAI productions either a good fairy or a nourishing mother-figure. If so, the function of guidance can be transferred over to this particular figure.

When the patient manifests kind and helpful images, their existence suggests often the presence of hitherto repressed childhood experiences with a positive mother-figure. This new and positive development can benefit the patient by providing him with new strength. Paradoxically, these feminine images can help to develop the sense of masculinity in a male patient. The improvements will be expressed both in his feelings and in the transformed content of his imagery.

CONFRONTATION. Confrontation[23] is one way of dealing with the archaic, symbolic figures which emerge from the forest, the cave, and the swamp. When a patient imagines that a big snake is coming out of a swamp and is attacking him, it is often difficult for the therapist to decide what remedy to suggest. Should one tell him to run away or should one tell him to fight it? Neither action seems to be therapeutically helpful. The first suggestion would encourage the patient to act in a cowardly fashion while the latter would be unrealistic because one does not know whether the patient would really be able to overwhelm the snake. Confrontation is a subtle alternative and using a very active technique. Its use requires an experienced therapist who is able to tolerate intense emotional outbursts from his patients. In the case of an aggressive snake, the therapist would insist that the patient neither run away from the animal nor struggle with it. (This latter alternative appeals to many patients, but they should usually be discouraged because it may be dangerous.) Instead, the therapist tells the patient to hold his ground, to stay put, to suppress his anxiety, and to apply a very old practice—to neutralize the creature by staring at its eyes. The patient is constantly encouraged to combine staring at the creature with a detailed description of every single spot of its head and facial features: the mouth, the teeth, the eyes, the movement, the emotional quality of the facial expression, and so forth.

An important feature of the method of confronting frightening symbolic images is the persistent staring into the eyes of the frightful creature. Its purpose is to discover the message or meaning which the creature's existence conveys and to banish the creature henceforth from one's daydreams. During this confrontation, the therapist actively supports the patient by listening to his description of the monster, by repeating the above-mentioned instructions, and by holding his hand, if necessary, to give him moral support.

Although the confrontation procedure may last only from 10 to 30 minutes, something very remarkable happens during this time. A genuine transformation occurs. The frightening animal may become weaker and smaller, and it may sooner or later be transformed into another creature. As a rule, this new animal stands higher in the line of phylogenetic development than the earlier one. The snake, for instance, may be transformed into a bird, later on into a mammal, and, finally, into the threatening mother-in-law of the patient who may stand in front of him, showing that the original symbol was a mother-derivative. Psychoanalytically speaking, the end result of successful confrontation is a strengthening of the ego.

FEEDING. Feeding is the mildest way to deal with the frightening symbolic figures that emerge from the forest, the cave, or the swamp. It is therefore suitable for use by less experienced therapists. It is a good way for a patient to deal with aggressive or dangerous symbolic figures. For instance, suppose a giant comes out of a cave. He is angry and wants to kill the patient. What can the patient do? It would probably be impossible even to try the principle of confrontation. So I tell the patient to imagine feeding the creature. Of course, the food should be provided in sufficient quantity, and the therapist should be ready to offer suggestions as to what kind and how much food should be fed to the creature. In the case of a giant, I might tell the patient that a convoy of trucks is arriving and that each is loaded with beef carcasses. The patient's task is to feed all this meat to the giant. It is possible that the giant may at first refuse to eat. But with the help of some suggestions, he will start to do so. Now it is the task of the patient to feed the giant as much as possible. That means that the giant has to be fed much more than one might think he needs. This overfeeding is very important. What typically happens is that the giant loses his aggressiveness, gets drowsy, lies down, and goes to sleep.

In this symbolic fashion, the patient learns subconsciously that he can face frightening aspects of his own psyche, he can give them their due recognition, and he can work out a modus vivendi with them. Subsequent confrontations may well lead to transformations of the frightening giant into a milder, more benign symbol.

RECONCILIATION. The technique of reconciliation can in some cases be used as a supplementary tool to the principles of confrontation and feeding. All three can often be combined. The essential purpose of reconciliation is to make friends with hostile symbolic figures by addressing them, by touching them physically (e.g., stroking them), and by showing tenderness toward them in different ways. Of course, the patient can be expected to show resistance to these suggestions and may even refuse to imagine doing any of these things. He may be too frightened at first to touch an animal, and he may even have to be pushed a little and to be encouraged by a therapist. Here is an example to illustrate these techniques:

A twenty-one-year-old student of chemistry had failed an important examination. He showed good knowledge of his subject when examined by a junior faculty member, but when he was subsequently tested by his professor, he was emotionally so disturbed that he was unable to demonstrate his competence. He came to see me late in the afternoon of the day before he was scheduled for a reexamination. I knew his family quite well. He had a very authoritarian father who had caused some of his neurotic difficulties. In discussing the situation with the young man, I found my suspicion confirmed when he confessed that his chemistry professor was an older and quite strong-looking man toward whom he felt quite ambivalent. We then engaged in the following guided daydream. After imagining the meadow, I asked the young man to look into the darkness of the forest and to wait until his professor would emerge from it. There was dinstinct resistance, and it took me some time and several suggestions before the professor appeared. And when he did so, he ignored the patient completely. My young man was too shy to meet him and to greet him. So I had to develop new suggestions to encourage the patient. At last he tried to address his teacher and to shake hands with him, but the teacher reacted negatively. After the patient had started a conversation, he seemed well on the way to success in his efforts to make friends with the professor. But this did not seem enough to make sure of the result I wanted, namely, to enable the young man to do a good job at the examination the next morning. I then brought in the feeding technique and told the patient to unpack all the things which would be desirable for a really nice picnic. He reached into his pockets where he found, with the help of suggestions, sandwiches, a chicken, and a bottle of good wine. He invited his teacher to a picnic. After some hesitation, the professor agreed and both were soon enjoying the meal. At this point, the patient's task was to imagine feeding the teacher as much as possible giving him more than one would think that he would be able to eat. After the imaginary picnic, they separated in a good mood, laughing and slapping each other on the back. After the daydream was over, the patient was told to repeat this feeding daydream at home before falling asleep. The next morning he was quite relaxed and experienced no emotional disturbance during the examination. He passed with a fairly good mark.

Without going into the details of theory, I believe that I was able to shift the balance of the patient's ambivalent emotional attitudes concerning the father–professor image by literally overcoming the hostile feelings which the patient projected onto the imagined person. In the case above, this image of the feared professor is a part of the patient himself; namely, a derivative of the introjected father. The imaginary act of making friends with the professor assimilates this introject which has beeen rejected, split off from the young man's psyche, and projected onto the professor. It also separates this particular father–derivative, "professor," from the more powerful father-introject and differentiates between the two.

EXHAUSTING AND KILLING.   The technique of exhausting and killing is the most dangerous tool in the management of GAI. This tool should only be used by experienced therapists. It can be very powerful and helpful, but there is the risk that it may be experienced by the patient as an attack against himself. This will depend on whether the attacked symbolic figure is a more peripheral derivative of an introject or the introject itself.

As a consequence of an automobile accident, a thirty-four-year-old woman suffered from a hypochondria which made her feel she would soon die. Although free from any organic trouble, she remained weak and would not leave her bed. In her imagery, she saw Death emerge out of the trunk of the tree against which her husband had driven his car. Death was brought forth into the daydream, and now was forced (by suggestion) to run into the countryside with the intention to exhaust him. When he wanted to sit down for a rest, he was pushed on. At one time, he tried to hide in a cornfield; on another occasion, he ran into the patient's home and wanted to rest on her couch. Arriving at the market place of the town, he was derided by the crowd. At last he arrived at a stream and fell into it. The waters dissolved his bones which fell away from each other. The next day, the patient's fear of death had vanished. She got up and for the first time since becoming ill, she began to do some housework.

MAGIC FLUIDS.   The imaginary use of magic fluids has already been discussed in connection with the spring. But it is by no means only at a spring where the patient can experience the comfort of fresh water. I know some fine examples of the benefit a patient gets from an imaginary bath in the brook or from a swim in the sea. Besides spring water, there are other magic fluids such as cow's milk, mother's milk, spittle, and urine. The imaginary application of these various fluids for the relief of bodily aches and pains must always be done carefully because the reactions can be ambivalent. Much depends on whether a patient feels comfortable subjectively with what we are trying to accomplish in a given instance. In other words, the patient must understand and accept the purpose and goal of treatment.

The Psychoanalytic Method.   In psychoanalysis, the patient's productions are of two distinct kinds. There are the nightdreams, which are reported during the therapeutic hour as memories, and there are the free associations to the contents of these dreams. Each occurs at different times, under different circumstances, and at different levels of consciousness. Bridging these gaps depends on the interpretive skill of the psychoanalyst. By contrast, GAI offers a more integrated therapeutic procedure; "dreamwork" (as daydreams) and "couchwork" of various kinds are combined in a single session. This permits the patient to experience different levels of consciousness in the course of the session itself. Under the protection and guidance of the therapist, the patient can move back and forth between image and concept, between feelings and understanding, between the fears of the past and the potentialities of the future.

It is my impression that GAI is an effective treatment method because it juxtaposes the repressed aspects of the personality that are associated with a regressive mode of ego-functioning with the more mature ego; it promotes their interaction, and in so doing, it encourages a productive integration of primary and secondary processes. The combination of psychoanalysis with the GAI method is especially useful for dealing with difficult cases of longstanding character neuroses.

The GAI can be applied to psychoanalytic therapy in two ways:

1.   One can have the patient develop chains of associations to the various images which arise in the daydream.

2.   The GAI may be used when a patient is unable to recall his dreams or when signs of persistent resistance are encountered.

In the case of apparently insolvable resistance, therapist and patient can often get useful information about the reasons for resistance through the imagery which spontaneously arises within the standard motifs.

To check the therapeutic effect of GAI, a controlled study has been made on 14 unselected patients with character neurosis, phobias, and psychosomatic disorders.[33] To prove the value of GAI as a short-term therapy individual treatments were limited to 15 sessions (50 minutes each, two per week). The therapist was a first year student having passed the training program for general practitioners to acquire the supplementary term "Psychotherapy" (enabling him to practice psychotherapy). He was supervised by the author. The method of GAI was limited to the technically simple elementary approach (Unterstufe), especially designed for trainees in psychotherapy with the goal to guide the patient through the first four standard motifs promoting abreactions, spontaneous associations, and insights. No interpretations, no analysis of resistance and transference were given (the latter mainly remains "positive" in the course of short-term psychotherapy with GAI). The study was designed especially to examine the value to the elementary approach for short-term therapy.

Besides a 3-hour semistandardized interview, a test battery was applied before and after therapy, consisting of Raven[37]; Scale for Intro-extraversion, Neuroticism and Rigidity; Pf (Brengelmann and Brengelmann)[3]; Manifest anxiety (Taylor)[44]; MMPI[49]; Scale for Psychosomatic complaints (Giessener Beschwerdenliste)[45]; and Mental symptoms (Göttinger Beschwerdenliste).

Two groups of patients were formed: (1) GAI group and (2) control group without any psychotherapeutic care (waiting list), 14 subjects each.

The results summed up for this study are given in compared schemes of Pf and MAS.

The summary profile (Figure 1) gives little evidence in the efficacy of GAI, since in a small group of neurotics such as the one presented here, because of its heterogeneity, the individual cases suspend each other. Therefore, for better clinical transparence, two abbreviated case histories are outlined.

CASE 1 (J. F.).   Eighteen year old male Gymnasium student. For two years excessive use of Haschisch and LSD, dealer and prominent figure in the drug scene of a small town, drop out, broken home situation, neurotic depressive state, instable, immature personality, fairly well motivated for therapy for which he himself asked the doctor, Raven III.

Results of 15 sessions GAI elementary approach within 15 weeks follow:

CLINICAL EVALUATION.   Decrease of symptoms; socially less depressive, left drug scene and stopped drug abuse, left his neurotic mother and decided by himself to continue his studies in a boarding school (Gymnasium) with good results (follow-up period half year).

CASE 2 (J. B.).   Thirty-nine-year-old female, married, two children: for 9 years periodically neurotic depressive states and obsessive deathphobia, chronic disturbance in sleep, spastic pain of gall bladder and abdomen, acné excoriée, a very rare psychosomatic skin disease, instable personality, infantile character traits, Raven I.

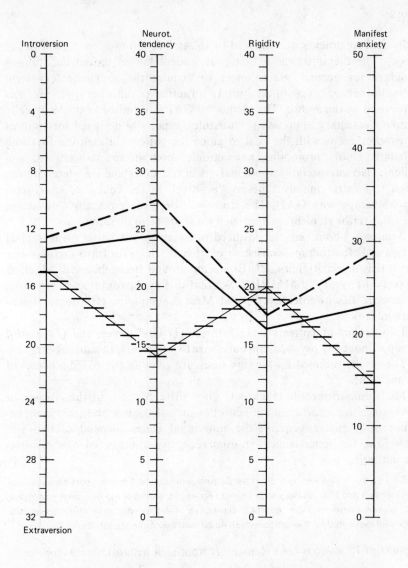

Figure 1. Profile of 14 cases before and after 15 sessions of treatment with GAI (54 days). In neuroticism and rigidity a tendency of reduction is evident. Manifest anxiety is significantly reduced.

PF and MAS:

E   12.5 → 13.2
N   27.9 → 24.7   (−11.46%)
R   17.9 → 16.4   (−8.3%)
A   28.9 → 23.5   (−19.4%)

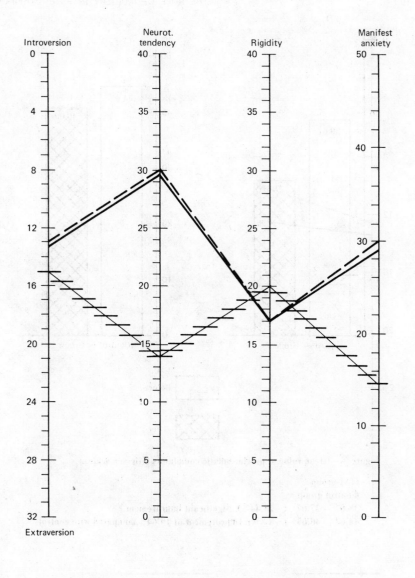

Figure 2.   Profile of the control group (waiting list 46 days). In none of the scales even a slight tendency of change can be seen.
PF and MAS:

E   13.9 → 13.3
N   30.0 → 29.6
R   17.0 → 17.0
A   29.7 → 29.9

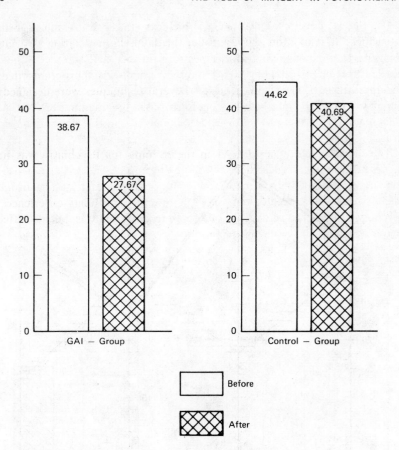

Figure 3.   Mean value of psychosomatic complaints (Giessen scale).

GAI-group
Control group
38.67 → 27.67   (−28.44%). Significant improvement.
44.62 → 40.69   (−8.8%). Improvement of 19.64% compared with control.

Results of 15 sessions GAI follow:

CLINICAL EVALUATION. Obsessive phobias as well as the above-mentioned spastic symptoms disappeared totally, improvement of sleep disturbance and depressive states, also marked improvement of the acné excoriée (proven by independent examination University Hospital for Dermatology).

The latest development of GAI includes the use of music which intensifies the relaxation and intensifies the daydream activating associated imagery. It expands the indication spectrum for this method.[27, 32, 34] Playing music (tapes or records) of selected and specially prepared programs[34] led to the application of GAI with groups.[36] Several techniques were designed to develop close group interaction being mirrored in the imaginations of GAI[39] This method also has proven to be highly effective in the psychotherapy of drugabusers.[14, 31]

The didactic relevance of GAI in the training for Psychiatry was first described by Kosbab (Medical College of Virginia).[19] The self-experience of the trainees in symbolism, experiencing associations and gaining insights under supervision, results not only an intensive personal experience in psychodynamics, in a way comparable with training analysis, but also effects changes in character patterns of the subject.

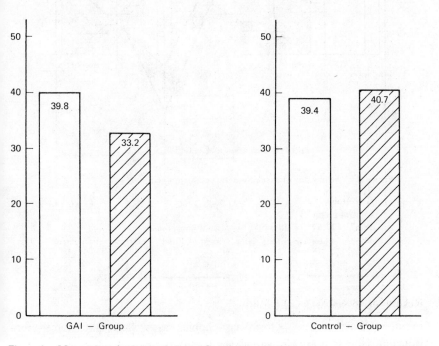

Figure 4.   Mean value of mental symptoms (Goettingen scale).
   39.8 → 33.2   (– 16.58%). Control group.
   39.4 → 40.7   (+3.29%). Difference between active and control group with 19.87% (significant) improvement.

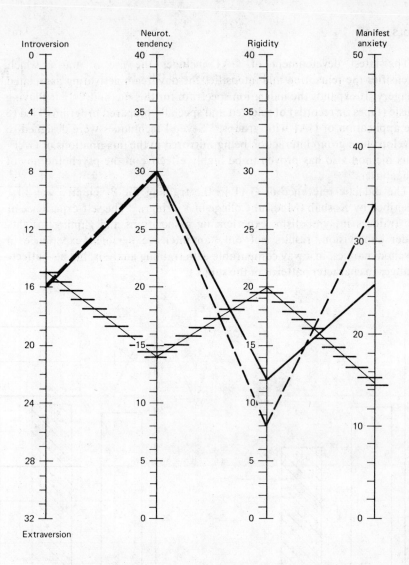

Figure 5.   Pf and MAS.

     E   **16 → 16**
     N   **30 → 30**
     R   **8 → 12** **(+50.0%)**

The increase of rigidity of 50% can be considered as improvement of ego strength.

     A 34 → 25 **(−26.5%)**

Shows a significant reduction of manifest anxiety.

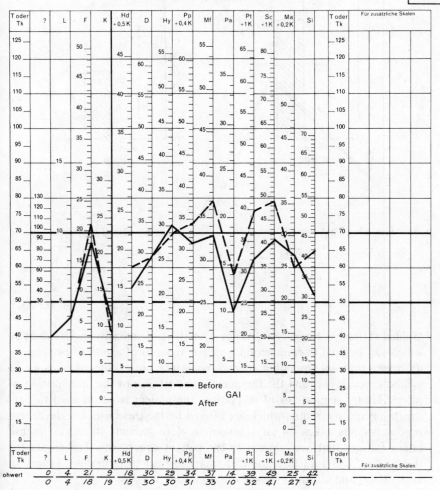

MMPI - SAARBRÜCKEN
Profilblatt

M
Männlich

T oder Tk	?	L	F	K	Hd +0,5 K	D	Hy	Pp +0,4 K	Mf	Pa	Pt +1 K	Sc +1 K	Ma +0,2 K	Si	T oder Tk	Für zusätzliche Skalen

Before GAI

After

ohwert	0	4	21	9	18	30	29	34	37	14	39	49	25	42		
	0	4	18	19	15	30	30	31	33	10	32	41	27	31		

Figure 6.   MMPI. Significant improvement in Mt, Pa, Pt, Sc, and Sci.

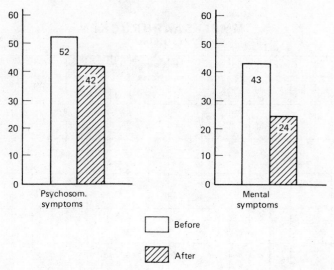

Figure 7.   Psychosomatic complaints.   Figure 8.   Mental symptoms.

52 → 42   (– 19.23%)   43 → 24   (C44.00%)

SUMMARY

Guided Affective Imagery (GAI) is a method of intensive psychotherapy which can be used in conjunction with any theoretical aspect of personality dynamics that acknowledges subconscious motivation, the significance of symbols, resistance, and the therapeutic importance of the mobilization of affect. Under suggestions of relaxation, the patient is encouraged to day-dream on specific motifs which are offered by the therapist. The daydream process usually takes on an autonomous development. It evokes intense latent feelings that are relevant to the patient's problems. Techniques for the guiding and transformation of imagery lead to desirable changes in both affects and attitudes toward life situations.

The GAI has been applied successfully in patients with neuroses, psychosomatic disturbances, and in borderline states. It seems to be contra-indicated either with psychotics or with addicts. Therapists who are psychoanalytically trained and who are skilled in dream interpretation will find this method congenial. An abbreviated form is especially useful for training student therapists. The GAI is suitable for short-term psychotherapy. Also, it is less dependent on the patient's ability to verbalize accurately his emotional problems than is the case with conventional methods.

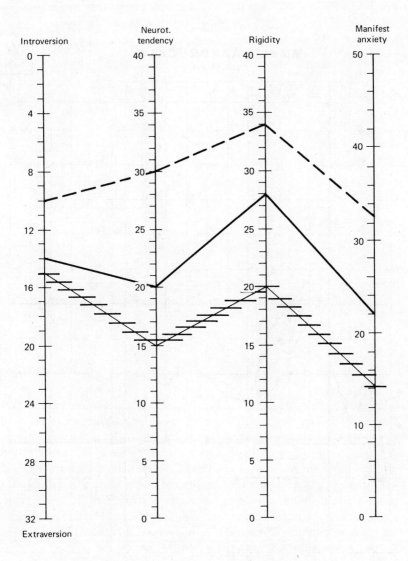

Figure 9. Pf and MAS.

E   10 → 14   (+40.0%)
N   30 → 20   (−33.3%)
R   34 → 28   (−17.6%)
MA 33 → 22.5 (−31.8%)

All scores show a significant improvement, only R shows a tendency to reduction.

MMPI - SAARBRÜCKEN
Profilblatt

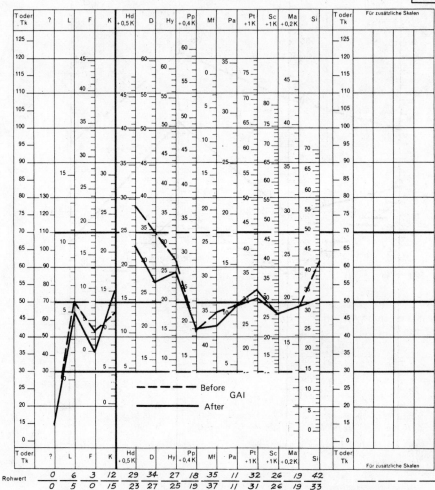

Figure 10.   MMPI Improvement in HD, D, Si which is significant.

196

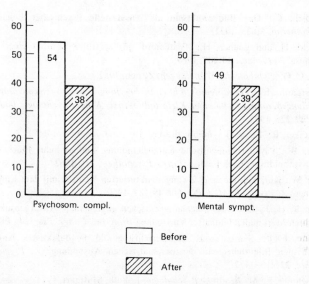

Figure 11. Psychosom. compl., improvement 29.62%.

Figure 12. Mental symptoms, improvement 20.4%.

A controlled study with GAI is briefly outlined, including two case histories. The method can also be used in a Group Setting. Music intensifies the daydream and so expands the indication spectrum.

REFERENCES

1. Barolin. G.: Spontane Altersregression im Symboldrama und ihre klinische Bedeutung. *Z. Psychother. Med. Psychol.* **11**:77, 1961.

2. Beck, M.: Rehabilitation eines chronischen Trinkers mit der Methode des Katathymen Bilderlebens. *Praxis Psychotherapie* **12**:97, 1968.

3. Brengelmann, J. C. and Brengelmann, L.: Deutsche Validierung von Fragebogen der Extraversion, Neurotischen Tendenz und Rigidität. Z. exp. angew. Psychol. **7**:291, 1960.

4. Boss, M.: Herkunft und Wesen des Archetypus-Begriffes. *Psyche* **4**:584, 1952–1953.

5. Breuer, J. and Freud, S.: *Studien über Hysterie,* Deuticke, Leipzig and Vienna, 1895.

6. Desoille, R.: *Le rève eveillé en psychothérapie,* Paris, 1945.

7. Erickson, M. H. and Kubie, L. S.: The successful treatment of an acute hysterical depression by a return to a critical phase of childhood. *Psychoanal. Quart.* **10**:583, 1941.

8. Frank, L.: *Affektstörungen,* Springer, Berlin, 1913.

9. Freud, S.: The Ego and the Id. *SE:* **13**:280 (German).

10. Fromm-Reichmann, F.: *Principles of Intensive Psychotherapy,* The University of Chicago Press.

11. Happich, C.: Das Bildbewubtsein als Ansatzstelle psychischer Behandlung. *Zbl. Psychotherap.* **5**:633, 1932.

12. Holfeld, H. and Leuner, H.: "Vatemord" als zentraler Konflikt einer psychogenen Psychose, *Nervenarzt* **40**:203, 1969.

13. Jung, C. G.: *Symbole der Wandlungen,* Zürich, 1952.

14. Klessmann, E.: *Therapiemöglichkeiten bei jungeren Drogenkonsumenten in der Erziehungsberatungsstelle einer Kleinstadt, Praxis Kinderpsychologie und Psychiatrie,* 1974, **22**:225, 1973.

15. Krojanker, R.: Leuner's symbolic drama. *Am. J. Hypn.* **9**:56, 1965.

16. Koch, W.: Psychotherapeutische Kurzbehandlung somnambuler Fluchtzustände mit dem Symboldrama nach Leuner. *Praxis Psychother.,* **7**:1, 1962.

17. Koch, W.: Kurztherapie einer Zwangsstrukturierten Neurose mit dem Katathymen Bilderleben. *Z. Psychoth. Med. Psychol.* **19**:187, 1969.

18. Kornadt, H. J.: Der Zusammenhang zwischen allgemeinem Anspruchsniveau und bestimmten Merkmalen bildhafter Vorstellung *Proc. Int. Congr. Psychol.,* Bonn, 1960.

19. Kosbab, F. P.: Symbolismus, Selbsterfahrung und die didaktische Anwendung des katathymen Bilderlebens in der psychiatrischen Ausbildung. *Z. Psychother. Med. Psychol.* **22**:210, 1972.

20. Kretschmer, E.: *Medizinische Psychologie,* 1. Aufl., Stuttgart, 1924.

21. Leuner, H.: Kontrolle der Symbolinterpretation im experimentellen Verfahren. *Z. Psychother. Med. Psychol.* **4**:201, 1954.

22. Leuner, H.: Experimentelles katathymes Bilderleben als ein klinisches Verfahren der Psychotherapie *Z. Psychother. Med. Psychol.* **5**:186, 233, 1955.

23. Leuner, H.: Symbolkonfrontation, ein nichtinterpretierendes Vorgehen in der Psychotherapie. *Schw. Arch. Neurol. Psychiatr.* **76**:23, 1955.

24. Leuner, H.: Symboldrama, ein aktives nicht-analysierendes Verfahren der Psychotherapie. *Z. Psychother. Med. Psychol.* **7**:221, 1957.

25. Leuner, H.: Das Landschaftsbild als Metapher dynamischer Strukturen. In: *Arzt im Raum des Erlebens,* Speer, E., (Ed.), J. F. Lehmanns Verlag, München, 1959.

26. Leuner, H.: Die Leistungen, Indikationen und Grenzen des Symboldramas. *Z. Psychother. Med. Psychol.* **10**:46, 1960.

27. Leuner, H. and Nerenz, K.: Das musikalische Symboldrama und seine psychotherapeutische Wirkung. *Heilkunst* **77**:330, 1964.

28. Leuner, H.: Das assoziative Vorgehen im Symboldrama. *Z. Psychother. Med. Psychol.* **14**:196, 1964.

29. Leuner, H.: Über den Stand der Entwicklung des Katathymen Bilderlebens. *Z. Psychother. Med. Psychol.* **19**:177, 1969.

30. Leuner, H.: *Katathymes Bilderleben (Unterstufe) - kleine Psychotherapie mit der Tagtraumtechnik - Ein Seminarkurs,* Thieme, Stuttgart, 1970.

31. Leuner, H.: *Therapeutische Möglichkeiten mit dem Katathymen Bilderleben (Tagtraumtechnik) bei RM-Konsumenten* (Ref. Fortbildungsverantst. Nervenklinik Tübingen 1971, unveröff.).

32. Leuner, H.: *Die Bedeutung der Musik in imaginativen Techniken der Psychotherapie.* Vortrag gehalten auf dem Ostersymposion der Herbert von Karajan-Stiftung, Salzburg, 1972 in: Revers, W. J., Harrer, G., Simon, W. C. M. (Hrsg.): Neue Wege der Musiktherapie, Econ Düsseldorf, Wien 1974.

33. Leuner, H., Wächter, M., and Pudel, V.: Die "15-Stunden-Therapie," kontrollierte Untersuchung einer Kurzpsychotherapie mit dem Katathymen Bilderleben. *Z. Psychother. Med. Psychol.* 1974 (in print).

34. Nerenz, K.: Das musikalische Symboldrama als Hilfsmethode in der Psychotherapie. *Z. Psychother. Med. Psychol.* **19**:28, 1969.

35. Leuner, H.: Das Katathyme Bilderleben in der Psychotherapie von Kindern und Jugendlichen. *Z. Kinderpsychologie Kinderpsychiatrie.* **19**:212, 1970.

36. Plaum, G.: Erste Ergebnisse des musikalischen katathymen Bilderlebens in seiner Anwendung als Gruppentherapie. *Med. Diss. Goettingen,* 1968.

37. Raven, J. C.: *Standard Progressive Matrices,* H. W. Lewis Co., London 1960.

38. Rechenberger, H.-G.: Das Symboldrama in der psychotherapeutischen Praxis: ein Fallbericht. *Z. Psychother. Med. Psychol.* **13**:239, 1963.

39. Sachsse, H.: Gruppentherapie und Gruppendynamik mit dem Katathymen Bilderleben im Versuch mit führerlosen Gruppen. *Med. Diss.* Göttingen, 1974.

40. Schneck, J. M. G.: Spontaneous regression to an infantile level during self-hypnosis. *J. Genet. Psychol.* **86**:183, 1955.

41. Silberer, H.: Symbolik des Erwachens und Schwellensymbolik überhaupt. *J. Psychoanal. Psychopath. Forsch.* **3**:621, 1912.

42. Spreen, O.: *MMPI Saarbrücken,* Handbuch, Zur deutschen Ausgabe d. Minnesota Multiphasic Personality Inventory von S. R. Hathaway, J. C. McKinley, Huber, Bern, 1963.

43. Swartley, W.: *Initiated Symbol Projection, In: Psychosynthesis by R. Assagiol:* Hobbs, Dorman and Co., New York, 1965.

44. Taylor, J. A.: A personality scale of manifest anxiety. *J. Abnormal Social Psychol.* **48**:1953.

45. Zenz, H.: Empirische Befunde über die Giessener Fassung einer Beschwerdenliste. *Z. Psychother. Med. Psychol.,* **21**:1971.

CHAPTER NINE

MODERN HOSPITAL MILIEU
TREATMENT OF SCHIZOPHRENIA

OTTO F. KERNBERG, M.D.

A TREATMENT MODEL FOR SCHIZOPHRENIA

I have in earlier papers[4-6] suggested a theoretical frame of reference for integrating the various etiological factors of schizophrenia into a model of psychopathological functioning that has direct relevance for the treatment of schizophrenic patients. This frame of reference combines psychoanalytic object-relations theory with an open-systems theory stemming from A. K. Rice's[12] model for integrating individual, group, and organizational functioning.

Within Rice's conceptualization, the individual is thought of as an open system importing from, converting, and exporting into the environment. His basic tasks in these interactions with the environment are to gratify his internal needs by means of utilizing environmental resources and to adjust this gratification to environmental demands. The intrapsychic world of object relations (the internalized fixations and elaborations of past interactions with others) may be regarded as the principle depository of the individual's internal (instinctual) needs, that is, of his past experiencing of the gratification and/or frustration of instinctual needs. The ego would represent the control system that carries out the boundary functions between this intrapsychic world and the external social environment.

Schizophrenia might be conceptualized as a breakdown of the individual's capacity to gratify his intrapsychic needs because of the breakdown of the ego, that is, of the control system correlating the intrapsychic and interpersonal worlds. The failure of the ego to carry out these boundary functions may be described chiefly in terms of the failure of affect control, with subsequent disruption of psychic functioning (especially of cognitive processes) under the effect of excessive anxiety; and the failure of perceptual control, with a subsequent distorted perception of the intrapsychic and the external interpersonal world and the incapacity to maintain the boundary differentiation between them (loss of reality testing). To survive, the individual has to carry out the task of interchange (import–conversion–export) with the environment. Breakdown of the control system interferes with this basic task, and, therefore, with normal psychic survival: the individual can no longer establish his goals and carry out the specific tasks that will lead him to these goals. In other words, at such a point, the strivings for emotional gratification and for effecting a creative adjustment to the environment with optimal autonomy and self-respect must fail.

Psychological malfunctioning in schizophrenic patients may be formulated within this framework as taking place at two levels: a first level is that

* Presented at the Symposium, "The Meaning of Madness," New York, November, 1973.

of the defective perception, defective cognitive structures, defective affect experience and control, and defective external and internal thresholds. A second level of malfunctioning is that of the psychological structuring of interpersonal experiences, namely, the building up and reshaping of the intrapsychic world of object relations. Evidence appears to be accumulating that schizophrenic patients may present lower thresholds to perceptual input, leading to information-input overload and excessive arousal; and/or lower anxiety thresholds, leading to diffuse, massive affective reactions, and secondary cognitive disorganization. A disequilibrium in autonomic reactivity may underlie both types of lower thresholds; in turn, these lower thresholds determine excessive reactivity, withdrawal, and disorganization under the impact of affect-laden interactions. These defects may seriously affect the building up of those normal intrapsychic structures that reflect the interpersonal field. In turn, excessive stress in in the interpersonal field itself, such as the pathological family structure so typically seen in schizophrenic patients, may directly bring about a faulty structuring of the intrapsychic world of objects and, subsequently, a defensively determined disorganization of perceptual, cognitive, and affective controls. This conceptualization allows for a complementary (constitutional-environmental) series of etiological factors, determining a defective control system (ego weakness). Thus faulty building up of internalized object-relations is the crucial common element in the interaction of various etiological factors and may be the consequence of both faulty ego maturation and development, on the one hand, and pathological psychosocial (particularly intrafamilial) interactions, on the other.

In other words, it may be that what happens in future schizophrenic patients (for genetic, constitutional, or psychosocial reasons, or a combination of them) is that the early control system, as represented by the ego's transactional functions between internal needs and the environment, is faulty and brings about a distortion of the psychological structuring of the experiences with others (a distortion of the internal world of self- and object-representations and of the structures derived from them). Such a distortion predisposes the future patient to discrepancies between his internal needs and expectations and the actual interpersonal environment. This discrepancy would represent a common final path in the predisposition to schizophrenia, and the eventual breakdown of the originally damaged control system would signal the actual beginning of the psychotic episode. The implication is that primitive defensive operations activated in the context of pathological structuring of the internal world of object relations contribute to, or even usually may bring about, breakdown of the control system (ego). The polar opposites of "process" and "reactive" schizophrenia might reflect a continuum from a predominance of defects in the control system (ego) on the one end to a predominance of defects in the intrapsychic world of object relations on the other.

In applying these formulations to the integration of various treatment modalities for schizophrenia,[5] I have stressed that drug treatment needs to be integrated within a comprehensive conceptual frame of reference that encompasses the pharmacological, psychological, and social treatment of schizophrenic patients during both the acute or psychotic stage and the convalescent or "sealing over," or latent stage of illness. From a clinical viewpoint, there seems to be good evidence that phenothiazines reduce the level of anxiety and increase affective thresholds; they may also indirectly normalize perception by decreasing information input. In any case, the effect of phenothiazines would be a direct reinforcement of the control system, that is, of ego structures involved in perceptual, cognitive, and affective control. Improvement of the control system brought about by ataractic drugs may, in turn, permit the ego (1) to reestablish the boundaries between the intrapsychic world and the external interpersonal one, and (2) to reexamine goals and tasks in the light of the now less distorted perceptions of self and nonself. If, at the same time, the patient is provided with therapeutic interpersonal relations so that his improved control system may better evaluate the interactions between his internal and interpersonal worlds, further improvement may occur as internal needs are gratified in new social interactions and the control systems' effectiveness increases with new experiences in the interpersonal field. In short, ataractic drugs may improve the patient's control system to a point where his ego could make use of the psychotherapeutic examination of his intrapsychic and interpersonal fields and reassume the basic task of gratifying his internal needs in interactions with the environment.

Thus the treatment of a patient with an acute schizophrenic reaction would be geared to reestablishing the control system to a level sufficient for him to be able to reexamine the relations between his intrapsychic world (distorted as it might be) and his interpersonal one (distorted as it might be experienced at first). Treatment with ataractic drugs may be a crucial breakthrough in obtaining a reversal of the more disorganizing defects of the ego (especially the excessive arousal and affect diffusion, and the lowered perceptive thresholds).

Psychotherapy should start out as a straightforward, here-and-now examination of the patient's interactions with other people, with several tasks to be carried out simultaneously. First, the particular defects in the patient's perceptions and affective reactions may be diagnosed and monitored within the psychotherapeutic interaction; second, the patient's chronic distortions of his intrapsychic world of object relations may be diagnosed and their implications incorporated into a comprehensive plan for social rehabilitation; third, and most important, a meaningful therapeutic relationship may be established in the process, which may help to carry the patient along from a situation of maximum external control (hospitalization) to one in which he will again have to autonomously monitor his life in relating to others. An intensive psychotherapeutic approach along current psychoanalytic lines may be the end point of a long relation with a therapist that starts out as psychotherapeutic management.

Psychotherapy with a schizophrenic patient would start out, therefore, as a psychotherapeutic monitoring of his ego and of his internal world. Only gradually, as the patient's ego becomes stabilized, would psychotherapy proceed toward focusing more on the conflicts within this intrapsychic world. In this process, psychotherapy may gradually expand its scope in the sense of increasing the patient's understanding of his intrapsychic life. Eventually, psychoanalytic psychotherapy should help the patient to achieve structural changes in his internalized object relations. Unfortunately, such a highly specialized type of psychoanalytic psychotherapy by particularly skilled therapists, probably endowed with special personality characteristics enabling them to deal with severely regressed patients, will, at best, require years of treatment. Although this kind of treatment may be prohibitive from the viewpoint of social resources, from the viewpoint of research into the origins of schizophrenia—into the relations of very early structures and defensive operations of the mind to later pathological and normal development—such an approach seems to me a highly valuable clinical research instrument. For some patients with chronic schizophrenic reactions, it may be the only road to a significant recovery.

Recent psychoanalytic theories of schizophrenia have been applied in the psychotherapeutic approaches of Rosenfield,[14] Searles,[16] and Bion.[3] It is interesting to observe that the Sullivanian-based approach of Searles, stemming from a theoretical background completely different from that of Rosenfeld and Bion, has evolved into technical formulations quite similar to those of these two Kleinian authors. All three of them stress the importance of the analyst as a real person who has to tolerate uncertainty, lack of contact, and confusion for a long time before the psychotic patient is able to fully activate an infantile-dependent relationship in the therapeutic interaction. The first, "out of contact" phase, in Searles' terms, later gives rise to a highly shifting, symbiotic kind of relation in which primitive affect states are activated, and the patient cannot differentiate himself from the therapist. The building up of gradual tolerance of the therapeutic interaction as the patient loses his fear over the destructive nature of his primitive rage gradually permits a better delimitation of boundaries in the interaction between patient and analyst. Finally, a phase of integration may occur in the patient so that he can accept himself as distinct and different from the therapist and integrate his loving and hateful feelings for him.

It needs to be stressed that these psychoanalytic approaches to the intensive psychotherapy of schizophrenic patients focus mostly on the pathology of internalized object-relations, in apparent contrast to the predominant focus on ego functions of contemporary ego psychology. However, insofar as intensive psychotherapy with schizophrenic patients deals with their characteristic primitive defensive operations—which influence all their object relations to a direct focus on the control system— ego is always involved. In practice, intensive psychotherapy deals with both the internal world of object relations and the ego; this holds equally true for a contemporary conception of hospital milieu treatment of schizophretions of contemporary ego psychology. However, insofar as intensive psychotherapy with schizophrenic patients deals with their characteristic primitive defensive operations—which influence all their object relations— a direct focus on the control system (ego) is always involved. In practice, intensive psychotherapy deals with both the internal world of object relations and the ego; this holds equally true for a contemporary conception of hospital milieu treatment of schizophrenia.

As I have pointed out, this integrative model for treatment of schizophrenia takes into account recent research on the psychological functioning of schizophrenic patients, research which indicates defects in their perception, cognitive structures, affect experience and control, and in their external and internal perceptive thresholds. The approach I outline, however, is in contrast to a naive interpretation of complex clinical findings in schizophrenia directly in the light of the general psychological and psychophysiological defects mentioned: the intrapsychic world of the schizophrenic patient needs to be understood in terms of his pathological intrapsychic structures (particularly his distorted internal world of object relations). The problem is how underlying defective psychophysiological and psychological structures influence the consolidation of a pathological world of internalized object relations. These psychophysiological defects, moreover, may also seriously interfere with the immediate functioning of the patient in the interpersonal realm, and their correction may improve the patient's capacity to work psychotherapeutically and change his intrapsychic as well as his interpersonal life. This treatment approach combines the use of psychopharmacological, psychotherapeutic, milieu, and rehabilitation measures: it is in contrast to a mechanistic treatment approach which loads the patient with medication to eradicate target symptoms and which conceives as the main goal of treatment to get the patient out of the hospital, rather than to develop a long-range treatment strategy that will gradually expand his autonomous functioning and social rehabilitation.

Within this overall treatment approach, the psychotherapist carries out a "boundary function"[12] between the intrapsychic life of the patient on the one hand, and the external reality impinging on the total psychotherapeutic situation on the other. This approach is in contrast to the temptation of a magical or messianic isolation of the psychotherapeutic relation from the rest of the patient's environment; it also implies a gradually developing, cautious interpretation of the transference in the "here and now," rather than a forceful, premature introduction of "depth" interpretations which may act in magical (as opposed to communicatively meaningful) ways.

THE HOSPITAL AS A SOCIAL SYSTEM

Abundant research of the last 20 years indicates that pathological interactions within the family as a social system are of great importance in the psychosocial development of the future schizophrenic patient. The work of Bateson et al.,[1] Laing and Esterson,[9] Lidz,[10] Wynne et al.[18] all coincide in pointing to pathological interactions among the family members of schizophrenic patients as a crucial factor in the functions and meaning of the patient's behavior, thinking, and affect. Wynne and Singer[19, 20] have demonstrated that disordered thinking in schizophrenic patients is related to the peculiarities in the styles of thinking and communication of their parents. This raises the question as to what extent genetic factors in schizophrenia might be reflecting, in part, the cultural transmission of psychopathology in schizophrenic families—a question that has been convincingly analyzed by Rosenthal[15] and others, with the conclusion that most probably both genetic and psychosocial factors are involved in the etiology of the syndrome. The question I wish to raise is the nature of the mutual influences of the patient's interpersonal world of object relations within the family and/or other intimate social groups, on the one hand, and his intrapsychic world of object relations, on the other. An examination of the functioning of schizophrenic patients within psychiatric hospitals that specialize in the psychoanalytic study of these phenomena seems relevant.

Insofar as the hospital represents a social structure organized around group processes with varying degrees of structuralization, the patient is faced with participation in a setting that reinforces in varying degrees the activation of primitive object relations. There exists impressive clinical evidence to indicate that, regardless of the degree of the individual's maturity and psychological integration, small, closed, unstructured groups—as well as large groups with minimal structure and no clearly defined task relating these groups to their environment—tend to bring about an immediate regression of the people involved toward activation of primitive defensive operations and primitive interpersonal processes reflecting primitive object relations.[6]

In other words, a potential exists in all of us for activating primitive levels of psychological functioning when the ordinary social structure is lost, when suspension of ordinary social roles occurs, and when multiple objects are present simultaneously in an unstructured relationship (thus reproducing in the interpersonal field the multiplicity of primitive intrapsychic object relations). Our theoretical understanding of why this surprising development takes place in groups is still insufficient, but the fact that it does occur and particularly in patients with severe character pathology, with borderline or psychotic syndromes, makes the hospital an impressive diagnostic (and potentially therapeutic) tool for understanding primitive levels of internalized object relations and for modifying them in a controlled social system. It may well be that the potential for regression from higher level identifications to the underlying more primitive introjections is quite prevalent, and that the role enactments of ordinary interpersonal relations protect the higher level identifications from such a regression. Also, there may be a normal potential for reestablishing a certain identification after some temporary regression to a component introjection. This might explain part of the rapid regression that occurs in certain group situations and the rapid recuperation from such regression: groups may induce such regression by eliminating the usual role protection of normal interpersonal interactions.[6]

Bion's analysis of the regressive phenomena that occur in small groups when their task structure ("work group") fails is relevant here.[2, 13] He described the emergence of certain basic emotional reactions within the group ("basic-assumptions group"), reactions that exist potentially at all times but become activated particularly at times of breakdown of the work group. What is particularly impressive is that the defensive mechanisms activated within the basic-assumptions group correspond to the defensive operations characteristic of primitive internalized object relations. Indeed, impulses, defenses, and object relations of that primitive level of intrapsychic development become evident in the basic-assumptions group. The practical importance of these findings seems to warrant a brief summary of the relevant observations of groups.

The psychotherapists' focus on the development of individual psychopathology (particularly the manifestations of individual character pathology) in a group setting tends to activate transference developments among the group members and a group situation that resembles something of a modified psychoanalytical situation—there is dramatic intensification and observability of some transference manifestations (while other transference aspects go "underground" because of their realistic flavor in the middle of generalized transference acting-out in the group). In contrast, when the psychotherapist focuses predominantly on the total emotional situation of the group and treats the group as a whole, an entirely different set of developments and processes occurs: surprisingly primitive emotional conflicts and resistances are activated, which resemble primitive object relations and transferences of borderline conditions, and even psychotic reactions. In other words, the exploratory focus provided by the psychotherapist's acting as a group leader has fundamental influences on group phenomena.

This emergence of primitive emotional reactions and defenses in group situations is further complicated when the group situation occurs in the context of an institutional setting. For example, a group psychotherapy or group dynamics group developed within a psychiatric hospital or a university setting tends to reflect, within the total group process, the emotional issues and conflicts permeating the institution at large. It is as if "hidden agendas" of the institution were intimately connected with the primitive levels of emotional reactions and defenses mentioned before. It would appear that the focus on individual psychopathology and characterological defenses protects the group and its members both from regression into more primitive emotional layers ordinarily only seen in more regressed patients, and from full awareness of the latent social conflicts characteristic of the institution within which the group process takes place.

Bion described the development of several emotional reactions within the group ("basic-assumptions group"), reactions that exist potentially at all times, but become activated particularly at times of breakdown of the task structure of the group. These are the "dependency" assumption, the "fight-flight" assumption, and the "pairing" assumption.

In the "dependent" group, the members perceive the leader as omnipotent and omniscient, while they consider themselves inadequate, immature, and incompetent. The idealization of the leader on the part of the members is matched by their desperate, greedy, but futile efforts to extract knowledge, power, and goodness from him. The failure of the leader to live up to such an ideal of perfection is met first with denial, then with a rapid, complete devaluation of him and a search for substitute leadership. Thus primitive idealization, projected omnipotence, denial, envy, and greed and defenses against them characterize the dependent group. Members feel united by a common sense of need, helplessness, and fear of an outside world they dimly experience as empty or frustrating.

The "fight-flight" group is united against vaguely perceived external enemies as well as to protect the group from any infighting. Any opposition to the "ideology" shared by the majority of the group cannot be tolerated, and the group easily splits into subgroups which fight each other. Frequently, one subgroup becomes subservient to the idealized leader while another subgroup attacks that subgroup or is in flight from it. The group's tendency to forcefully control the leader, or to experience itself forcefully controlled by him; to experience "closeness" in a shared denial of intragroup hostility; and to project aggression onto an outgroup are all prevalent. In short, splitting, projection of aggression, and "projective identification" are predominant, and the search for nurture and dependency on the part of the dependent group is replaced by conflicts around aggressive control, with prevalent suspiciousness, fight, and dread of annihilation.

In the "pairing" group, a couple (frequently but not necessarily heterosexual) symbolizes the hopeful expectations of the group that the selected pair will "reproduce itself"—thus preserving the current threatened identity and survival of the group. The fantasies experienced about this selected pair express the group's hope that, by means of a magical "sexual" union, the group will be saved from the conflicts related to both the dependent and fight-flight assumptions. In the pairing group, in short, generalized intimacy and sexual developments are experienced as a potential protection against the dangerous conflicts around dependency and aggression (which, we may add, have a pregenital character, in contrast to the genital one of the pairing group).

Main,[11] in analyzing the group reaction of nursing staff involved in the treatment of predominantly borderline and some psychotic patients ("special cases") within the hospital, found that the patients managed to activate group phenomena in the nurses' group similar to those characterizing Bion's basic-assumptions group. The implication is that regressed patients may, under certain conditions, activate their intrapsychic object relations in the interpersonal relations of the hospital staff: the patient induces in his social field a reenactment of the conflicts in his intrapsychic world. The combination of massive projection, omnipotent control, denial, primitive idealization, and, above all, splitting of staff, reflects both the intrapsychic mechanisms involved and the behavioral means by which staff relationships are distorted in terms of the patient's intrapsychic world. Stanton and Schwartz,[17] in turn, demonstrated how splits and covert conflict in the hospital's interpersonal and social field may intensify intrapsychic conflict and disorganization in "special" patients (particularly in borderline conditions and some psychotic patients). In short, a reciprocal reinforcement develops between the patients' intrapsychic conflicts and the potential cleavages and stresses within the social system of the hospital.

The social system is crucial in bringing about regression and in activating pathological primitive object relationships in those forming part of such a social system. The intrapsychic structures of the regressed patient also influence and bring about regressive features in the immediate social environment with which he interacts. These complementary phenomena illustrate the general boundary function of regressive symptoms in the sense that such symptoms may both reflect the impact of the social environment (particularly the influence of his family) on the patient's intrapsychic structures and/or induce a kind of replication of the intrapsychic structures in the patient's social environment.

It is difficult enough to integrate such a complementary view of schizophrenic regression in our theoretical thinking. These difficulties increase in the practice of treating schizophrenic patients. Often, it is as tempting to formulate a simplistic theory that regards the psychosis as derived entirely from the influences of the environment (the family) upon the patient, as it is to attribute the patient's symptoms exclusively to his "endogenous" personality predisposition, and thus free ourselves from the puzzling and complex reciprocal influences operating between the immediate familiar and psychosocial environment and the schizophrenic syndrome.

The view that the psychotic patient is a victim, and his symptoms are a potential expression of protest within and against a "mad" society continues to be an attractive formulation. Clinically, one can observe that, in the course of a schizophrenic regression, many of the contradictory elements within the patient's total social situation become activated and strangely dramatized in his subjective experience; it is as if the psychotic patient becomes a receptacle for the explosive, irreconcilable aspects of social and political conflicts within his familial and social world. That which ordinary man must suppress, repress, adapt to, protest against, or come to terms with, explodes in an open and contradictory, dissociated way in some schizophrenic patients. Bion[3] has suggested that the role of the analyst of severely regressed patients is that of a "container," in the sense of empathizing with and attempting to integrate subjectively what the patient projects onto him in a myriad of disconnected, mutually conflictual fragments. At times, it is tempting for the therapist to empathize with, submerge himself in, and even adopt the strange reorganization of the life experience of the psychotic patient, with its implicit dramatic promise of independence from the ordinary constraints of reality. When engaged in psychotherapy with such patients, it is sometimes easy to forget the terrible impoverishment of the psychotic patient's life and the psychic sterility that is the price he pays for such a primitive type of "containing" what ordinarily cannot be integrated. Sometimes it is difficult to become aware of the extent of the patient's responsibility in preserving what he experiences as "mad" in his environment. In broader terms, one therapeutic task is to help the patient explore his responsibility in supporting, by his very escape into illness, that which he is in protest against or escaping from.

At times, it is as if the entire history of a patient's past life and family experience is reenacted in the relationships among hospital staff. For example, one patient with chronic paranoid schizophrenia presented an idealization of a primitive father image conceived as a tyrannical, cruel, omnipotent suppressor of both sex and violence. The patient feared and yet admired this image of his father, and saw him as an indispensable protection against the oubreak of uncontrollable violence in himself and others. In the hospital, the patient presented periods of relative "integration" (with little thought disorganization and rather "appropriate" behavior on the ward) during which he meekly submitted to staff, identified himself consciously with political groups of the extreme right, had homosexual fantasies (linked to his submission to powerful men), and was terrified of women. At such times, he saw the director of the hospital service as a tyrant whom he admired and paid homage to. This submissiveness had an almost mocking quality to it; and he angrily defended the need for "law and order" on the ward, demanding punishment for all aggressive behavior of other patients. At other times, he was "disorganized"—that is, he presented a marked thought disorder, became openly aggressive with authority figures, approached in seductive ways women with "motherly" featues, and, indeed, was not sure whether these women were his mother. In other words, primitive rebellion against oedipal father figures and sexual seductiveness toward mother images was acted out in the context of psychotic regression.

After some time, conflicts which replicated these problems developed among the staff on the service. Conflicts developed particularly among staff directly in charge of this patient's treatment, but eventually spread over the service at large, as this patient became a "special case." A psychiatric resident experienced one senior staff consultant as a dangerous tyrant who would punish him if he disagreed with the consultant's recommendation. Subtle competition simultaneously developed among other senior male consultants around the figure of the (apparently) "submissive" female staff member who was a special counselor to the patient. The entire staff perceived this woman counselor as a kind of reluctant, somewhat passive, but crucial judge of this case, and the male staff members involved eagerly sought her favorable opionion. At the same time, more generalized sexual and aggressive acting out was occurring among patients on the service. All this seemed related to the "testing" of a new service director, with fears shared by staff and patients alike about whether he would become a harsh, tyrannical suppressor of sex and violence, or a dangerous "libertarian" who would cause a chaotic disorganization of the service because of general loosening of impulse control. At one point, the staff's fantasies and fears regarding the new service director became condensed with the competition of senior consultants for the "favors" of the female staff member involved in the patient's treatment. The service director was now seen as the male figure who, in effect, had established a personal "pairing" with this woman counselor, thus triumphing over the other male consultants, and there was widespread fear that the new director would impose his ideas tyrannically over the treatment team of this patient. These fantasies were eventually shared by patients and staff alike, as patients expressed in community meetings their wishes for and fears of a strong father figure who would control sex and violence which would otherwise destory the social fabric of the service.

The analysis of the patient's contributions to these fantasies shared by groups of patients and staff permitted both a reduction in anxiety and conflicts among staff and a sharper focus on the intrapsychic dynamics of the patient, all of which led to a more integrated and focused combination of psychotherapy and hospital milieu treatment for him.

In the psychotherapy, the patient was confronted with his fear about his aggression and sexual excitement and his fantastic conviction that either all his impulses were suppressed or he would kill his father and rape is mother. In the hospital milieu approach, he was permitted some expression of his anger, and the more primitive and destructive aspects of it were controlled by staff while pointing out to him that this was not done in punitive or retaliatory fashion. More contacts with female patients were implicitly fostered in his daily program of activities, while his more primitive, seductive behavior toward some women was discouraged. This example illustrates: (1) activation in the patient's object relations in the hospital of regressive condensation of oedipal conflicts with pregenital conflicts around aggression; (2) reciprocal activation of latent conflicts among the hospital staff in the interactions with the patient; and (3) therapeutic utilization of the understanding reached by hospital staff of these dynamics. The analysis of the distortions of the social structure permitted first a decrease in hospital conflicts, and then the utilization of a better understanding of the patient in his overall psychotherapeutic and milieu treatment.

The treatment modality implied in this example is geared to avoid and to repair the damaging influences on the treatment of individual patients of covert conflicts within the various echelons of the hospital administration and to utilize, diagnostically and therapeutically, the negative effects of the patient's intrapsychic conflicts on the social structure of the hospital. The proposed treatment modality requires, it must be stressed, on optimal, open examination both of the total social field surrounding the patient's treatment and of the reciprocal effects of the patient's intrapsychic life and this social field. All this information, made available to the psychotherapist, may then be incorporated into the psychotherapy, as well as directly utilized by the hospital treatment team at large. Such a treatment approach requires the establishment and protection of a functional, in contrast to an authoritarian, administrative hospital structure. Many of the criticisms that have been directed against the intensive treatment of regressed patients within a hospital setting have been directed against old-fashioned, overcrowded, understaffed, primitive treatment settings which do not reflect what a contemporary, psychoanalytically oriented hospital treatment approach may add to intensive psychotherapy.

Reality testing is a major anchoring point in the differential diagnosis between the psychoses, particularly schizophrenia, and nonpsychotic conditions, particularly borderline personality organization. While both borderline and psychotic patients present a predominance of pathological internalized object relations and primitive defensive operations (which distinguish these two categories of patients from less disturbed neurotic and characterological conditions), the functions of these primitive defensive operations in borderline conditions differ from those in schizophrenia[5]. In patients with borderline personality organization, such primitive operations (particularly splitting, projective identification, primitive idealization, omnipotence, denial, and devaluation) protect the patients from intense ambivalence and a feared contamination and deterioration by hatred of all love relations. In schizophrenic patients, on the other hand, these defensive operations (and particularly the pathological development of splitting mechanisms leading to generalized fragmentation of intrapsychic experiences and interpersonal relations) protect the patient—with their lack of differentiation of self- and object-images—from total loss of ego boundaries and dreaded fusion experiences.

The diagnosis of the social field surrounding a schizophrenic patient in the hospital can often be arrived at more easily than in the case of borderline conditions, because the higher level, relatively less fragmented splitting operations of borderline patients are typically reflected in their perception of some staff members as "all good" and others as "all bad." (Thus the total transference situation of borderline patients as reenacted within the hospital milieu can be diagnosed only by an interpretive integration of all the contradictory relations of the patient with others.) Contrariwise, in severely regressed schizophrenic patients, fragmentation of all human experiences tends to blur any sophisticated distinction between different members of the staff, particularly in the early stages of treatment. The disturbing, "uncanny" effect of these splitting mechanisms on staff often leads the latter to withdraw and to avoid the patient.

In short, the relations of regressed schizophrenic patients with most staff members and other patients are at first quite repetitive in their chaotic quality; and the complex splitting of staff into opposite groups, the subtle manipulation of staff members and patients against each other, so characteristic of borderline patients, is less of a problem with severely regressed schizophrenic patients. Paradoxically, the more regressed the patient, the more similar are the experiences that different staff members and other patients have in their interactions with him.

As the schizophrenic patient establishes, over a period of time, individually differentiated relations with others (which has positive prognostic implications), various members of the treatment team begin to see him in very different ways. It is at this point that the varying relationship patterns of the patient with staff members and the related countertransference reactions need to be observed, diagnosed, and integrated. Open communication between the psychotherapist and all other members of the treatment team permits a comprehensive view of the patient, which can be included both in the work of the psychotherapeutic relation and the hospital milieu treatment, and has a prognostically helpful implication. The opposite is true when psychotherapy is isolated from the rest of the patient's experiences in the hospital, or when the psychotherapist becomes engaged in a power struggle with the hospital team managing the patient's daily life in the hospital.

The degree to which severely regressed schizophrenic patients tolerate interactions with their human and inanimate environments varies greatly. Schizophrenic patients need opportunities to relate themselves regularly and routinely to staff members and other patients around activities in such a way as to promote greater socialization, while providing an "escape hatch" for withdrawal into the impersonal aspects of the task and away from its interpersonal implications when the latter become too threatening or too close.

Severely regressed schizophrenic patients may experience intensive group situations, particularly within large groups, as very threatening. They may not be able to participate in the therapeutic community structures that are part of the total milieu treatment program for most patients. On the other hand, the tolerance by patient groups of "deviants" or "outsiders" may be therapeutic to the group as well as to the schizophrenic patients themselves. A combination of open communication within the group, clarification of the here-and-now situation within the group—including the role and effects of the schizophrenic patient's interactions with the group—and tolerance of varying degrees of "nonparticipation" of the part of individual patients, are some of the potentially helpful aspects of a group-centered hospital milieu program.

NEW CONCEPTIONS IN HOSPITAL MILIEU TREATMENT

The conceptualization of the overall treatment of hospitalized schizophrenic patients presented so far, and, particularly, the conceptualization of the hospital milieu as a complex social system (composed of various group processes involving staff as well as patients) reflects a departure from the traditional view of hospital milieu treatment.[7] Traditionally, the daily life of the schizophrenic patient in the hospital was organized in terms of scheduled activities and establishment of routines that would help him become aware of space and time boundaries and thus be more able to differentiate himself from the environment. The nursing, occupational, recreational, artistic, and education activities offered were geared to provide the patient with specialized skills that would, hopefully, be relevant to his social rehabilitation and prevent his regression into a passive, practically irresponsible recipient of the ministration of others.

Recent trends in hospital milieu treatment, outlined in this paper, incorporate the studies mentioned regarding the impact of the hospital as a social system on the patient, and the potentially helpful aspects of the diagnosis and therapeutic utilization of this social system. Within this approach, the various helping professions in the hospital—the nursing service, the activities department, the social service, in addition to the psychiatric and psychological diagnostic and therapeutic approaches—all provide three types of therapeutic functions.

1. Each profession contributes with specialized skills to the rehabilitation of the patient, not only within the hospital setting, but also, particularly, for the rehabilitation of the patient at the time of aftercare. The activities prescribed by the activities department center around work; they need to be relevant to the patient's life outside of the hospital, and they provide skills commensurate with his tasks in reality. The social service focuses on the social field of the family and other small social groups and organizations with whom the patient interacts; it should provide tools to the patient and his family for improved communication and negotiation of their mutual needs. The nursing service deals with the patient's immediate physical and human environment; it should provide the patient with more appropriate and gratifying ways of going about his daily life, and create a homelike atmosphere, which combines appropriate intimacy, privacy, and sharing.

2. In addition to the provision of specialized skills, each of the professions should provide the patient with opportunities for meaningful, individualized human interactions and for better understanding of the emotional conflicts that are activated in such human interactions. Hospital staff must all be able to utilize their own personalities in diagnosing the emotional implications of the patient's interactions in the hospital; they provide the material that leads to the understanding of transference and countertransference in the hospital. From this viewpoint, the total field of each patient's emotional reactions in the hospital can be utilized for an on-

going here-and-now thereapeutic management, and can be fed back into the specialized psychotherapeutic relationship itself (as a background against which the primitive transference reactions of the psychotic patient can be diagnosed and integrated psychotherapeutically).

3. Lastly, and most important, the total impact of the patient's particular psychopathology on his immediate social milieu in the hospital can be diagnosed and utilized therapeutically by means of an open examination of the group processes involving patients and staff. Therefore, all staff must acquire skills in diagnosing the functional and regressive characteristics of groups, the symptoms of effective and distorted administrative structures, and the manifestations of shifts in morale of the hospital community at large. This last function of the various professions in the hospital constitutes, in my opinion, a most powerful tool in the treatment of schizophrenic patients. Not only can it utilize the understanding of the distortions of social processes around the patient for understanding the conflicts within his intrapsychic world, but it can also utilize these same social factors in group situations for powerful confrontation with and modification of these conflicts.

Following a first stage of non-involvement, gradually, powerful emotional reactions evolve within and around the patient, typically culminating in what appears as an almost uncanny reproduction within the hospital setting, of the patient's family constellation and conflicts. At this second stage of development, it is as if the patient's intrapsychic conflicts and those potential conflicts among hospital staff that are activated by the patient's impact would powerfully reinforce each other. It is as if some kind of "click" integrates the hospital's social atmosphere and the patient's past life into one solid, conflictual, compromise formation. It is at this stage that the possibility of an open examination of the hospital's social system and of its utilization for diagnositic and therapeutic purposes become optimal.

Under the best circumstances, a third period may follow, wherein staff actively work at resolving the distortions in the social system created by the patient. At this stage, the combination of confronting the patient and clarifying with him what is implied in these conflicts, and how he can better deal with his emotional needs expressed through them, may become of crucial therapeutic importance.

Under unfavorable circumstances, when lack of sufficient understanding, skill, or human resources within the hospital makes such diagnostic appraisal and therapeutic utilization of its social system impossible; or when an excessively authoritarian structure exists; or when a generally chaotic atmosphere prevails—precluding integration of the split-off aspects of information about the patient into one comprehensive picture—endless repetition within the hospital of the patient's past conflicts within his family may ensue and even end with therapeutic stalemate or termination of treatment.

At times, of course, special unfavorable factors within the patient's personality interfere with the optimal utilization of the hospital for therapeutic purposes. The most important of these are severe types of negative therapeutic reaction, characterized by the patient's primitive identification with a savagely hostile parental introject (which forbids any improvement, and permits the patient to achieve security only by defeating those who try to help him and who would bring about a dreaded separation from such a primitive introject).

For practical purposes, the most important factor limiting the utilization of the hospital milieu therapeutically in terms of its social system is an authoritarian administrative hospital structure. Although patients may improve under very different hospital social "regimes," the potentially damaging consequence of hospitalization for treatment where an authoritarian administrative structure of the hospital prevails is impressive. Also, authoritarian hospital structures typically underutilize their human resources; this becomes evident when a shift occurs from authoritarian to functional hospital organization.

I now turn to some disadvantages or dangers in utilizing the social-systems approach recommended. Powerful and potentially valuable as the analytical approach to the emotional processes in groups within the hospital setting may be, a note of caution against excessive use of this method is warranted. A continuous examination of group processes involving patients and staff puts tremendous stress on the staff and is potentially dangerous in terms of reducing the spontaneity of staff reaction within the hospital. Then too, acting out, emotional breakdown, and defensive withdrawal on the part of staff may occur. The delicate fabric of the social net of staff and patients requires periods of rest, so that spontaneous reactions may develop without premature interpretation or disruption of privacy. Such periods should alternate with periods in which serious distortions of the social field are explored, analyzed, and reduced. An optimal balance is needed between openness and exploration of group processes, on the one hand, and tolerance of privacy and of informal, casual interactions among staff as well as between staff and patients, on the other. This requires experience and skill. What is particularly dangerous is the possibility that a pseudotherapeutic culture will develop, in which intimate and primitive emotional phenomena are discussed so frequently and so freely that words relating to deep emotions lose their meaning and become one more intellectual system to be used for defensive purposes.* Paradoxically, therefore, there

---

* Personal communication from Dr. Paulina Kernberg.

are times when the persistence of splitting mechanisms among staff involved in the treatment of one patient and among staff and patients in general may have a protective function against this particular deterioration of communication of emotionally significant material.

One other danger of the hospital milieu therapy approach consists in the relative role diffusion among professionals from the various disciplines involved. Ideally, each discipline should have specific skills and tools that distinguish its approach to patients from that of other disciplines; however, the commonly shared utilization of human skills by all helping professions in evaluating transference and countertransference reactions in the here-and-now, and the shared communication and analysis of emotional reactions in the group processes in the hospital, tend to blur the limits between the functions of various disciplines, to threaten individual staff members with role diffusion, and to exacerbate conflicts of interest among the professions. It is therefore important to reevaluate from time to time what the specific contributions of each profession within the hospital are and should be. This is particularly important in the treatment of schizophrenic patients, who usually have difficulties in differentiating the social role of themselves and others.

At present, it seem that schizophrenia is here to stay with us for a long time and that the expectations of eradicating this illness by massive psychopharmacological approaches, at the one extreme, or by massive psychosocial manipulations, at the other, are highly exaggerated, to put it mildly. My final plea is, at the theoretical level, for a tolerance of complexity and, at the clinical level, for the training and professional development of highly skilled clinicians, able and willing to enter with openness and respect the world of schizophrenic patients and at the same time, able to withstand getting lost in that world.

REFERENCES

1. Bateson, G. and Jackson, D., et al.: Toward a theory of schizophrenia. *Behavioral Sci.* **1**:251–264, 1956.
2. Bion, W. R.: *Experiences in Groups,* Basic Books, New York, 1959.
3. Bion, W.: *Second Thoughts; Selected Papers on Psychoanalysis,* Heinemann, London, 1967.
4. Kernberg, O.: Early ego integration and object relations. *Ann. N.Y. Acad. Sci.:* **193**:233–247, 1972.
5. Kernberg, O.: Clinical observations regarding the diagnosis, prognosis and intensive treatment of chronic schizophrenic patients. In *Traitements au Long Course des États Psychotiques,* Colette Chiland, M.D. and Paul Bequart, M.D. (Eds.), Eduard Privat, Paris, 1974, pp. 215–233.

6. Kernberg, O.: Psychoanalytic object-relations theory, group processes and administration. *Ann. Psychoanal.* 1:363–388, 1973.

7. Kernberg, O.: A crisis in the adjunctive therapy department. *Hosp. Community Psychiatr.* 24:225–230, 1973, With Ann Appelbaum, M.D.

8. Kernberg, O.: A Systems Approach to Priority Setting of Interventions in Groups. Presented to the American Group Psychotherapy Association, Detroit, February, 1973 Unpublished.

9. Laing, R. D. and Esterson, A.: *Sanity, Madness and the Family,* Penguin Books, Baltimore, 1964.

10. Lidz, T.: The family, personality development, and schizophrenia. In *Origins of Schizophrenia,* J. Romano, (Ed.), Excerpta Medica Foundation, New York, pp. 131–138.

11. Main, T. F.: The ailment. *Brit. J. Med. Psychol.* 30:129–145, 1957.

12. Rice, A. K.: Individual, group and intergroup processes. *Human Relat.* 22:565–584, 1969.

13. Rioch, M. J.: The work of Wilfred Bion on groups. *Psychiatry* 33:56–66, 1970.

14. Rosenfeld, H. A.: *Psychotic States, A Psychoanalytic Approach,* International Universities Press, New York, 1965.

15. Rosenthal, D.: *Genetic Theory and Abnormal Behavior,* McGraw-Hill, New York, 1970.

16. Searles, H. F.: *Collected Papers on Schizophrenia and Related Subjects,* International Universities Press, New York, 1965.

17. Stanton, A. A. and Schwartz, M. S.: *The Mental Hospital,* Basic Books, New York, 1954.

18. Wynne, L. C., Ryckoff, I. M., Day, J., and Hirsch, S. I.: Pseudo mutuality in the family relations of schizophrenics. *Psychiatry* 21:205, 1958.

19. Wynne, L. C. and Singer, M. T.: Thought disorder and family relations of schizophrenics: I. A research strategy. *Arch. Gen. Psychiatr.* 9:191, 1963.

20. Wynne, L. C. and Singer, M. T.: Thought disorder and family relations of schizophrenics: II. A classification of forms of thinking. *Arch. Gen. Psychiatr.* 9:199, 1965.

CHAPTER TEN

INSTITUTIONAL PSYCHIATRY

HENRY BRILL, M.D.

As this chapter is being written, the future of the large mental hospitals appears more uncertain than ever before in their history. Some writers call for their total and unconditional liquidation.[4, 10, 40] Other writers, and they are now a vocal majority, are asking what will replace these hospitals and whether the new services should be created before the older ones are withdrawn.[9, 12, 20, 22, 23] They are asking also whether the replacement can be total and if not how large a population will be better served in the mental hospitals. Finally it remains to be seen what part these hospitals will play in the system of mental health care which is now evolving. Such questions are being raised in the context of attacks on the state hospitals, and it is curious that these institutions which are still being assailed for having allowed themselves to become "a dumping ground for the rejects of the community" are at the same time under fire for precisely the opposite reason—for dumping their patients into the community.[12, 17, 36] This says many things about the nature of the problem, but it also shows that society will not accept in practice, what was once accepted in theory— that virtually any alternative is preferable to the mental hospital. The ideal of community placement has not by any means been given up, but the emphasis has shifted from merely "running down" the hospital population to creating adequate community based alternatives. This represents a relatively new phase in the history of the mental hospitals and the events which led to it are of relatively recent date.

THE FALL OF MENTAL HOSPITAL
POPULATION AND ITS REPERCUSSIONS

The year 1955 will undoubtedly be recorded by medical historians as the start of a revolution in mental hospital practice and perhaps in psychiatry generally. This was the year when a confluence of social, political, and technological events initiated a series of major mental hospital changes which are still in the process of evolving. Like revolutions generally, the origins of this one Revolution, date back many years, and the entire process can be reconstructed only in part.

A series of momentous professional advances had been registered in the previous 50 years and all of them had their impact, but they had had no visible effect on overall population trends. Among these one may list the development of psychoanalysis; the introduction of new somatic therapies such as insulin and electric shock; the creation of a greatly improved series of sedatives and anticonvulsants; and the development of antiluetic drugs, vitamins, hormones, and other substances of value in certain psychiatric disorders. Furthermore, a strong mental health movement had been organized; the public appeared to have adopted a more constructive attitude about mental illness than ever before; and in the United States the Federal Government with its National Institute of Mental Health had reentered the field. This was especially significant because the Federal Government had avoided this area since the failure of the 1854 bid by Dorothea Linde Dix for a Federal land grant to support mental hospitals. In Britain the mental hospitals had been brought into the National Health Service in 1948 and this had led to great improvement in the status of these hospitals with a promise of much more to come.[43]

Yet in spite of all this the population of the mental hospitals had until 1955 continued to rise relentlessly in the United States, Canada, Britain[6] and other countries where admission was not restricted. In those countries which did restrict admissions the waiting lists grew longer; the pressure for more mental hospital beds was universal. This was as true in states like New York which provided over 600 beds per 100,000 of its general population as it was in localities with a fraction of that number. Facilities seemed to "silt up" as fast as they were opened, and some observers felt that as long as more mental hospital beds were provided they would be filled. Still other developments also had failed to have a visible effect on the relentless growth of state hospital figures. Child guidance clinics were proposed as prevention[39]; family care was launched as an alternative[30]; large increases took place in the psychiatric units of general hospitals, and the number of private psychiatrists rose spectacularly, but the mental hospitals grew faster than ever.

By 1955 the census of United States mental hospitals had reached 560, 000 and had doubled every 25 years since 1900. In Britain the figure had reached 152,000 by the end of 1954[16], and in New York State it was some 93,000[6] in March 1955.

It was at this point that the first large scale use of the new tranquilizing agents chlorpromazine and reserpine took place. And that year saw the beginning of a fall in population of United States mental hospitals that has continued ever since and has now reduced their size by more than 50%. A similar reduction has been registered for the state of New York, but it is noteworthy that while the decrease began at the same time[16] in Britain it has proceeded more slowly, producing a reduction of a third even though Britain has been a leader in hospital reform through this entire period.

Patton and Brill analyzed the data for the first years of population fall in the New York State's mental hospitals and concluded that it was due to the large scale use of the new drugs. They based their conclusion on the observation that decreases were noted only in those patient groups where the drugs were effective, and on the fact that no other change in the mental hospital situation was identified to offer an alternative explanation.

Furthermore, through the use of these drugs the atmosphere of the mental hospitals had changed simultaneously and regressive and disturbed behavior had virtually disappeared.[5] Reports that so many other states and countries had a similar experience at the same time seemed to support their conclusion.

The years following 1955 saw an acceleration of the population fall. In New York, the first decrease, registered in fiscal year 1955 to 1956, was under 500, but in the year 1968 to 1969 it amounted to over 7000. This acceleration may be seen at least in part as a secondary reaction to the drug induced improvements in the hospital situation. At that time the public gained confidence that mental illness was in truth an illness like all others, that it could be treated, and that the mentally ill could and should be given more freedom. Liberalized release procedures, open hospitals, and an increasing support for the rights of psychiatric patients followed.

THE JOINT COMMISSION REPORT AND THE COMMUNITY MENTAL HEALTH CENTERS ACT

A second and unrelated development of 1955 was the establishment, by Congress, of the Joint Commission on Mental Illness and Health. One of the main motives of this move was dissatisfaction with the mental hospitals which had always been understaffed, underfinanced, overcrowded, and a traditional target for public attack.[8] The Commission report issued in 1961 paid little attention to the improvements which had gotten under way in the mental hospitals after 1955, and its recommendations led to the Community Mental Health Centers Act of 1963 which had as one of its main purposes the eventual replacement of the large mental hospitals by a locally based comprehensive system of prevention and treatment although President Kennedy's message to Congress on the subject dared only to predict that "if we launch a broad new mental health program now [1963] it will be possible with a decade of two to reduce the number of patients now under custodial care by 50% or more."[19]

STATE MENTAL HOSPITALS SINCE 1955

Since 1955 many other conditions have changed and each of these might be considered as having contributed to or produced the population fall in state hospitals. The number of outpatient clinics has almost doubled while the number of psychiatrists, psychologists, and psychiatric social workers has more than doubled.[1, 25] Finally, the use of outpatient clinics has risen by more than 600%. By 1972 the number of reported outpatient episodes was 2,317,000 as compared with some 200,000 in 1961[32] and if one includes the number of patients seen in private practice some 2% of the total United States population now has some type of psychiatric attention each year.[1] Thus the vast expansion of other mental health services, the introduction of the Community Mental Health Centers, the increase of mental health professionals, the mass use of psychotropic drugs, and the liberalized mental hospital practices all have occurred since 1955, and there is room for much debate as to what part, if any, each played in the mental hospital changes.

The available evidence seems to point to the drugs as the initiators of the process,[5] and the liberalized practices and policies of the mental hospitals themselves as the reason for the subsequent marked acceleration in population fall. It does not seem that the CMHC's or the other alternative psychiatric services contributed in any major way. The effect of the CMHC's is perhaps the easiest to rule out. The earliest of these facilities were not opened till 1966 eleven years after the population fall had begun; by 1969 only 200 of the planned 2000 of these centers were open, and even in 1971 these centers served only 19% of the United States population; by that time the mental hospital census had fallen by 44%.

The effect of other psychiatric services is somewhat more difficult to evaluate, but if they were to have an influence, it would have to be either by decreasing admissions to the mental hospitals or by facilitating discharges through providing treatment for patients leaving the hospitals. Neither of these occurred. Mental hospital admissions were not reduced; instead they rose steadily from 185,000 in 1955 to over 400,000 in 1971, although there has been a small decrease in the last 2 years.[2] Furthermore, the fall could not have been produced by after-care services in community facilities because it is a matter of common experience that such facilities have tended not to accept state hospital type patients either before or after they have been in a state hospital.

CREDIT FOR POPULATION FALL AND BLAME FOR DUMPING PATIENTS

We are thus left with the conclusion that the state hospital changes were due to changes in the policies of the hospitals themselves. The average hospital stay dropped from 6 months to 41 days in those years, and whatever after-care the discharged patients received was given by the hospitals and not by community facilities. This has been the view of those who consider the after-care inadequate and characterize the release of many of these patients as "dumping" into the community.[12, 41] At this time no one seems to be inclined to claim the credit (or share the blame) for the state hospital decreases. The criticisms, which have mounted sharply in the last 2 years, are directed not against release per se but against inadequate preparation of the patient in the hospital, inadequate placement, and inadequate follow-up. Nevertheless, in spite of the way in which the objections are verbalized community reaction leaves little doubt[9, 17] that an additional underlying motivation is the old deep-rooted community reluctance to have groups of ex-patients housed nearby. At the center of the controversy is the problem of the unrecovered patient who cannot care for himself adequately in the community; he is looked upon with sympathy but suspicion and anxiety as well. It has often been tacitly assumed that community placement in itself would be therapeutic for such persons but recent studies now report that it may instead involve rejection by the public, regimentation by landlords, and an overall state which may be worse than it was in the mental hospital.[23, 24] This last is supported by newspaper exposées describing horror stories of such persons being victimized by rooming house operators who seize their welfare checks and maintain the patients at the edge of survival.[12, 17]

Demands are now being made that adequate alternative facilities be created before such patients leave the mental hospitals and that proper conditions for living and for social and economic rehabilitation be provided by a responsible agency and not be left to spontaneous "community" action. Experts seem to agree that it is possible and desirable for many mental hospital cases, but they warn that this will be at least as costly as mental hospital care. The problem of the patient who is not cooperative with such programs remains as yet unsolved and virtually undiscussed, even though clinical experience indicates that many such patients seem to seek a regressive pattern of existence by preference and may not be amenable to voluntary community programs. Such persons are disruptive to society far in excess of their numerical importance and because of social and economic pressure they are driven to cluster in low grade rooming houses, and deteriorating hotels and skid rows. They are often not certifiable under current laws, but they do require social as well as fiscal support and must in some way be protected from the effects of their own negligence, and from the depredations of the unscrupulous who are attracted by the regular welfare type cash allowance which they receive. Even if such patients do have a responsible family there are many problems, and it is now generally conceded that both the family and the patient require far more assistance then they have had in the past.

These negative aspects of hospital operations should not be allowed to overshadow the very real advances which have taken place in patient treatment, care, and rehabilitation.

GERIATRIC PSYCHIATRY

Another aspect of mental hospital policy which was roused considerable criticism is the resistance against accepting geriatric cases on the grounds that simple senile deterioration does not constitute a psychosis and that such cases should not be sent to a state hospital. It is a paradox that the state mental hospitals had previously been vigorously condemned because they did receive such cases. Now they are under attack because they do not receive them. The intent has, of course, been to encourage the development of alternate facilities for the aged located in their own communities, and there has indeed been a considerable increase in the numbers of such facilities, but these in turn are now being criticised as inadequate in quality, unsafe, and still insufficient in number.[14, 15, 26, 27, 42] It appears that here as elsewhere in the mental hospital situation the real issue is upgrading of care and not the sign over the door of the facility. It is too easily lost to sight that transferring the patient from one type of facility to another is a pseudo solution unless care is improved. The history of the mental health movement is replete with examples of such pseudo solutions.[8] What is lacking in one facility cannot be supplied merely by moving the patient to another type of installation.

ANTIPSYCHIATRY AND THE STATE HOSPITAL

The state hospital type facility has been a prime target of the movement which has come to be known as "antipsychiatry."[4, 10, 35, 40] The political orientation of most of the writers seems to be toward the left although some years ago a right wing group in the south western part of the United States also attacked the mental health movement and the hospitals as communist in orientation.

For a long time the issues raised by antipsychiatry had to do with the principle of involuntary hospitalization and the effects of hospital life as portrayed by such writers as Goffman, Foucault, and Rothman. Their writings reactivated and reinforced preexisting fears, suspicions, and dislike of mental hospitals which date from the eighteenth century, reactions which had become dormant with the state hospital improvements of the 1950s. Basically the reaction contained much that can be seen as a displacement of the fears of mental illness onto the hospitals. With this background it was easy to persuade many influential persons that what psychiatrists call chronic schizophrenia was purely an artifact of long hospital residence. More recently the displacement has broadened its scope and has produced attacks on everything connected with organized psychiatry including psychiatrists, all types of psychiatric hospitals, and psychiatric procedures. Antipsychiatry is at many points closely linked to the counter-culture and one finds almost as many view points as there are writers, but they all seem to agree in their total condemnation of the mental hospital. This writer knows from personal experience that their statements have had a major impact on laws, judical decisions, and administrative regulations. Unfortunately their views are essentially negative; and they consist of persuasive logic only; the antipsychiatrists offer no positive alternatives and present no scientific data to show that abandoning current procedures would produce better results, or otherwise improve the lot of the mentally disabled patient. One would think that antipsychiatry must be on a collision course with those who deprecate the "dumping" of hospital patients, but up to the present time both sides seem to avoid direct conflict and have contented themselves with attacking the hospitals.

The most direct practical expression of the antihospital sentiment is found in such programs as those of Saskatchewan and California which have moved to close their large mental hospitals. A full scientific evaluation of their experience still remains to be done and anecdotal accounts are contradictory. We can say only that the California program which reduced the hospital population from a high of some 36,000 in the mid-1950s to some 7000 in 1973 came under attack when that state announced a plan for the total liquidation of the state hospitals and the state schools. As a result the plan has now been withdrawn.[7, 33]

ADMINISTRATIVE AND OTHER CHANGES

In all this discussion one must not forget that the mental hospital of today has undergone revolutionary changes and improvements since 1955; the average cost per diem has risen from $3 in 1956 to $20 in 1972[1]; the overcrowding has, of course, been abolished by the drastic cut in population; and overall staff ratios have risen by 300% in 10 years.[25] In addition the mental hospitals have become largely or wholly open facilities; a large proportion of cases are on voluntary status; and patients' rights are strictly defined and protected by a variety of formal mechanisms. In New York a Mental Health Information Service which is a branch of the courts operating within the hospitals maintains contact with all patients and stands ready to assure that any contested issues are brought before a judge. The old fears of peonage of patients have been eliminated by court decisions and other legal action which requires that patients who work for the benefit of the hospital must be paid minimum wages.[31] This has produced some enforced idleness which certain patients resent bitterly, but it should at least put to rest one old suspicion about hospital practices. Termination of unpaid work has incidentally not been followed by any visible exodus of "working patients" from the hospitals of which I have personal knowledge.

Finally, the total atmosphere of the state hospital has been radically changed; regressed and disturbed wards have disappeared and today it is unusual even to hear a "disturbed" patient. Moreover, as one makes hospital rounds he sees that restraint, seclusion, and tube feeding have been reduced to the vanishing point, and one is struck by the extent to which the residual mental hospital population today is made up of older persons who entered the hospital many years ago, almost 50% being over 65 in New York.

Another major change in hospital operations that gets little notice has to do with nutrition. The application of scientific principles has within the past decade or two eliminated the nutritional edemas, and the "acrocyanoses" that were a traditional part of the old state hospitals. Good nutrition too has played a major role in eliminating various infections, although here the antibiotics have, of course, been of great value. In spite of all these developments, the old "snake pit" legend still colors the popular sterotype of the mental hospital, and many persons are even today reluctant to visit "such places" although volunteer workers are coming to these hospitals in greater numbers every year and are encouraged by hospital arrangements such as formal volunteer departments.

Another change in mental hospital practice has been the regionalization of services, that is, the subdivision of the total geographical area of the institution into several catchment areas each of which is assigned to its corresponding hospital division or unit. In this instance as in many other aspects of social and administrative psychiatry, United States practice was much influenced by British example, since the pioneering work with "catchment areas" was done in that country. In 1958 the Veterans Administration in Topeka Kansas took the lead in the United States and regionalized its services, and the movement gradually gained ground in the next few years. It probably received much of its current impetus from the 1964 Federal regulations for CMHC's which specified that each center would serve a region containing 75,000 to 200,000 population.[29] The aim of regionalization is to make the hospital relationships less impersonal, to provide continuity of service, to allow the treatment team to become familial with the agencies and conditions in its own area, and to fix responsibility for area services on a single group. The concepts of the CMHC have influenced mental hospital practice and many of these hospitals have begun to broaden their range of services to their own areas and some have actually established formal CMHC's. Regionalization has been criticized on the grounds that it is used to exclude patients which limits their freedom of choice[29] and that it is monopolistic and stifles healthy competition. Nevertheless division into catchment areas is now the dominant pattern in United States mental hospital services.

The corresponding internal division of the hospitals has taken a wide variety of forms. For the most part the hospital unit which corresponds to a catchment area is clinically quite autonomous. At first the concept called for a radical mixing of all patients from a given geographical area, and all patients, acute and chronic, young and old, were housed together on the same ward. This did not work out well,[37, 38] and today the tendency is again to treat acute patients on special wards separate from long-term cases— and special wards are also usually set aside for geriatric and infirm cases, sometimes in a single psychogeriatric unit that serves several catchment areas. Medical-surgical services and units for children and adolescents are, of course, also centralized. A difficult question is how far administrative and support services should be unitized. In some instances there is complete separation producing the so-called colocated hospitals—two or more independent hospitals on the same grounds. In others, there are varying degrees and patterns of separation but costs rise as separation is more complete, and this is a limiting factor.

Associated with unitization is the development of the treatment team, a multidisciplinary grouping of personnel which allows for "blurring of roles" amomg various disciplines. This involves a conscious egalitarianism which may include everyone in the unit, patients as well as staff. Some of the problems which may occur in this connection have been described by Panzetta[29] and it must be admitted that certain professional and human issues which tend to be raised by this movement have not been fully resolved.

ACTIVITY AND REHABILITATION

The rehabilitative programs of the state hospital have changed radically in the last decade. The old basket weaving type of occupational therapy has been replaced by a vocationally oriented program which seeks to progress the individual through formal vocational rehabilitation to paid employment, often with some form of sheltered work as an intermediate step. Recreation stresses socialization and the sexes are purposely brought into contact with each other not only at dances but in dining rooms and in day-to-day hospital life. In spite of fears which were expressed about such practices, they have not resulted in orgies of promiscuity nor epidemics of pregnancy. Homemaking classes, academic education, patient projects, and bus trips to recreational points are among the other features of current mental hospital programs.

TREATMENT

The state hospital innovations with respect to the more narrowly defined techniques of treatment have recently been extended to include the application of social and psychological principles. In this category one finds a variety of procedures for behavior modification using positive and negative reinforcement methods that range from token economies to electrical aversive stimuli.[3] The latter have been vigorously criticized and negative conditioning is now largely confined to withdrawal of privileges. In the field of the somatic therapies where the state mental hospitals led the field since the introduction of insulin shock therapy in the 1930s, there has been a pronounced decrease of initiative much influenced by current suspicions of new psychiatric drugs, by the attacks of antipsychiatry and by legal restrictions on human research generally. Several of the older somatic methods have been completely abandoned, and these include insulin and metrazol therapy. Psychosurgery too has virtually disappeared and some think this has been premature; one occasionally still sees a patient suffering from intractable behavior disorder, which is not responsive to any of the available therapies and cannot help but wonder whether the British may not be justified in continuing their work with modified psychosurgical techniques.[18] ECT still survives though it is being given to far fewer patients. The courses of treatment tend to be brief and would in the past have been considered inadequate, but the use of the psychotropic drugs has changed the indications. ECT is almost universally modified by the administration of such substances as succinylcholine and thiopental. Younger psychiatrists tend to be quite reluctant to use ECT, and the current climate of public opinion also limits the use of most of the somatic methods except for the tranquilizing drugs. No doubt electric shock therapy has been overused, and indeed abused, but the immoderate views of the antipsychiatrists seem quite unwarranted and have contributed to the opposite error of underuse with its hazards of suicide and chronicity.

PHARMACOTHERAPY

The early history of drug therapy was written in the large mental hospitals, and this form of treatment is still employed in some 60 to 70% of cases. In the course of years the number of available drugs has multiplied and so has the variety of medications in common use. Unfortunately interest in the technical side of pharmacotherapy has not kept pace with the drug supply, and it is necessary to combat a tendency to polypharmacy and routinization of prescribing. Perhaps the most important recent practical advance has been the introduction of prolonged action parenteral phenothiazines such as the enanthates. These are particularly useful in cases who cooperate poorly. Lithium too has been generally accepted but at this time finds only limited use. Tardive dyskinesia has emerged as a significant problem in the mental hospitals because many patients must be treated for long periods of time and are particularly vulnerable because of age and complicating organic states. Drug holidays, minimum dose levels, and careful selection of drugs offers a partial solution to these problems, but it must be admitted that currently available drugs do not meet the needs of many long-term patients especially the need for something to reverse defect states, apathy, and lack of response to stimulation of rehabilitation.

AFTERCARE

The aftercare of patients leaving the mental hospitals is a problem which has had varying solutions. Some states like New York have long maintained an organized after care, but this has always called for a great deal of cooperation by patients since the legal basis for compulsion was always tenuous and today the dependence on cooperation is even greater. The relationship between the patient and the hospital is not at all that of a parolee to a correctional facility. Most patients are discharged as they leave the hospital and have only a voluntary contact with the after-care service, and even if they are still under a judicial certificate this provides only very limited authority and can be used to return the patient to the hospital only if his mental condition clearly requires it. In many states distance interferes with after care, but satellite and traveling clinics are used to fill the gap or, the patients are referred to local physicians. A fully comprehensive community service seems to be the only real answer to the need for after-care.

The state hospitals have long maintained an interest in transitional facilities, the first being family care which dates back to the 1930s.[30] In the past 10 years the hospitals have taken an increasing initiative in the development of the transitional facilities which are especially needed for long-term patients. Some hospitals are now operating hostels, others have set up day and night hospitals while still others have rented ordinary furnished apartments where they place and support small groups of patients until these can get work or welfare.[11, 21] Community resistance to such installations remains a constant problem, and sometimes it is insuperable.

WHAT OF THE FUTURE?

As this chapter is being written, the future of the large mental hospital seems uncertain. Some feel that all large mental hospitals will soon be decommissioned; others, more radical, see the end of all medical psychiatry as inevitable. It is hard to find two writers who have exactly the same opinion as to what the future holds although virtually every possibility seems to be espoused by one or another. On one point only does one find virtually unanimous agreement—that further major change is inevitable. All of this is of great practical significance because of the current emphasis on redesign of systems of delivery of mental health services as well as health services generally. In this connection much attention has been given to the psychiatric units of general hospitals which will undoubtedly continue to increase their activities, but as Jones has stated: "It is hard to see how [they] . . . could fully replace the large mental hospitals."[16] They suffer from serious disadvantages in dealing with patients who need more than a few weeks of treatment because their quarters are cramped, and they are not large enought to provide the needed variety of rehabilitative services. Finally, their costs are three to four times as high as those of the larger facilities. This could change somewhat in the future if we follow the example of certain European countries where a small mental hospital of up to several hundred beds may be attached by a corridor to an ordinary general hospital. As yet only 20% of United States general hospitals have psychiatric units[1] and with their 10,000 beds and their out-patient departments these hospitals still see only 18% of all psychiatric cases in the United States. Three-quarters of their cases are out-patients and the average stay is about 3 weeks. So far they have tended to limit admissions to nonorganic, nondrug, nonalcoholic, adult, and short-term cases and to admit others only when they serve as screening centers providing triage for state hospital admission.

Another alternative that is now being vigorously pursued is to do away with the need for long-term mental hospital care altogether and substitute brief crisis intervention followed by full community support. The success of this plan must depend on stable financing and on a large degree of public tolerance for aberrant behavior. If either of these is lacking the only alternative is a breakthrough in technology which will provide a quick and reliable final treatment which will in fact end chronic mental disability of the schizophrenic pattern. After that we shall be in a position to reassess our position with respect to the other long-term mental disorders.

Finally, of course, the possibility remains that the mental hospital will undergo further change and will be adapted to the new conditions of psychiatric practice serving as a community mental health center for a specific region and a long-term facility for a larger one. It may be significant that at this time New York State hospitals see 10% of all out-patients in the State not counting their own after-care services.

REFERENCES

1. American Hospital Association: *Hospital Statistics 1972,* Chicago, Ill., 1973.

2. Bethel, H. E.: Provisional patient movement and administrative data state and county mental hospital inpatient services July 1, 1971–June 30, 1972. *Statistical Note* 77, N.I.N.H. Biometry Branch, Washington, D.C., March 1973.

3. Birk, L. et al.: Report of A.P.A. Task Force on Behavior Therapy. American Psychiatric Association, Wash. D.C., July 1973.

4. Boyers, R. and Orrill, R.: *R. D. Laing and Anti Psychiatry,* Perennial Library, Harper & Row, New York, 1971, p. 229.

5. Brill, H. and Patton, R. E.: Analysis of population reduction in New York state mental hospitals during the first four years of large scale therapy with psychotropic drugs. *Am. J. Psychiatr.* 116(6):494–508, December 1959.

6. Brill, H. and Patton, R.: *The Impact of Modern Chemotherapy on Hospital Organization, Psychiatric Care and Public Health Policy,* Proceedings of the Third World Congress of Psychiatry, Vol. 3, University of Toronto Press, 1964, p. 433–437.

7. *Buffalo Courier Express:* Reagan shelves plan to phase out mental hospitals. November 11, 1973, p. 38.

8. Caplan, R. B.: *Psychiatry and the Community in Nineteenth Century America* Basic Books, New York, 1969.

9. Cryer, D.: Bizarre acts bring hostility. *Newsday,* December 13, 1973, pp. 34–35.

10. DeGalard, H., (Ed.): *L'antipsychiatrie La Nef,* Librairie Jules Tallandier, Paris, January–May 1971, p. 42.

11. Dykens, W. et al.: *Strategies of Mental Hospital Change,* Commonwealth of Massachusetts, Boston, Mass., 1964.

12. Esman, A. H.: Discharge of state hospital patients constitutes 'a grotesque Fraud'. *The Bulletin,* New York State Branches, American Psychiatric Association, Vol 16, No 4, November 1973, p. 8.

13. Glasscote, R. M., Sussex, J., N., Cumming, E. and Smith, L.: The community mental health center an interim appraisal. The Joint Information Service of the American Psychiatric Association and the National Association for Mental Health, Wash., D.C., 1969.

14. Hanson, K.: Alone and afraid in a tiny room. *N.Y. Daily News,* February 27, 1973, p. 34.

15. Hanson, K.: The setting adrift of the old and unit. *N.Y. Daily News,* February 26, 1973, p. 32.

16. Jones, K. and Sidebotham, R.: *Mental Hospitals at Work,* Routledge and Kegan, Paul, London, 1962.

17. Keeler, B.: Long beach to limit ex-patients (proposal would ban hotels and boarding houses for former mental patients) *Newsday*, December 13, 1973, p. 3.

18. Kelly, D. et al.: Stereotactic limbic leucotomy. *Brit. J. Psychiatr.* **123**:141–148, 1973.

19. Kennedy, J.: Mental illness and mental retardation. Feb. 5, 1963, 88th Congress, House of Representatives, Document No. 58, U.S. Government Printing Office, Wash., D.C., 1963.

20. Lamb, H. R. and Goertzel, V.: The demise of the state hospital—A premature obituary. *Arch. Gen. Psychiatr.* **26**:489–495, June 1972.

21. Landy, D. and Greenblatt, M.: Half way house. H.E.W. Vocational Rehabilitation Administration, Wash., D.C., 1965.

22. *Mental Hygiene News:* Seek better programs for former patients. Oct. 12, 1973, p. 3.

23. Murphy, H. B. M., Pennee, B., and Luchins, D.: Foster homes, the new back wards? *Canada's Mental Health Suppl.* No. 71, September–October 1972, pp. 1–17.

24. Murphy, H. B. M.: Results from evaluating a canadian regional mental health program, *Hosp. Comm. Psychiatr.* **24**(8):533–542, August 1973.

25. N.I.M.H.: Staffing of mental health facilities United States 1972, Series B, No 6, Mental Health Statistics, Analytical and Special Study Reports (draft copy).

26. *N.Y. Daily News:* Eleven men die in Philadelphia nursing home fire. September 14, 1973, p. 6.

27. O'Brien, J. and Nolte, R.: Elderly left alone plead for aid in boarding house. *Chicago Tribune*, February 3, 1972, Sec. 1, p. 19.

28. Ozarin, L., Taube, C. and Spaner, F. E.: Operations indices for community mental health centers. *Am. J. Psychiatr.* **128**(12):1511–1516, June 1972.

29. Panzetta, A. F.: *Community Mental Health, Myth and Reality*, Lea and Febiger, Philadelphia, 1971.

30. Pollack, H. M.: *Family Care of Mental Patients*, State Hospitals Press, Utica, N.Y., 1936.

31. *Psychiatric News:* Court orders wages paid for in-hospital labor. December 5, 1973, p. 1.

32. Redick, R. W.: Patient Care Episodes in Psychiatric Services. United States 1971, Statistical Note 92, National Institute of Mental Health Survey and Reports Section, August 1973.

33. Rinsley, D. B.: *California hospitals, Psychiatric News*, June 20, 1973, p. 2.

34. Rosen, B., Kramer, M., Redick, R., and Willner, S. G.: Utilization of Psychiatric Facilities by Children. Public Health Service Pub. No 1868, U.S. Government Printing Office, Wash., D.C. 20402.

35. Rothman, D. J.: *The Discovery of the Asylum*. Little Brown, Boxton, 1971.

36. Saltus, R.: New day ahead for mentally ill, *Long Island Press*, June 14, 1973, p. 9.

37. Snow, H. B.: Aspects of decentralization of a state hospital. *Psychiatr. Quart.* **39**:607–620, 1965.

38. Snow, H. B.: The Dutchess county project after five years. *Milbank Mem. Fund Quart.*, January 1966, Vol. XLIV, No 1, part 2, p. 57–78.

39. Stevenson, G. S. and Smith, G.: *Child Guidance Clinics*, The Commonwealth Fund, New York, 1934.

40. Szasz, T.: *The Myth of Mental Illness*, Hoeber and Harper, New York, 1961.

41. *Time:* Crack up in mental care. December 17, 1963, p. 74.

42. U.S. Senate Report by the Subcommittee on Aging: Mental Health Care and the Elderly—Shortcomings in Public Policy, Report No. 92-433, November 8, 1971, pp. 13–16, U.S. Printing Office, Wash., D.C. 1971.

43. Vail, D. J.: *The British Mental Hospital System*, Charles Thomas, Springfield, Ill., 1965.

PART THREE

NEW OR NOT WIDELY KNOWN FORMS OF PSYCHOTHERAPY*

MORITA THERAPY: ITS SOCIOHISTORICAL CONTEXT

MEDITATION AS AN ADJUNCT TO PSYCHOTHERAPY

VALUE OF PATANJALI'S CONCEPTS IN THE TREATMENT OF PSYCHONEUROSIS

PARADOXICAL INTENTION AND DEREFLECTION: TWO LOGOTHERAPEUTIC TECHNIQUES

* Harold Kelman, M. D., is thanked for his contribution to the idea, organization, and editing of this chapter.

CHAPTER ELEVEN

MORITA THERAPY: IT'S SOCIOHISTORICAL CONTEXT

AKIHISA KONDO, M.D.

In Japan Past and Present, *Reischauer writes,*[4] *the two centuries of strictly enforced peace under the watchful eye and firm hand of the Edo government have left an indelible mark upon the people. The bellicose, adventurous Japanese of the sixteenth century became by the nineteenth century a docile people looking meekly to their rulers for all leadership and following without question all orders from above.*

His view is based mostly on political observation.

JAPANESE PERSONALITY AND RICE CULTURE

T he docile attitude of the Japanese was, however, also generated by their agricultural methods, especially of rice production, which has been their main staple food. Restricted by the limited available arable land, they were forced to rely on intensive cultivation of what they had. This required the collective efforts of the whole village. A farmer was dependent on the help of the villagers especially at the times of planting and harvesting. Likewise because each villager had to be so closely and mutually interdependent on the others for the necessities of life, he had to be very careful not to offend their feelings, otherwise he could not expect their help in the next season. When in fact someone did commit such an offense and hurt others' feelings, he was sure to be ostracized and to become an outcast.

IMPOSED MUTUAL SURVEILLANCE

Also since the Edo government strictly prohibited people leaving the country, they had no other choice. They had to stay and be docile and not offend others. In addition, the Edo government enforced a system of mutual surveillance. Each villager was responsible for every other neighbor; any individual deriliction resulted in punishment for all.

FEUDAL CLASS SYSTEM

Under these circumstances, it is easy to understand that sensitive attentiveness to others' feeling expressed in the attitudes of docility and obeyance to the superiors had to be developed. Also during the Edo era, in the most feudalistic days, the Tokugawa were the rulers. Reischauer states that "They created a hierarchy of four social classes, the warrior-administrator, the peasant, the artisan, and the merchant, and the members of this new fixed aristocracy who were known as samurai, meaning 'feudal retainers,' and their badge was the long and the short sword each samurai wore at his side."⁵ In reality the sword was not only a simple badge that showed their status but also an actual tool authorized to be used, if necessary, to kill people of inferior status whenever they felt insulted by those people, who, being totally deprived of any effective weapon to defend themselves, had no power to rebel against their superiors.

PATTERNS OF CONDUCT—RITUALS OF ETIQUETTE

Under such a circumstance, people under the Samurai class had to be sensitive to the superiors' feelings for the sake of their security. However, it is almost impossible to have the proper response on every occasion and not to hurt another's feelings even after exquisite sensitivity has been developed. A human being would have to be equipped with supersensitivities and to be the ultimate chameleon. Forms had to be invented to help people have a feeling of security which would aid them in giving the appearance of docility and of not intending to hurt anyone's feelings. Partly because of the governmental edict and partly because of these psychological factors, according to Reischauer "They [the Japanese] grew accustomed to firmly established patterns of conduct." He adds, "A thousand rules of etiquette, supplemented by instructions from their rulers, governed all their actions."⁶ As long as they followed these patterns, at least they had the advantage of feeling much more secure. Also they did not have to consume so much of their human energies in maintaining sensitivity so as not to hurt another's feelings.

THE MEIJI REFORMATION

After the Meiji Reform which took place in 1868, Japan opened her doors to the world. She began to orient herself toward modernization or Westernization with the goal of increasing her national wealth and bringing it up to the level of civilized countries in the West. The methods used were those of industrialization and of building up the armed forces. With this new orientation, she was abandoning the class system of the prior era. However, even though the systems were dropped, the life patterns which had been so strongly established in the Japanese mind were not so easily done away with. Actually a new hierarchy system was established.

Politically and socially, it centered in the Emperor with his governmental bureaucrats. Financially and economically wealth was concentrated in the hands of the strong financial groups called Zaibatsu. Instead of the samurai class, high government officials and the management of the Zaibatsu now became the superiors.

The established pattern of obedience to superiors and sensitivity to their feelings were still alive and active in every organization including family life. Just as the constitution was given to the people as an act of grace by the Emperor, similarly a worker's salary was "given" by superiors to their subordinates in organizations. The spirit of these attitudes was a continuation of what obtained during the Edo era. The big difference from the former society now lay in the fact that as long as a subordinate was docile and faithful to the orders of his superiors and fulfilled his given share of work diligently, he had the prospect of becoming a superior according to the rule of seniority preference. This was one of the governing rules in family life thoughout the society in the Edo period. This prospect gave a member of an organization not only the feeling of security but also a goal for which to work. And the organization in turn gave many kinds of protection to their employees' welfare as long as the latter were faithful to their organizations.

MODERN ORGANIZATION: REPLICA OF OLD FAMILY RELATIONSHIPS

The nature of human relationships in organizations whose forms were introduced from the West can be understood as an extension of the relationship between the feudal lord and his retainers, but even more as a replica of the relationships among Japanese family members and of the spirit of these relationships. Competitiveness, which was characteristic of the industrialized societies, was therefore much more prevalent among various organizations than among the individuals in the organization. In other words, competitiveness was openly admitted between organizations, but suppressed among the individuals in the organization. Their attention was chiefly directed toward not hurting the feelings of group members, especially those of their superiors.

JAPANESE ARCHITECTURE AND HYPERSENSITIVITY TO OTHERS' FEELINGS

It has been my observation that one of the factors that contributed to the formation of hypersensitivity to others' feelings among the Japanese is related to the interior conditions of the Japanese house structure. The interior of a Japanese house, generally, is partitioned by paper screens, and/or thin walls through which sounds are easily audible. Sounds in the house are not only noises; they convey other persons' feelings as well as their presence. Being brought up in such a house, a baby can sense the presence of his mother by the sounds in the kitchen and feel secure, but at the same time very often he can sense the irritation of his mother by the harsh clattering sounds of the plates she is washing. And, conversely, his mother can easily sense her baby's feelings by his crying, mumbling, or being silent.

Development of this sort of sensitivity is increased by imagination because of the partitions that hinder the direct visual observation of the other's facial expressions. Because of this situation, the modus operandi of Japanese communication depends much more on sensing than on explicit verbal expressions. As a consequence the structure of Japanese communication produces certain characteristics.

COMMUNICATION BASED ON EMOTIONAL SENSING

Since this sort of sensing is primarily central around sensing others' feelings, the communication to be achieved in this way is on the emotional level. The accuracy of sensing of others' feelings of course depends on the frequency of such experiencing and practicing. But as it is sharpened, even the personality of others can be sensed, especially in terms of their emotional inclinations. Therefore, it is an effective and efficient way of communicating in a closely related group such as a family. In this way, the members can share common feelings with each other, often without making use of or having to rely on overt verbal expressions, gestures, and facial expressions. But because of this very characteristic, sensing is not as effective for understanding the ideas or notions which others may have cognitively and which can be much more accurately expressed by verbal communication.

SENSING WHILE VERBALLY COMMUNICATING

Even while verbally communicating in Japanese, sensing plays a very important role. As frequently observed in Japanese expressions, there are many sentences which have no subject or definite object articulately stated. In terms of Western grammar, they are incomplete sentences. These sentences can only be understood and become meaningful by sensing not only the context but also the situational factors which vary in each case. In understanding and appreciating Japanese literature and art, such as Haiku,

Sumie, and Noh play, this sort of sensing of what is not expressed or is omitted is especially necessary.

READING BETWEEN THE LINES IS BASIC

Therefore, reading between the lines is not only necessary in reading Japanese but also important in understanding Japanese verbal communication. It is a faculty that is useful and effective in understanding symbols, allusions, cues, hints, implications—what is subtle but meaningful. This structure of communication also produces, when it is distorted, many misunderstandings and confusions, resulting in projections, externalizations, or subjective distortions as understood in Western psychiatry. It is a fact that the interactions between the daily use of such a language as a tool for communication, and the constant functioning of sensitivity to feel and understand the many shades of meaning and emotional connotations of what is expressed complemented with what is not expressed, lead to the further development of a sensitivity of this kind.

SENSITIVITY AND SELF-IMAGE

The same factor that contributed to this development of sensitivity to others' feelings plays an important role in the formation of one's individuality, ego, or self-image in the Western sense. As a Japanese room has no keys with which to lock it, anyone who lives in such a room is not only sensitive to what is going on outside the room in connection with others' activity, but also has to be sensitive to and always to expect others coming into the room.

THE JAPANESE EGO-FIELD

The so-called ego-field which is considered as vital to one's self-feeling in the Western sense is in constant danger. When another person comes into the room, one has to share the room space with the new arrival. Put in mathematical terms, one's ego-field is divided by half and when the other leaves the room, one's ego-field is enlarged and ego-space recovered. As previously mentioned, Japanese family life is more or less ordered in a hierarchical system, or in a vertical order. It is not arranged in a horizontal system of equality as in the United States. Therefore, one's ego-field is contracted especially when a superior enters one's room. Accordingly, because of the constant decreasing and increasing of one's ego-field, to which one gets accustomed, one's self-feeling fluctuates.

THE JAPANESE SELF

In other words, the "ego" or the "self" of Japanese people is determined by their relation to others in each given situation. This has two consequences: one is the development of a flexible self or ego that adapts itself to the nature of human relationships or situations; the other is the establishment of certain formalities or patterns of being, which, even though not overtly expressed, help each individual feel secure and stable about his ego-field as long as he conforms to these patterns or formalities. These two effects, which seemingly are contradictory, maintain harmonious relationships among the Japanese.

Actually the Japanese word for self or ego can be translated as "one's own share," and the word for man or a human being as "being among men," connoting the existence of a whole or a basic space that is shared in common by each individual.

However, it takes quite a time to achieve and establish this sort of self or ego. The learning process for developing one's sensitivity to the nature of the situation with others is an extended one. While a baby may feel secure by virtue of simply being with others, for an adolescent it is a different matter. He may feel awkward and uncomfortable with others. Although he is sensitive, he has not yet acquired the dexterity and the flexibility required to adjust himself to the situation and find his own "share" as a "being among men," because he is split between his dependency needs and his upsurging desire for independence. We have observed certain sociocultural characteristics of Japanese people which obtained before World War II. They are as follows:

1. Their tendency toward or emphasis on interdependence.
2. Their sensitivity to others' feelings.
3. Their sense of self or ego as "one's own share."
4. The introduction and implatation of competitiveness as the result of their strenuous efforts to become Westernized, which more or less contradict the above-mentioned attitudes.

MORITA THEORY AND THERAPY

Morita[1-3, 7, 8] was born in 1874, 8 years after the Meiji Reformation had begun and Japan's Westernization had started. He died in 1938, 3 years before the outbreak of the Pacific War, and lived in the period which had the above-mentioned sociocultural characteristics. Correspondingly, the patients he treated were the people who more or less had come under the influences of the same sociocultural climate. His theory and therapy about *Shinkei-shitsu*, the term he gave to a Japanese type of neurosis, were developed through his observations and contact with these patients. After observing those who were hypochondriacal, manifested anxiety states, or obsessive and compulsive symptoms, he brought them all under the category of *Shinkei-shitsu*. He did so according to his understanding of those symptoms which he saw as the outcome or the expression of this specific type of personality.

He also observed that there is a vicious circle between the patients' sensitivity to their symptoms and the attention they paid to them. He noted that the more attention that is paid to symptoms, the more heightened the sensitivity to them, and the more the sensitivity to symptoms, the stronger the attention to them becomes, creating a vicious circle of psychic-interaction.

THE *SHINKEI-SHITSU* PERSONALITY

The *Shinkei-shitsu* personality,the neurotic personality of Morita's time, was characterized first, according to his view, by its introvertive tendency. The *Shinkei-shitsu* person, instead of blaming external factors for his symptoms, thus including others, he tends to accuse himself. The second characteristic is his tendency to hypersensitivity. He is very sensitive not only to others but also to his own mental and physical condition. The third characteristic is establishing and clinging to a certain ideal state of mind and/or emotion, or of a physical state of being which he feels he should live up to so that his life will not become endangered. This characteristic is called the idealistic attitude.

MORITA'S IDEALIZED SELF-CONCEPTION

According to Morita, the idealized self-conception stemmed from the desire or need of a person to perserve the security in life that is common to all human beings. But in the case of the *Skinkei-shitsu* person, his need or desire is so extraordinarily strong that he builds up an ideal state or condition as a standard necessary to attainment of his security. The content of ideal states or conditions, if scrutinized, boils down to an abstract rather vague notion or ideal, such as he should be a person who always is liked by others, he should have a stable, serene state of mind whenever and wherever he is, he should always feel pleasant, happy, comfortable, and safe, he should never be inferior to any person, his physical condition should be always nice, or he should keep an undisturbed, purely concentrated mind in reading and studying, and so forth.

With this ideal notion established in his mind, he is constantly and vigilantly attentive, and checks up on his mental or physical condition all the time. To any flaw, even the slightest, he responds or reacts with heightened sensitivity and anxiety. His "shoulds" are strict because of his desperate need for security. These ideals demand that no flaw be allowed and that their fulfillment be perfect. From these shoulds and standards arise the fourth characteristic of the *Shinkei-shitsu* personality. It is called the perfectionistic attitude. Its guiding principle is "all or nothing."

PERFECT FULFILLMENT OF "SHOULDS"

Because the *Shinkei-shitsu* person believes that his security depends on the perfect fulfillment of his shoulds, he subordinates himself to their demands and clings to them desperately instead of depending on himself or his intrinsic life force. Also his self-esteem always depends on the evaluation of others. What he sees as his security need and the evaluation of others is reflected in the content of his shoulds. This dependent attitude is the fifth characteristic of the *Shinkei-shitsu* personality.

Through all these characteristic attitudes, it can be observed that the *Shinkei-shitsu* person is always and totally concerned with the fulfillment of his shoulds, his security, and his self-preservation without regard for the well-being or security of others. Comparing himself to others, he complains and feels himself as the most anxiety-stricken, the most helpless, the most suffering, the most unhappy, and therefore the most wretched, inferior person in the world. Morita pointed out this attitude in the *Shinkei-shitsu* personality. He called it the ego-centered attitude which constitutes the sixth characteristic of the *Shinkei-shitsu* personality.

INTELLECTUALIZING OF *SHINKEI-SHITSU* PERSONALITY

Morita also observed an intellectual tendency in the person of the *Shinkei-shitsu* personality. However, in his case his intellect is put in the service of establishing and rationalizing his shoulds. Most frequently, it is subordinated to the futile attempt to control his feelings and his symptoms by objectifying and alienating them as something foreign to his whole entity, to be rejected and eradicated.

These are the attitudes that characterized the neurotic personality of Morita's time, the *Shinkei-shitsu* personality, that was produced by and reflects the sociocultural climate of Japan between 1900s and 1940s.

SELF-PRESERVATION VERSUS FREEDOM

As mentioned before, Japanese people have a tendency, generated and fostered in the Japanese sociocultural matrix, to be particularly sensitive to others' feelings and actions. To maintain their security, they learned to comply with formalities and adjust themselves to a given situation to have their own share in relation to others, at the expense of self-assertiveness in the Western sense. As a result, instead of asserting their freedom in the external world, their mental energy is directed and used toward preserving themselves within the framework of their ego-space which is proportionate to their status or position. This does not interfere with their working hard or with their zealous activities in the external world. If observed closely, it is easily seen that they are working hard or acting zealously within the confines of the share of the work assigned to them by the organizations to which they belong. Against this background we can see that Japanese people have a tendency to direct and discharge their energy centripetally.

INTROVERSIVE TENDENCY OF THE JAPANESE

In personality, Japanese have an introvertive tendency. In the light of this sociocultural matrix, we can understand that the basic traits of an introvertive tendency and sensitivity which Morita observed in the *Shinkei-shitsu* personality are an extension of the general patterns of Japanese culture. Regarding the establishment of the ideal state or condition, or "shoulds," in the *Skinkei-shitsu* personality, we can see almost a parallel picture in the pattern of Japanese culture in terms of their establishment of formalities or rules of life which they could feel they should follow. Actually in learning the arts such as of the tea ceremony, flower arrangement, or calligraphy, the teacher is supposed to show his work of art to the student as a paragon to be followed by the latter.

Even in introducing foreign civilization, the same attitude was taken by the Japanese. When Chinese civilization was introduced, the Japanese people took it as a paradigm which they should live up to. It was the same with the introduction of Western civilization in the Meiji era. Therefore, the very attitude of following and obeying the demands of their shoulds was nothing new to the Japanese.

SHINKEI-SHITSU IDEAL REFLECTS IDEALS OF JAPANESE ETHOS

When we check the content of the ideal state or condition, or the "shoulds" of the *Shinkei-shitsu* personality, we can find almost the same notions or ideals which are prevalent in Japanese culture. The notion or ideal that one should be liked by others is exactly the notion or ideal that is stressed in the Japanese sociocultural climate as mentioned above. A perfectionistic attitude is also one of the characteristics of the Japanese people as witnessed in their way of cleaning house, in the tea ceremony, in their meticulous care of Bonsai, or in their minutely detailed craftsmanship. As to the dependent attitude of the *Shinkei-shitsu* personality on others, we have already observed the identical pattern in Japanese culture as discussed before in connection with the interdependence in the village life, dependence on formalities and rules in daily life, and particularly dependence on others in defining "one's share"—one's self or his ego-field—in various situations.

WESTERNIZED JAPAN: COMPETITIVENESS FOSTERED BY BUSINESS ORGANIZATION—INDIVIDUALISTIC ASSERTIVENESS STILL CHECKED

The ego-centered attitude is also not so strange to a competitive society. Since the Meiji Reformation, Japan took Western society, the competitive society, as her model to follow and imitate. As industrialization has proceeded, competitiveness has become routine in the business world and it has been gradually pervading the individual mind. Actually, the notion that one should be superior to others as seen in the content of shoulds of the *Shinkei-shitsu* personality is a common notion for any individual in a competitive society and can be interpreted as an expression of his ego-centered attitude. From these points of view, we can see that the characteristics which Morita observed in the *Shinkei-shitsu* personality are closely related to the characteristics of Japanese culture representing the latter but exaggerated in a condensed form like a caricature.

MORITA: *SHINKEI-SHITSU* SHOULD BE TREATED AS A NORMAL PERSON

According to information obtained from one of his students, Morita used to say that the *Shinkei-shitsu* person is to be treated as a normal person because essentially he is not different from a normal person. His remark can be understood most clearly in the light of the foregoing observations, although it has another implication; namely, the *Shinkei-shitsu* person has in common with a normal person the life force to develp his intrinsic potentiality as a human being. In other words, the *Shinkei-shitsu* person is governed by the same kind of patterns of thinking, feeling, and acting, experiences the same kind of conflicts, problems, and anxieties, as his fellowmen. The difference is not in quality but in quantity.

In the Japanese sociocultural climate, as has been observed, the need for security plays the dominant role in determining the patterns of life of the Japanese, and contributes a great deal to the formation of their characteristics. But if we put freedom as the antonym to security and observe from that point of view, we find that the traits of self-assertiveness, competitiveness, and independence are not so strongly emphasized in Japanese life, and that they are much less developed in comparison with Western society where self-assertiveness, competitiveness, and independence foster the freedom of individuality.

CONFLICTS CAUSED BY WESTERNIZATION

Of course, Japanese, being human, manage to maintain their individuality, their self, in their own way. However, in contrast to the Japanese notion of self, the freedom of individuality was a totally new concept when it was introduced as a result of Westernization. It was in those days, when the Japanese were struggling for absorbing and adjusting this idea to their sociocultural patterns, that the *Shinkei-shitsu* persons developed their symptoms. The traditional patterns that demanded obedience, docility, conformity to one's superiors and formalities, and sensitivity toward others not to hurt their feeling, clashed with the new demand to be competitive, harsh, aggressive, self-assertive, and individualistic to achieve success or at least survival in the competitive industrialized new Japan. The Japanese as a whole had to experience this conflict.

TYPES PARTICULARLY SENSITIVE TO CULTURAL CONFLICTS

The ones who suffered from this conflict were those who were more acutely brought up in a tight family system where traditional patterns were stressed, those who had the special privilege of being very much protected as only children or as a favorite child. In a similar way the conflict was more intensely experienced by the people who came to the city for a job where competitiveness was a matter of routine, in contrast to their village life where traditional patterns prevailed. In the case of governmental and industrial organizations, the adjustment was made more easily than when an individual attempted the adjustment on his own. Within the organizations, the traditional patterns were maintained which made it easier. But for an individual, it involved quite an ordeal.

VILLAGER VERSUS URBAN RESIDENT

Take the instance of a student who came to Tokyo from a rural district. Though his father was a farmer, he was no longer bound by the feudal class system. He was given the freedom to enter a good school that would enable him to get a job in a big firm or as a governmental official. His parents as well as the people of the village expected him to become successful. He was sensitive enough to feel that he should live up to their expectation. To fulfill this "should" imposed on him by his parents and the village, he had to pass the entrance examination for a certain top-ranking university. It meant being intensely competitive with his fellow students. As he had been brought up in a warm cooperative atmosphere of village life, competitiveness was something alien to him. It made him feel uncomfortable and insecure.

To defend himself against his anxieties, he felt he should have a concentrated mind in his studying to prepare properly for the entrance examination, otherwise he would fail. Driven by his should and anxiety, he tried to have a concentrated state of mind. But the more he tried to concentrate, the more he felt distracted from his studies. He tried to wipe the disturbing ideas away from his mind, but to no avail. He found his attention was completely caught in his futile struggle against distracting ideas and was not focused on his study. The fear of failing and of the prospect that he might be unable to fulfill the "should" imposed by his parents and villagers finally overwhelm him. He became entirely anxiety ridden. This is a simple case history of a student who visited Morita.

FIRST BORN IN A COMPETITIVE SOCIETY

A young businessman, being born as the eldest son, had the traditional privileges of being overprotected from any unpleasant or burdensome work and of being respectfully and carefully treated by his family on every occasion. He was a good boy to his parents—docile and pleasant. When he was supposed to enter a famous university, he failed the entrance examination, which hurt his pride, but somehow he was able to enter a university and later he graduated and got a job in a stock company with the help of his father. In working as a salesman, he found himself anxiety-ridden and unable to express his opinions whenever he faced his clients. He felt tight, blushed, and was overwhelmed by the presence of others. Naturally he did poorly in the amount of stock that he sold in comparison to others. He could not stand the situation, but he could not quit his job because his father had helped to arrange the job by asking his friend, the president of the company, to find work for his son. He began to be absent from the office frequently and spent hours in a coffee shop. Around that time he developed insomnia, constant sweating, and diarrhea together with anxiety; finally he sought therapy.

SHINKEI-SHITSU—COMMON CHARACTERISTICS

Both patients studied above fell in the category of *Shinkei-shitsu* according to Morita. They were both introvertive and oversensitive to others' feelings. In the former case, the student's primary "should" was imposed by others and internalized as a dictum that he "should" be successful. In the case of the young businessman, he took it for granted that he "should be" successful and that he was entitled to be the center of attention and therefore should be treated kindly and with deference in every situation because of his upbringing. They both wanted perfect fulfillment of their "shoulds," and they were chiefly concerned with their security. Both were manipulating their intellect to decrease their anxieties.

We can understand, also from a sociocultural point of view, that they were very sensitive to others' feeling in terms of how they were looked at or esteemed by others which is a typical Japanese characteristic as previously mentioned. Their "shoulds" were based on what they were expected to be and what they wanted to be, because of these expectations and because they wanted to be that kind of person or do that kind of work. We can see conformity to and subsequent internalization of external demands including others' feelings, expectations, and formalities as well as the rules and requirements of their culture. In both cases there is the tendency to withdrawal from competition.

SHINKEI-SHITSU—ALL-OR-NOTHING THINKING

As mentioned before, in Japan, the ego or one's ego is determined by one's relation to others. A person can feel secure as long as he knows his appropriate and definite share or place in his relations with others. Patients had felt quite secure when they were in their village or with their family, where they knew their definite share, position, or status, where they knew exactly what was expected of them. On the other hand, competition put them into a situation in which they could not assess what their part was. It put them into a world of uncertainty which caused them to jump to the conclusion that there were only two extremes, to win or to lose, to be a success or to be a failure—an all-or-nothing frame of mind. People who are brought up in an atmosphere of security and stability are naturally staggered and become anxious when they find themselves in a competitive situation. In this sense, the *Shinkei-shitsu* patients are people who suffer from the conflict between the traditional patterns which foster stability and security and the newer pattern of competitiveness introduced during the Westernization of modern Japan.

Perhaps, from the Western point of view, the *Shinkei-shitsu* personality is to be explained as the neurotic personality of a weak or underdeveloped ego or an ego lacking in aggressiveness, and the therapeutic approach will be made according to one's various orientation. However, Morita approached these patients from his own understanding of human nature.

MORITA PHILOSOPHY OF HUMAN NATURE

Morita postulated and observed the existence of a life force as the basic source of development and growth in every sentient being.[1]

> First return to your own real nature, and you can see in every sentient being the existence of a life-force and the desire for development and growth. It is an undeniable force. A worm is a worm, an animal is an animal, and a man is a man. They may have different dispositions, but they have this desire in common.

According to Morita death is a completion and termination of life. Life and death are a process. We are afraid of death because we want to live as long as we are alive.

According to Morita, the person with a *Shinkei-shitsu* personality does not realize the existence of this force within him and is always concerned with how to preserve his security, his life. He is caught in futile attempts to get rid of anxieties and fears which are actually expressions of his life force. Morita believes that man is destined to live his life according to the realities of life, including psychic realities, which are based on their own principles and cannot be manipulated or controlled by one's intellect or emotional desires. He considers that feeling, even if unpleasant, cannot be eradicated by intellectual understanding.

PRINCIPLES OF MORITA THERAPY

Morita therapy has its own principles: (1) When a certain emotion comes up, it will take its due course of up and down, making a convex curve until it disappears, if you leave it alone and let it take its natural process. (2) An emotion will stabilize and disappear as soon as it is fully expressed. (3) An emotion will lose its intensity, diminish, and disappear as it gets accustomed to the same stimulus. (4) An emotion becomes strongly felt when there are repeated stimuli and attention is focused on it. (5) One can get a new feeling by having a new experience. His feeling will be enriched by the increase of his experiences. These principles, at first sight, look very simple, almost like ordinary common sense. Nevertheless they are based on psychological facts, and they are very effective in practice for handling emotions. In explaining the first principle, Morita says that even in the case of various kinds of pain and anxiety, if they are left to take their own course and an attitude of endurance is assumed by the person who suffers from them, they will gradually soon disappear. This is the common experiences of those who experienced the first stage of the bedrest period in Morita therapy. Also as regards the nature of the intellect and its functions, he has the following ideas.

HOW INTELLECT FUNCTIONS

Our intellect produces notions, ideas, concepts, or thoughts. According to his understanding, notions, ideas, and concepts are the nomina or denominations for facts viewed from various standpoints. Thought is composed of descriptions, explanations, and reasoning about facts, using notions, ideas, or concepts. Morita strictly differentiates them from facts. He compares notions and the others with the images that are reflected on a mirror. The image is different from the substance or fact of our own face. Likewise, notions, ideas, concepts, and thoughts are different from the bare reality of the facts. However, our intellect has a tendency to try to fabricate facts, manipulate and change them in terms of notions, ideas, concepts, and thoughts, falling into inevitable contradictions against facts. Especially in the case of the person with a *Shinkei-shitsu* personality, this tendency is quite strong. He tries to fabricate facts, or change them according to the demands of his "shoulds," or control his psychological facts as well as change and control objective reality to meet his needs and expectations.

According to Morita, all the activities of our mind and body are natural phenomena, which can never be changed by our will except in a few cases such as the movements of out voluntary muscles. What we can do, therefore, says Morita, is to accept natural phenomena as they are and live according to the principles and nature of these phenomena. This attitude is expressed as "being true to the facts," or "being in accord with nature." This attitude is exactly the opposite of the attitude of the person with the *Shinkei-shitsu* personality who is trying to control or change psychic and objective reality by his intellection.

DICHOTOMOUS NATURE OF INTELLECT

Our mind, Morita also contends, because of the dichotomous nature of our intellect, tends to have bipolar notions or feelings which contradict each other, such as the idea of fearlessness versus fear, humbleness versus pride, the idea of waste versus the desire for abundance, and suppression versus fulfillment of impulse. According to Morita, only in our mind are these feelings contradictory. In the reality of life, just as flexors and extensors complement each other in effecting smooth muscle movement, these seemingly contradictory notions and feelings help the stream of life flow in a balanced harmonious way, if no artificial, intellectual intervention by the "either-or" principle is introduced. He expressed this function of the mind as the counterbalancing function of the mind. The extreme "shoulds" of the *Shinkei-shitsu* personality, force him into following an either-or principle and thus he is not free to realize this counterbalancing function of mind. Therefore, Morita believes that mere intellectual understanding cannot be the deepest understanding effective for human life.

Real understanding can be achieved only by actual practicing and experiencing in reality, and this is the fundamental process of self-realization. In the process of actual practicing and experiencing, Morita adds, there is no "I" that observes, criticizes, and is conscious of "me" or itself, but there is a functioning, acting, un-self-conscious being in motion that is always becoming, and that is pure subjectivity—this is the self.

THE SELF ACCORDING TO MORITA

With his understanding of human nature, Morita brought out a new picture of the self, which is different from the conventional Japanese notion of self

as one's own share and different from the Western notion of the self—"I"
that observes "me" and that stands against others. On the other hand, Morita's notion of self also has a feature in common with the Japanese
Buddhist notion of the self, if the latter is interpreted in terms of one's
share of the universal life force which is expressed in the form of each individual, and also has some similarity with the Western notion of self which
is based on freedom and independence. Morita's notion of the self is one
charged with an intrinsic life force that is shared with all sentient beings,
free and independent in its spontaneous process of being and becoming.

Morita attempted to free his patients from the fallacy of their "shoulds"
so that they could accept what he believed to be the principles of psychic
reality, experience, and realize their intrinsic life force. To help his patients
live their own dynamic, un-self-conscious "self," independent and free from
being overdependent on others' feelings and evaluation, Morita provided
his patients with a therapeutic environment which he called a homelike setting consisting of four therapeutic periods. The following is a brief description of these periods.

MORITA THERAPY—PRACTICAL ASPECTS

1. Bed rest period. About a week. Patients are requested to remain in
bed resting and having no human contact except with the doctor. The
patients experience psychological relief. They are told to just accept and
experience their symptoms as they come and go as natural phenomena
operating according to psychic principles. The patients eventually feel
bored and begin to feel hunger for activity which is an expression of their
life force. The differential diagnosis is also made during this period.

2. A period of light work. About a week. Patients are requested to
write a diary, spend time out of doors, and continue with the same attitude
toward their symptoms. This period is designed to enhance their spontaneous impulses toward engaging in activities. Participating in casual conversation and hobbies is prohibited. As the patients feel bored with the
nonactive situation and spontaneously desire to do something, a little work
is allowed, beginning with light work such as pulling out weeds, picking up
fallen leaves, and gradually heavier work. The choice of work and time are
entirely left up to the patients' spontaneous desire.

3. A period of heavier work. About a week. This period is designed to
develop the patient's endurance, self-confidence, and courage by
experiencing the joy of accomplishment as they complete some activity or
work which they chose moved by their spontaneous desire for activity. The

patients feel occupied and content with what they are doing and accomplishing, regardless of the value or quality of their work according to any conventional frame of reference.

4. A preparatory period for returning to actual life. In the third period, patients are motivated to work guided by their spontaneous desire for or interest in activities. This period is designed to develop their capacity for dealing with things freely, to the best of their ability in every given situation, free not only from their "shoulds" but also from their personal likes or dislikes. Patients are encouraged to read books about practical matters, go out shopping, follow practical pursuits.

POSTWAR JAPAN

In short, through their experiences in these periods, it is hoped that patients have become able to develop and realize a new way of life, which is experienced in the spontaneous outflow of their life force. No longer bound by their "shoulds" nor by the traditional conventional notion of the self, they have found their genuine self, independent and free, and are no longer self-conscious.

Twenty-eight years have passed since the surrender of the Japanese Empire and her transformation into a democratic country under the guidance of the United States. With a new constitution, everyone is treated equally, no hierarchical system is allowed, and no one can be superior to another just because of his status or position, at least theoretically and legally speaking. During those years, many reforms and changes were made according to democratic principles. Space limitations preclude their being described here. Suffice to say that Japan utilized those reforms and changes for furthering the process of industrialization which was set as one of the main national goals at the time of the Meiji reformation.

INDIVIDUALISM VERSUS GROUP MORES

Today we see the results of industrialization and Westernization, an affluence never experienced before in her long history. Success and prestige have been the goals of the Japanese people in those years and are even more so in the present day of affluence. It is true that competitiveness among individuals is more openly admitted than before. Urbanization is tremendously accelerated due to industrialization and creates more individualistic attitudes among people in big cities.

CHANGES IN FAMILY PATTERNS

In family life, the father has lost his former position of prestige and status. This change in turn has resulted in the elevating of the mother's or wife's position especially in relation to the upbringing of their children. Mothers have become more concerned and involved with the education of their children as a preparatory step for the success and prestige of their beloved ones. This tendency was enhanced by the fact that mothers have fewer children because of the planned birth control and that they have more time for attending to their children because of the time saved by electric appliances and devices. Children are highly protected by supervising and controlling mothers in place of the strict fathers of former days. This tendency is particularly strong in urban families.

NEW TYPES OF PATIENTS

Now among the patients who visit Morita therapists, besides the typical patients with a *Shinkei-shitsu* personality who have generally a rural life background, there are an increased number of the patients who have an urban family situation. These patients are anxiety-ridden, sensitive, and intelligent, but are more temperamental or moody and show a tendency to withdraw from competitive situations. It is interesting to see their reactions to therapy. They take the first stage of bed rest very easily, but in the second period, when they are not given instructions regarding what work to do and are told to find anything they want to do spontaneously, they feel quite at a loss. In other words, they show less spontaneity or initiative than the ordinary *Shinkei-shitsu* patients, and they expect that Morita therapy will give them some definite patterns or rules to follow and to depend on. It means that despite the fact their environment (family, school, and community) has provided freedom which their seniors never experienced, they have used it for seeking pleasure in a world of affluence. They have indulged in their dependence on their protective parents, and have not used their freedom to develop their "self"—a firm, independent self that would enable them to face the reality of life squarely. Morita therapy can give such patients a new environment in which they can develop their independent self in the process of experiencing their intrinsic life force.

STUDENT RIOTERS: THEIR NEUROTIC PROBLEMS

During the 1960s, there were rampant upsurges of student riots, which were in a sense an expression of the self-assertiveness and aggressiveness of young students who had been brought up within the new democratic, educational system. Unfortunately their self-assertion, in the form of antagonism and revolt against the establishment and especially against the Japanese pro-American government, was extremely destructive and resulted in failure. Not a few students felt frustrated, dismayed, and dropped out of these activities. They became despondent, depressed, and visited Morita therapists. In the case of these patients, Morita therapy helped them experience and realize their spontaneous, dynamic self, which was different from their idealized self that used to stand against others being molded by rigid ideological notions.

OLD JAPAN IN NEW JAPAN

In present-day Japan, despite the fact that Westernization and industrialization have been pushed forward since the Meiji Reformation and particularly after World War II, there still pulses, through large segments of the population, traditional sociocultural patterns. Even the many who now work and live in cities because of the recent drastic urbanization have not moved far from their traditional rural cultural patterns. However, at the same time it is a fact that the younger generation who have more flexible minds are, gradually, with trial and error, taking in Western ideas. The Japanese must still solve or integrate the difference between their own traditional cultural patterns and those notions implanted from the West. Perhaps it is not a problem to be solved by an either-or way decision. In this regard, Morita's views may give some suggestions for a new orientation for Japanese people, for their freedom and independence, since views are the result of his struggle in those days when there was a severe clash between Western ideas and Japanese culture.

REFERENCES

1. Kora, T.: Morita therapy. *Int. J. Psychiatr.* 1:611–640, 1965.
2. Levy, N. J.: Discussion of east meets west: Moritists and freudian psychotherapies. In *Science and Psychoanalysis*, J. Masserman, (Ed.) Vol. 21, Grune and Stratton, New York, 1972, pp. 193–195.
3. Morita, M.: *Shinkei-suijaku to Kyohaku-Kannen no Konchi-ho (The Fundamental Therapy for Neurasthenia and Compulsive Ideas)*, Hakuyo-sha, Tokyo, 1955.
4. Reischauer, E. O.: *Japan Past and Present*, 3rd ed. rev. Knopf, New York, 1964, pp. 93, 94.
5. Ref. 4, pp. 85–86.

6. Ref. 4, p. 94.

7. Reynolds, D. K.: Directed behavior change: Japanese psychotherapy in a private mental hospital, Ph.D. dissertation, Department of Anthropology. University of California, Los Angeles, 1969, University Microfilm No. 70-14319.

8. Reynolds, D. K. and Yamamoto, J.: East meets west: Moritist and Freudian psychotherapies. In *Science and Psychoanalysis,* J. Masserman, (Ed.) Vol. 21, Grune and Stratton, New York, 1972, pp. 187-193.

CHAPTER TWELVE

MEDITATION AS AN
ADJUNCT TO PSYCHOTHERAPY

PATRICIA CARRINGTON, Ph.D. and
HARMON S. EPHRON, M.D.

With growing popular interest in the meditative techniques, the attention of mental health professionals has been increasingly attracted to these disciplines. On a practical level, many psychotherapists need to evaluate the impact of meditation on their patients who have taken up this practice, and some psychotherapists see the use of meditation as a promising adjunct to psychotherapy, especially where nonverbal conditionings remain unresponsive to more conventional forms of therapeutic intervention.

Contributing to the rising interest in the meditative techniques is the fact that these techniques are related to the biofeedback techniques (which also emphasize a delicately attuned awareness to *inner* processes) and to relaxation techniques used with behavior modification. The meditative disciplines also promise to help the patient in an area peripheral to the conventional psychotherapies—the fostering of communication between the patient and his own self, *apart from* his interpersonal environment. In a world where spiritual enrichment from any source is scarce, many patients hunger for a more profound sense of self than is implicit in merely "getting along with others." Such people seek an awareness of their identity as *being* (as distinct from identity as *doing*).

The inner communion of meditation offers hope of fulfilling this need, thus promising to heal an aspect of the psyche which may be as needful as any other presently identified. The use of meditation along with psychotherapy may be an inevitable accompaniment of the latter's trend toward encompassing more and varied aspects of man.

In this chapter, we explore, in a preliminary manner, various ways in which psychiatry and meditation may interact.

THE MEDITATIVE PROCESS

Theoretically, it is possible to list a large number of practices under the term "meditation,"* each having its own method of inducing a special kind of free-floating, attentional state which is essentially nonverbal and nonconceptual in nature.

Techniques used to bring about this state may be as diverse as gazing quietly into a candle flame; attending to the mental repetition of a sound (*mantra*); following one's own breathing or proprioceptive sensations; concentrating on an unanswerable riddle (*Koan*); scanning one's inner experiential field; or others.

---

* For a comprehensive review of the various forms of meditation, see J. Naranjo: "Meditation: Its spirit and technique." In J. Naranjo and R. Ornstein, (Eds.), *On the Psychology of Meditation*, Viking Press, New York, 1971.

Whatever the technique used, it seeks to alter the meditator's interaction with his sensory world, often doing this through inducing a state of partial sensory isolation as the meditator is instructed to attend to a relatively constant source of stimulation, the "focus" or object of meditation, maintaining a passive-receptive attitude toward it. The pull is to be centripetal (inward) in nature.

Each meditative technique must cope, however, with an intrinsic property of meditation which can best be described as a counter tendency, or centrifugal (outward) push. Even the calm and centered mind seeks periodically renewed contact with the external environment, or its verbal-conceptual representations (thoughts). Meditational systems have various ways of dealing with this "outward stroke" of meditation.

Some systems are coercive with respect to the handling of so-called distractions of the mind during meditation. A coercive form of meditation will demand strict concentration on the meditational object, directing the practitioner to banish intruding thoughts from his mind by an act of will, to pinpoint his attention, and to return immediately and forcefully to the object of focus whenever he finds his attention has wandered. This approach is seen in extreme form in instructions given to a meditator in a fifth-century Buddhist treatise dealings with thoughts that may intrude into the meditation[10]:

> . . . with teeth clenched and tongue pressed against the gums, he should by means of sheer mental effort hold back, crush and burn out the (offending) thought; in doing so, these evil and unwholesome ideas, bound up with greed, hate or delusion, will be forsaken, then thought will become inwardly calm, composed and concentrated.

In contrast to the above, some meditative systems are distinguished by their permissiveness toward intruding thoughts. In certain of these noncoercive techniques, the meditator is instructed to return gently and without effort to the object of focus.

Although there are no experimental findings dealing with the effects on the meditator of coercive versus noncoercive forms of meditation, effects may be expected to differ according to whether the meditator practices one approach or the other. A coercive form of meditation might foster repression in a meditator, increasing superego pressure in the form of guilt about "not meditating correctly," as well as guilt concerning the nature of intruding thoughts. A noncoercive directive, on the other hand, might encourage resolution of emotional conflicts during meditation through lifting repression (encouraged by an acceptant attitude toward thoughts or feelings arising during meditation) and through catharsis brought about by this state. This calm, reassuring state might also afford an opportunity for unconscious derivatives which surface at this time to become integrated into the personality.

Because the specific directives of a form of meditation may determine its clinical effectiveness, we have chosen to investigate an extremely *non*coercive meditative technique known as transcendental meditation. Probably the most effortless of the meditative techniques, it encourages the practitioner to treat thoughts that he may have during his meditation (no matter how unusual) as entirely natural and as serving to reduce stress, a point of view consistent with that adopted by psychoanalysis toward free association.

TRANSCENDENTAL MEDITATION

Transcendental meditation (TM) is a standardized form of mantra meditation adapted for Western use from an ancient Indian technique.[25] It is readily available as an adjunct to psychotherapy, being taught by an organization of instructors trained in an uniform method of instruction.* There are TM centers in and around most of the major cities of the United States and Europe; and the technique itself is exceedingly easy to learn, being mastered in four lessons taught over a period of 4 days. It does not require adoption of any particular life-style or set of beliefs, not does it use special postures or methods of breathing.

When he is instructed in TM, the student is assigned a Sanskrit word (*mantra*), said to possess soothing properties, which he is asked to repeat silently to himself for 20 minutes, sitting quietly in a chair with eyes closed. This he does twice daily. When the meditator finds that his attention has wandered, he is told to exert no effort to deliberately return to his mantra, but to resume its repetition in a passive manner by "favoring the mantra" over his other thoughts. The TM instructors give considerable reassurance to practitioners with regard to the nature of thoughts that arise during meditation, with the meditator taught to look upon the spontaneous emergence of thoughts, feelings, images, or somatic sensations during meditation as evidence of a process said to have therapeutic properties, termed *unstressing*. By means of unstressing, residual tensions produced by previous traumatic or stressful events in a person's life are said to be released spontaneously.

Although reassurance about the normality and desirability of unstressing reactions is given by the TM instructor and is usually sufficient to handle

* The Students International Meditation Society (SIMS).

any temporary disturbance that they may cause, we have on occasion seen "unstressing" bring about sufficient discomfort to cause a meditator to stop the practice of meditation altogether, even though he has been experiencing gratifying gains from it. If such a person is given an opportunity, through psychotherapy, to work out the emotional problem which has surfaced during meditation, he may be able to resume his practice of it. We discuss this more fully when we consider various forms of resistance to meditation.

THE PHENOMENOLOGY OF MEDITATION

In order to become acquainted with meditation, the authors learned TM and we have been practicing it regularly for close to a year. During this time we have kept a journal of our meditative experiences and compared them with observations of meditating friends and patients. It is our impression, based on these journals, that each 20-minute session tends to be a new and different experience, just as each dream is unique. Every meditator also appears to have his own characteristic "style" of meditating despite the similarity of instruction. This style may change and develop over time. As one meditator writes:

> . . . The waves of the mantra wash over me repeatedly. I feel them physically, slowly pulsing through me. . . . At various times the mantra may be a soft spread of light; a cushion caressing my face; a cloud of mist rhythmically dispersing; the echoing toll of a distant bell; a faint sensation over and around my eyes; or just quiet beats. Sometimes I have no imagery. At such times, it is as though the mantra were some deep biological presence existing amidst profound silence.

Meditators frequently experience a string of memories which drift through their minds during meditation, seemingly "carried along" by the mantra. These may be scenes of tranquil, nostalgic places from childhood, carrying with them a strong sense of pleasure. On occasion, the memories during meditation may be disturbing, but if so, they tend to lose their painfulness through the soothing influence of the mantra, changing under its rhythm. These meditation memories, unusually vivid and realistic, are often described as a form of *reliving*, rather than remembering. Meditators report that they can actually feel the kinesthetic or temperature sensations involved, smell the scents, reexperience details that they may not have recalled since the original event. These relivings are without plot or elaborations of dream-like character, nor are they identical with the vivid imagery of hypnogogic hallucinations.

The mantra may be experienced by different persons at different times as loud, fast, soft, slow, melodic, resonant, clear, barely discernible, or in some other fashion. One meditator describes a form of thought during meditation which is deeply absorbing and during which the mantra is absent for long periods of time. When he develops a tendency to engage actively in such thought rather than "flow with it", however, the mantra reappears spontaneously and continues along with his thinking, or supersedes it, leading the experience.

The mantra may play a significant orienting and synthesizing function during meditation:

> . . . I searched for the mantra, and having found it, felt 'pulled together' (as being oriented by the North Star). I was coalesced.

Yielding to internal rhythms without expending effort and without trying for a result is another common experience:

> . . . You are in a state of alertness, yet without grasping or making any effort to cope. You do not try to succeed, nor can you fail. Distant feelings, images, uninvitedly float into your ken, but there is no effort to define what you hear, see, sense . . . .

Some meditators experience spontaneous insights during or following meditation. The authors find these insights to be essentially similar to the deeper insights which may occur during psychotherapy, with the difference that the preliminary conscious "work" leading up to the therapeutic insight is not present during meditation. Those meditators who have reported such insights in meditation were persons presently undergoing some form of psychoanalytically oriented psychotherapy, or who have done so in the past. We do not know whether the meditative process fosters similar insights in psychologically naive persons.

Meditators may also report vivid, hypnogogic-like imagery in which they see a succession of faces dissolving into one another in continuous progression, and some experience primary process transformations of a primitive nature with imagery that is described as dream-like or even "psychedelic" in nature, although it is typically without plot or dramatic action and does not seem to possess the "reality" of a dream.

During meditation there may be a progressive refinement of the mantra toward a more subtly perceived sound, depending on the vicissitudes of any particular meditative session or the state of responsiveness of the meditator. The mantra becomes in such instances increasingly indiscernible, then, no longer needed, may give way to profound quiet.

At this point, the mind is said not to be focused on either thought or image, but to be fully aware, conscious, alert without having any object of alertness. This experience of utterly still awareness, termed by the teachers of TM "transcending," is by no means experienced by all meditators (the authors, for example, if they have experienced it at all, have not identified it as being any special state of consciousness).

While "transcending" is not necessary for a personality change to take place, for those who do experience it, it seems to be deeply meaningful. One investigator has described this fleeting state, possibly the ultimate goal of meditation, as follows:[39]

> When, in full wakefulness, all inner activity comes to a stop, all thinking, all fantasy, all feeling, all images—everything—even the urge to think or to feel or to act; when all of this stops, stops on its own, without suppression or repression, one thing remains: a vast, inner stillness, a clear peace, and the firm realization that this, at the very least, is how it feels to be, simply, alive.

RELATIONSHIP TO FREE ASSOCIATION

Transcendental meditation and free association have a number of points in common. Both techniques attempt to lessen external stimulation, to refocus attention *inwardly*. The free-associating patient and the TM meditator are also both instructed to remain nonjudgemental with respect to the nature of thoughts during their session. They are asked to allow the mind to accept whatever enters it, thus encouraging openness to emotionally charged experience not ordinarily accessible to consciousness.

There are several sharp points of difference between these techniques, however. In free association, all thoughts are supposed to be *verbalized*, thereby filtering out areas of experience which cannot be converted rapidly enough (if at all) into word symbols. The vast flow of ideation available to the meditator is curtailed in the free associating patient because he must continually translate experience into language *while it is occurring*.

Another point of difference is that free association is used to *pinpoint* areas of conflict while meditation offers a comprehensive approach to the resolution of broad field-tension states. For this reason nonverbal conditionings, out of the reach of the verbal techniques of free association, may be altered in the meditative state.

In addition, while the psychoanalytic patient free associates with a clear *purpose* in mind—to reveal to the analyst and to himself certain concerns now hidden to him—the meditator is encouraged to allow thoughts to drift with *no goal*; they need serve no purpose; and there is no attempt to contemplate their meaning. Free association might thus be said to approximate a type of work, and meditation a type of play, two complementary modes of experiencing.

A final difference stems from the fact that psychotherapy is fundamentally interpersonal in nature while meditation is predominantly *intra*personal. Transference reactions, as part of the normal psychotherapeutic process, tend to restrict the free associative process but not the meditative one. Only gradually, through the progression of psychotherapy itself, can the influence of the superego during the therapeutic session (and outside of it) be mitigated. During meditation, on the other hand, lessening of superego dominance may occur automatically with a particular kind of freedom unavailable at other times because the meditator is alone, beholden to no one while on his "inward voyage."

THE PHYSIOLOGY OF MEDITATION

Research has shown that in transcendental meditation the body enters a profound state of rest, oxygen consumption being lowered during 20 to 30 minutes of meditation to a degree ordinarily reached only after 6 to 7 hours of sleep.[42] Heart and respiration rates also tend to decrease during meditation,[2, 41] while forearm blood flow and forehead skin temperatures increase,[34, 43] suggesting a shift toward parasympathetic dominance.

Since electrical resistance of the skin is generally considered to be an involuntary indicator of the subject's level of anxiety, with low resistance (palmar sweating) reflecting a high-level of anxiety, and high resistance, a nonanxious state (the basis for the "lie detector" test), it is interesting that during TM skin resistance appears to increase markedly.[41] The meditating subject thus may operate at a low-anxiety level.

Also suggestive of lowered anxiety is a sharp decline in the concentration of blood lactate during meditation.[42] High concentrations of lactate in the blood have been correlated with anxiety—patients with anxiety neuroses tending to show a rise in blood lactate when placed in stressful situations[23]; and an infusion of lactate has been shown to bring on anxiety attacks in anxiety neurotics as well as triggering anxiety symptoms in normal subjects.[32] Conversely, low blood lactate levels have been associated with tranquility. The fact that during meditation there is a decline in blood lactate level which is three times as great as that during ordinary rest with eyes closed,[42] and that this decrease is maintained for 10 minutes after meditation (only slowly returning to premeditation levels) suggests reduction in anxiety at this time.

A number of studies have shown that the physiology of meditation differs from that of ordinary rest with eyes closed, from sleep, and from hypnotic states.[9, 41, 42] During meditation the EEG shows an alert-drowsy pattern with high alpha and occasional theta wave patterns[11, 42] and an unusual pattern of swift shifts from alpha to slower (more sleep-like) frequencies and then back again.[3] These findings suggest that meditation may be an unusually fluid state of consciousness, partaking of qualities of both sleep and wakefulness.

Because during meditation deep physiological relaxation similar to that occurring in the "deepest" non-REM sleep phase may occur in a context of wakefulness, Wallace et al. have termed TM a "wakeful hypometabolic state"[42] and Gellhorn "a state of trophotropic dominance compatible with full awareness."[15]

EFFECTS OF MEDITATION

Based on data from our own cases and those reported to us by colleagues interested in exploring meditation as an adjunct to psychotherapy, our overall clinical impression is presented in the following.

Tension-Reduction

We have observed that after commencing meditation, there frequently seems to be a lessening of tension in the meditator with inappropriate "alarm" responses dropping out of his behavioral repertoire. The result of this amelioration of the alarm response may be more relaxed and efficient handling of both large and small tasks and less of a sense of urgency in matters which formerly caused distress.

Our clinical observations appear related to the laboratory finding that meditators tend to recover from stress more quickly than nonmeditators (as measured by more rapid habituation of the Galvanic Skin Response to stressful stimuli).[29] In addition, the initial orienting response does not appear to "reverberate" in persons who are meditating regularly. Instead, an appropriate calm ensues in the meditators after only a brief initial orienting reaction to the stress.[29] It is not surprising therefore that meditating patients frequently report a feeling of being "protected" from strains formerly encountered in the office or home.

The increased coping ability which is often seen in meditators differs in several respects from effects brought about by psychotropic drugs. Taking such drugs may *restore* a patient to feeling "normality" or more "like himself" but does not seem to promote *growth*. By contrast, the meditator frequently reports that meditation leads him to react in ways quite new to him. Relaxation brought about by drugs may slow a patient down, causing grogginess, while the relaxation resulting from meditation does not bring with it loss of alertness. On the contrary, meditation seems, if anything, to sharpen alertness. Groups of meditators have been shown to have faster reaction times,[38] increased refinement of auditory perception,[19] and to perform more rapidly and accurately on perceptual-motor tasks[6] than nonmeditating controls. Interestingly, Glueck,[16] in a preliminary study conducted with a group of psychiatric in-patients, found that dosages of psychotropic drugs could be greatly reduced after the patients had been meditating for several weeks and in the majority of cases, sedatives could be reduced or eliminated for these patients following meditation.

Greater Productivity

As Jacobson[22] noted some years ago, successful relaxation may bring about increased efficiency by eliminating unnecessary expenditures of energy, such as that used in maintaining excessive muscle tension or the effort wasted in straining to do something "well." The manner in which anxiety and emotional conflict drain energy has been noted in the psychiatric literature, with clinical observations indicating frequent increases of available energy in patients following the successful resolution of disabling conflicts. Similarly, we have noted that the practice of TM appears to bring about a striking increase in energy and productivity in certain patients.

Lowered Anxiety

Evidence that meditation serves to lower anxiety may be found in some preliminary studies which have shown that TM has positive effects on such psychosomatic conditions as bronchial asthma[44] and hypertension,[5] and in experimental studies which show sharp reductions in trait-anxiety as measured by personality tests given before, and again some months after, learning TM.[12, 13, 21, 28] It has been our clinical observation that certain patients, after commencing meditation, seem able to tolerate emotionally charged material during their psychotherapy sessions with less anxiety than formerly. There also seems to be less necessity to spend time helping the patient cope with his everyday pressures, leaving him now free to concentrate on problems more central to the psychotherapeutic process.

Modification of Superego

Meditation appears to lead to an increased self-acceptance on the part of the patient, evidenced in the analytic hour as a lessening of self-criticism. Corollaries of this may be increased tolerance for the human frailties of others and decreased self-defensiveness. It is our observation that this amelioration of the punitive superego increases in direct ratio to the number of months an individual has been meditating; that is, it is a cumulative gain.

Antiaddictive Properties

A potentially useful property of meditation is its apparent tendency to lessen certain forms of addiction. In a study of 1862 subjects who had been practicing transcendental meditation for 3 months or more, Benson and Wallace[4] found that following the start of the practice of TM, there was a marked decrease in the amount of abuse of marijuana, amphetamines, barbiturates, and hallucinogens (such as LSD). For example, in the 6-month period before the start of the practice of meditation, about 80% of the subjects (mostly college students) used marijuana, and of those about 28% were "heavy users" (i.e., were using the drug once a day or more). After practicing TM for 6 months, only 37% used marijuana and of those only 6.5% were heavy users. After 21 months of the practice, only 12% continued to use marijuana and of those only one individual remained a heavy user. The decrease in the use of LSD was even more marked, and similar results were reported for other hallucinogens, narcotics, amphetamines, and barbiturates.

The antiaddictive effects of meditation also appeared to extend to other areas. In the Benson and Wallace study, the number of hard liquor users are reported to have decreased from an initial 50% before meditation to 25% after 21 months of meditation. Forty-eight percent of the persons studied were reported as smoking cigarettes before starting meditation, with 25% described as "heavy users" (i.e., as smoking one or more packs a day). After 21 months of meditation, these percentages had decreased to 16% who were smoking cigarettes and only 5.7% still heavy cigarette users. TM is described by these authors as being more acceptable than other forms of intervention for youthful drug abusers, since it is offered as a program for personal development and not specifically as treatment for drug abuse. Thus it may not threaten those beliefs of the committed abuser who condones the use of drugs.

The Benson and Wallace study did not, however, have a matched control group to determine the degree to which nonmeditating persons spontaneously reduce their use of drugs over a similar period of time. In a more recent study of the effects of TM on the use of marijuana, other nonprescription drugs, and cigarette smoking, Shafii et al.[36, 37] used a control group consisting of persons of comparable age, socioeconomic level, and interests, who had never meditated. These investigators found that *before starting meditation* the meditators were using twice as much marijuana and hashish as the controls, but that after having meditated 1 to 39 months, marijuana usage in the meditating group was reduced to nearly one-third the original amount, whereas the figures for the control group stayed the same. In addition, 71% of the meditators who had practiced meditation more than 2 years significantly decreased their use of cigarettes and 57% totally stopped smoking by that time, while cigarette usage figures for the control group remained almost the same.

These studies appear to indicate that meditation may be effective in combatting some forms of addiction, providing the person is sufficiently motivated to continue meditating for a substantial period of time, there being an apparent relationship between the amount of time the person has been meditating and the effectiveness of this practice in combatting addiction. Since Shafii et al. report a 30% drop-out rate among practitioners of TM (over a period of 3 years), this factor must be taken into account when evaluating the potential effects of TM on "soft" drug abusers and on heavy users of alcohol and cigarettes. As yet, there have been no systematic studies of the effects of TM on "hard" drug usage, although relevant research is underway.

Clinically, we have noted lessened interest in excessive use of marijuana in three of our patients after they commenced meditation, lessened interest in alcohol in two of our patients, and have seen no decrease in cigarette smoking to date in any of our patients who are heavy smokers.*

PSYCHOLOGICAL DIFFERENTIATION

One of the most striking clinical changes to occur in our meditating patients has been a sharp increase in *psychological differentiation*, a personality attribute which reflects the ability of a person to separate himself from his surroundings. Someone possessing this attribute is said to experience himself in a more articulated, less global fashion; to be "innerdirected" rather than "outerdirected"[33]; to be better able to use his own self as reference point when making judgments or decisions; to have a clear sense of his separate identity; and to be aware of needs, feelings, and attributes which he recognized as his *own* distinct from those of others. *Internal* frames of reference serve as guides for definition of this sense of identity and Witkin et al.[45, 46] have termed such persons "field inde-

---

* Since the Shafii study reports that most reductions in cigarette smoking tended to occur after the subjects had been meditating 13 months or more, and none of our smoking patients have been meditating more than 7 months, we cannot consider our experience to be any test of the efficacy of TM in reducing smoking.

pendent." Persons with a less-developed sense of separate identity—those who tend to rely on external sources for definition of their attitudes, judgments, sentiments, and their views of themselves—have been termed field dependent.

Several highly reliable testing instruments have been developed to measure field dependence-independence, two of the best known being the Embedded Figures Test and the Rod and Frame Test.[45] Both of these require the subject to deal with part of an organized field *independently of the field as a whole.* In light of the stability of these measures, it is interesting to find that where meditators have been tested for field dependence-independence before learning to meditate, and then retested several months later, preliminary studies, emerging from several different laboratories, have shown changes in the direction of greater field *independence* following several months of meditation.[20, 31] These studies suggest that a fundamental change in the person's perception of his self may take place as a result of meditation.

Such experimental findings closely parallel the changes which we have observed in our patients, as well as our meditating friends and ourselves. Persons meditating over a period of time frequently report experiencing an increased sense of their own *identity.* They may find that they identify their own opinions and feelings more sharply, sense their personal "rights" in situations where formerly they were unaware of them, and are better able to withstand social pressures without abandoning their own opinions. As a consequence, they may become more decisive, express opinions more openly, disagree with others, or demand their own rights in situations where they would formerly have been submissive.

Changes in degree of psychological differentiation may be experienced by a patient as exhilarating or threatening according to whether his self-image successfully adjusts to include this new sense of separateness and the increased self-assertion it sometimes entails. We discuss the problems which can be encountered with such an increase in differentiation when we consider the various kinds of resistance to meditation.

Availability of Affect

Patients frequently report that they feel strong emotions during meditation. Feelings of love, hate, rage, tenderness, longing, grief, and joy can, it seems, be intense during the self-communion of this state. Even more significant from a therapeutic point of view, however, is the generally enhanced emotional responsiveness which is frequently seen *outside* of the meditative sessions.

We have seen meditating patients experience emotions formerly repressed or suppressed and be surprisingly able to communicate these emotions, showing greater openness to both pleasurable and painful experiences. Such changes in the availability of affect may facilitate the psychotherapeutic process, helping the patient cut through intellectual defenses to deal with more deep-seated emotional problems.

Referring to the surfacing of unconscious material in meditation and its effects on his own psychoanalytic patients, Glueck[17] suggests that TM may be "a new window into the unconscious." As patients meditate, he points out, the usual tension associated with repressed material may lessen with formerly painful material now surfacing and being better tolerated.

We have noted that this may be particularly true when the patient has meditated just prior to commencement of his psychotherapeutic session, or if patient and therapist meditate together during the session. In the immediate postmeditative period, the patient's free association seems particularly rich in content with much of the sham and role-playing of ordinary life absent and the patient often seems to have increased tolerance for his own impulses at this time. We would thus agree with Glueck that TM offers a promising avenue to unconscious material.

Seemingly related to the emotional aliveness that some persons experience with meditation is an increased fluency of ideation and greater productivity (often creative in nature) that may result from this practice. In several instances, we have seen a disabling creative block dissolve entirely with the commencement of meditation. In one case, this block represented a virtual impasse in the person's life. The use of TM in the treatment of a creative block, whether this be in an artist, businessman, student, or other, appears promising.

Effect on Mood

Many patients who commence TM experience mood elevation, greater stabilization of mood, and a pervasive sense of well-being. While these alterations in mood are clinically beneficial when they occur, we have noticed that they are more likely to occur and be tolerated in neurotic patients suffering from mild, low-grade, chronic depressions. Patients in a state of acute depression may refuse outright to learn meditation or if they do learn it may discontinue it quite rapidly. This apparent resistance to the mood-elevating, pleasurable properties of TM may be rooted in the character structure of the depressive as delineated by Bonime.[8] We discuss this problem when we consider resistances to meditation.

Miscellaneous Effects

Paranoid tendencies may become lessened in some persons after commencement of meditation. A withdrawal of projections appears to be a corollary of readmittance into the self-system of previously disowned aspects of the self; and we have noticed that meditators may view their own formerly compulsive complaints about others with a new found sense of perspective. There is some evidence that this antiparanoidal effect may be experienced even by psychotic patients. When conferring with the research team studying the effects of TM on psychiatric in-patients at the Institute for Living in Hartford, we observed a paranoid schizophrenic patient who had recently learned to meditate state that meditation was making him feel "less paranoid."

Other effects noted in some of our meditating patients are increased spontaneity, increased self-confidence, greater ability to take risks, and decreased obsessive-compulsive behavior.

We now consider the theoretical rationale for some of the effects noted above.

THEORETICAL CONSIDERATIONS

Rhythmicity

The rhythmic component of meditation is obvious in *mantra* meditation (such as TM) where a lilting sound is continuously repeated, but rhythm seems to be a component of *all* forms of meditation. The inner stillness involved in this practice tends to make the practitioner profoundly aware of his own bodily rhythms. In the unusual quiet of the meditative state, breathing may be intimately sensed, pulse may be faintly perceived, and other bodily sensations generally obscured by the activity of daily life may become apparent. Some meditative techniques even take bodily rhythms as their object of focus. In Zazen meditation, for example, the meditator is instructed to concentrate on his own natural, uninfluenced breathing.

Regularly repeated sounds or rhythmic movements have long been recognized as soothing. In attempting to quiet an agitated baby, the parent may rock him gently, sing a lullaby, recite a nursery rhyme, repeat affectionate sounds in a lilting fashion, or bounce him rhythmically on the lap with intuitive awareness of the soothing effects that these rhythmic activities have on the infant.

In the psychological laboratory, Salk[35] has shown that neonates respond to a recorded normal heartbeat sound (played to them without interruption day and night) by greatly lessened crying (as compared to a control group of infants who were not played the sound) and by gaining more weight than the controls.

Salk suggests that during the period in the uterus the infant may have built an association between the rhythmical heartbeat sound (the most prominent sound heard by the fetus) and the tension-free intrauterine state (or possibly there may be an "imprinting" of these heartbeat rhythms) so that similar rhythmical sounds later in life have a "functional connection with the original (intrauterine) experience" and become "permanently associated with a feeling of well-being."

Writing in a somewhat similar vein, Meerloo[26] conjectures that conditioning to intrauterine heartbeat rhythms may be the basis of the profoundly soothing effects of poetry, music, and dance, these rhythmic experiences being grounded in "various reminiscent feelings of a lost long ago and far away happiness" (i.e., the intrauterine experience).

It may be that the subjective feeling of deep well-being which tends to occur during meditation is related to the rhythmical nature of this experience. As Salk and Meerloo suggest, we may be conditioned to respond to deep regular rhythms with a sense of tranquility. It is, however, also possible that certain regular rhythms may be *innately* soothing to a biological organism. In the latter case, the rhythmic component of meditation would constitute an unconditioned stimulus to which the *mantra* (as conditioned stimulus) would then be linked.

If contacting deep biological rhythms in oneself is a prominent component of meditation, then regular meditation might be expected to have important effects on personality. Metaphorically speaking, it might be akin to periodically returning to a source of well-being from which one would come back strengthened to deal with an outer environment where the rhythms are, more often than not, out of phase with one's own.

Desensitization

We might liken meditation, on one level, to the behavior modification technique known as *systematic desensitization*. In the latter technique a relaxed state is induced by visualizing a "calm scene" (or by use of *progressive relaxation*). When thoroughly relaxed, the patient is then exposed to anxiety-provoking stimuli related to his problems. These stimuli are presented to him in small increments—never so much at one time that his state of relaxation is dispelled. In this manner, anxiety-laden stimuli gradually lose their "charge," becoming reconditioned to the pleasant, soothing atmosphere.

In meditation, as in systematic desensitization, a state of deep calm forms the background mood, while anxieties and concerns that come to mind at this time often seem to lose their urgency. The two techniques differ, however, in several important respects. In desensitization, the therapist *pinpoints* several anxiety areas and then laboriously desensitizes each in turn. In meditation, it would seem that the vast computer of the human brain selects many pieces of information to be "desensitized" at once, in an entirely automatic manner. Goleman, noting this possibility, has suggested that TM may be a "*global* desensitization procedure."[18]

Instead of one discrete response being worked on in a single session (as in behavior modification), during TM a string of many related images and thoughts stream through the mind during a meditative session. Each in turn may be partially "desensitized" by the soothing meditative mood that prevails. As we visualize this process, it would be analogous to a tape which is being demagnetized on a tape recorder, with vast amounts of information run through the demagnetizing circuits at high speeds and thereby erased or "uncharged."

An advantage of meditation over systematic desensitization might be that in TM the selection of material to be processed in any given session is made *by the responding* organism itself. An individual may be expected to be more sensitive to his idiosyncratic tolerance thresholds for specific anxiety-provoking material than an external therapist could be.

If meditation serves as a form of automatic desensitization, as postulated, this could explain the effect often noted by meditators that a particular meditation session has seemed to lessen the urgency of current problems and conflicts, rendering them less anxiety-provoking and more manageable. It could also explain the *cumulative* personality change which is frequently seen, over time, in meditating persons.

A Learning Exercise

Regular meditation, practiced twice daily, might be conceived of as a learning exercise with important implications for personality development. During TM, a solid block of time is spent contacting a profound self-awareness which is ordinarily obscured by activity. The individual may have an opportunity, during this special state of being, to experience a new sense of his own identity, one rooted in his very act of existing. Unlike other experiences of waking life, in meditation he is supremely important to himself, but this only because he *exists* and not because he *acts*. His identity is self-evident in this state—external affirmation is superfluous. A simple but profound lesson of the meditative session might be expressed in the following hypothetical formulation:

I exist even though I am separated from others . . . .I do not disappear when they are removed . . . .I am *separate* from mother, father, lover, friend, analyst, whomever . . . .But this separateness is not loneliness . . . it is closeness to myself, to life . . . .

Occurring in a completely conscious state, this new-formed identity can be remembered and applied to life outside of meditation—the life of action. It is our conjecture that it is this repeated lesson concerning one's own identity as "being" that forms the basis of the increasing individuation often noted in meditators, a growing sense of self as *separate from* others.

Paradoxically, a rediscovery of one's own identity is frequently coupled with a growing awareness of others and a greater sensitivity to their needs. The person no longer fears loss of identity when he centers his attention elsewhere. Such a change in the experiencing of the self may manifest itself in a lessened need to command attention and an increased tolerance of others' opinions.

Change in Cognitive Mode

Recent research on the discrete functions of the cerebral hemispheres[7, 14, 40] suggests that each hemisphere controls its own special kind of thinking, with the left hemisphere mediating verbal, sequential, analytic, rational thinking, and the right hemisphere controlling spatial perception, and holistic, simultaneous, synthetic thinking of the type involved in many creative activities.

This hemispheric specialization may play a role in the effects of meditation. While no systematic study of possible shifts (during meditation) of hemispheric dominance has as yet been made, there is strong subjective evidence of a shift in mode of thinking during meditation in the direction of that type of thought which is generally felt to be controlled by the right hemisphere (i.e., nonverbal, holistic, nonsequential thought). Ornstein[30] considers a shift toward "right hemisphere" modes of thinking to be one of the dominant features of meditation and of Eastern methods of thought in general.

At the least there would seem to be, during meditation, a greater *equalization* in the workload of the two hemispheres. Verbal, linear, time-linked thinking frequently is minimized during meditation (compared to the role it plays in everyday life) while holistic, intuitive, wordless thinking is maximized. Some of the effects of meditation may reflect this shift in emphasis.

Superego values are largely rooted in verbal-conceptual frames of reference. Restrictive moral systems are for the most part transmitted verbally, and complex role-modeling is largely dependent upon verbal concepts. The effects of meditation on the punitive superego, previously noted, may therefore be partially explained by this basic shift away from the *verbal mode* during meditation. Minimizing verbal-conceptual experience (during a state of wakefulness) may afford the individual temporary relief from his superego injunctions which are, for the most part, internal verbalizations. Having obtained a degree of relief from these injunctions during meditation, when returning to active life, the meditator may now find himself less subject to severe self-criticism and/or guilt reactions, the change in the strength of his superego having generalized from the meditative state to the life of action.

CLINICAL APPLICATIONS OF MEDITATION

Having considered the theoretical rationale for the effects of meditation, let us look at some practical problems inherent in its use as an adjunct to psychotherapy. Meditation is not a panacea. Not every patient wants to learn meditation, and not every patient who learns it benefits from it; but we believe the success ratio is sufficiently high to warrant consideration of this technique as a facilitator of the psychotherapeutic process.

Refusal to Learn to Meditate

There are a number of reasons why certain patients respond negatively to a suggestion that they learn to meditate:

1. Meditation may be seen as incompatible with the life-style of the patient. This is particularly apt to occur with persons having an undue need for achievement. Such persons may be threatened by the concept of "letting down" or being "tranquil" even though intellectually they may realize that a more relaxed existence would be advantageous to them. These same people are also likely to resist a physician's advice to take prolonged vacations when necessary or to lessen their work schedules, since compulsive overactivity is often used by them as a means of avoiding self-confrontation. Meditation may thus be refused because it is sensed as a threat to the defensive system.

2. The patient who fears loss of control may equate meditation with hypnosis or forms of coercive mind control. If he does learn to meditate, he may unconsciously experience the meditative session as punishment, surrender, loss of dominance, or as threatening to a need on his part to manipulate others and will probably soon discontinue the practice unless therapeutic intervention brings about sufficient change in attitude.

3. The patient may view the psychotherapist's suggestion to learn meditation as proof that the therapist wants to "get rid of him." He may feel that learning to meditate will rob him of a fantasied control which he believes his symptoms exert over the therapist, or other transferential problems may cause rejection of the suggestion.

Resistance to Continuing Meditation

Resistance to continuing meditation, once the technique has been learned, stems from a number of sources:

1.   Transference reactions may interfere with the patient's acceptance of meditation. A need to prolong a dependent child-parent role vis-a-vis the psychotherapist may, for example, cause the patient to become threatened by the growing independence fostered by meditation. A form of "transference reaction" to the meditative process itself also seems to occur. The mantra may be treated by certain persons as though it were a "good parent" when the meditation is going satisfactorily, and as a "bad parent" when it is not. One of our patients became enraged at his mantra because it would not readily enter his mind during meditation. Analysis of this reaction revealed that this patient had in the past experienced similar fury at his mother who had often been preoccupied with siblings during the patient's childhood and frequently unavailable when he needed her.

Another patient who seemed to be deriving considerable benefit from meditation complained bitterly that the meditation had "deserted" her when she became ill with the flu and particularly needed comfort.* She became so angry at this that she would not resume meditating even after she became well. Therapeutic exploration of this problem revealed that the patient, who had been one of 11 children, felt that she had been neglected whenever she was ill as a child, her overworked mother finding a sick child in the family a great burden with which she could seemingly only cope by removing herself, emotionally, from concern for the child. Now, finding herself ill and alone once more (the patient was at the time divorced) and being unable to meditate at this time, the patient felt that the meditation had changed from an idealized "good mother," which it had seemed up to this point, into an indifferent "unavailable mother."

2.   Patients with rigid or puritanical backgrounds may make out of the meditation-ritual a new tyranny. Simple instructions of when, where, and how to meditate are construed by such a patient as authoritarian *commands* and he then must rebel against what is felt to be an increasing enslavement by the meditation. It may be necessary in such cases for the therapist to instruct the patient to vary his meditation ritual in a more flexible manner, perhaps encouraging him to move his body rhythmically during meditation, or to open his eyes during the session. Such maneuvers may help him become less compulsive in his approach to the meditation, but the response is best handled by insight obtained through psychotherapy.

---

* Physically ill patients frequently find themselves unable to meditate.

In the meanwhile, frequency and/or duration of meditation may have to be temporarily decreased.

Despite such problems as the above, we have encountered no instances in which meditation was used by a patient to resist the psychotherapeutic process itself, that is, where it was used in lieu of psychotherapeutic work by the patient. Nor have we seen any patient terminate psychotherapy or psychoanalysis because they entered meditation. In all cases that we have observed, meditation was used in a manner that contributed to the therapy rather than detracted from it. In three instances, we have seen persons enter psychiatric treatment *after* they had been meditating for awhile, stating that they now felt less anxious about the prospect of dealing with deep-seated problems.

Resistance of Self-Image to Change

Changes from meditation, when they occur, may be more sudden and dramatic than those resulting from psychotherapy and thus, even when salutary, may not always be easily assimilated by the patient. Untreated, such a person may discontinue meditation.

An example of such a reaction is a patient who was referred for TM by her psychotherapist because her chronic tension-headaches had consistently resisted treatment, even though other psychosomatic symptoms had abated with psychotherapy (e.g., gastric ulcer and colitis), and she had made important positive changes in her life. After she commenced meditation, her headaches worsened for a period of about a week (temporary symptom acceleration is not unusual following commencement of meditation) and then abruptly disappeared, the patient remaining entirely free of headaches for 4 months (for the first time in many years).

During this period, however, she noticed personality changes which disturbed her and which she attributed to the meditation. Formerly self-sacrificing and playing the role of a "martyr" to her children, she began to find herself increasingly aware of her own rights and impelled to stand up for them, sometimes so forcefully that it alarmed her. Though she was apparently effective in this new self-assertion (her adolescent daughters began to treat her more gently, with far fewer scathing comments), she complained that "meditation is making me a hateful person."

This patient also found that she was no longer talking compulsively, a change for which she received favorable comments from others but which bothered her because she was now able to sense the social uneasiness that had been hidden beneath her compulsive chatter. Unable to assimilate these personality changes, the patient stopped meditating despite the fact that her tension headaches then returned.

It was necessary to trace the origins of this patient's need to be self-effacing before she could consider reinstating the practice of meditation. In doing so it was discovered that her competition with an older sister was at the root of much of this difficulty. This sister had been considered by the parents as a "saint" while the patient had always been considered a troublesome, irritating child. During her childhood she had despaired at this state of affairs; but in her adolescence, she developed an intense compulsion to become more "saintly" than her exalted sister, though this often meant total sacrifice of her own wishes or needs for those of others. Even the simple pleasure of a meditation session seemed to this patient to be a self-indulgence out of character for so "self-sacrificing" a person.

Following some therapeutic working through of these problems, the patient agreed to resume daily meditation, but it was soon discovered that the meditative process was once again pushing her toward self-assertion at too rapid a rate for her to handle. The therapist then suggested that she reduce her meditation to *once weekly*. Her meditation session was to take place at the start of a psychotherapeutic session and the therapist was to meditate *with the patient* at these times, giving tacit support to the patient's right to independence and self-assertion. These weekly joint meditative sessions proved extremely productive, the patient describing her TM sessions with her therapist as being "deeply restful" and seeing them as pleasurable and constructive. Since her emotional responses to each meditation session was promptly dealt with in the discussion which followed, guilt was prevented from accruing. With this approach, the patient's headaches again disappeared and she began to experience personality changes typical of regular *daily* meditators, such as marked enrichment of a previously impoverished fantasy life. She repeatedly stated, however, that this weekly meditation session was all she could "take" of meditation at one time without feeling "pounded by it." In this moderate dose, the patient appeared well able to assimilate the changes in self-concept brought about by the meditation and the patient–therapist relationship was used, through the joint meditation sessions, to enhance the effectiveness of the meditation.

Patients with depressive trends seem particularly prone to resist TM because it may threaten their self-image or pathological life-style. One such patient spontaneously commented that she did not want to learn TM because "it might make me feel better and in a way I may not really *want* to feel better." Another such patient was a woman in her thirties who suffered from chronic depression and obsessive indecision concerning her marital relationship. This patient communicated little during her therapeutic sessions, attempting to force the therapist to solve her problems while simultaneously resisting any constructive suggestions given to her.

The therapist suggested to the patient that she learn TM in the hope that meditation might replace her attitude of resignation with a more active stance which would enable her to resume a constructive struggle. Somewhat to the surprise of the therapist, the patient consented to learn TM and found to her own bewilderment that she began to feel decidedly positive effects from meditation. Her mood lightened considerably, compulsive crying spells ceased, and she began to make decisions of a meaningful sort. She also reported that she felt more energetic and was becoming more active. She stated that meditation was making her feel "much better"; but at this point (it being summer) both she and the therapist left for vacation.

During her vacation, the patient stopped meditating completely, later explaining that she had become "angry" at the meditation because it was "making me cope" and also because "it made me feel calm so that I could no longer cry or feel sorry for myself." Feeling that she must cry and must complain, she discontinued meditating and was able to resume her despair, weeping, and self-pity. In her own words, "I had my own feelings back again."

Several factors seemed to play into this negative reaction. The vacationing therapist was clearly requiring that she become more independent. Resentment at this may have been displaced onto meditation which was a therapist-suggested activity. A pervasive tendency on the part of the patient to make every new activity into a form of slavery also seemed to have included the meditation which began to be a new "ordeal" and "duty" for her. Probably the most important factor, however, was the fact that the meditation threatened to rob this patient of her role as a "helpless" being whose misery was used unconsciously as a club with which to control others (husband, friends, therapist, etc.). In effect, the meditation was working "too well" by fostering a genuine change of attitude for which she was not emotionally prepared.

In a related vein, Glueck[16] has noted that certain patients seem unable to accept the pleasurable feelings which result from TM, and may stop meditating rather than face the guilt engendered. In such instances, it is sometimes useful to confine meditation to sessions conducted immediately prior to or during the patient's psychotherapy session so that any guilt reactions to the pleasure can be immediately worked through.

Overmeditation

Excessive use of meditation is sometimes encountered. Too much time spent in meditation may lead to unconscious material surfacing so rapidly that it cannot be properly assimilated. Fortunately this eventuality is guarded against by the Meditation Society's insistence that the practice of TM be limited to no more than two 20-minute sessions daily.

Not everyone obeys instructions however. On the theory that if "one pill makes me feel better, taking the whole bottle should cure me" some persons may decide to meditate 4 or 5 hours a day! These people often show histories of severe addictive disorders or other psychiatric problems of a serious nature. Taken in such heavy doses in a person with an adverse psychiatric history, meditation may precipitate psychotic symptoms and thus is decidedly contraindicated. Although it is not certain that overmeditation leads to such serious results in relatively stable people, the Meditation Society does not advise any form of extended meditation except in special settings (such as a retreat) where careful supervision is available.

The fact that meditation may be a tonic and facilitator when taken in short, well-spaced dosages but have an antitherapeutic effect when taken in unduly prolonged sessions, is essential to consider when reviewing a psychiatric case history where any form of meditation has been practiced by a patient. Certain flamboyantly promoted forms of meditation currently in vogue in this country *demand* up to 4 hours daily of meditation from their followers, an important piece of information for a therapist dealing with a patient involved in such practices.

Unstressing

Even the mild, generally conservative, and limited meditation regime of TM cannot be handled by *all* patients. In a minority of persons, it may lead to too rapid release of emotionally charged material ("unstressing" reactions) with attendant increase of symptomatology, or to poor impulse control. One of our patients emerged from each of his meditation sessions so angry that he described his day as "ruined" afterwards and because of this had discontinued meditating. This patient, who had a depressive personality, had been suppressing a great deal of rage which apparently was released by the meditation. Since the therapist deemed it desirable to bring this rage into the treatment session, he instructed the patient to resume meditation *once* daily instead of twice to slow down the speed of emotional release) and advised him to meditate immediately prior to coming to therapy so that any affect which surfaced during meditation could be made available to the therapy. The latter proved to be an effective maneuver, bringing into the treatment a wealth of reactions of an alive, nonintellectual sort which could be worked on. This strategy was found to be even more effective when psychiatrist and patient meditated together at the commencement of the treatment hour, making the contemplative postmeditative state an integral part of the treatment.

Impulsive or acting out behavior may stem from other causes as well. Some meditators, when undergoing unstressing, experience exceptional restlessness and because of this may terminate a meditation session abruptly without waiting the recommended 2 to 3 minutes with eyes closed following meditation. In such instances their turbulent mood may be carried over into activity instead of resolved in the quiet of the meditative state. It may be useful to advise such a patient to take an even *longer* than usual time coming out of meditation when he feels the session has been a "rough" one, allowing a postmeditative rest of 4 to 5 minutes or more with eyes closed until some resolution of tension is experienced.

Clinical Results

Although problems frequently arise in the treatment of meditating patients which must be handled with appropriate modifications in the meditation regime, in some instances meditation contributes in a direct fashion to the patient's therapeutic progress with few, if any, complications. At such times, the therapist finds it a distinct contribution to the healing process.

A patient in her midthirties originally entered psychoanalytically oriented psychotherapy for an agitated depression which had been entirely dissipated through her treatment. After a year and a half of therapy, the patient had been able to return successfully to work, was supporting herself and her five children (her divorced husband had defaulted in child support), and was enjoying her new found strength. She was also growing in her ability to relate to her children with considerably less guilt and anxiety. A continuing unresolved problem for her, however, was a relationship with an emotionally disturbed lover.

The lover was possessive and jealous of the patient's relationship to her children, drank heavily, and on several occasions had threatened violence to her and her family. At one point he had been hospitalized for several weeks after he made physical threats against the patient and also threatened to take his own life. She had long felt that she must end this relationship both for her own sake and that of her children, but was unable to seriously think of doing so without uncontrollable weeping and an intense sense of guilt at "throwing him out."

As her therapy proceeded, the patient began to experience a growing conflict between a new-found sense of personal dignity and her continuing dependence on this lover. At this point, she found herself becoming unusually tense and on several occasions she alarmed herself by drinking so heavily that she later had no memory of the events that had transpired—a pattern unfamiliar to her.

The therapist was concerned by these episodes of uncontrolled drinking in a patient who had been in a rather precarious emotional state when she had commenced therapy, and suggested that the patient learn TM in hopes that this might help to bring the anxiety and excessive drinking under control. The patient accepted the suggestion readily, stating that she hoped TM would also help her with an insomnia which had been increasing in severity.

TM was almost immediately effective in relaxing the patient. Within a few days after commencing meditation, she slept restfully throughout a whole night (for the first time in years) and her sleep remained restful, even under stress, for the past 9 months since she commenced meditating.

The sporadic drinking ceased immediately following commencement of meditation, and unexpectedly the patient also lost all sense of urgency about smoking marijuana, which she had formerly used somewhat compulsively. She reported a greatly increased composure and sense of calm at work which helped her to stay "on top of" situations at the office, and said that she experienced a generally quieter, more understanding relationship with her children. The children had also learned to meditate and the family now frequently meditated together, an activity which brought them closer to each other.

The most notable change in the patient following commencement of TM, however, was a marked increase in her sense of independence. A few weeks after commencing meditation, the patient was able to ask her lover to leave the house and insisted that he do so (despite his protests). She arranged for police assistance should he become violent, took a firm but nonpunitive stand, and followed through with it without her usual guilt and self-recrimination. She grieved appropriately after he left but despite this was able to sleep well and continued working the next day. Her ability to carry through this decision with a minimum of anxiety she attributed directly to TM which, she said, enabled her to *carry out* the decision which her therapy had, over a long period of working on her problems, helped her reach— namely to terminate this destructive relationship.

While this same patient some months later was reunited with this lover, the new relationship seems to be on a different footing. She is now more independent, having in the interim built up a number of outside activities, interests, and relationships of her own which she has in no way abandoned for him. Unlike previously, she is now insistent on her rights and those of the children and clearly ready to resume living alone if necessary. Apparently sensing this change, the lover has become more controlled, less demanding, less jealous, more of a socially participating family member.

The final outcome of this relationship is uncertain at the present writing. The lover, who was originally strongly opposed to the patient's meditating, has, interestingly, recently expressed an interest in learning TM himself, but whether he will do so and whether he could benefit from meditation without the additional support of psychotherapy, is unknown at this time.

TM as Therapy

While undoubtedly many well-integrated persons can benefit from TM in terms of optimizing their *personality growth*, it is not certain whether this technique can be considered a form of therapy. Preliminary observation suggests that it has only limited usefulness as *sole* therapeutic agent. As noted, meditators may have the same forms of resistance to the therapeutic effects of meditation as patients do to psychotherapy. They are at a disadvantage, however, in not having help in understanding or handling this resistance similar to the help offered in a conventional psychotherapeutic setting.* Without insight into the anxieties which may underlie their resistance to meditation, such persons may simply stop meditating. While there are, as yet, no official figures on the attrition rate among practitioners of TM, one study[36] found a 30% dropout from the practice over a 3-year period (in a normal population). Based on the limited clinical sample we have seen, we would estimate the attrition rate to be higher in psychiatric populations. It is possible that such dropping out from the practice will be found to be a major detriment to its use with psychiatric patients *unless* meditation is accompanied by psychotherapy. Such psychotherapy should be conducted by a therapist aware of the difficulties involved and able to help the patient work through resistances to the meditative process.

Hitherto unavailable emotion-laden material brought to the surface by meditation seems to be assimilated by a disturbed person more constructively if it is exposed to the acceptant attitude of another person, as in the psychotherapy session. In the latter instance, a bridge may be formed between a growing *inner* acceptance of self and an experience of acceptance by a significant other. In addition, the rich insights and changes fostered by TM may be encouraged to take permanent root through the deeper understanding of them gained in psychotherapy.

The remarks above apply specifically to clinical populations. Persons who are reasonably well-adjusted may have the emotional resources needed to integrate the material which surfaces as a result of meditation, into their life, unaided.

* While the SIMS organization offers instruction in the meditative technique and regular checking to make sure the person is meditating correctly, the TM teachers, not being psychotherapists, quite properly refrain from any form of psychodynamic interpretation or analysis of meditators' problems and do not give advice of a psychological or psychiatric nature.

INDICATIONS FOR USE OF MEDITATION

Depending on the psychotherapist's evaluation of the situation and the patient's readiness to accept such a program, we would be inclined to recommend meditation adjunctively for the following:

- Tension states and/or anxiety reactions
- Psychophysiologic disorders
- Chronic fatigue states
- Insomnias and hypersomnias
- Abuse of "soft" drugs, alcohol, or tobacco
- Paranoid tendencies
- Obsessive-compulsive tendencies
- Chronic low-grade depressions or subacute reactive depressions
- Low frustration tolerance (we would use TM in cases of organic as well as psychogenic irritability, since preliminary clinical observations[1, 16] suggest that meditation was useful in increasing overall adjustment in several isolated cases of brain injury)
- Strong submissive trends and/or poorly developed psychological differentiation
- Blocks to productivity
- Inadequate contact with affective life
- To shift emphasis from the patient's reliance on the psychotherapist to reliance on self (of particular use when terminating long-term psychotherapy or psychoanalysis)

Because rapid surfacing of unconscious material may occur during unstressing in meditation, we are not recommending that borderline psychotic or psychotic patients be referred for meditation unless their practice of it can be supervised by a psychotherapist familiar with meditation (particularly with respect to handling unstressing or release phenomena). Such a therapist would be competent to guide the patient in terms of frequency of meditation and to institute variations in the meditational regime, when necessary.

CONCLUSIONS

In summary, we would conclude that, correctly used, a responsible meditative technique such as TM can offer valuable assistance to the psychotherapeutic process. We recommend, however, that psychotherapists interested in using meditation as an adjunct in their work with patients, first learn it themselves* Laing[24] has suggested that the psychoanalyst may derive considerable personal benefit from meditating and that meditation may, in addition, make him more receptive to the communications of his patients, a point of view with which we concur. Because of his own professional training and background, a psychiatrist will hopefully have the tools to enable him to work through unconscious material which may surface during his own meditation, and he should be in a position to derive particular benefit from the deep insights which sometimes occur at this time. In addition, since meditation frequently brings about a value change in the practitioner which may include a greater acceptance of many aspects of life, it seems advantageous that both therapist and patient be on the same "wavelength" with respect to the philosophical implications of this practice.

Whether in the future it will be found advisable for psychiatrists to teach their own patients one of the various forms of meditation awaits further study. At present, there appear to be distinct advantages in *not* doing so, but rather using the official TM organization, SIMS, to instruct the patient. Not only are its instructors carefully trained in the teaching of the techniques involved, but the atmosphere of group participation at the TM centers, the dignity which these centers impart to the meditation process, the systematic classroom repetition of the proper attitude required for meditation, and the somewhat dramatic emphasis given by the organization to the actual process of initially experiencing meditation appear to be central components of the learning experience, ensuring that the practice is viewed seriously and adhered to. Meditation training also involves an intense relationship between pupil and teacher at the time of initiation into the practice and its complete separation from the psychotherapeutic session therefore appears desirable from a transferential point of view.

If interest in meditational techniques continues to grow at its present rate over the next few years, we can expect a considerable increase in the number of psychiatric patients who are also meditators. The therapeutic management of meditation will therefore no doubt become increasingly important to psychiatrists. We believe that the latter can play a prominent role in exploring the therapeutic possibilities of this technique, with a rapprochement between psychiatry and meditation a fruitful opportunity for all concerned.

---

* SIMS offers instruction in TM to psychiatrists and psychologists but requires of all mental health practitioners that they first sign a relase-form indicating that they will not teach TM to their patients (i.e., that they will not impart knowledge of the TM *mantras*). This is a fairly straightforward agreement which we have found in no way a hindrance in our work with patients. Approval by SIMS of the application of any mental health practitioner takes about 2 weeks to process and is largely automatic.

REFERENCES

1. Allen, C.: Possible psychological and physiological effects of transcendental meditation on aphasic patients. Unpublished paper, University of Michigan, 1973.

2. Allison, J.: Respiratory changes during the practice of the technique of transcendental meditation. *Lancet* **7651**:833–834, 1970.

3. Banquet, J. P.: EEG and meditation. *J. Electroencephalography Clin. Neurophysiol.* **33**:454, 1972.

4. Benson, H. and Wallace, R. K.: Decreased drug abuse with transcendental meditation: A study of 1862 subjects. *Congressional Record*, 92nd Congress, First Session, June, 1971, Serial #92-1, U.S. Government Printing Office, Washington, D.C., 1971.

5. Benson, H. and Wallace, R. K.: Decreased blood pressure in hypertensive subjects who practiced meditation. Supplement II to *Circulation*, Vols. XIV and XLVI, p. 130, 1972.

6. Blasdell, K.: The effect of transcendental meditation upon a complex perceptual motor task. Unpublished paper, Department of Kinesiology, University of California, Los Angeles, Calif., 1972.

7. Bogen, J. E.: The other side of the brain: I, II, III. *Bull. Los Angeles Neurological Soc.* **34**(3): July 1969.

8. Bonime, W.: The psychodynamics of neurotic depression. In *American Handbook of Psychiatry*, Vol. 3, S. Arieti, (Ed.), Basic Books, New York, 1966, pp. 239–255.

9. Brown, F. M., Stewart, W. S., and Blodgett, J. I.: EEG Kappa rhythms during transcendental meditation and possible perceptual threshold changes following. Paper presented to the Kentucky Academy of Sciences, November 13, 1971.

10. Conze, E.: *Buddhist Meditation*, Harper and Row, New York, 1969, p. 83.

11. Das, N. N. and Gastaut, H.: Variations de l'activite electrique du cerveau, du coeur, et des muscles sequelletiques au cours de la meditation et de l'extase yogique. *J. Electroencephalography Clin. Neurophysiol.* Suppl **6**:211–219, 1957.

12. Doucette, L. D.: Anxiety and transcendental meditation as an anxiety reducing agent. Unpublished paper, McMasters University, Hamilton, Ontario, Canada, 1972.

13. Ferguson, P. D. and Gowan, J.: The influence of transcendental meditation on anxiety, depression, aggression, neuroticism and self-actualization. Unpublished paper, California State University, Northridge, Calif., 1972.

14. Gazzaniga, M. S.: The split brain in man. *Sci. Am.* **1967**:24–29, Offprint No. 508.

15. Gellhorn, E. and Kiely. W. F.: Mystical states of consciousness: Neurophysiological and clinical aspects. *J. Nervous Ment. Dis.* **154**:399–405, 1972.

16. Glueck, B.: "Current research on transcendental meditation. Paper delivered at Rensselaer Polytechnic Institute, Hartford, Conn., March 1973.

17. Glueck, B.: Quoted in the *Hartford Courant*, May 27, 1973.

18. Goleman, D.: Meditation as a meta-therapy: Hypotheses toward a proposed fifth state of consciousness. *J. Transpersonal Psychol.* **3**:1–25, 1971.

19. Graham, J.: Auditory discrimination in meditators. Unpublished paper, University of Sussex, Brighton, England, 1972.

20. Hines, M.: Meditation and creativity. Senior thesis, Princeton University, Princeton, N.J., 1973.

21. Hjelle, L. A.: Transcendental meditation and psychological health. Unpublished paper, State University College, Brockport, N.Y., 1972.

22. Jacobson, E.: *You Must Relax*, McGraw-Hill, New York, 1934.

23. Jones, M. and Mellersh, V.: Comparison of exercise response in anxiety states and normal controls. *Psychosom. Med.* **8**:180–187, 1946.

24. Laing, R. D.: Keynote address of the American Academy of Psychoanalysis, quoted in *Frontiers of Psychiatry* 3(3):1–2, February 1, 1973.

25. Mahesh, M. Y.: *Transcendental Meditation*, New American Library (Signet), New York, 1968.

26. Meerloo, J. A.: The universal language of rhythm. In *Poetry Therapy*, J. J. Leedy, (Ed.), J. Lippincott, Philadelphia, Pa., 1969.

27. Naranjo, C. and Ornstein, R. E.: *On the Psychology of Meditation*, Viking Press, New York, 1971.

28. Nidich, S., Seeman, W. and Siebert, M.: Influence of transcendental meditation on state anxiety. *J. Consulting Clin. Psychol.*, in press.

29. Orme-Johnson, D.: Autonomic stability and transcendental meditation. *Psychosom. Med.* **35**:341–349, 1973.

30. Ornstein, R. E.: *The Psychology of Consciousness*, Viking, New York, 1972.

31. Pelletier, K. R.: Altered attention deployment in meditation. Unpublished paper, University of California, Berkeley, Calif., 1973.

32. Pitts, F.: The biochemistry of anxiety. *Sci. Am.* **220**:69–75, 1969.

33. Reisman, D.: *The Lonely Crowd*, Yale University Press, New Haven, 1950.

34. Ritterstaedt, H. and Schenkluhn, H.: Measuring changes of the skin temperature during the practice of transcendental meditation. Unpublished report, Max Planck Institute, Germany, 1972.

35. Salk, L.: The role of the heartbeat in the relations between mother and infant. *Sci. Am.* **228**:24–29, 1973.

36. Shafii, M.: Smoking following meditation. Unpublished paper, University of Michigan Medical Center, Ann Arbor, Mich., 1973.

37. Shafii, M., Lavely, R., and Jaffe, R.: Meditation and marijuana. *Am. J. Psychiat.* **131**:60–63, 1974.

38. Shaw, R. and Kolb, D.: One-point reaction time involving meditators and nonmeditators. Unpublished paper, University of Texas, El Paso, Tex., 1972.

39. Smith, J. C.: Transcendental meditation and anxiety. Dissertation proposal, Michigan State University, Ann Arbor, Mich., 1973, p. 29.

40. Sperry, R. W.: The great cerebral commisure. *Sci. Am.* **1964**:42–52, Offprint No. 174.

41. Wallace, R. K.: Physiological effects of transcendental meditation. *Science* **167**:1751–1754, 1970.

42. Wallace, R. K., Benson, H., and Wilson, A. F.: A wakeful hypometabolic physiologic state. *Am. J. Physiol.* **221**:795–799, 1971.

43. Wallace, R. K. and Benson, H.: The physiology of meditation. *Sci. Am.* **226**:84–90, 1972.

44. Wilson, A. F. and Honsberger, R.: The effects of transcendental meditation upon bronchial asthma, *Clin. Res.*, in press.

45. Witkin, H. A., Dyk, R., Faterson, H. F., Goodenough, D. R., and Karp, S. A.: *Psychological Differentiation*, Wiley, New York, 1962.

46. Witkin, H. A. and Oltman, P. K.: Cognitive Style. *Int. J. Neurol.* **6**:119–137, 1967.

CHAPTER THIRTEEN

VALUE OF PATANJALI'S CONCEPTS IN THE TREATMENT OF PSYCHONEUROSIS

N. S. VAHIA,
D. R. DOONGAJI, and
D. V. JESTE

At this time, when many new therapeutic procedures are being devised and assessed, a technique based on principles of Patanjali (Circa, 400 B.C.) deserves careful consideration because of its novel concept and its holistic therapeutic approach. Patanjali's theory is that as long as a person's behavior is primarily conditioned by environmental stimuli, he is prone to personality dysfunction. However, if the primary motivational force guiding all his behavior is to make the most of his capacities, without constant preoccupation with the resultant gain, the nature of the environmental feedback will not disturb the harmonious functioning of his personality. Patanjali has presented a method for maintenance of such personality function by the gradual development of control over various expressions, thought processes, bodily functions, and social relationships. According to him, it is possible to develop, by practice, an ability to observe these functions in a detached and objective manner, so that one can control and modify them to maintain a harmonious relationship with the environment.

CONCEPTS

From childhood an individual becomes a prey to the external environment so that his or her feelings of well-being are influenced by the reactions of others. Thus adequate or inadequate adaptation becomes the yardstick for the concept of normality. However, this makes one vulnerable to the danger of greater or lesser disharmony among the various psychophysiological functions, depending on the nature of the environmental feedback.

Patanjali[11] suggests that one should gradually, by practice, learn to control one's social relationships, bodily functions, and psychological processes so that their harmony is not disturbed by this external feedback. To control them adequately, one must be able to observe these processes in a detached and objective manner. It is comparatively easy to observe others' thoughts, emotional reactions, and behavior, but it is difficult to be an observer of one's own psychological, physiological, and social behavior because of subjective involvement. Patanjali has presented a method for developing the ability to observe different aspects of one's personality function with the same objectivity, with which one can study the function of others. He recommends that an appealing symbol be selected by the individual (with the help of the therapist), and that the individual learn how to concentrate all his thought processes on this selected symbol. He would then be able to appreciate that although the object of concentration was appealing to him, in actual practice, his concentration would be disturbed constantly by external factors. He would now realize that although he thought that he was in full control of his thinking and behavior, the controlling factors were really around him and not within himself. His subjective involvement with the environment disturbs his capacity to control himself. The frustrations of inability to achieve desires, the fear of loss of what he has achieved, or the repercussions of his behavior have dominated his thinking to such an extent that he is unable to control his thought processes and their impact on the bodily functions and social relationships.

With practice, he would be able to develop greater and greater freedom from external influences and learn to control his thought processes and other functions. He would learn to observe in a detached manner the link between the environmental influences, his reactions to them, and their impact on his behavior, psychological, physiological, and social. The increased ability to observe and acquire control would help him modify his reactions by realistic assessment of the environmental feedback, resulting in the utilization of his faculties to an optimum capacity.

Eight measures have been described for this purpose—Yama, Niyama, Asana, Pranayama, Pratyahara, Dharana, Dhyana, and Samadhi. The first two measures represent guidelines for social behavior. The third, fourth, and fifth measures are meant for development of control over voluntary and autonomic functions. The last three represent developing the ability to observe, control, and modify thought processes, so that optimum personality function is maintained.

1.   Yama and (2) Niyama are rules and regulations for social behavior, such as

Satya.   Truthfulness.
Ahimsa.   Nonaggression (thought, word, or action).
Astheya.   Honesty.
Brahmacharya.   Sexual moderation.
Aparigraha.   Nonpossessiveness, nonacquisitiveness.
Shaucha.   Purity (thought, word, and action).
Santosh.   Contentment.
Tapa.   Self-denial.
Swadhyaya.   Self-enlightenment, objective study of self.
Ishwarpranidhana.   Submission to God's will, being one with God.

3.   Asana.   Practice of certain postures for relaxation of voluntary musculature.
4.   Pranayama.   Breathing practices for voluntary control of inspiration, expiration, and retention of breath.
5.   Pratyahara.   Restraint of the senses by voluntary withdrawal from external environment.

6. Dharana. Selection of an object for concentration and development of increasing concentration on the same, with decreasing preoccupation with external stimuli.

7. Dhyana. Undisturbed concentration on a selected object to the complete exclusion of all other thought processes and later, identification of that object with the internal observing and integrating mechanism present within all of us.

8. Samadhi. Observing and maintaining harmonious functioning of psychological, physiological, and social aspects of the personality.

INDICATIONS AND CONTRAINDICATIONS

The patients who get maximum benefit from this therapy are acute or chronic psychoneurotics and patients with psychosomatic complaints or diseases. Preliminary observations have shown that schizophrenics are not suitable for this treatment because of their increasing withdrawal from reality leading to exacerbation of their initial symptoms. Patients with personality disorders are also not suitable, as they are likely to dramatize and elaborate their symptoms rather than concentrate on recovery. Mental patients with some degree of retardation are not suitable candidates because of their inability to comprehend fully the instructions and to cooperate during treatment. Manics and hypomanics are difficult subjects as they do not cooperate or continue with the treatment, and for obvious reasons, this treatment is contraindicated in severe depression.

THE TECHNIQUE

A technique based upon the concepts outlined earlier was devised. An initial explanation about the psychological nature of the illness is given to the patient. It is emphasized that the drugs will give only symptomatic relief, in contrast to this therapy which may bring about lasting benefits. Since the therapy acts gradually, it would have to be continued for some time before the patient would find relief. After the initial explanations and establishment of a working relationship, the treatment is begun. The patient attends treatment every morning, each sitting lasting for about an hour. He is taught the practice of Asana in the first week, pranayama during the second week, and the other steps in the subsequent weeks; the total treatment period lasts 6 weeks.

Asanas

These practices are meant for the relaxation of voluntary musculature. They consist of adoption of different kinds of relaxing postures, and are not exercises for strengthening the muscles. They are to be performed in a smooth and steady manner and with minimum effort, in such a way that a feeling of relaxation occurs, unaccompanied or followed by tension or exhaustion.

Sukhasana and Shavasana are taught initially, followed gradually by four other Asanas—Talasana, Konasana, Yogamudra, and Vakrasana. The last four Asanas are centered around movements of the spinal column. The first two Asanas are practiced for 10 to 15 minutes, while the remaining four Asanas are each practiced for 5 minutes. The total time taken is approximately 30 minutes. The patient is advised to disregard the presence of the therapist and to imagine that he is far away, near a beach, alone under the clear sky. Some patients prefer to concentrate on the precordium during the Asanas. The important point is that the patient learns to keep his thoughts away from the immediate environment.

Pranayama

Pranayama is taught during the second week. It consists of voluntary control of inspiration, retention, and expiration of breath. It should also be performed in as effortless a manner as possible without the patient becoming tense and tired. Pranayama is practiced while the person is in the Sukhasana (sitting) posture. He is asked to close one nasal orifice with his thumb and gradually breathe in through the other nasal orifice until he is in full inspiration. He is then asked to close both the nasal orifices and hold his breath for as long as possible without feeling uncomfortable. He then gradually exhales air from the opposite nostril. After expiration he is instructed to hold his breath as long as he can before beginning the next inspiration. This procedure of inhalation, retention, and exhalation, which is one Pranayama, is repeated as many times as is possible without feeling tense or tired. The important point in the practice of Pranayama is that it is to be performed as gently and as rhythmically as possible. The therapist notes the duration of each phase in seconds. This duration for each of the three phases should be same, and should be progressively increased. The total number of Pranayama at one sitting is also gradually increased. During both Asana and Pranayama, the same visual imagery (e.g., sky and the sea) is maintained.

To find out whether these steps are performed satisfactorily, the therapist lifts up one limb of the patient. If he is completely relaxed, it shoud fall like "dead weight." If the patient has succeeded in maintaining unawareness of the presence of therapist, his eyes will not wander toward or away from the therapist, while his face would appear calm and peaceful, with no flickering of eyelids, and all the phases of respiration will be smooth and rhythmic. The initial tendecy to get the sitting over and to go back to work as soon as possible will gradually subside, and instead, the patient would enthusiastically look forward to the next session because of the increasing feeling of relaxation.

Pratyahara

Pratyahara is an integral part of Asana and Pranayama, and consists of keeping one's thoughts as free from all distractions as is possible. Realizing that environmental stimuli are related to tension, anxiety, restlessness, and other symptoms, and also that this preoccupation with the external environment disturbs functioning, the person learns to consciously inhibit distraction. He subsequently finds that it also improves the performance of Asana and Pranayama.

Dharana, Dhyana, and Samadhi

The thought processes are controlled by Dharana, Dhyana, and Samadhi. Dharana consists of the selection of an appealing object for concentration. It may be a visual image of a religious symbol like a god, a goddess, a prophet, "Om," a cross, a crescent, the moon, or a nonreligious entity like a "flower" or a "star." He may also select words like "mantras."

Usually in the third week of treatment, the patient is asked to select the object on which he would like to concentrate, one that appeals to him most so that he feels happy while contemplating it and concentrating on it. Concentration is to be maintained on the same object during all the sittings for as long as possible until such a time that the patient is unable to continue or until the time for concentration is over. In the beginning, concentration on the selected object is disturbed by intruding thoughts, but concentration gradually improves with practice. The patient is instructed to write down all thoughts that disturb his concentration during each sitting. The therapist does this in case of illiterate patients.

The patient's notebook is studied later, and the nature of the distracting thoughts is noted. Initially most of the recorded material consists of description of symptoms. As time progresses, three types of distracting thoughts are described—worries about the future, problems of the present, and mistakes of the past. At times pleasant experiences are recorded as distractors, while at other times the nature of distractions are stray events in daily life which are neither pleasant nor unpleasant, for example, an incident in the street or a movie. During subsequent interview, the patient is shown the relationship between symptoms and disturbing thoughts. The patient is told that just as his concentration during the sitting is disturbed by these thoughts, his concentration at work is also likely to be distracted by similar external factors.

With practice, the person learns to be in complete unison with his object of concentration for a desired length of time, completely excluding external distractions. There are likely to be ups and downs in his efforts to improve his concentration, but he gradually acquires this ability. Next he must identify the selected object with the conceptualized observer within himself, which activated and integrated all his psychophysiological functions and social behavior. He is told how if his behavior is guided by the inner observing mechanism, undistracted by the external feedback, he can maintain harmonious personality functioning, because he is less vulnerable to the mechanism of external feedback.

Samadhi

Only a few patients who would follow previous steps satisfactorily were taught this step.

Yama and Niyama

Principles of Yama and Niyama are explained during the latter part of therapy to decrease distractions and improve concentration.

RESULTS

During the last 10 years, over 700 patients in psychiatric department of King Edward VII Memorial Hospital, Bombay, have been treated. The results have been published elsewhere. This work has been conducted in three phases.

Phase I

An attempt was made to study the extent to which the therapy was useful in psychoneurosis. The patients were assessed before and after the treatment, the criteria for improvement being relief of target symptoms and increased work efficiency as reported by patients, relatives, and colleagues. Out of the 102 patients treated for 6 weeks and longer, over 50% improvement was obtained in 70% of the patients with the diagnosis of anxiety state, hysteria, and reactive depression.

Phase II

A double blind controlled study compared psychophysiological therapy with placebo therapy. The variables of suggestion, time, and milieu were similar for index and control groups. Fifteen patients were treated with psychophysiological therapy and 12 with placebo therapy. Psychophysiological therapy was found to be significantly superior to placebo therapy.

The same physiotherapist carried out both treatments. Clinical evaluation was based on clinical (as in Phase I) and psychological testing (Taylor's Anxiety Scale, Hamilton Rating Scale for depression, and Bell's Social Adjustment Inventory) were done before, during, and at the end of the treatment.

Phase III

A double blind controlled study compared psychophysiological therapy to drug therapy, which included anxiolytics, antidepressants, and placebo. Patients were evaluated clinically using standardized rating scales (Taylor's Anxiety Scale, Hamilton's Depression Rating Scale, and Bell's Social Adjustment Inventory) before, after 3 weeks, and after 6 weeks of treatment. A follow-up was obtained for an average period of 6 months. Nineteen patients were treated with psychophysiological therapy, and 14 with drugs. Although there was a suggestion that the psychophysiologically treated patients did better than the drug treated ones, the difference was not statistically significant.

DISCUSSION

In spite of considerable advances in the understanding and treatment of psychiatric disorders during last few decades, no real progress has been made in the management of psychoneurotic and psychosomatic disorders. In the treatment of psychoneurosis, treatment is largely concerned with the usual drugs, various types of psychotherapies, and behavior therapy. Drug therapy is of relatively minor importance as it gives symptomatic relief and is not curative.[8] Moreover, there is always a danger that drug dependency will develop. Environmental modification is of value in a small percentage of patients. However, it does not increase an individual's ability to face the environmental stress. Psychotherapy is considered to be the most important treatment for psychoneurosis. However, on critically evaluating published literature on different types of psychotherapy, Eysenck[2] failed to detect the superiority of either psychoanalytical psychotherapy or supportive psychotherapy over the rate of spontaneous remissions. Strupp et al.[13]

failed to detect the superiority of one type of psychotherapy over another, when psychoanalytical, existential, and Rogerian client-centered therapies were compared. They were not able to find any specific factors related to the patient's improvement. The most nonspecific factors associated with improvement were the establishment of rapport, therapeutic suggestibility[1], and hope.[3] Although behavior therapies have been found to be useful in some cases, their exact rationale is not established,* and according to Glick, "they are still not what the world is waiting for."[5]

There are two possible reasons for this state of affairs. According to the existential school,[10] the weakness of most of the systems of psychotherapy being practiced today is their goal. Their idea of "cure" is for the patient to become satisfactorily adjusted to society. Sol Levine,[9] for instance, states that psychotherapy is an institution that resembles the other institutions involved in the socialization of the adult. May[10] feels that this type of thinking will make psychotherapists agents of their culture, and psychotherapy will become an expression of the fragmentation, alienation, and other neurotic trends in our time rather than an enterprise for overcoming them. In existential therapy (Daseinsanalyse), the aim is adjusting to the existence (instead of to the society), experiencing one's potential, and being able to act on the basis of this potential. In spite of this laudable goal, Daseinsanalyse has failed to have a wider application. He has been criticized for diffuseness in concepts and lack of regularity in process.[19]

The other major shortcoming in current psychotherapeutic techniques is that most of them concentrate on an isolated aspect of behavior rather than on the total individual as a psychobiosocial entity. In psychotherapies, it is hoped that altered thinking (i.e., with insight) will lead to altered behavior (i.e., nonneurotic). In behavior therapies, in contrast, altered behavior is expected to result in altered thinking.[16] Critics of behavior therapy state that a change in behavior without a gain in insight cannot cure neurosis. On the other hand, psychoanalysed patients with insight into their unconscious may fail to improve because of inability to translate insight into action. Jacobson[6] treats neurosis with voluntary muscle relaxation, but the results with this therapy are unsatisfactory.[8]

The psychophysiological therapy based on Patanjali's concepts differs from the existing therapies because of its aim and its holistic approach.

According to Patanjali, any treatment that is motivated by the need for environmental adjustment would still be unsatisfactory, because dependence on a changing environment for well being would make a person vulnerable to a state of tension, not only when the environment is frustrating but also when it is gratifying. He therefore suggests that if the goal

---

* See the leading article in *Brit. Med. J.*, 1972.

of functions, psychological, physiological, and social, is their harmonios utilization by the development of voluntary control over them and their suitable modification without constant preoccupation with the resultant feedback, then the personality would not be vulnerable to the impact of a constantly changing environment.

Any therapeutic process should look at a man in his environment as a psychobiosocial unity. The eight steps in the present therapy are meant to modify physiological, psychological, and social aspects of personality.

Physiological (voluntary and autonomic) functions are controlled through the steps of Asana, Pranayama, and Pratyahara. Dharana, Dhyana, and Samadhi serve to bring the psychological processes under control. During these latter steps, insight is developed about the likely cause of the illness (namely, preoccupation with environmental feedback). Finally, Yama and Niyama are guidelines for social behavior. The therapy concentrates not only on behavior modification but also on instilling insight and reconstructing the personality. Like existential therapy, it aims at experiencing and fulfilling one's potential, but unlike the former, its concepts and technique are well defined.

Alteration in the psychophysiological state with this therapy can partly be explained on the basis of Gaarder's[4] homeostatic adaptive control system. A major determinant of a psychophysiological state is the nature of information transmitted between subsystems. Control of this state is therefore achieved through control of such information—transmission. Meditation alters the psychophysiological state, mainly by controlling sensory feedback through relative sensory deprivation (by being in a quiet, calm environment) and focussing on a single potential input in a single way.[4] Pavlovian theory has also explained changes in brain functioning as a result of contemplation. By emptying the mind of all extraneous matter and concentrating on a single subject, there is peripheral inhibition and focal excitation of the brain. This leads to "paradoxical" and "ultraparadoxical" disturbances of function, finally resulting in the acquisition of faith.[12]

However, the psychophysiological therapy does not depend on such artificially induced alterations in a psychophysiological state. The total therapy concentrates on gaining insight and conscious control of behavior.

It must be mentioned that Patanjali did not present his concepts as a therapeutic method for the treatment of psychiatric disorders. He described measures for harmonious personality function. he advocated their use throughout the life time. These concepts have been modified into a technique for the treatment for psychoneurotic and psychosomatic disorders. The duration of the treatment was arbitrarily fixed at 6 weeks for practical reasons. As defined by Ticho,[15] treatment goals concern the removal of obstacles to the patient's growth and the discovery of what his potentialities are. However, to achieve life goals, (i.e., the goals the patient would arrive at if he could put his full potentialities to use), the patient is advised to continue the therapeutic practice at home beyond the period of 6 weeks.

The World Health Organization[7] has defined health as a state of complete physical, psychological, and social well-being and not merely absence of disease and infirmity. According to Patanjali, such health can be developed and maintained by the observation, control, and modification of psychological processes, physiological functions, and social relationships for their integrated and harmonios functioning in a constantly changing environment.

The results of Phase I study suggest that the 70% improvement in those who took the treatment for 6 weeks compares favorably with the response to other psychotherapies.[2]

However, this comparison is rather crude because of differences in the type of population and criteria for diagnosis and improvement.

The results of Phase II study indicate that the therapy is superior to what would be expected from nonspecific factors like hope, suggestibility, placebo response, milieu and natural remissions.

Finally the Phase III study shows that the therapy is at least as effective as drug therapy, and that the good results are maintained at the time of follow-up, 6 months later.

REFERENCES

1. Calestro, K. M.: Psychotherapy, faith healing and suggestion. *Int. J. Psychiatr.* 10:83–113, 1972.

2. Eysenck, H. J.: The effects of psychotherapy. *Int. J. Psychiatr.* 1:142, 1965.

3. Frank, J.: The role of hope in psychotherapy. *Int. J. Psychiatr.* 5:383–395, 1968.

4. Gaarder, K.: Control of states of consciousness: I. Attainment through control of psychophysiological variables. *Arch. Gen. Psychiatr.* 25:429–435, 1971.

5. Glick, B. S.: Conditioning: A partial success story, critical evaluation. *Int. J. Psychiatr.* 7:492–519, 1969.

6. Jacobson, E.: *Progressive Relaxation.* Chicago University Press, Chicago, 1938.

7. Jus, A.: Social systems and the criteria of health as defined by the World Health Organization. *Am. J. Psychiatr.* 130:125–131, 1973.

8. Lader, M.: The nature of anxiety. *Brit. J. Psychiatr.* 121:481–491, 1972.

9. Levine, S.: Psychotherapy as socialization. *Int. J. Psychiatr.* 8:645–665, 1969.

10. May, R.: The existential approach. In *American Handbook of Psychiatry.* Vol. II, S. Arieti, (Ed.), Basic Books, New York, 1967, pp. 1348–1361.

11. Patanjali's yogasutra. In *Raja Yoga*, Vivekananda Swami, (Ed.) Advaita Ashrama, 5 Dehi Entally Road, Calcutta—14, 1966, pp. 123-286.

12. Sargant, W.: The physiology of faith. *Brit. J. Psychiatr.* **115**:505-518, 1969.

13. Strupp, H. H., and Bergin, A. E.: Some empirical and conceptual bases for coordinating research in psychotherapy. *Int. J. Psychiatr.* **7**:18-90, 1969.

14. Strupp, H. H.: Specific Vs. nonspecific factors in psychotherapy and the problem of control. *Arch. Gen. Psychiatr.* **23**:393-401, 1970.

15. Ticho, E. A., Termination of psychoanalysis: Treatment goals, life goals. *Psychoanal. Quart.* **41**:315-333, 1972.

16. Urban, H. B., and Ford, D. H.: Behavior therapy. In *Comprehensive Text Book of Psychiatry*, Alfred M. Freedman and Harold I. Kaplan, (Ed.), The Williams and Wilkins Company, Baltimore, 1967, pp. 1218-1219.

17. Vahia, N. S., Doongaji, D. R., Jeste, D. V., Kapoor, S. N., Ardhapurkar, I., and Ravindra, N. S.: Further experience with the therapy based upon concepts of Patanjali in the treatment of psychiatric disorders. *Ind. J. Psychiatr.* **15**:32-37, 1973.

18. Vahia, N. S., Doongaji, D. R., Jeste, D. V., Kapoor, S. N., Ardhapurkar, I., and Ravindra, N. S.: Psychophysiological therapy based on the concepts of Patanjali—A new approach to the treatment of neurotic and psychosomatic disorders. *Am. J. Psychother.*, **27**:557-565, 1973.

19. Wolberg, L. R.: *The Technique of Psychotherapy*, Vol. I, 2nd ed., Grune and Stratton, New York, 1967, p. 721.

CHAPTER FOURTEEN

PARADOXICAL INTENTION AND DEREFLECTION: TWO LOGOTHERAPEUTIC TECHNIQUES

VIKTOR E. FRANKL, M.D., Ph.D.

Logotherapy[9, 15, 17, 19, 20,-23, 35, 62] is usually subsumed either under the category of humanistic psychology,[5, 25a] or regarded as belonging to the movements called phenomenological psychiatry[55] and existential psychiatry.[1, 48-50] It is the contention of several authors, however, that among the existential-psychiatric schools, logotherapy is the only one that has succeeded in developing a psychotherapeutic technique in the proper sense of the word.[35, 39, 40, 56-58] Obviously, they thereby refer to that logotherapeutic technique which is called paradoxical intention.[18]

Paradoxical intention has first been described by this author as early as in 1939[10] and later on elaborated by evolving its methodology[12] and tying it in with the logotherapeutic system.[14, 16] In the meantime, it has shown to be an effective therapy in cases of obsessive-compulsive and phobic conditions[26, 34, 36, 37b, 38, 44, 46, 54a, 60, 63] in which it sometimes even lends itself to short-term treatment.[27]

To understand how it works one best takes as a starting point the phenomenon called anticipatory anxiety: A symptom evokes, on the part of the patient, a response in terms of the fearful expectation that it might recur. Fear, however, always tends to make come true precisely that which one is afraid of; thus anticipatory anxiety is likely to trigger off what the patient so fearfully expects to happen. A self-sustaining vicious circle is thereby established: a symptom evokes a phobia; the phobia provokes the symptom; and the recurrence of the symptom reinforces the phobia.

One of the targets of fear is fear itself. Our patients often refer to it as "anxiety about anxiety." Upon closer investigation, however, it turns out that this "fear of fear" is often caused by the patient's apprehensions about the potential effects of his anxiety attacks. More specifically, the patient is afraid that such an attack may eventuate in collapsing or fainting, in a coronary, or in a stroke.

These are the usual reasons for "fear of fear." What then is the typical reaction to it? Most of our patients react to their "fear of fear" by "flight from fear": the patient begins to avoid situations that arouse his anxiety. However, "fear of fear" still increases fear, and "flight from fear" thus proves to be the starting point of anxiety neurosis.[14]

This reaction and behavior represents the first of three pathogenic patterns as they are distinguished in logotherapy,[16] namely, the phobic pattern. The second is the obsessive-compulsive pattern. Whereas in phobic cases the patient displays "fear of fear," the obsessive-compulsive neurotic exhibits "fear of himself." He is caught by the idea that he might commit suicide, or even homicide, or that the strange thoughts that haunt him might be signs of imminent, if not present, psychosis.

While "flight from fear" is a characteristic of the phobic pattern, the obsessive-compulsive patient is characterized by his "fight against obsessions and compulsions." However, the more he fights them, the stronger they become. Pressure induces counterpressure, and counterpressure, in turn, increases pressure. Again, we are confronted with a vicious circle.

How then is it possible to break up such feedback mechanisms? This is precisely the job to accomplish by paradoxical intention: *the patient is encouraged to do, or wish to happen, the very things he fears.* Thereby, the pathogenic fear is replaced by a paradoxical wish. At the same time, the phobic patient stops fleeing from his fears, and the obsessive-compulsive patient stops fighting his obsessions and compulsions.

The following quotation from a letter may serve as an illustrative example.*

I am 40 years old, and I have been suffering from a neurosis for at least 10 years. I sought psychiatric help, but did not find the relief that I had looked for (I had about 18 months of therapy). After one of your lectures in 1968 I heard one of the men asking you how to treat his fear of flying. I listened all the more carefully since this was also my phobia. With what I assume to have been your "paradoxical intention" technique, you told him to let the plane explode and crash and see himself crushed to bits in it! Scarcely a month later I was to fly about 2500 miles, and as usual I was scared. My hands were sweaty and my heart was palpitating, and your prescription to the other man came to mind. So I imagined that the plane exploded; I was tumbling through the clouds, headed for the ground. Before I could finish the fantasy, I realized that I was suddenly thinking very calmly about some of the business I had transacted. I tried several more times until I managed to splatter myself in a bloody heap on the ground. When the plane landed, I was calm and even enjoying an eagle's view of the land. Being a Freudian in training and therapy, I have found myself wondering about the deeper levels of one's pathology that paradoxical intention does not touch. Yet I am now wondering if there are not therapeutic resources that are even deeper than the pathological ones, resources that are basically human and that can be released by paradoxical intention.

Another case, which was of compulsive rather than phobic nature, was reported by Darrell Burnett[7], a counselor.

A man came to the community mental health center complaining of a compulsion he had for checking the front door at night before he went to bed. He had reached the point where he was checking and rechecking the door 10 times within a 2 minute span. He said he had tried in vain to talk himself out of locking and rechecking the door, but to no avail. I asked him to see how many times he could check the door within the two minute span, to try and set a new record! At first he thought it was silly, but after 3 days the compulsion had disappeared.

* As to other illustrative cases, the reader is referred to the literature in the field[15, 19, 21, 23]; in this paper, only unpublished material is quoted.

The following report was included in a paper read by Godfrey J. F. Briggs[4] at a meeting of the Royal Society of Medicine.

I was asked to see a young man from Liverpool, a stutterer. He wanted to take up teaching, but stuttering and teaching do not go together. His greatest fear and worry was his embarassment by the stuttering so that he went through mental agonies every time he had to say anything. He used to have a kind of mental rehearsal of everything he was going to say, and then try to say it. Then he would become frightfully embarassed about it. It seemed logical that if this young man could be enabled to do something which previously he had been afraid to do it might work. I then gave him the following suggestions. "You are going out into the world this weekend and you are going to show people what a jolly good stutterer you are. And you are going to fail in this just as you have failed in the previous years to speak properly." He came up the following week and was obviously elated because his speech was so much better. He said, "What do you think happened! I went into a pub with some friends and one of them said to me 'I thought you used to be a stutterer' and I said 'I did—so what'!" It was an instance where I took the bull by the horns and it was successful. I do not claim any credit for this case, if it should go to anyone but the patient it should go to Viktor Frankl.

In this case, paradoxical intention was deliberately combined with suggestion; suggestion cannot be completely eliminated in therapy, anyway. And yet it would be a mistake to dismiss the therapeutic successes obtained by paradoxical intention merely in terms of suggestive effects. The following report, concerning another case of stuttering, might cast some light on this issue. It was written by a student at Duquesne University.

For seventeen years, I stuttered very severely; at times I could not speak at all. I saw many speech therapists, but had no success. One of my instructors assigned your book, *Man's Search for Meaning*, to be read for a course. So, I read the book and I decided to try paradoxical intention by myself. The very first time I tried it, it worked fabulously—no stuttering. I then sought out other situations in which I would normally stutter, and I applied paradoxical intention and it successfully alleviated stuttering in those situations. There were a couple situations thereafter when I did not use paradoxical intention—and the stuttering quickly returned. This is a definite proof that the alleviation of my stuttering problem was due to the effective use of paradoxical intention.

Its use may be even effective in cases where negative suggestion was involved, that is to say, when the patient did in no way "believe" in the effectiveness of the treatment. Let us take up, as an example, the following report delivered by Abraham George Pynummootil,[51] a social worker.

A young man came to my office with a severe case of eye winking problem. He was winking his eyes in a rapid fashion whenever he had to talk to someone. People began to ask him why he was doing so and he began to worry about it. I advised him to consult a psychoanalyst. After many hours of consultation he came back saying that psychoanalyst could not find the reason for his problem and that he could not help to solve the problem. I told him, the next time when you talk to someone wink your eyes as rapidly as possibly and as fast as you can deliberately to show that person just how much more you can really wink your eyes. He said that I must be crazy to suggest this to him for he thought that he will get more into the habit of winking his eyes rather than get out of it. So he stomped out of my room. I did not hear from or see him for a few weeks. Then one day, he came again. This time he was full of joy and told me what happened. As he did not agree with my suggestion, he did not think about it for a few days. During this time his problem became worse and he was almost going out of his mind. One night as he was going to bed, he thought about my suggestion and said to himself, "I have tried everything I know to get out of this problem but failed. Why don't I try the one thing the social worker suggested"? So the next day, it just happened that the first person he met was a close friend. He told him that he was going to wink his eyes as much as he could when he talked to him. But to his surprise, he could not wink his eyes at all when talking to him. From then on he became normal in his eye winking habit. After a few weeks he did not even think about at all.

The cases reported above are intended to elucidate the principle of paradoxical intention rather than to elicit the impression that this technique is effective in each and every case, and even more, that its effects are easy to obtain. Paradoxical intention, or for that matter, logotherapy is no panacea. There are no panaceas in the field of psychotherapy. And yet, paradoxical intention may be effective, at least to some extent, even in severe and chronic cases. Pertinent reports have been published by Kocourek, Niebauer, and Polak,[36] H. O. Gerz,[27] and Victor and Krug.[60] One of Niebauer's cases was a 65-year-old woman who had suffered from a hand-washing compulsion for 60 years; Gerz treated a woman who had a 24-year history of phobic neurosis; and the case treated by Victor and Krug was one of compulsive gambling that had lasted for 20 years. Even in these chronic cases, success could be obtained. The following report, will show that in severe cases, success is available only at the expense of total personal involvement. This report was published by Friedrich M. Benedikt[3] and constituted part of his dissertation at the University of Munich Medical School.*

The case concerns a 41-year-old lawyer, who retired early because of his obsessive-compulsive neurosis. His father had a bacteriophobia which may indicate a hereditary facet of his illness.† As a child, the patient used to open doors with his elbows from fear of possible contamination (European doors have handles that have

* For the translation of the following report from the German into English, I am indebted to Dr. Joseph B. Fabry, Instructor of Logotherapy, University of California at Berkeley Extension.

† I subscribe to the conviction of Peter Hays[32] "that genetic predisposition is almost a sine qua non," at least as far as severe cases are concerned.

to be pushed down, not twisted as American doors.) He was overly concerned with cleanliness and avoided contact with other children because they might have been diseased carriers. During his elementary and high school years he remained isolated. He was shy and his schoolmates teased him because he was so withdrawn. The patient recalls one of the first symptoms of his illness: In 1938, walking home one night he found a postcard he felt compelled to read six times. "If I hadn't read it, I would have found no peace." Evenings he felt compelled to read books until "everything was in order." He avoided bananas which, coming from primitive countries, he associated with harboring bacteria, especially those of leprosy. In 1939 he began to suffer from a "Good Friday craze," a fear he might have unknowingly eaten meat or violated some other religious rule. In high school, while discussing Kant's "Critique of Pure Reason," he was exposed to the thought that the objects of this world may not be real. "This sentence was the truly decisive blow for me, all else had been only a prelude," he complained. It became the central theme of his illness. The patient began worrying about doing everything "one hundred percent" correctly.* He constantly kept searching his conscience, according to a strict ritual. "I established a formalism," he stated, "which I still have to observe." He felt compelled to make a wide detour around every cross, for fear to touch something that is holy. He began to repeat certain phrases such as "I have done nothing wrong" to escape punishment. During the war his symptoms somewhat receded. His comrades teased him about not going with them to brothels. He had remained sexually naive and did not know that intercourse required an erection. One girl told him that there was something wrong with him because he lacked masculine aggression. Some psychoanalytical treatment and hypnosis proved successful inasmuch as he achieved an erection. These treatments, however, did not make his obsessive-compulsive symptoms disappear. In 1949 he married. Initial trouble with potency disappeared after renewed treatment. By that time he had concluded his studies and graduated from the university. He worked for the police force and later in the Ministry of Finance, but lost his job because he was slow and inefficient. Renewed consultation with the doctor brought no improvement. He found a job with the railroad. During this period he did not allow his daughter to come near him because he was afraid he might abuse her sexually. His obsessive-compulsive symptoms increased since 1953. In 1956 he read about a schizophrenic nurse who had gouged out her own eyeballs. He began to fear that he might do the same to himself or to small children. *The more I fought the thought the worse it became,*" he stated. Numbers took on significance. At night he felt obligated to put three oranges on the table, or he couldn't find any rest. Again he changed jobs. In 1960 he received treatment from a psychologist but treatments were unsuccessful. In 1961 treatment by a homeopath, and acupuncture, both failed. In 1962 he became a patient in a mental hospital where he received 45 insulin shocks after he was diagnosed a schizophrenic. The night before dismissal he suffered a breakdown, and he was overwhelmed by the thought that everything was unreal. "From that day on," the patient stated, "this central theme of my illness has been threatening me and I have been in deep

---

* For "hundred-percentness" as a constitutive feature of the obsessive-compulsive character structure, see Frankl.[15]

trouble." Treatments abroad followed. Within one year he changed jobs 20 times including such jobs as tourist guide, ticket agent, and printer's helper. In 1963 he received a work therapy which he considered at least partly successful. However, from 1964 on, his obsessive-compulsive symptoms become stronger and he is unable to work. His most frequent thought during this period is, "I might have gouged out somebody's eyes. I have to turn around every time I pass someone on the street to make sure I didn't do it." His illness became unbearable for his family. He was admitted to the Poliklinik with a diagnosis of "severe obsessive-compulsive neurosis." The examination revealed no organic disturbances. Drug treatments were given to the patient to calm him. Day 1 of the psychotherapeutic treatment: The patient is restless, tense, keeps looking at the door to see if he has not gouged out anybody's eyes. He makes a wide detour around each child in the corridor who is passing by from the nearby nose-ear-and-throat clinic. He constantly goes through certain "ceremonial" motions to make sure he has not hurt anyone. He keeps looking at his hands, fearful that he might have gouged out eyes so that vitreous humor was drained. Day 2 initiates a long and rather general discussion which is continued during the entire period of treament. Dr. Kocourek concentrates his efforts on the patient's guilt feelings, his relationship to his mother, wife, and children, his continuous changing of jobs, his obsession that everything is unreal, and such. When the patient expressed his fear that he would end up in an institution or that he would be driven to attack children and then be locked up as "insane." Dr. Kocourek explained to him the difference between a compulsive action and an obsessive thought. He then pointed out to the patient that exactly because of his illness he was unable to hurt anyone. His illness, being an obsessive-compulsive neurosis, was a guarantee that he would not commit criminal acts: his very fear that he might gouge out other people's eyes was the reason that he would be unable to carry out his obsessive thought. On day 4 the patient seems more quiet and relaxed. Day 5: The patient is not certain, he says, that he understood everything correctly. Again and again he demands assurances that the explanations of Dr. Kocourek are valid "everywhere in the whole world and at all times." Days 6 to 10: The conversations with the patient are continued. He asks many questions which are answered in detail. He appears to be less anxious than on previous days. Day 11: The essence of paradoxical intention is explained to the patient: he is not to repress his thoughts but rather to let them well up in him; they would not result in the actions he feared. He is to try to meet his thoughts with irony, or to meet them "with humor"—then he would no longer fear his obsessive thoughts, and if he would not fight them, they would fade away. Whatever he feared he should plan to actually do—as obsessive-compulsive neurotic he could afford to do that. Dr. Kocourek himself would take the responsibility for whatever the patient would do. Day 15: The active exercises begin. Accompanied by Dr. Kocourek, Herr H. walks through the hospital, practicing paradoxical intention. First he is instructed to voice certain phrases, such as "All right, let's go and gouge out eyes! First we'll gouge out the eyes of all patients here in the room, then we'll get the doctors, and in the end the nurses, too. And to gouge out an eye only once is not enough, I'll do it five times to every eye. When I get through with these people here, there will be nobody left here but blind folks. Vitrious humor will be all over the place. What do we have clean-up women here for? They'll have something to clean up, all right." Or another set of phrases: "Ah, there is a nurse, she's a likely victim for gouging out her eyes. And on the ground floor there are lots of visitors, there is much for me to do. What an opportunity to gouge out eyes *en masse*! And some of them are important people, it pays to go to work on them. . . . When I get through with them, nothing is going to be left here but blind people and vitrious humor. . . ." These phrases are practised in variations and applied to every one of his compulsive thoughts. In these exercises it was necessary for Dr. Kocourek to get personally involved with the patient because in the beginning the patient showed great resistance to actually practicing paradoxical intention. He was afraid he still might fall victim to an obsessive thought, and besides he did not really believe in the success of the method. Only after Dr. Kocourek had showed him what to do, the patient agreed to cooperate. He repeated the suggested phrases and practiced "a funny way of walking" through the hospital which, as he later admitted, he actually enjoyed. After these preliminary exercises he is sent to his room and asked to keep on practicing paradoxical intention. In the afternoon of that day the first shy smile crossed his lips, and he remarked: "For the first time I see that my thoughts are really 'silly'!" On day 20 the patient states that he is now able to apply the method without trouble. He is instructed to practice paradoxical intention from now on not only when meeting someone whose eyes he thinks he has gouged out but to forestall his obsessive thought by thinking about it ahead of time. During the following days he practices paradoxical intention, alone and also with the help of Dr. Kocourek. The area in which he practices is extended to the children of the nose-ear-and-throat clinic. The patient is encouraged to go to that clinic, with some excuse, and to intend paradoxically: "All right, now I'll go and make a few children blind, it's high time that I fill my daily quota. Vitrious humor will stick to my hands, but I don't give a damn, especially about my obsessive thoughts." Or: "I've got to have a lot of obsessive thoughts. They'll give me a chance to practise paradoxical intention so I am well prepared when I can go home again." Day 25: The patient informs Dr. Kocourek that he has hardly any obsessive thoughts within the hospital, neither in the presence of adults nor of children. Occasionally he even forgets about paradoxical intention. When he does have an obsessive thought, it doesn't seem to scare him any more. His obsessive thought that everything is not real is also being attacked with paradoxical intention. He practices such phrases as "Okay, so I live in an unreal world. The table here is not real, the doctors are not really here either, but even so this 'unreal world' is not a bad place to live in. By the way: My thinking about all this proves that I really am here. If I were not real I could not think about it." On the 28th day the patient is allowed for the first time to leave the hospital. He is frightened and does not think he can use the phrases outside. He is advised to formulate his thinking in this manner: "So I'll go out now and cause disaster in the streets. For a change I'll do my gouging out of eyes outside the hospital. I'll get every one of these people, not one will escape me." He leaves the hospital with great misgivings. Upon return he reports happily that he was successful. Despite his apprehensions he was able to use the phrase as learned. Unlike his experiences within the hospital he did have obsessive thoughts on the street but they didn't scare him. During a walk of one hour he had to turn around only twice. In these cases he had thought of using paradoxical intention too late. During the next days he continues paradoxical intention outside the hospital. "I hardly have obsessive thoughts, but if I do they don't bother me," he reports on day 32. On day 35 the patient is sent home and continues his treatment through visits to the hospital. He participates in group therapy. His condition at the time of his dismissal from the hospital: Inside the hospital he has no more obsessive thoughts; he still has some during his walks on the street but he has learned to formulate his own phrases to deal with them. They are no longer an impediment in his daily routine. The patient immediately finds work which he accepts. During the first 2 weeks Herr H. visits Dr. Kocourek every day to report on his work and to receive advice as to how to handle himself. After that his visits are reduced to three times a week, and after 4 months once a week. He visits his group therapy only irregularly. The patient is well adjusted to his job. (His boss is satisfied with his performance.) He was able to practice paradoxical intention every day. During working hours he hardly noticed any obsessive thoughts; they only turned up when he was overly tired. During the fifth month of his treatment, shortly before Easter, he developed anxiety about Good Friday. He was afraid he might eat meat on that day without knowing it. He discussed the impending situation with Dr. Kocourek, and they agreed on the following phrasing: "I am going to gulp down a lot of soup, with meat in it. I can't see it but, being an obsessive neurotic, I am sure it's there. For me, eating such a soup is no sin but therapy to get cured." The next week he reports that he had no trouble during the Easter week. He didn't even need the paradoxical intention. In the sixth month of the treatment he suffered a relapse. Obsessive thoughts returned, and paradoxical intention is practiced again. Two weeks later the patient has regained his self-control and is free of obsessive thoughts. He does have occasional relapses which, however, can be straightened out in a few therapy sessions. The patient is advised to immediately see Dr. Kocourek when he fears a turn for the worse. During the seventh month the patient claims his obsessive thoughts have vanished in thin air, and only show up when he is under pressure or physically exhausted. For one weekend he gets a job as tourist guide—an assignment he loves. After the trip—the first outside of Vienna in years—he reports that it had been a great success. "I can now master every siutation," he declares, "my thoughts no longer bother me." At the end of the seventh month he goes on a vacation with his family, which he can spend without any trouble. After that he doesn't show up at Dr. Kocourek for 3 months. As he explained later, he felt well and did not need any doctor. He felt no need to use paradoxical intention during that time. For 3 months he had been free of obsessive thoughts. "That had never happened before," he declared. Although obsessive thoughts sometimes recur, he no longer feels compelled to actions. He also learned to react to occurring obsessive thoughts with equanimity. They no longer interfere with his daily life. The success of the treatment can be seen from the fact that Herr H. was able to work the entire 14 months since his release from the hospital and did not change jobs.

There are a few instances in which paradoxical intention has been tried even with psychotic manifestations such as auditory hallucinations. The following is a quotation from a paper by Mohammed Sadiq.[53]

Frederick was a 24-year-old patient suffering from schizophrenia. The predominant symptomatology was auditory hallucinations. He heard voices making fun of him and ridiculing him, and he felt threatened by them. He was in the hospital for 10 days when I talked to him. Fred came out of his room around two o'clock in the morning and complained that he was not able to sleep because the voices wouldn't let him.

Patient: I cannot sleep. Could you please give me some sleeping pills?
Therapist: Why can't you sleep? Is something bothering you?
P.:   Yes, I hear these voices making fun of me and I just can't get rid of them.
T.:   Well, did you talk about these to your doctor?
P.:   He asked me not to pay any attention to them. But I just can't do it.
T.:   Did you try not paying attention to them?
P.:   I have been trying all these days, but it just doesn't seem to work.
T.:   How would you like to do something different?
P.:   What do you mean?
T.:   Go, lie down on your bed and pay all the attention you can to these voices. Don't let them stop. Try to hear more and more.
P.:   You are kidding.
T.:   I am not. Why not try to enjoy these God damn things.
P.:   But my doctor. . . .
T.:   Why don't you give it a try?

So he decided to give it a try, I checked him after about 45 minutes, and he was sound asleep. In the morning, I asked him how did he sleep last night. "Oh, I slept alright," was the answer. I asked him if he did hear voices for long, and he said, "I don't know, I think I fell asleep soon."

This case is somewhat reminiscent of what Jack Huber,[33] having visited a Zen psychiatric hospital, described in terms of an "emphasis on living with the suffering rather than complaining about it, analyzing, or trying to avoid it." In this context, he mentions the case of a Buddhist nun who had become acutely disturbed:

The major symptom was her terror at the snakes she saw crawling over her body. Physicians and then psychologists and psychiatrists were brought to see her but they could do nothing for her. Finally a Zen psychiatrist was brought in. He was in her room for only 5 minutes. "What is the trouble?" he asked. "The snakes crawl over my body and frighten me." The Zen psychiatrist thought a bit and then said, "I must leave now, but I shall come back to see you in a week. While I am gone, I want you to observe the snakes very carefully so that when I return you will be able to describe their movements accurately to me." In 7 days he returned and found the nun doing her duties she had been assigned before her illness. He greeted her and then asked, "Did you follow my instructions?" "Indeed," she answered, "I centered all my attention on the snakes. But alas, I saw them no more, for when I observed them carefully they were gone."

If the principle of paradoxical intention is of any worth, it would be improbable if it had not been discovered long ago, and again and again. Logotherapy had to make it into a scientifically acceptable methodology.

Incidentally, also other forms of "ethnopsychiatry seem to apply principles that later on have been systematized by logotherapy," as was stated by J. M. Ochs.[47] This holds not only for another Eastern method such as Morita therapy as was evidenced by I. Yamamoto.[64] But also "the principle underlying the therapy of the Ifaluk is logotherapeutic," and the Shaman of Mexican-American folk psychiatry, "the curandero, is a logotherapist. Wallace and Vogelson point out the fact that ethnopsychiatric systems often use psychotherapeutic principles which only recently have been recognized by Western psychiatric systems. It appears that logotherapy is one nexus between the two systems."[47]

For long it has been observed that the paradoxical intention technique lends itself, last but not least, to the treatment of sleeplessness. As an example I would like again to quote from the paper by Sadiq[53], a case of a 54-year-old lady who had become so addicted to sleeping pills that he decided to use paradoxical intention with her.

She came out of her room about 10 p.m. and asked for sleeping medicine.

Patient: Can I have my sleeping pill?
Therapist: I am sorry I can't give you the pill tonight as we ran out of it and forgot to get a fresh supply in the evening.
P.:   Oh, how would I go to sleep now?
T.:   Well, I guess you have to try it without the pill tonight. (She went into her room, kept lying on her bed for about 2 hours and came out again.)
P.:   I just can't sleep.
T.:   Well, then why don't you go to your room, lie down, and try not to sleep. Let's see if you cannot stay awake all night.
P.:   I thought I am crazy, but it looks like you are too.
T.:   It is fun to be crazy for a while. Isn't it?
P.:   You really meant that?
T.:   What?
P.:   Trying not to go to sleep.
T.:   Of course, I meant that. Go try it. Let us see if you can keep awake all night? And I will help by calling you everytime I make a round. How about that?
P.:   O.k.

In the morning, when I went to wake her up for the breakfast, she was still asleep.*

The credit for having used paradoxical intention to influence not only the

* What comes to mind is the following episode reported by Jay Haley[29]: "During a lecture on hypnosis a young man said to Milton H. Erickson, 'You may be able to hypnotize other people, but you can't hypnotize me!' Dr. Erickson invited the subject to the demonstration platform, asked him to sit down, and then said to him, 'I want you to stay awake, wider and wider awake, wider and wider awake.' The subject promptly went into a deep trance."

patient's sleep but also his dreams goes to R. W. Medlicott[44] who applied the technique of paradoxical intention especially in phobic states and found it extremely helpful even to an analytically oriented psychiatrist. What is most remarkable, however, is "the attempted application of the principle to nightmares along the lines apparently used by the African tribe and reported some years back in *Transcultural Psychiatry.* The patient had made excellent progress in hospital where she was sent because of a severe neurotic depressive state. Encouraging her to practice paradoxical intention had resulted in her being able to go back home, take over responsibilities, and meet her conscious anxieties quite effectively. However, some time later she returned complaining that her sleep was disturbed by dreams in which she was pursued by persons who were going to shoot her or knife her. Her husband's sleep was disturbed by her screaming and he would wake her. She was firmly instructed to try and dream further such dreams, but stand and be shot or knived, and her husband was instructed that under no circumstances was he to wake her if she screamed. The next time I saw her she told me there had been no more nightmares, although her husband complained that he was wakened by her *laughing* in her sleep."[54]

The reader may have noticed that it is essential in practicing paradoxical intention to do what Sadiq did, namely, to utilize and mobilize in the patient the exclusively human quality called humor.* This becomes even more obvious in a third case in which he used the paradoxical intention technique.

Mrs. N., a 48-year-old lady, diagnosed as hysteric, had body shaking and trembling. She would have this trembling fits to the extent that she was not able to hold a cup of coffee or water without spilling it over and over. She could not write or hold a book firm enough to read. One morning, she came out of her room and was sitting in front of me on the other side of the table when she started trembling and shaking. There were no other patients around, so I decided to use paradoxical intention in a really humorous way.

---

* Arnold A. Lazarus[37b] thinks that "an integral element in Frankl's paradoxical intention procedure is the deliberate evocation of humor. A patient who fears that he may perspire is enjoined to show his audience what perspiration is really like, to perspire in gushes of drenching torrents of sweat which will moisturize everything within touching distance." He also points out "that when people encourage their anticipatory anxieties to erupt, they nearly always find the opposite reaction coming to the fore—their worst fears subside and when the method is used several times, their dreads eventually disappear." Most remarkably, however, I. Hand, Y. Lamontagne and I. M. Marks[28a] report on "patients with chronic agoraphobia" who "were treated effectively by group exposure *in vivo* . . . An impressive coping device used by the groups . . . was humour (*vide* the paradoxical intention of Frankl, 1960). This was used spontaneously and often helped to overcome difficult situations. When the whole group was frightened, somebody would break the ice with a joke, which would be greeted with the laughter of relief."

Therapist: How would you like to compete with me in shaking, Mrs. N.?
Patient: [She was shocked for a while.] What?
T.:   Let us see who can shake and tremble faster and for how long?
P.:   Are you suffering from these shakes too?
T.:   No, I am not suffering from them, but I can tremble if I want to. [I began to shake.]
P.:   Gee. You are doing it faster. [Trying to speed up and smiling.]
T.:   Faster. Come on, Mrs. N., faster.
P.:   I can't. [She was tired after a while.] Quit it. I can't do it any more. [She got up, went in the day room, and brought herself a cup of coffee. She drank the whole cup without spilling it once.]
T.:   That was fun, wasn't it?

Afterwards, whenever I would see her shaking, I would say, come on, Mrs. N., let's have a race; and she would say 'O.k. It sure works.'"

In concluding his paper, Sadiq remarks: "It should be noted that in all the above cases, there was no inquiry made about the psychodynamic factors. The patient, in no case, was asked to talk about her childhood, the relationship with father and mother and so on. Further, it should be kept in mind that these were not formal therapy sessions, but were dealt with informally as the situations arose."

As logotherapy teaches, humor is a manifestation of "the human capacity of self-detachment,"[18] which—along with "the human capacity of self-transcendence"[24]—is an intrinsically and definitely human phenomenon and as such eludes any attempt along the lines of reductionism to trace it back to subhuman phenomena. By virtue of his capacity of self-detachment, man is capable of joking about himself, laughing at himself, and ridiculing his own fears. And by virtue of his capacity of self-transcendence, he is capable of forgetting himself, giving himself, and reaching out for a meaning to his existence. To be sure, he then is also liable of being frustrated in his search for meaning.[25] Anyway, these "capabilities" and "liabilities" are only understandable on the human level. Psychiatric approaches that stick either to "the machine model" or to "the rat model," as Gordon Allport[2] called them, give away therapeutic assets. After all, no computer is capable of laughing at itself. Nor is a rat capable of asking itself whether its own existence has a meaning.

This criticism is not in the least to detract from the importance of learning theoretical concepts and behavior therapeutic approaches. As early as in 1947, this author[12] attempted to interpret neurosis in reflexological terms. In this context, he pointed out that "all psychoanalytically oriented psychotherapies are mainly concerned with uncovering the primary conditions of the 'conditioned reflex' as which neurosis may well be understood, namely, the situation—outer and inner—in which a given neurotic symptom had emerged the first time. It is this author's contention, however, that the full-fledged neurosis is not only caused by the primary conditions but also by secondary conditioning. This reinforcement, in turn, is caused by the feedback mechanism called anticipatory anxiety.* Therefore, if we wish to recondition a conditional reflex, we must unhinge the vicious cycle formed by anticipatory anxiety, and this is the very job done by our paradoxical intention technique."

As compared with behavior therapy, logotherapy just adds another dimension—the distinctively human dimension—and thus is in a position to muster resources that are only available in this human dimension. Seen in this light, the Norwegian psychologist Bjarne Kvilhaug[37] was justified in contending that logotherapy might accomplish what he called the "humanization" of behavior therapy. For the time being, much of the logotherapeutic practice and theory has been empirically corroborated and validated by behavioristically oriented research.

In the meantime, paradoxical intention has been confirmed even on experimental grounds. L. Solyom, J. Garza-Perez, B. L. Ledwidge, and C. Solyom[54a] who are affiliated with the Allan Memorial Institute, McGill University, Montreal, Canada, successfully treated chronically ill patients who had suffered from obsessive neurosis for 4 to 25 years. One had had a 4½-year lasting psychoanalysis, four had had electroshock treatment at one time or another during their sickness. The authors now chose two symptoms that were approximately equal in importance to the patient and in frequency of occurrence and applied paradoxical intention to one of the obsessive thoughts; the "control thought" was left untreated. Well, it turned out that, although the treatment period was short (6 weeks), there was an improvement rate of 50% in the target thoughts. "Some subjects later reported that after the experimental period they had successfully applied paradoxical intention to the other obsessive thoughts." On the other hand, "there was no symptom substitution; no new obsessive thought replaced the successfully eliminated obsession." The authors conclude that "paradoxical intention alone or in combination with other treatments, may be a relatively fast method for some obsessive patients."

At the outset of this paper, for example, it was noted that, according to logotherapy, "fear of fear" is due to the patient's apprehensions about the potential effects his fear might have. In the meantime, this logotherapeutic hypothesis has been confirmed by an experiment conducted by Valins and Ray[59]: "Students with snake phobias were given false auditory feedback of their heart sounds while watching slides of snakes. They were led to believe

_____

* Cf. Leonard I. Lapinsohn[37a].

that their heart rate did not increase on seeing the snakes. This procedure led to significantly decreased avoidance of snakes."

At the beginning, it was also stated that, according to logotherapeutic teachings, "fear of fear" induces "flight from fear," and that a phobia really starts when this "pathogenic pattern" of avoidance has been established. Paradoxical intention then obviates such avoidance by generating a total inversion of the patient's intention to "flee from fear."* This is in perfect accordance with what much later was evidenced by Isaac M. Marks,[42] namely, that "the phobia is maintained by the anxiety reducing mechanism of avoidance, and the phobia can then be properly overcome only when the patient faces the phobic situation again." Later on, this principle was also implemented by behavioristically oriented techniques such as "flooding" and "implosive therapy." As Rachman, Hodgson, and Marks[52] explain it, during flooding treatment the patient is "encouraged and persuaded to enter the most disturbing situation." In the setting of another behavioristically oriented treatment called "prolonged exposure" and discussed in a paper by Watson, Gaind, and Marks,[61] the patient is "encouraged to approach the feared object as closely and as quickly as he can, and avoidance is discouraged." This is said to "produce better results in less time than desensitization." Isaak M. Marks himself[41] recognizes expressly that the "flooding" technique "has certain similarities to the paradoxical intention technique." Apparently in view of such "similarities," Dilling, Rosefeldt, Kockott, and Heyse[8] of the Max Planck Institute of Psychiatry think that "the good, and sometimes very fast, results obtained by paradoxical intention, can be explained along the lines of learning theory."

Incidentally, there are a few instances in which both logotherapy and behavior therapy have been tried. One pertinent report reads as follows.

Vicki, a junior in high school, came into my counseling office. She cried and said she was flunking speech but was a straight A student in all of her other courses. I asked her why or if she had an idea why she was flunking. She said that each time she stood up to make a speech she became more and more afraid. How she couldn't give any speeches, nor stand up in class. She had many signs of anticipatory anxiety. I then suggested role-playing, she the speaker and I would be the audience. I used behavior modification techniques, using positive reinforcement each time we role-played on 3 days. She set the goal that after her first successful speech in class she would receive an off-campus pass, something she wanted very much. The next day she could not make her speech in class and came into my office sobbing. Since behavior modificative approaches had failed I tried paradoxical intention. I firmly

* Or, as Briggs said, the patient is invited to "take the bull by the horns."

told Vicki that the next day she would show the whole class how fearful she is; she should cry, sob, shake, and perspire as much as possible and I demonstrated. During speech she attempted to demonstrate how fearful she was but could not. Instead she gave a speech that her teacher graded A.

Also Barbara W. Martin,[43] a high school counselor, has "first used the behavior modification techniques, and later found logotherapeutic techniques much more successful and helpful in working with high school students." Milton E. Burglass[6] of the Orleans Parish Prison Department of Rehabilitation even instituted an experimental program of 72 hours of therapeutic counseling. Four groups of 16 subjects each were established. One group was selected as a control group to receive no therapy at all; one group was assigned to a psychiatrist trained in Freudian analysis; one group was assigned to a psychologist trained in behavior or learning therapy; and one group was assigned to a therapist trained in logotherapy. "Posttherapeutic interviews revealed a general dissatisfaction with the Freudian therapy, a rather apathetic attitude toward the behavior therapy; and a quite positive feeling about logotherapy and the benefits derived therefrom."

What is true of the behavioristically oriented approaches holds true for the psychodynamically oriented ones. Some psychoanalysts not only use paradoxical intention, but also try to explain its success in Freudian terms.[26, 27, 31, 62, 63] More recently, J. L. Harrington[30] expressed the conviction that "paradoxical intention is an attempt to consciously initiate the automatic defense erecting counterphobic attitude described by Fenichel. In a psychoanalytic model, paradoxical intention may be viewed as releaving symptoms by utilizing defenses which require less expenditure of psychic energy than the phobic or obsessive-compulsive symptom itself. Each time paradoxical intention is successfully applied, the id impulses are gratified, the superego becomes an ally to the ego, and the ego itself gains strength and becomes less restricted. This results in decreased anxiety and diminished symptom formation."

From the "three pathogenic patterns" that are distinguished by logotherapy, so far two have been discussed: the phobic pattern, "flight from fear," and the obsessive-compulsive pattern, "fight against obsessions and compulsions." What then is the third pattern? It is the sexual neurotic pattern, again characterized by the patient's fight, but instead of fighting *against* anything as the obsessive-compulsive neurotic does, the sexual neurotic is fighting *for* something, namely, sexual pleasure. However, as logotherapy teaches,[15] the more one aims at pleasure the more he misses the aim. It is the very "pursuit" of happiness that dooms it to failure. Happiness must ensue, and that is why it cannot be pursued. Happiness is a by-product of self-transcendence. This also holds for sexual pleasure. Sexual performance (male potency) and sexual experience (female orgasm) are thwarted by being made a target. The more a male patient cares for demonstrating his potency the more he falls prey to impotence. And the more a female patient is concerned with her own orgasm, the more likely she winds up with frigidity.

Usually, however, potency and orgasm are made not only a target of intention but also the target of attention as well. In logotherapy, this is referred to in terms of "hyperintention" and "hyperreflection",[19] respectively. To counteract the latter, another logotherapeutic technique— alongside paradoxical intention—has been developed: "dereflection."[15] Along with counteracting the patient's self-defeating "fight for pleasure," dereflection plays a decisive role in the logotherapeutic treatment of impotence. The respective technique has first been described by this author in 1946[11] in German and in 1952[13] in English. In these publications it was also pointed out that, according to this author's findings, hyperintention as well as hyperreflection are often due to the fact that the patient approaches sexual intercourse as something that is demanded of him. In some cases, it is the partner from whom this "demand quality" irradiates and emanates, even if only subjectively; in other cases, the demand character originates from the situation; and finally, the patient himself can place the demand on himself.

From this it can be understood that some patients are potent only as long as, and only as soon as, they can have the initiative* rather than being confronted with a situation that calls of *Hic Rhodus, hic salta!* The question is how to arrange this. In his paper published in *The International Journal of Sexology* in 1952, this author described the following "trick."

We advise the patient to inform his partner that he consulted a doctor about his difficulty who said that his case was not serious, and the prognosis favorable. Most important, however, is that he tells his partner that the doctor also has absolutely forbidden coitus. His partner now expects no sexual activity and the patient is 'released.' Through this release from the demands of his partner it is possible for his sexuality to be expressed again, undisturbed and unblocked by the feeling that something is demanded or expected from him. Often, in fact, his partner is not only surprised when the potency of the man becomes apparent, but she goes so far as to reject him because of the doctor's orders. When the patient has no other goal before him than a purely fragmentary, mutual sexual play of tenderness, then, and then only, in the process of such play is the complete sexual act accomplished, and he is faced, as it were, with the *fait accompli*. The vicious circle is broken.

* As understandable, on the human level, as this need to take the initiative is, there is an analog on the subhuman level: There is a fish species whose females are used "coquettishly" to swim away from the males that seek cohabitation. However, Konrad Lorenz succeeded in training a female to do the very contrary; that is, to approach the male forcefully. The latter's reaction consisted in a complete incapacity to cohabit.

William S. Sahakian and Barbara Jacquelyn Sahakian[54] think that this idea has been corroborated in 1970 by Masters and Johnson in their research on human sexual inadequacy.

G. Kaczanowski[34] has contributed illustrative case reports regarding the logotherapeutic technique of dereflection. In the following case, however, Kaczanowski[35] treated impotency by counteracting hyperintention rather than hyperreflection.

A young couple came for help. They were married for several months; the husband was impotent. He was downhearted and ashamed; the wife believed that it was her fault. They loved each other very much and their life together was most satisfactory, except in the sexual sphere. The husband's examination by two urologists had not revealed any organic abnormality. The husband stated that since he had been the lucky one to get the most glamorous girl of his acquaintance as his wife, he wanted to give her the greatest possible sexual pleasure which she deserved and certainly expected. The therapist let the patient ventilate his feelings and ideas about love and marriage. After a few sessions, the patient became aware of his desperate striving for sexual perfection and of his obsessive preoccupation with his failures. Guided by pointed questioning, he began to suspect that his hyperreflection upon the sexual situation and his hyperintention of virility could be the reason for his impotence. He accepted the explanation that the sexual act was an automatic function and could easily be disturbed by higher emotional processes, like worries and anxieties. The therapist helped him to see that real love had many aspects worthy of cultivation. The patient learned that if he loved his wife he could give her himself, instead of trying to give her a sexual climax. Then her pleasure would be the consequence of his attitude, not an aim in itself. The doctor had told the patient and his wife that no attempt at intercourse should be made for an undetermined period of time. This instruction relieved the patient's anticipatory anxiety. A few weeks later, the patient broke the doctor's order; the wife tried to remind him but, fortunately, she disregarded it too. Since that time, their sexual relations have been normal.

One is tempted to add: and they lived happily thereafter for years.

Paralleling a case for frigidity whose history was published by this author,[19] Darrell Burnett[7] reported the case of "a woman suffering from frigidity, who kept observing what was going on in her body during intercourse, trying to do everything according to the manuals. She was told to switch her attention to her husband. A week later she experienced an orgasm." In fact, it would seem that today the pathogenic demand quality mentioned above is engendered, last but not least, by the overemphasis on sex and sexual achievement as it is at present so predominant and prevalent in the cultural climate of the Western world. In addition, "the effect of increased sexual freedom of women on their male partners," as Ginsberg, Frosch, and Shapiro[28] have pointed out only recently, is that "these newly free women *demanded* sexual performance," and the consequence is, again to quote from Ginsberg, Frosch, and Shapiro,[28] that "young men now appear more frequently with complaints of impotence."* This observation, in full accordance with many other observations on various continents, seems to corroborate on a mass scale the logotherapeutic hypothesis on the etiology of impotence as presented above.

REFERENCES

1. Allport, G. W.: Preface to Viktor E. Frankl, *From Death-Camp to Existentialism*, Beacon Press, Boston, 1959.
2. Allport, G. W.: *Personality and Social Encounter*, Beacon Press, Boston, 1960.
3. Benedikt, F. M.: Zur Therapie angst- und zwangsneurotischer Symptome mit Hilfe der "Paradoxen Intention" und "Dereflexion" nach V. E. Frankl, Dissertation, University of Munich, 1968.
4. Briggs, G. J. F.: Courage and identity. Paper read before the British Society of Medical and Dental Hypnosis.
5. Bühler, C. and Allen M.: *Introduction to Humanistic Psychology*, Brooks/Cole, Monterey, 1972.
6. Burglass, M. E.: Personal communication.
7. Burnett, D.: Unpublished paper.
8. Dilling, H., Rosefeldt, H., Kockott G., and Heyse, H.: Verhaltenstherapie bei Phobien, Zwangsneurosen, sexuellen Störungen und Süchten. *Fortschr. Neurol. Psychiatr.* **39**:293–344, 1971.
9. Fabry, J. B.: *The Pursuit of Meaning: Logotherapy Applied to Life*, Beacon Press, Boston, 1968.
10. Frankl, V. E.: Zur medikamentösen Unterstützung der Psychotherapie bei Neurosen. *Schweizer Archiv Neurolog. Psychiatri.* **43**:26–31, 1939.
11. Frankl, V. E.: *Ärztliche Seelsorge*, Deuticke, Vienna, 1946.
12. Frankl, V. E.: *Die Psychotherapie in der Praxis*, Deuticke, Vienna, 1947.
13. Frankl, V. E.: the pleasure principle and sexual neurosis. *Int. J. Sexology* **5**:128–130, 1952.
14. Frankl, V. E.: Angst und Zwang. *Acta Psychotherapeut.* **1**:111–120, 1953.
15. Frankl, V. E.: *The Doctor and the Soul: From Psychotherapy to Logotherapy*, Knopf, New York, 1955.
16. Frankl, V. E.: *Theorie und Therapie der Neurosen*, Urban and Schwarzenberg, Vienna, 1956.
17. Frankl, V. E.: On logotherapy and existential analysis. *Am. J. Psychoanal.* **18**:28–37, 1958.
18. Frankl, V. E.: Paradoxical intention: A logotherapeutic technique. *Am. J. Psychother.* **14**:520–535, 1960.

* Dr. J. M. Stewart, [55a] reporting in the medical magazine *Pulse* on impotence at Oxford, supports this view, saying, "Females run around *demanding* sexual rights." Some males are fearful of critical analysis of their sexual performance by women with greater experience.

19. Frankl, V. E.: *Man's Search for Meaning: An Introduction to Logotherapy*, Beacon Press, Boston, 1962.

20. Frankl, V. E.: Logotherapy and existential analysis: A review. *Am. J. Psychother.* **20**:252–260, 1966.

21. Frankl, V. E.: *Psychotherapy and Existentialism: Selected Papers on Logotherapy*, Washington Square Press, New York, 1967.

22. Frankl, V. E.: logotherapy. *Israel Ann. Psychiatr.* **7**:142–155, 1967.

23. Frankl, V. E.: *The Will to Meaning: Foundations and Applications of Logotherapy*, World, New York, 1969.

24. Frankl, V. E.: Self-transcendence as a human phenomenon. In *Readings in Humanistic Psychology*, J. Sutich and M. A. Vich, (Ed.), Free Press, New York, 1969.

25. Frankl, V. E.: The feeling of meaninglessness. *Am. J. Psychoanal.* **32**:(1):85–89, 1972.

25a. Frankl, V. E.: Encounter: The concept and its vulgarization. *J. Am. Academy Psychoanal.* **1**:(1)77–87, 1973.

26. Gerz, H. O.: The treatment of the phobic and the obsessive-compulsive patient using paradoxical intention sec. Viktor E. Frankl. *J. Neuropsychiatr.* **3**(6):375–387, 1962.

27. Gerz, H. O.: Experience with the logotherapeutic technique of paradoxical intention in the treatment of phobic and obsessive-compulsive patients. *Am. J. Psychiatr.* **123**(5):548–553 1966.

28. Ginsberg, G. L., Frosch, W. A., and Shapiro, T.: The new impotence. *Arch. Gen. Psychiatr.* **26**:218–220, 1972.

28a. Hand, I., Lamontagne, Y., and Marks, I. M.: Group exposure (flooding) *in vivo* for agoraphobics. *Brit. J. Psychiat.* **124**:588–602, 1974.

29. Haley, J.: *Strategies of Psychotherapy*, Grune and Stratton, New York, 1963.

30. Harrington, J. L.: Unpublished paper.

31. Havens, L. L.: Paradoxical intention. *Psychiatr. Soc. Sci. Rev.* **2**(2):16–19, 1968.

32. Hays, P.: Determination of the obsessional personality. *Am. J. Psychiatr.* **129**(2):217–219, 1972.

33. Huber, J.: *Through an Eastern Window*, Bantam Books, New York, 1968.

34. Kaczanowski, G.: Introduction and Epilogue. In *Modern Psychotherapeutic Practice*, A. Burton, (Ed.), Science and Behavior, Palo Alto, 1965.

35. Kaczanowski, G.: Logotherapy: A new psychotherapeutic tool. *Psychosomatics* **8**:158–161, 1967.

36. Kocourek, K., Niebauer, E., and Polak, P.: Ergebnisse der klinischen Anwendung der Logotherapie. In *Handbuch der Neurosenlehre und Psychotherapie*, V. E. Frankl, V. E. von Gebsattel, and J. H. Schultz, (Eds.), Urban and Schwarzenberg, Munich, 1959.

37. Kvilhaug, B.: Klinische Erfahrungen mit der logotherapeutischen Technik der paradoxen Intention. Paper read before the Austrian Medical Society of Psychotherapy, July 18, 1963.

37a. Lapinsohn, L. I.: Relationship of the logotherapeutic concepts of anticipatory anxiety and paradoxical intention to the neurophysiological theory of induction. *Behav. Neuropsychiat.* **3**:(3–4) 12–14 and 24, 1971.

37b. Lazarus, A. A.: *Behavior Theory and Beyond,* McGraw-Hill, New York, 1971.

38. Lehembre, J.: L'intention paradoxale, procédé de psychothérapie. *Acta Neurologica Psychiatr. Belgica* **64**:725–735, 1964.

39. Leslie, R. C.: *Jesus and Logotherapy: The Ministry of Jesus as Interpreted through the Psychotherapy of Viktor Frankl,* Abingdon Press, New York, 1965.

40. Lyons, J.: Existential Psychotherapy. *J. Abnormal Soc. Psychol.* **62**:242–249, 1961.

41. Marks, I. M.: *Fears and Phobias,* Academic Press, New York, 1969.

42. Marks, I. M.: The origins of phobic states. *Am. J. Psychother.* **24**:652–676, 1970.

43. Martin, B. W.: Behavior modification and logotherapeutic techniques as used in high school counseling. Paper presented to the Advanced Seminar in Logotherapy, US International University, 1972.

44. Medlicott, R. W.: The management of anxiety. *N. Zealand Med. J.* **70**:155–158, 1969.

45. Medlicott, R. W.: Personal communication.

46. Müller-Hegemann, D.: Methodological approaches in psychotherapy. *Am. J. Psychother.* **17**:554–568, 1963.

47. Ochs, J. M.: Logotherapy and religious ethnopsychiatric therapy. Paper presented to the Pennsylvania Sociological Society at Villanova University, 1968.

48. Patterson, C. H.: Frankl's logotherapy. In *Theories of Counseling and Psychotherapy,* Harper and Row, New York, 1966.

49. Pervin, L. A.: Existentialism, psychology, and psychotherapy. *Am. Psycholog.* **15**:305–309, 1960.

50. Polak, P.: Frankl's existential analysis. *Am. J. Psychother.* **3**:517–522, 1949.

51. Pynummootil, A. G.: Unpublished paper.

52. Rachman, S., Hodgson, R., and Marks, I. M.: The treatment of chronic obsessive-compulsive neurosis. *Behav. Res. Ther.* **9**:237–247, 1971.

53. Sadiq, Mohammed: Application of logotherapeutic concepts in a variety of neurotic and psychotic disorders. Paper presented to the Advanced Seminar in Logotherapy, US International University, 1972.

54. Sahakian, W. S. and Sahakian, B. J. Logotherapy as a personality theory. *Israel Ann. Psychiatr.,* **10**:230–244, 1972.

54a. Solyom, L., Garza-Perez, J., Ledwidge, B. L., and Solyom, C.: Paradoxical intention in the treatment of obsessive thoughts: A pilot study. *Comprehensive Psychiat.* **13**:291–297, 1972.

55. Spiegelberg, H.: *Phenomenology in Psychology and Psychiatry,* Northwestern University Press, Evanston, 1972.

55a. Stewart, J. M.: Quoted from *Psychology and Life Newsletter* **1**:(1)5, 1972.

56. Tweedie, D. F.: *Logotherapy and the Christian Faith: An Evaluation of Frankl's Existential Approach to Psychotherapy,* Baker Book House, Grand Rapids, 1961.

57. Tweedie, D. F.: *The Christian and the Couch: An Introduction to Christian Logotherapy,* Baker Book House, Grand Rapids, 1963.

58. Ungersma, A. J.: *The Search for Meaning,* Westminster Press, Philadelphia, 1961.

59. Valins and Ray: Quoted from Ref. 41.

60. Victor, R. G. and Krug, C. M.: Paradoxical intention in the treatment of compulsive gambling. *Am. J. Psychother.* **21**:808–814, 1967.

61. Watson, J. P., Gaind, R., and Marks, I. M., Prolonged exposure. *Brit. Med. J.* **1**:13–15, 1971.

62. Weisskopf-Joelson, E.: Some comments on a viennese school of psychiatry. *J. Abnormal Soc. Psychol.* **51**:701–703, 1955.

63. Weisskopf-Joelson, E.: The present crisis in psychotherapy. *J. Psychol.* **69**:107–115, 1968.

64. Yamamoto, I.: Die japanische Morita-Therapie im Vergleich zu der Existenzanalyse und Logotherapie Frankls. In *Abendlandische Therapie und östliche Weisheit*, W. Bitter, (Ed.), Klett, Stuttgart, 1968.

CHAPTER FIFTEEN

ANALYTICAL AND IRRATIONAL ASPECTS OF POLITICAL SEDUCTION AND READINESS TO BE SEDUCED

ANTON SCHELKOPF
Translated by Leo Katz

In the course of human history, the rational has conquered an ever greater part of what people can understand intellectually and emotionally and probably will be able to accomplish. The irrational is therefore the remainder of what is not yet rationally understandable or perhaps also of what we shall not be able to comprehend in the future with our present intellectual apparatus.

From this point of view, psychoanalysis is a science that, within the social sciences, was and is most dedicated to root out the irrational in human conduct in the field of what can be known in the human psyche and to replace it by a consistent search for the causality of human development within the narrow confines of the family or in the expanse of archaic systems of relatedness.

We must admit that when we examine human behavior, whether in the consulting room and clinic or in the larger area of history and politics, we are always confronted by phenomena which we may be able to observe rationally at least today, but which we can—explain would already be the wrong word—make thinkable by including the irrational. A part of our human repertoire, to be active or to remain passive, without being able to clear up rationally all of the individual phenomena, is the ability of human beings to be seduced not in the diadic relationship, but within the relatedness of groups, especially in the idiological political area.

Human beings in my country and in other European nations who were born during the approximate time between 1910 and 1920 have begun to ask themselves, at the latest in 1945, whether, without considering themselves to be stupid or devoid of character, they have become seduced by a political regime whose arrogance and crimes have shaken our world. They have experienced how the world became solidified, in a previously not imaginable way, against the crime and how this world changed decidedly. This generation asks itself why human beings have not learned either through the experience of horror nor through the common defense, and why a new cycle of political ideologic seduceability could begin in the world, as manifested by the nonfunctioning of the individual and group conscience, the projections used as alibis, and thus the brutal application of new power and terror in all parts of the world.

This question, asked by one generation, has to become a new obligation for us to apply our knowledge of individual human drives to the examination of mass phenomena, that is, to contemplate once again the malleability of the individual within the group. In the future, it will also have to be our task to examine whether the theory which is now available to us permits us to elucidate the methods by which political seducers induce paranoid projections in the ego thus to make it possible for the ego to throw off acquired guilt feelings, resulting in a veritable explosion of archaic id impulses into the ego. We might find that when we examine what we might call a group id or a group ego, our present instruments are not sufficient and that we have to acquire into irrational circumstances. Strangely, politics have hardly, or not at all, been the concern of classical psychoanalysts. This is so even though the first massive resistances confronting psychoanalysis arose largely from political-ideological roots. The great seducers of our time were already on the way, the seduced became a mass. It is possible that understandable repressions as well as irrational influences, whose origins we cannot know, played a part in the disregard of politics by psychoanalysts.

I now want to proceed to offer a chronological scheme, to complement this scheme with two case histories, and, subsequently, to derive conclusions from the foregoing material. Political-ideological seduction proceeds stepwise in an ever recurring scheme:

1.   Insecure and frustrated individuals, usually compromised by a significant figure who indulged them, seek comrades in their misery or kindred spirits. The small group is formed, the initiating group, which provides the leader who may sometimes also be replaced by the leader of another initiating group.

2.   The group finds and solidifies a mass, being formed by shared experiences of frustrations. The frustrations of the initiator or initiators are to be found in the personal area, whereas those of the mass in the economic or political area.

3.   The mass is split into its mobile part (schizoid or hysterical) and into its sedimentary part (depressive or compulsive).

4.   The appearance of what seems to be an idealistic elevated goal, actually an ideological goal vis-a-vis the mobile group. The first expression of an enemy system. (In the formulation of the elevated goal, the word "freedom" is almost never absent.)

5.   Further structuralization of the mobile part into schizoid and depressive groups by the formation of a lower and middle hierarchy and strict hierarchical selection.

6.   The activation of subordinate groups through training demands for performance and through the command:

a.   to produce an ego-flooding determination to climb up the rungs of the hierarchical stepladder to get closer to the "leadership."

b.   for indoctrination of the manifest elevated aim and the conviction that the effort for achieving it and the unconditional subordination to the command of "leadership" are identical.

7.   The commitment of the seduced into the mass, thus expanding

geometrically the base of command receptivity and suggesting to the mass that the elevated aim is their own wish.

8.   The agitation of the seduced mass by means of appeal and command, such that the mass is moved like an avalanche and moves in ever increasing speed toward the goal fixed by the initiating group.

Two very brief developmental histories follow. First is the case of Paul.

Paul was born in October 1897 in a German town on the left bank of the Rhine. A few months after his birth, his father, the offspring of peasants, who progressed in a small factory from office boy to manager, is able to move with his family into a row house, bought by his savings. The mother is the daughter of an artisan and is described as unassuming and devoted. She remains this way to the end of her days, even after the steep public ascent of her son. The father is industrious, serious-minded at work but with a sense of humor at home. Mother and father are loved by the children. Paul has four siblings, two older brothers, one sister 12 years his junior and another sister who died when Paul was 18. The parents live by the motto: We want our children to have a better life than ours. Paul and his mother had a particularly good relationship; she worried about him constantly. Paul had a loving, respectful attitude toward father at first, later becoming more distant. Four years after the father's death, Paul called him "a well-meaning Spiessbuerger."

Paul's childhood stood in the shadow of a deformed left foot and leg, such that it was about 8 centimeters shorter than the right. We are not sure how this deformity developed, but we may assume that it was not congenital but was due to an accident. Paul was otherwise not a good-looking child either. Above all, a disproportionately large head rested on a rickety body. At any rate, since he could not play nor later dance, could neither wrestle like a boy nor participate in sports, he was often alone, isolated from his peers, a condition which further strengthened the closeness to his mother. All the children of the family attended the gymnasium but only Paul graduated. At school it was possible for him for the first time to become noticed and to gain respect through his talent in acting.

While still a student, he volunteers for the war in 1914, is rejected, locks himself crying into his room and refuses all food for a day. His Abitur (final exam), falling into the period after the beginning of the war, is accordingly easier, permits him to shine with the best German composition. This in turn accords him the honor of being the valedictorian.

At this time his parents express the wish that he study theology and become a priest. At first Paul agrees, but first begins to study archaic philology and later Germanistics. Through the aid of an ecclesiastic student-aid society for Catholic students and the Catholic student organization Unitas, he is able to study at Bonn, Freiburg, Würzburg, and München, and he finally graduates in Heidelberg after 10 semesters. In Freiburg he meets his first great love. The affair is over after 6 months but we don't know why. It is certain, however, that very soon women are strongly attracted to Paul, largely due to his eyes, his deep warm voice, which could also become hard melodic, his capability to charm, but above all, his way with words which afforded him successes.

Munich, however, becomes decisive in his mental development, where he meets up with the ideology of Marx, Engels, Lenin, and Walter Rathenau. Here, a friend from his Rhenish homeland becomes his mentor and object for identification, a friend who has many military battlefield decorations, seriously wounded, discharged with the odium of a German hero, tall and blond in appearance, imbued with Marxist-mystical views of the world. Under the influence of this friend, Paul dissociates himself at this time from the church, wants to leave the church. His father writes him to warn him from taking this step, but tells him that he would not "condemn" his son. Paul, moved by his father, although he does not change his view toward the church, never leaves the church. Instead, he even deepens his capacity for religious experience to the point of an ecstatic Christ frenzy.

In 1920, Paul comes under the influence of Friedrich Gundolf's circle, the greatest teacher of literature of his time and follower of the poet Stefan George, in whose work appears, "the first ray of the vision of the coming Fuhrer," possessed of the "chaste, clear, barbaric eye."

Paul tried his hand at poetry, taking from Faust, Christ, and Zarasthustra, writing at unsuccessful epic poem whose hero reads the Bible, lies awake at nights and thinks of the "still, pale man from Nazareth." Paul finds that there is no speech more powerful than the Sermon on the Mount, which "should be studied by every propagandist." But something is defined in this first attempt at being a writer of great significance for Paul: socialism as he sees it:

"To be a socialist means to subordinate the I to the Thou, to sacrifice one's person to the community. Socialism in its deepest sense is service, self-denial for the individual and commitment to the whole."

All of this is in a state of ferment in 1924, the year in which he applies as editor to the Berliner Tagblatt and, as we may assume, in which he is quite routinely rejected. Ten years later he is Hitler's minister of propaganda, destroys the Berliner Tagblatt, and becomes subsequently the effective technocrat of one of the greatest mass-seductions of our millenium.

His idealized goal remained to the end a special, not closely defined type of socialism, an aim which he occasionally lost sight of in his unconditional subordination to Hitler, but from which his spirit never wandered. Paul Joseph Goebbels, whose course I do not want to follow further, was a seduced person before he became a seducer. As a spoiled and indulged seduced person, he betrayed his intellect. As a frustrated seducer, he betrayed his principles, accumulating during phases of frustration through Hitler in a shameless way property, money, and women, working at other times to the point of exhaustion during phases of self-indulgence by denying his weak physical condition.

Let us now look at parts of another life history, the case of Andreas.

Andreas was born in 1915 in a large southwest German city. The father, at that time an official of the lower civil service, came from a Catholic family of peasants and artisans. The mother, a very religious Lutheran, mostly quiet and inspired but sometimes dramatically vehement, came from a family of artisans, church people but also occasional musicians. Andreas remained an only child. Father was industrious and easy-going, but in order to maintain his patriarchal ideas, he could, at times, become strict and resort to severe corporal punishment. More severely felt, however, were humiliation and derision by the father, who, in this way, compensated for jealousy of his son, who was indulged as an only child by the mother, but who was also beaten by her in occasional unbridled anger.

The child was able to read one and one-half years before entering school, was the best in his class in the first grade of elementary school. Already in the third grade he drew attention to himself because of his restlessness. His first year in secondary school again was brilliant, but then he got into difficulties which became more pronounced up until his Abitur. His German examination was the best of his class. He passed mathematics only after an oral examination and the indulgence of a number of teachers who respected his efforts in music. Andreas was much encouraged in the muses by his mother; he was taken along at an early age to plays, operas, and concerts. Since the father was politically active, he travelled a good deal. He belonged to an actual conservative party in a Christian trade union.

When the National Socialists came to power in 1933 and were able to use radio broadcasting in the service of political seduction, when a wave of martial music, nightly torch parades, mass demonstrations, and working projects cascaded upon the population, and when while secret followers among pupils and teachers appeared in uniform, Andreas felt isolated and lonely. As he said later, he felt that a fateful hour in the life of the nation passed without his participation. The others sang and marched, the flags were waving, and he found himself excluded from the celebration as the son of a "reactionary" father and a "strictly Protestant" mother. Despite a suspension of new admissions to the party, Andreas tried to become a party member, an undertaking in which he was successful with his characteristic stubborness. Shortly thereafter, recruited by a friend from school, he entered a technical communications unit of the SS, here again with difficulties because he had not yet acquired the sufficient height for the elite guard of Hitler's. Andreas, whose decision was at first severely judged by his parents, served whenever it was demanded of him. Although he had no bent for mechanical things, he learned radio transmission and Morse code. He gave up concerts and the theater and participated in nocturnal field maneuvers in order to gain the respect of the tall ones despite his short stature.

At this point, a remark about the SS is appropriate. The SS, which, as Hitler's Honor Guard, at that time had a better reputation than the SA, had an overly developed code of honor. The smallest infractions against the common good, against the spirit of comradeship, were punished very severely. This is not without significance because there is certainly a relationship between the elitist esprit de corps as produced by the code of honor and the faith of subsequent SS units in the justification of the inhuman orders of the leadership. Examples from recent historical events in the United States (and surely also from other countries) show a similar relationship.*

In the worst possible condition, weakened by lack of sleep and distractions of all

* Added in 1973.

kinds, Andreas sat for his final examinations (Abitur) and was drafted into the Labor Service. After discharge from this Service, he entered the University, where he found friends for the first time; indeed something seemed to have changed. He now no longer had to make efforts, friends sought him out, and, fortunately for him, they were generous, open-minded, partly even sophisticated liberal friends and especially older friends who attracted him and who found him attractive. Suddenly the party receded in the background, his service was neglected; silently tolerated by his unit commander, the conversations and get-togethers with his friends gained in importance. They discussed the regime dispassionately and with critical sarcasm. Soon Andreas got into trouble and finally received a disciplinary transfer. Even at the University he soon thereafter was involved in a serious confrontation with the regime when Andreas, who chaired a seminar, was expected to drop a friend from the seminar whose grandfather was a Jew. Because of Andreas's refusal and the resulting confrontation with the party functionaries, a proceeding was initiated aiming at suspension from all universities. Andreas became distressed and asked his faculty advisor for help, which was refused with the contention that these were student affairs in which he did not want to interfere. But Andreas found help through his former buddies from the technical unit, who first of all saw to it that the suspension proceeding was squashed and who subsequently, by means of several tricks, let his name disappear from the rolls of the SS, when, a new proceeding began to threaten before an SS court at this time.

From this time on, there was little difference between Andreas and other Germans who felt increasingly more alienated by the arbitrariness of the party, unless it was through his conviction that nothing could happen to him as a party member and his more frequent and loud criticism. Still, strangely, nothing happened to him. Andreas was drafted when war broke out and returned at the end of the war, with multiple decorations for bravery without injuries or ever having been a prisoner of war. After the war was over, he was brought before a denazification court, which classified him as a sympathizer (Mitlaeufer). This classification Andreas accepted with simultaneous feelings of relief and indignation.

I do not want to trace any further this patient's life history, which is also somewhat fragmented. I want to point out only that we are dealing here with one of the seduced who, because of oedipal insecurity, at first found the fathers and heroes he needed in the regime, but who later on, becoming increasingly critical, turned toward new fathers with whom an initial process of belated maturing could begin which was continued throughout the stress of the war, but which could only be somewhat concluded through a later psychoanalysis. He was able to avoid personal guilt involvement before and during the war, probably because at first he was too immature to obtain entry into an initiating group and because later his budding maturity saved him from being exploited by the group.

I briefly sketched this life history to present the not atypical conflict between the good will of young people to subordinate themselves and commit themselves to an abstract idea, and the reaction that sets in when increasingly mistakes are noticed as described very convincingly by *Milovan Djilas*.[5]

All the more tragic seems to us a discernible doubt which is surfacing anew among those who were at the time aiming at presumed idealized goals while being seduced *en masse*. I have in mind the doubt of those who, although ready for insight and remorse, are still today being pursued by collective abuse and are experiencing how their mentors at home and abroad are endangering the foundations of a more humanitarian world all over again. The doubt of the fathers already brings in train the protests of the sons and daughters.

Let me now return to the stepwise scheme, to raise the question whether this scheme and its functioning follow a certain theoretical lawfulness which can be conceptualized psychoanalytically.

The conception of seduction was used by Freud and his early students only in the sexual area. *Lampl-de-Groot*,[7] too, uses this concept in the same way when in another context she remarks that acts of aggression mainly (not usually) are caused by frustration whereas sexuality by seductions. If "too much love is equivalent to seduction," it becomes clear that what is meant here is the seductive impulse of excessive offerings, that is, indulgence. This is undoubtedly true not only in the area of sexuality, but also in all other cases where a person is exposed to an excessive offering of indulgence. If we consider further that the causal sequence frustration-aggression may be continued to include a renewed frustration, then we can conclude that the frustrated person may be spoiled by an excessive offering of attention and thus may also be seduced.

The initiating group, which is comprised as a rule of individuals who were originally indulged but later frustrated, forms from its own ranks the leader, the seducer, and has him return the group into a state of indulgence. In return for indulgence, the leader can then ask for performance.

When we examine the mass which is required to make the initiating group effective, we find that its members are recruited from various structures, that their experience of frustration is polymorphous, that external conditions may intensify or weaken the latent feeling of frustration without any genuine awareness being generated. Everything remains in the realm of the emotional.

Every feeling of dissatisfaction pushes toward a resolution and seeks power which allegedly accrues to the individual in a group. Added to this there is a *contagion mental*, as *Le Bon*[16] called it, a mental contagion which is produced by one or more initiating groups. There arises a group soul; the individual ceases to think and to feel as such.

If we can say that the psyche of an individual integrates uncritically the demands of the super-ego and thus becomes so essentially weakened in its ego that very deep id impulses can no longer find regular channels of discharge and can then in an unselected state of disarray pour themselves into the ego, then we could raise the question what laws are followed by the group soul which also finds itself confronted very soon by an overpowering super-ego demand, without, however, being in a position to decide whether it should integrate or defend itself against this demand. Moreover, the splitting of the mass into the mobile and sedentary component contradicts the original need of the mass and seemingly follows irrational relationships such that the appearance of the elevated aim under mostly magic aspects and the magic of commands seems to play a special part.

Let us remember here that *Riemanm* and others have shown that "two antinomical complementary types often exert an unconscious attraction, a fascination for each other." In the realm of the individual, the schizoid would thus attract the depressive and the compulsive the hysterical. In a group, however, schizoid and hysterical people seem to attract depressives and compulsives. The examples of Paul and Andreas showed that in each case it was an indulgent mother who started their life's course. Both were depressive, one, however, with compulsive, the other with hysterical un-underpinnings. The father of one of them seems to be strong at first but then fails when challenged by the son. The other father, because of his weakness, denies himself as an object for identification for his son. Paul seeks a father who punishes and rewards him capriciously, finds him in the great seducer, and becomes his tool. Andreas seeks "fathers," to achieve with their assistance maturity and is later in a position to accept mother and father as they were.

Paul becomes a seducer to prove himself. Andreas wants to prove himself, seeks indulgence and becomes seduced, is temporarily submerged in the mass, but then he rebels and saves himself through his inner freedom.

Elias Canetti[4] has shown that the command "which triggers off an act that differs from all other acts" plays a special role which can be understood rationally only in part. "When the power of command is not questioned, the power of the commander grows incessantly."

Canetti says that every command consists for the receiver of a goal and a sting, such that the sting remains constant when the command is carried out. In this connection, the dynamics of indulgence play a part again, since whoever carries out the command is rewarded by the commander. Here, too, the group obeys its own irrational laws, for "the command directed at the group leaves no sting."

Hau[13] speaks of the building of social illusions which is indispensable for any dictatorship which, in turn, cannot be imagined without a seducer. The indulgence of the group does not actually have to be carried out; it may remain an illusion and can still motivate the mass in the direction desired by the initiating group and its leader. *Hau* says further that "influencing the mass can become the means of building social illusions," and he refers to parades, mass meetings and festivals, shows, literature, advertising, radio, movies, and TV. He remarks that in these instances the individual is forced into receptivity and becomes exclusively a receiver. Actually, the mass can be restructured at will through the media of mass influence. A war-weary, exhausted people reacts to its seducer by roaring enthusiastic approval of total war. Once such phenomena are already in existence, the psychoanalytic method fails. We should ask, however, whether it must fail as a general rule. In his letter to Pfister, Freud[2] pointed out that in trying to have a therapeutic impact on a group, the enlightenment and exposing of errors would have more effect than curing of individuals. This would mean that psychoanalysis can contribute to the unmasking of the great seducers as long as it is possible to expose them in time.

The inherent irrational processes of large groups make it necessary, however, to immunize in time those who are ready to be seduced. This is not possible without planned social application of psychoanalytic methods.

In 1951, *René Laforgue*[12] called in vain for an offering of help to the endangered communities by applying the same knowledge to them that we have of individuals.

How do we see our task?

The seducers are to be deprived of power and those ready to be seduced are to be immunized.

But this task can be solved only partially. There are no means in this world by which the seduction as carried out by a seducer can be prevented. However, the positive application can be seen in heading off the seducibility as a reaction by the group. The prognosis for doing this is not favorable either, when we observe, as *Riemann* points out, how our world is becoming more schizoid, emotionally blunted and given to intellectualizing. He deplores synthetic freedom, the lack of love, and the dearth of considerateness and responsibility. But *Riemann*, too, hopes for "a new introspectiveness, which might lead to a new mysticism and thus to an awareness of the generally human and humane." He sees beginnings of a "schizoid freedom," which may perhaps elevate one to a new level of consciousness.

Is it possible to believe in the freedom of man who drags behind him his schizoid chains and thus remains susceptible to seduction?

The task remains to educate man to the point where he can escape the tendency to carry his frustration into the group instead of developing his own individual aggressiveness; to educate man, so that he can forego being indulged en masse by the great seducers and so that he can develop an openminded ability to love and thus to achieve pleasurable experience.

I am one of those who believe it is high time to fulfill Freud's demand and to carry the secure results of psychoanalysis on a broad basis into the nations. The social political application of psychoanalysis can become viable only if we are successful in developing "an analytic ethic of the evolutionary consciousness," of a consciousness whose internal mental economy can get along with small quantities of narcissistic gratification and which will more immediately diminish the initial frustration experience of large groups and thus decrease their readiness to be seduced.

REFERENCES

1. Freud, S.: *Complete Collected Works*, XIII, Group Psychology and the Analysis of the Ego, Imago Publishing Co., Ltd., London.

2. Freud, S.: *Letters 1909–1939*, S. Fischer Verlag, Frankfurt, 1963.

3. Fromm, E.: *The Revolution of Hope*, Ernst Klett Verlag, Stuttgart, 1971.

4. Canetti, E.: *The Mass and the Individual*, Claasen Verlag, Hamburg, 1970.

5. Djilas, M.: *Conversations with Stalin*, Harcourt, Brace and World, New York, 1962.

6. Elhardt, S.: On healthy and neurotic aggression. In *Aspects of Psychoanalysis*, Schelkopf and Elhardt, (Eds.), Verlag Vandenhoek and Ruprecht, Göttingen, 1969.

7. Lampl-de-Groot, J.: The formation of ideals in neurotics and delinquents. *Psyche* 19(7):October 1965 (1949).

8. Riemann, F.: *Basic Forms of Anxiety*, Ernst Reinhardt Verlag, Munich, 1961.

9. Riemann, F.: On the advantage of a concept of a pre-oral phase. *J. Psychosom. Med. Psychoanal.* 16:January/March 1971.

10. Reimann, V.: *Dr. Joseph Goebbels*, Verlag Fritz Molden, Vienna, 1971.

11. Monod, J.: *Chance and Necessity*, Editions de Leuil, Paris, 1970.

12. Laforgue, R. *Failure in the Life of Persons and Peoples*, Georg Thieme Verlag, Stuttgart, 1951.

13. Hau, T. F.: On social illusionizing. *Littera*, 5.

14. Picker, H. and Schramm, P. E.: *Hitler's Dinner Conversations at the Führer's Headquarters 1941/1942*, Percy Ernst Schramm in collaboration with A. Hillgruber and M. Vogt, (Eds.), Seewald Verlag, Stuttgart, 1963.

15. Boelke, W.: Do you want total war? In *The Secret Goebbels Conferences 1939/43*, Deutsche Verlagsanstalt, Stuttgart, 1969.

16. Le Bon, G.: *Group Psychology*, Alfred Kroner Verlag, Stuttgart, 1950.

17. Schelkopf, A.: Fritz Riemann—Attempts at a Biography. In *Aspects of Psychoanalysis*, Schelkopf—Elhardt, (Eds.), Verlag Vandenhoek and Ruprecht, Göttingen, 1969.

18. Schelkopf, A.: Resignation or evolution, the significance of conscience in [the Works of] Hans Zulliger. Address given in honor of the awarding of the Zulliger Prizes, 1971.

19. Reich, W.: *Mass psychology of fascism*, Kiepenheuer and Witsch, Cologne/Berlin, 1971.

20. Matussek, P.: Present-day ethics from a psychotherapeutic point of view. In *Possibilities of Modern Psychotherapy*, Schelkopf, (Ed.), Verlag Vandenhoek & Ruprecht, Göttingen, 1967.

21. Matussek, P. and Egenter, R.: *Ideology, Faith and Conscience*, Droemer-Knaur Verlag, Munich, 1965.

CHAPTER SIXTEEN

HYPNOTIZABILITY AND MENTAL HEALTH

HERBERT SPIEGEL, M.D.
JOSEPH L. FLEISS, Ph.D.
A. A. BRIDGER, M.D. and
MARC ARONSON, B.A.

For the average clinician concerned with diagnosis and therapy, hypnosis has unquestionably been a failure. Induction techniques have been mysterious, unclear, cumbersome, and too time consuming to be gracefully weaved into evaluation and therapy.

The purposes of the present report are (a) to call attention to a uniquely new 5 to 10 minute strategy of hypnotic induction recorded on a graded 15 point profile, the hypnotic induction profile (HIP), which can easily be scored in terms of hypnotic capacity[16]; (b) to describe the distribution of hypnotic capacity using this method in a patient population of 2000; and (c) to discuss a statistically significant correlation between scores on the HIP and independent psychological testing.

THE HYPNOTIC INDUCTION PROFILE

Various measures have been used to evaluate hypnotic capacity. A single index such as postural sway was suggested by Eysenck in 1944.[6] A currently popular measure is the Stanford Hypnotic Susceptibility Scale (SHS) developed by Weitzenhoffer and Hilgard which takes at least 45 minutes to administer and involves the actual induction of hypnosis.[18] Shor and Orne's Harvard Group Scale of Hypnotic Susceptibility, and Barber's Suggestibility Scale have been extensively utilized.[1, 14] All of these scales for hypnotic capacity were developed in the experimental laboratory with volunteers. Mental health was assumed, but not diagnosed in any critical manner. The phenomenon was measured by discrete test variables without accounting for a continuity of concentration throughout the test procedure. To our knowledge, none of the other current methods of hypnotic induction is easily applicable to the clinical setting because the measurements themselves cannot be used as part of the diagnostic and treatment process. A new measure was needed which could be appropriately incorporated into a clinical context. Such a test had to be rapid, clinically appropriate, and it had to give a critical measure of sustained, disciplined concentration.

The 5 to 10 minute strategy of hypnotic induction developed by Spiegel is an eye-roll, arm levitation method which elicits 15 points of information on the profile shown in Figure 1. Statistical analysis has shown that the most salient indicators of hypnotizability respectively are the eye-roll, control differential, and posthypnotic levitation.

The eye-roll is the degree to which a person can gaze upward while closing his eyelids. This capacity is one of the strongest single measures of potential hypnotizability. This measure alone correctly predicted the final grade in 75% of a patient population of over 2000 (see Figure 2).[15]

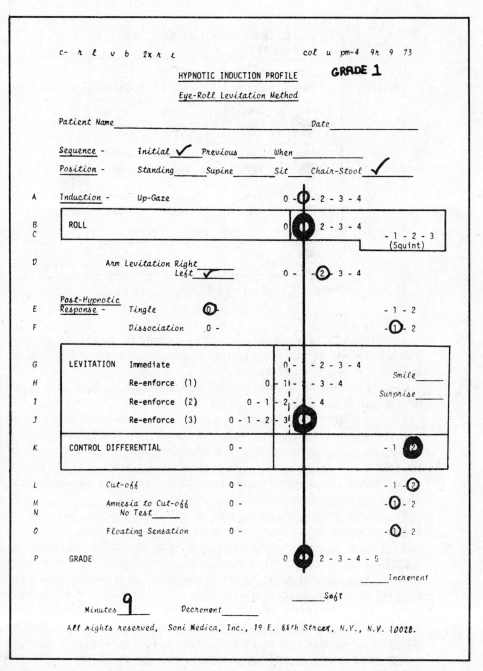

Figure 1. Grade 1, hypnotic induction profile.

EYE-ROLL TEST FOR HYPNOTIZABILITY

UP-GAZE   ROLL

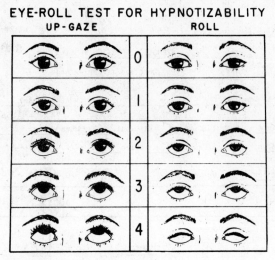

Figure 2.   Upgaze and eye-roll.

Arm levitation measures the patient's response to the posthypnotic signal that his arm will remain in an upright position and return to that position even when drawn down by the therapist.

Control differential is a measure of the relative difference in control the patient feels between his levitated hand and his nonlevitated hand.

The initial arm levitation, posthypnotic responses to tingling, dissociation, cut-off to posthypnotic signal, amnesia to cut-off, and floating sensation are less important measures which give a fuller clinical picture of the patient and are necessary parts of the induction procedure. The details of the method of the hypnotic induction and evaluation are discussed in the *Manual for Hypnotic Induction.*[16]

The profile grade is determined by the distribution of the three salient measures. Figure 3 illustrates the three most significant profiles.

A typical straight line profile, referred to as an "intact" profile, connotes hypnotizability, that is, the capacity for optimal, attentive, responsive concentration inherent in the patient as tapped by the examiner. Within the category of straight intact profiles there is a range from 0 to 5. Hypnotizability is not an either/or phenomenon, but rather it covers a range from nonhypnotizable (grade 0) to extremely hypnotizable (grade 5), including slightly hypnotizable (grade 1), moderately hypnotizable (grade 2), very hypnotizable (grade 3), and highly hypnotizable (grade 4). The profile can deviate in the following ways. A shift to the left, with a 0 at K (control differential) identifies a decrement profile. The decrement profile, considered a

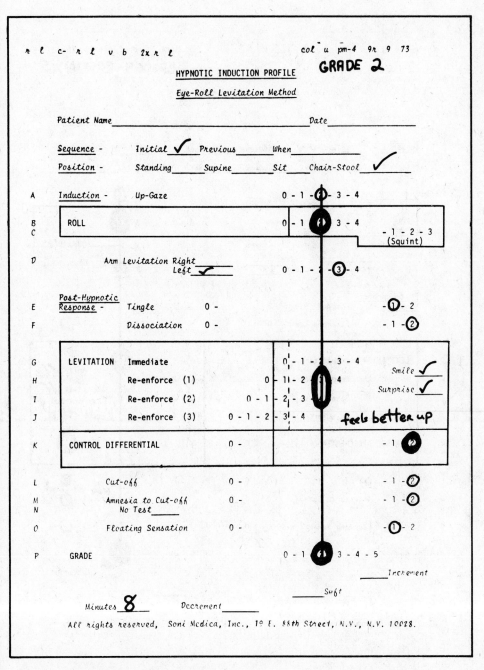

Figure 3. Straight grades 2 and 4, decrement and soft.

345

l   c- r l   v b   2x r l   *col u pm-4 9r 9 73*

HYPNOTIC INDUCTION PROFILE **GRADE 4 - POSSIBLY 5**

Eye-Roll Levitation Method

Patient Name _____ *Date* _____

Sequence -   *Initial* ✓ *Previous* _____ *When* _____

Position -   *Standing* _____ *Supine* _____ *Sit* _____ *Chair-Stool* ✓

A   Induction - Up-Gaze   0 - 1 - 2 - 3 - ⓪

B   ROLL   0 - 1 - 2 - 3 ❷
C   - 1 - 2 - 3
                                                        (Squint)

D   Arm Levitation Right
                    Left ✓   0 - 1 - 2 - 3 - ⓪

     Post-Hypnotic
E   Response -   Tingle   0 -   - 1 - ❷
F   Dissociation 0 -   - 1 - ❷

G   LEVITATION Immediate   0 - 1 - 2 - 3 ❶
H   Re-enforce (1)   0 - 1 - 2 - 3 - 4   Smile ✓✓
I   Re-enforce (2)   0 - 1 - 2 - 3 - 4   Surprise ✓✓
J   Re-enforce (3) 0 - 1 - 2 - 3 - 4   *That's cool*
                                                     I can't stop it.
K   CONTROL DIFFERENTIAL   0 -   - 1 - ❷

L   Cut-off   0 -   - 1 - ❷ *Now it's back*
M   Amnesia to Cut-off 0 -   - 1 - ❷
N   No Test ____
O   Floating Sensation 0 -   - 1 - ❷

P   GRADE   0 - 1 - 2 - 3 ❹ 5
                                                        _____ Increment
                                                  _____ Soft

        Minutes **5** ____   Decrement _____

Figure 3   (*Continued*)

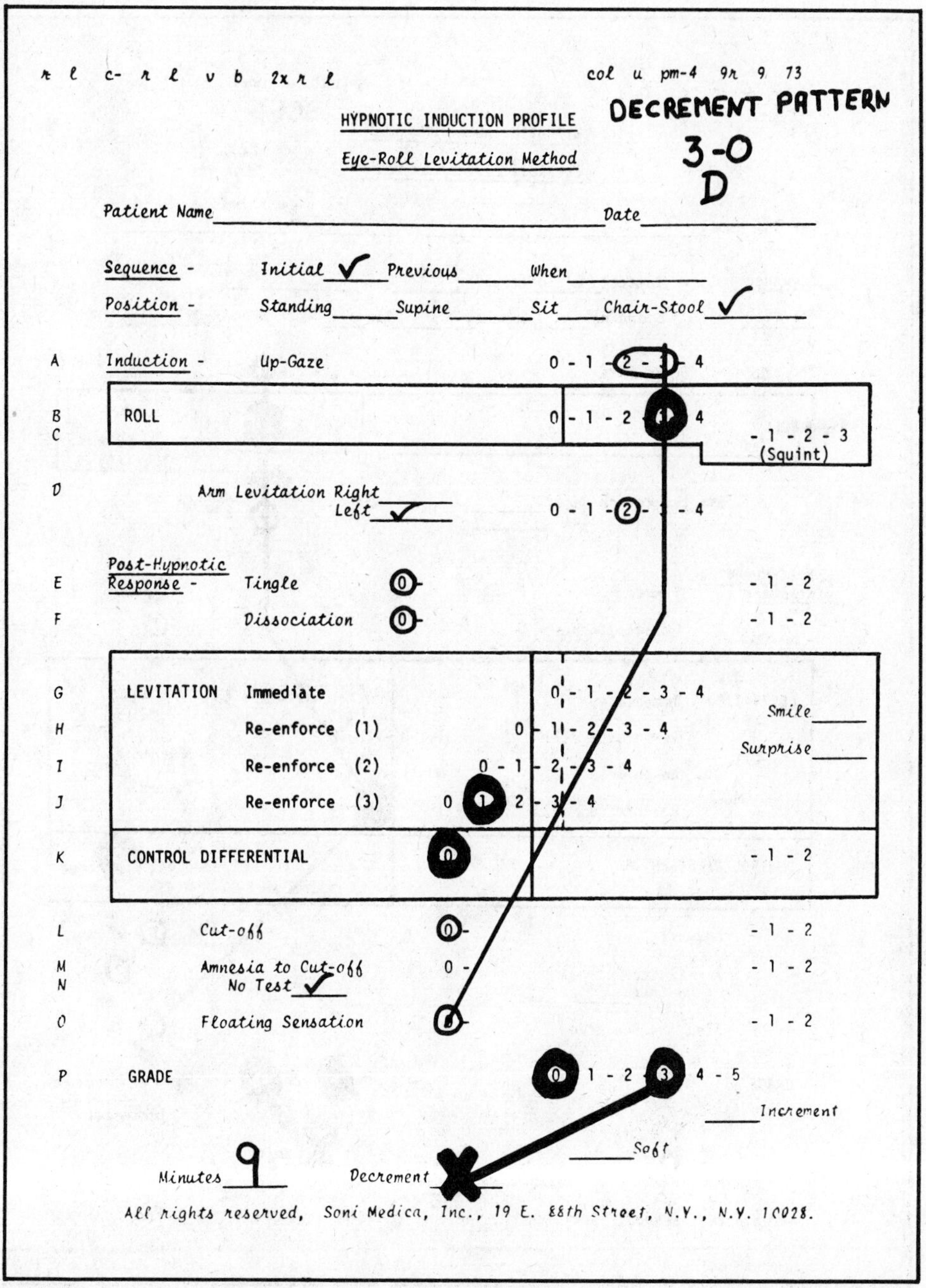

r l c- r l v b 2x r l   col u pm-4 9r 9 73

DECREMENT PATTERN
3-0
D

HYPNOTIC INDUCTION PROFILE
Eye-Roll Levitation Method

Patient Name ______ Date ______

Sequence - Initial ✓ Previous ______ When ______
Position - Standing ______ Supine ______ Sit ______ Chair-Stool ✓

A Induction - Up-Gaze 0 - 1 - 2 - 3 - 4
B ROLL 0 - 1 - 2 - 3 - 4
C - 1 - 2 - 3 (Squint)
D Arm Levitation Right ______ Left ✓ 0 - 1 - 2 - 3 - 4
E Post-Hypnotic Response - Tingle 0 - 1 - 2
F Dissociation 0 - 1 - 2
G LEVITATION Immediate 0 - 1 - 2 - 3 - 4
H Re-enforce (1) 0 - 1 - 2 - 3 - 4 Smile ______
I Re-enforce (2) 0 - 1 - 2 - 3 - 4 Surprise ______
J Re-enforce (3) 0 - 1 - 2 - 3 - 4
K CONTROL DIFFERENTIAL 0 - 1 - 2
L Cut-off 0 - 1 - 2
M Amnesia to Cut-off 0 - 1 - 2
N No Test ✓
O Floating Sensation 0 - 1 - 2
P GRADE 0 - 1 - 2 - 3 - 4 - 5

______ Increment
______ Soft
Minutes 9 Decrement X

Figure 3 (*Continued*)

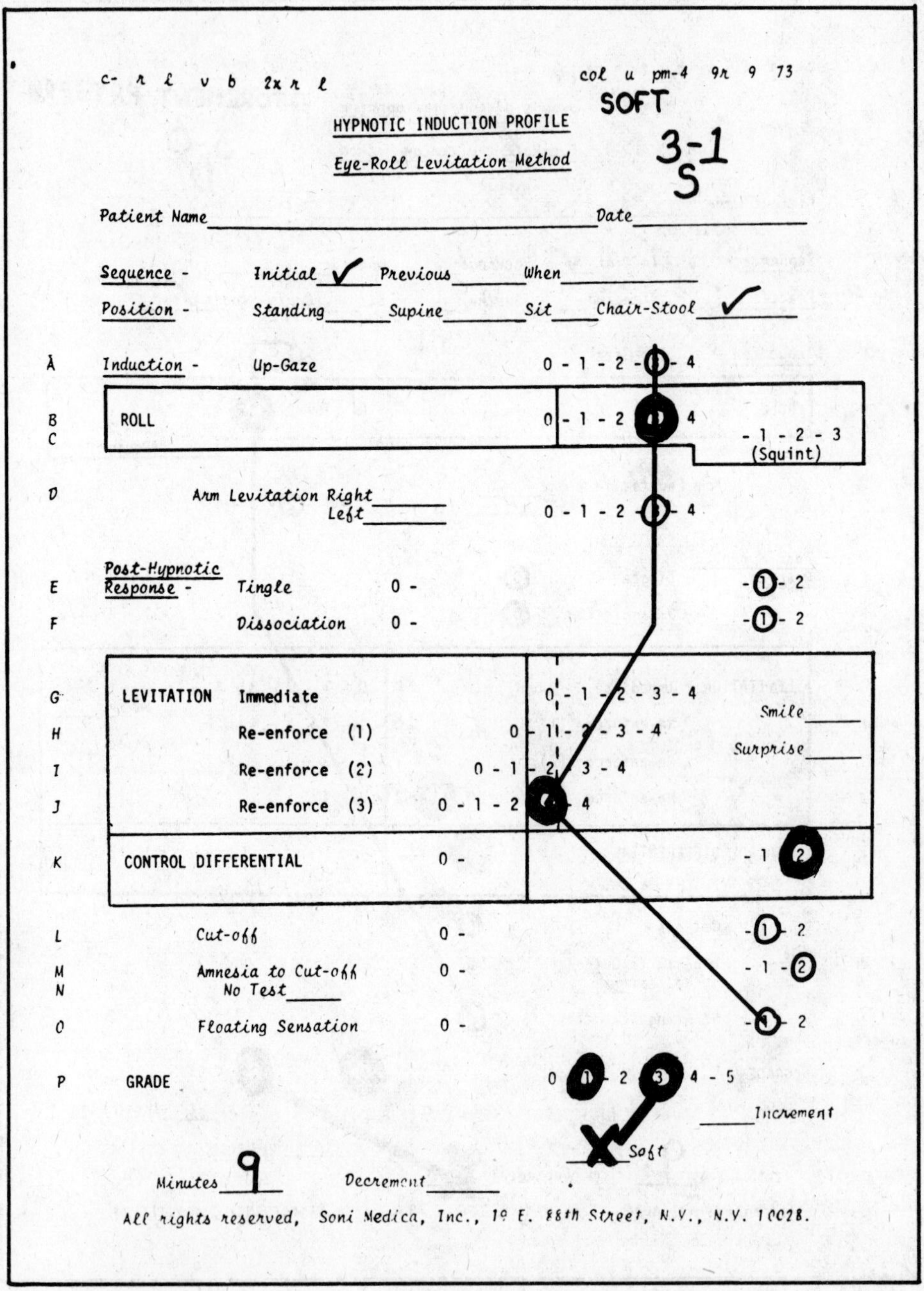

c- r l v b 2x r l   col u pm-4 9r 9 73
                                                       SOFT
                        HYPNOTIC INDUCTION PROFILE   3-1
                        Eye-Roll Levitation Method   S

        Patient Name_____ Date_____

        Sequence -   Initial ✓ Previous_____ When_____
        Position -   Standing____ Supine_____ Sit____ Chair-Stool ✓

A   Induction -   Up-Gaze   0 - 1 - 2 -③- 4

B   ROLL   0 - 1 - 2 -③- 4
C   - 1 - 2 - 3
                                                                (Squint)

D   Arm Levitation Right_____
                          Left_____   0 - 1 - 2 -①- 4

     Post-Hypnotic
E   Response -   Tingle   0 -   -①- 2
F   Dissociation 0 -   -①- 2

G   LEVITATION Immediate   0 - 1 - 2 - 3 - 4   Smile_____
H   Re-enforce (1)   0 - 1 - 2 - 3 - 4   Surprise_____
I   Re-enforce (2)   0 - 1 - 2 - 3 - 4
J   Re-enforce (3) 0 - 1 - 2 -③- 4

K   CONTROL DIFFERENTIAL   0 -   - 1 -②

L   Cut-off   0 -   -①- 2
M   Amnesia to Cut-off 0 -   - 1 -②
N   No Test_____
O   Floating Sensation 0 -   -①- 2

P   GRADE   0 -①- 2 -③- 4 - 5
                                                    _____Increment
                                        ✗   Soft

        Minutes 9   Decrement_____   .

Figure 3   (Continued)

348

"nonintact" pattern, indicates a break in the ribbon of attentive concentration which means, in effect, zero hypnotizability. A shift to the left in procedures G–J (posthypnotic arm levitation) with a positive K (control differential) indicates a soft pattern. This signifies that the ribbon of attentive concentration is intact, but not quite as intense as with those patients who have intact profiles.

INTERTESTER RELIABILITY

A reliability evaluation was done at the out-patient department of the Payne Whitney Clinic, Cornell Medical School, with the senior author and J. Haber, M.D., who was recently trained in the use of the HIP. The testers independently completed profiles on the same 53 patients. The raters had no knowledge of each other's evaluations and the order of the induction was systematically varied to eliminate biasing effects. Comparison of their scores provided the following table:

Grade A (H.S.)

Grade B (J.H.)	Hypnotizable	Not hypnotizable	Total
Agree	20	21	41
Disagree	6	6	12
Total	26	27	53

The proportion of agreement is

$$P = \frac{41}{53} = 0.77.$$

A fairly stringent correction statistic, κ, was used to adjust the observed agreement by the amount of agreement to be expected by chance alone. The possible values of κ cover a range from -1, complete disagreement, to $+1$, perfect agreement; a value of 0.00 indicates agreement neither better nor worse than chance. Kappa values assessing the agreement between well-trained clinicians in the diagnosis of mental disorders usually fall between 0.50 and 0.60. For this study, the corrected degree of agreement is $\kappa = 0.55$.[17]

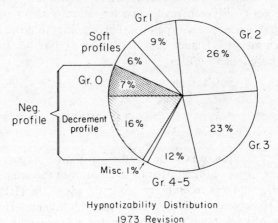

HYPNOTIZABILITY DISTRIBUTION
2000 CONSECUTIVE THERAPY CASES

Hypnotizability Distribution
1973 Revision

Figure 4.   Hypnotizability distribution.

HYPNOTIC DISTRIBUTION

Using this method of induction and grading, the hypnotizability distribution of 2000 consecutive therapy cases is shown in Figure 4.

This distribution of hypnotic capacity scores generally follows those reported by other experimenters, such as Hilgard, et al., and Lang and Lazovik; as such it is a rough indicator of intertest consistency.[10, 11] More rigid intertest correlation studies are in progress and the results will be published in the near future.

CORRELATIONS BETWEEN HYPNOTIC INDUCTION
PROFILE SCORES AND CLINICAL DIAGNOSIS

Although there has been much speculation concerning the relationship between personality and hypnosis, the findings have been conflicting.[2-9, 19] The hypothesis that differences in hypnotizability are related to differences among individuals' sociability, extroversion, or neuroticism has not been confirmed. Our focus has been on investigating the relationship between actual clinical pathology as assessed by independent, full scale psychological testing, and our method of induction.

THE PATIENT GROUP

A total of 110 patients, referred to our office for evaluation and psychotherapy, participated in the study. As part of our evaluation, the HIP was administered in the first interview. Shortly thereafter the patients were sent for full scale psychological testing, usually consisting of the Wechsler Adult Intelligence Scale, Figure Drawings, Sentence Completion, Bender Visual Motor Gestalt, Rorschach, and Thematic Apperception Test. Instructions to the patient consisted simply of advising him to call a consulting psychologist to request a "personality exploration." There was no communication between the referring physician and psychologist prior to the final psychological report. Of the total of 110 patients originally studied, 87 were evaluated by one psychologist, 18 by a second psychologist, and five patients, by five other psychologists.

Of the original 110 patients, only 105 were used for this analysis; five patients could not be graded clearly and were therefore not included in the study. Two of these had HIP's which were so internally contradictory that it was impossible to score them in any meaningful way. The remaining persons who were excluded presented such a confusing test pattern to the psychological evaluator that no definitive psychological statement concerning mental health–illness could be made. Of the 63 males and 42 females, 57 were married, 32 were single, and the remaining 16 were divorced, widowed, or separated. There was an inordinately high percentage of subjects with advanced education; 29 persons had completed graduate school, 36 were college graduates, and 19 had at least some college education. Fifty-five subjects were between the ages of 26 to 40, and 33 were over 40 years old. The remaining 17 subjects were under 26 years of age. Since this is a retrospective study, the patients were not aware that they were or would become part of a study group, and the implication both for therapist and patient was that psychological testing was part of the diagnostic survey and would be of benefit in the psychotherapeutic process.

PSYCHOLOGICAL TEST RATING

A five point clinical distribution was established, covering the continuum from healthy to obviously psychotic. The psychological reports were evaluated in terms of these five categories and the patients were appropriately distributed. This was done by either one of two authors (HS or AAB) who at the time of the assessment of the clinical categories was not aware of the patient's HIP grade.

TABLE 1.   DISTRIBUTION INTO FIVE CLINICAL
CATEGORIES

Category	Description	Number
A	Healthy	10
B	Moderate neurosis	31
C	Severe neurosis	22
D	Probable psychosis, Severe character disorder, depression, or latent schizophrenia	31
E	Obvious psychosis	11
Total		105

TABLE 2.   DECREMENT AND SOFT PATTERN
BY CLINICAL STATUS

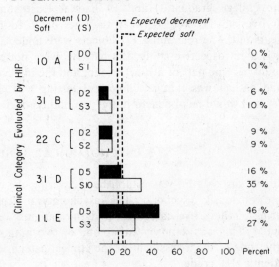

Table 1 presents the distribution across the five clinical categories of the 105 subjects.

Within each clinical category the distribution of the patients' HIP grades were computed and are presented in Table 2.

RESULTS

If there were no association between clinical status and the patients' HIP the expected HIP distribution for each clinical group would be 66% intact, 18% soft, 15% decrement, and 1% zero. If there were an association between the two indices we would expect a shift in the distribution, with either an increase or decrease in intact profiles along the continuum and a reverse shift in the decrement profiles, depending on whether hypnotizability was positively or negatively associated with clinical status. The data support the hypothesis that hypnotizability is positively correlated with nonpsychotic character structures and that decrement HIP's indicate a shift toward more severe psychosis. None of the healthy patients and only 6% of the moderately neurotic patients have clearly nonintact profiles. For the severely neurotic (but not psychotic) patients, the proportion is 10% decrement and 10% soft. For the borderline psychotic group the proportion of decrement profiles is 16%, with 32% soft. Finally for the severely psychotic group the proportion with a decrement profile jumps to 41%, with 27% soft. This shift from what would be expected if the null hypothesis were valid is highly significant (chi square $= 24.95$, $df = 8$, $p < .01$.)

DISCUSSION

The findings of the present study suggest that severe psychopathology, to the degree that it is clinically expressed, is strongly correlated with no capacity for hypnosis. Conversely, *hypnotic capacity implies reasonably good, nonpsychotic, mental health.* This contradicts the usual mythology that only "weak-minded" people are hypnotizable, and "healthy" people are not "susceptible."

Mitchell, in a series of experiments using the Harvard Group Scale of Hypnotic Susceptibility, investigated the relation between hypnotic "susceptibility" and the ability to resist distraction.[*][12] His results suggest that

---

* It is unfortunate how the old terminology still lingers. Concepts like "susceptibility" reflect the unfortunate biases of the traditional analytic and folk assumptions concerning hypnosis. They imply that hypnotizability is a vulnerability, or a weakness that mars the health or integrity of the person. Our study challenges such inferences. A more appropriate term would be hypnotic "capacity."

hypnotic capacity increases the establishment of optimal sympathetic and psychomotor means for overriding effects of exposure to irrelevant, unexpected stimuli. He proposes that the hypnotic subject does not ignore distracting stimuli, instead he seems to render them ineffectual as interfering with goal achievement.

Our definition of hypnosis—that it is a capacity for optimal, attentive, responsive concentration, inherent in the subject and tapped by the operator—is supported by the results of this study and Mitchell's work. The statistically significant gradient of increasing psychopathology with an increasing percentage of nonhypnotizable patients (decrement patterns) seems to imply that seriously disturbed patients have lost this capacity for peak concentration necessary for hypnosis. Shakow in his work demonstrated that the schizophrenic disturbance is characterized by an inability to exercise selective perception; schizophrenics do not differentiate between central and peripheral input and are therefore unable to exercise focused concentration.[13] In other words, the psychotic patient struggling with distracting internal and external stimuli is unable to set aside these stimuli sufficiently to focus his attentive concentration to shift into an altered state of awareness commonly called hypnosis.

The strong agreement between clinical categories and hypnotizability further suggests that this 5 to 10 minute evaluation of trance capacity can be of great merit in evaluating the degree of pathology and would make a worthwhile and significant contribution when used as a diagnostic tool or as part of a diagnostic test battery.

While this research project emphasizes the statistical relationship between intactness and nonintactness of the HIP and the mental health-illness continuum, it does not explore the relationship between HIP grades 1 to 5 and the mental health status of nonpsychotic patients. Our studies of this patient group and clinical observations of other patient groups lead us to suspect that this relationship is worth investigating. Data are now being gathered to evaluate it.

The results of this initial study indicate that the HIP is a quick, practical, clinical test for hypnotizability which can help clarify psychiatric diagnosis and facilitate decisions for appropriate treatment strategies.

SUMMARY

A new, brief, clinically appropriate test for hypnotizability, the Hypnotic Induction Profile, has been presented. Using this profile measurement the distribution of hypnotizability in a 2000 consecutive patient population was found to parallel the distribution of hypnotizability as determined by other experimenters using more time consuming scales. A study of a consecutive 105 patient sample suggests that this new measurement can elicit data about the mental health–illness status of a given patient. The major conclusion contradicts the common misconception that hypnotizability necessarily indicates psychological-emotional fragility; rather, capacity for trance concentration indicates a high probability of relative mental health.

Excerpts from the Psychological Reports Typifying Each Category

---

A: "Personality is essentially healthy and well-formed."

A: "Subject is a creative, dynamic individual capable of deep affection for others and insightful self-acceptance."

A: "She has free access to her feelings and uses her imagination in a free and creative way."

B: "Depressive reaction of middle age in a dependent, immature woman."

B: "Ideation is good and reality-testing skills seem to be of a psychoneurotic nature."

B: "She is an obsessively-oriented woman."

C: "Patient emerges as a constricted personality with a very high level of anxiety."

C: "An extremely obsessionally organized young woman . . . who is trying to cast *all* emotional feeling and expression aside."

C: "This is a picture of a depressive personality with marked anxiety features."

D: "Indications of incipient problems of reality-testing, thinking processes, and judgement."

D: "General picture resembles that of a probable schizophrenic process."

D: "Clinical impression is of a markedly schizoid, possibly schizophrenic person."

E: "This is a manic-depressive syndrome with pathology of a psychotic nature."

E: "She is maintaining a precarious hold on reality, and the picture points to a diagnosis of schizophrenia."

E: "He is actually psychotic at this time."

REFERENCES

1. Barber, T. X.: Measuring "hypnotic-like" suggestibility with and without "hypnotic induction"; Psychometric properties, Barber suggestibility scale (BSS). *Psychol. Rep.,* Mono. Suppl.: 3-V16, 1965.

2. Barber, T. X. and Calverley, D. S.: Hypnotizability, suggestibility, and personality: III. A study using teachers' ratings of children's characteristics. *J. Psychol* 57:275–280, 1964.

3. Davis, L. W. and Husband, R. W.: A study of hypnotic susceptibility in relation to personality traits. *J. Abnorm. Soc. Psychol.* 26:175–182, 1931.

4. Dorcus, R. M.: Fallacies in predictions of susceptibility to hypnosis based upon personality characteristics. *Am. J. Clin. Hypnosis* **5**:163–170, 1963.

5. Eysenck, H. J.: Suggestibility and hysteria. *J. Neurol. Psychiatr.* **6**:22–31, 1943.

6. Eysenck, H. J.: States of high suggestibility and the neuroses. *Am. J. Psychol.* **57**:406–411, 1944.

7. Heilizer, R. An exploration of the relationship between hypnotizability and anxiety and/or neuroticism. *J. Consult. Psychol.* **24**:432–436, 1960.

8. Hilgard, E. R. and Bentler, P. M.: Predicting hypnotizability from the Maudsley personality inventory. *Brit. J. Psychol.* **54**:63–69, 1963.

9. Hilgard, E. R. and Lauer, L. W.: Lack of correlation between the California psychological inventory and hypnotic susceptibility. *J. Consult. Psychol.* **26**:331–335, 1962.

10. Hilgard, E. R., Weitzenhoffer, A. M., Landes, J., and Moore, R. K.: The distribution of susceptibility to hypnosis in a student population: A study using the Stanford hypnotic susceptibility scale. *Psychol. Mono.*, 1961, 75 (whole No. 512).

11. Lang, P. J. and Lazovik, A. D.: Personality and hypnotic susceptibility. *J. Consult Psychol.* **26**:317–322, 1962.

12. Michell, M. B.: Hypnotizability and distractibility. *Am. J. Clin. Hypnosis* **13**(1):35–45, 1970.

13. Shakow, D.: Segmental set A theory of the formal psychological deficit in schizophrenia. *Arch. Gen. Psychiatr.* **6**:1–17, January 1962.

14. Shor, R. E. and Orne, E. C.: *The Harvard Group Scale of Hypnotic Susceptibility, Form A.* Consulting Psychologists Press, Palo Alto, Calif., 1962.

15. Spiegel, H. An eye roll test for hypnotizability. *Am. J. Clin. Hypnosis:* July 1972.

16. Spiegel, H. *Manual for Hypnotic Induction Profile*, Soni Medica, New York, 1973.

17. Spiegel, H.: *Hypnotic Induction Profile*, in preparation, 1973.

18. Weitzenhoffer, A. M. and Hilgard, E. R.: *Stanford Hypnotic Susceptibility Scale*, Conculting Psychologists, Palo Alto, Calif., 1959.

19. Weitzenhoffer, A. M. and Weitzenhoffer, G. B.: Personality and hypnotic susceptibility. *Am. J. Clin. Hypnosis* **1**:79–82, 1958.

CHAPTER SEVENTEEN

RECENT STUDIES CONCERNING PSYCHOSOMATIC SYMPTOM FORMATION IN OBSTETRICS AND GYNECOLOGY

HANS MOLINSKI

D oes present-day psychosomatic medicine, as far as it is psychoanalytically oriented, still fit into the traditional body of medical theory and practice? And why is it that exactly psychoanalysis, which contributed so much to the early development of psychosomatic medicine, has contributed increasingly less in recent decades? To answer these questions, this discussion of psychosomatics in obstetrics and gynecology focuses on the description of the different pathways of psychosomatic symptom formation.

PSYCHOSOMATIC MEDICINE IN LIGHT OF EGO- AND ID-PSYCHOLOGY

In the opinion of this author, psychosomatic medicine has been put at a disadvantage by the shift of emphasis that has taken place in the conceptual framework of psychoanalysis—a shift, however, that has brought about progress in other areas of application. In psychoanalysis, things can always be viewed from two sides, from the side of the instincts and from the side of the ego.

Freudian psychology benefited so greatly the gradual development of psychosomatic medicine because of its biological and instinctual orientation. Terms like psychogenic or psychosomatic awaken easily the misleading impression that the human being consists. of two distinct opposites, a soul on the one hand and a body on the other. In reality, psychoanalytically oriented psychosomatic medicine overcomes such a division through its central concept—the impulse. The impulse in contradistinction to the instinct is no longer an abstraction but a phenomenon that can be empirically grasped. The impulse has a somatic aspect, and it thus has a legitimate place in physiology and somatic medicine. The impulse, however, also has a psychological aspect. This is why psychotherapy is possible; that is, the concept of the impulse unifies physiology and psychology. In the case of repression, the impulse, while still operative in a hidden fashion, is detached from conscious experience. The repressed impulse therefore cannot be dealt with either through gratification or renunciation, but can find an outlet in certain impulse rudiments. In the psychoneurotic symptom, we are dealing with the breakthrough of the mental aspect of the repressed impulse. The physiological aspect of the repressed impulse may manifest itself, in a "psychogenic" physical symptom, for example, in a secretion, or in a muscular spasm. It was with the help of such notions that authors like Fr. Alexander[1] or H. Schultz-Hencke[2] were able to explore so successfully psychosomatic symptoms.

The impulses seeking outlets produce a realm of so-called derivatives: phantasies, mental images, reminiscences, ideas, and conceptions. Here, the controlling and regulating functions of the ego come into play. Viewed from the angle of the driving forces, the differences between various individuals are comparatively small. In fact, there are such recurrent similarities that the investigating physician can become bored with them. In the realm of the derivatives, however, there is variety and diversity. Here we find the uniqueness of each individual. The psychoanalyst is generally more interested in the personal, in individuality; and psychoanalysis has increasingly turned to ego-psychology and increasingly away from id-psychology. The more the interest of the analyst focuses on the ego, however, the less it focuses on the id, the instincts.

Psychoanalytic ego-psychology has been very fruitful, especially in the realm of psychiatry proper, that is, in the understanding and treatment of mental—neurotic and psychotic—symptoms and also in the realm of the social sciences. When it comes to grasping the whole of an individual's personality and even more so when it is a question of practical psychoanalysis as a treatment procedure, then the id-psychology is insufficient. Yet it is to the disadvantage of the understanding of psychosomatic symptoms if ego-psychology is overemphasized at the expense of id-psychology.

In discussing the pathways of psychosomatic symptom formation, it will be a central concern to show that both sides involved—medicine and psychoanalysis—will benefit if impulse and biology are given their proper emphasis in the conceptual framework. Since the majority of gynecological symptoms can be dealt with here only summarily, the usefulness of such impulse-oriented thinking shall at first be demonstrated by going into the details of a recent study on hyperemesis gravidarum and related symptoms[3] that lead to a new understanding of the psychology and psychosomatics of pregnancy and childbirth.

ORAL AGGRESSIVE SYMPTOMATOLOGY IN PREGNANCY AND CHILDBIRTH

Stimulation of Oral Impulses in Pregnancy

Healthy expectant mothers experience normal psychic changes during pregnancy, among others an increase of oral impulses. There are those women, for example, who suddenly show a strong bent for purchasing things for baby and the home. Such a stimulation of oral impulses during pregnancy is also well known in the colloquial idiom. There is that old and, of course, unfounded saying that as soon as a woman is pregnant, she should eat twice as much—one portion for the baby and one for herself. In fact, the mother-to-be tends to feel that now she is entitled to indulge herself.

To a certain extent, purely biological factors may play a role in this, since the body makes specific alimentary demands during pregnancy. But psychological factors play a much greater role as evidenced by the deliberate restraint many expectant mothers must exercise to avoid eating more than nature requires.

One of the normal psychological changes in pregnancy is the intensification of maternal emotions—among others, the need to give the child tenderness, to nourish it, to care for it. Thus one of the aspects of motherhood is the mother's participation in the oral needs of the child, which entails a mobilization of her own oral needs and impulses in the same way as a cook whets her own appetite when she prepares a meal with loving care.

A Study of Patients with Hyperemesis Gravidarum and Related Symptoms

A stimulation of oral impulses is also reflected by the frequency of the numerous symptoms in pregnancy that are a manifestion of repressed oral and aggressive impulses. Many pregnant women suffer from symptoms of the upper alimentary tract; hypersalivation, hyperemesis gravidarum, heartburn, excessive appetite leading to inordinate weight gain. Included here are the group of morbid cravings or aversions to particular foods. Related also are cases of functional rigidity of the cervix during childbirth, some depressions post partum, and cleptomania during pregnancy.

Observations and findings related to the foregoing symptoms were derived from 7 years full time psychiatric practice at Duesseldorf University's gynecological department. About 40 patients with hyperemesis gravidarum underwent intensive though short-term psychotherapy during the acute phase of the illness. A greater number of patients with hyperemesis gravidarum were observed while less intensive psychiatric care was given. In a number of cases, women with hyperemesis gravidarum were observed over an extended period of psychoanalytically oriented psychotherapy.

Personality Structure in Hyperemesis Gravidarum

At the outset, it was observed that all women with hyperemesis gravidarum had a well-defined personality structure. The term personality structure, often used so ambiguously, here refers only to habitual pathological ways of dealing with the impulse, that is, to inhibitions and attitudes and their elaborations. This term is not intended to conceptualize the entire diversity of an individual's personality. This personality structure, in the case of women with hyperemesis gravidarum, revolves around a dual set of inhibitions: first in the oral sphere and second in that of aggressive experience and behavior.

These women were orally inhibited; that is, oral impulses manifest themselves inadequately. Food and money, for example, seemed of little concern to them, at least in their conscious experience. Above all, such women are unable to experience satisfaction and pleasure from the good things in life. The aggressive inhibitions make them experience and handle their anger in a largely inadequate way. They lack the ability to assert themselves, and they shrink from any activity of their own that might be required in the pursuit of their affairs. Being unable to actively approach things—the English word aggression is derived from Latin adgredi, which means to step towards, to approach, to attack—means that they are inhibited in the constructive as well as destructive aspects of aggressivity.

But, as is always true of repressions, some rudimentary impulses remain in operation despite the inhibitions which could be designated, figuratively speaking, as undercurrent-effects of the repressed. That is, the personality structure of the women to be discussed here is not only characterized by voids in the sphere of oral and aggressive experience and behavior that were just mentioned. The remaining oral and aggressive impulses which continue to be effective in spite of the inhibitions manifest themselves in rigid behavior patterns that can be called attitudes. This term implies that such behavior patterns are not adjusted to reality and that they cannot be modified by volition.

In view of their oral inhibitions, these women feel unentitled to whatever good things are to be had in this world; they have an *attitude of modesty*. The inability to experience consciously wishes and desires goes along with immense and unrealistic expectations which are unknown to the women themselves. These expectations, combined with the inability to exert personal activity in the pursuit of their wishes, leads to an *attitude of passive expectation*. This attitude is combined with a compulsive *self-sacrificing attitude*, which, of course, is entirely different from a healthy voluntary readiness to make sacrifices in the interest of the baby. The attitude of passive expectation may turn into a *demanding attitude*; that is, despite their seeming modesty, these women constantly put forward claims, although in an unconscious and rather indirect manner. Because their surreptitious demands are never met, they also tend to have a *reproachful attitude*.

Oral inhibitions may find a still different sort of elaboration: they may result in greed and haste, or in seizing money and property, which, however, is not very common in hyperemesis. This form of oral attitude is more typically found in some of the other symptoms mentioned above. In women with hyperemesis, the inhibitions and the corresponding voids in the conscious experience outweigh by far the clandestine undercurrent-effects of the repressed impulses.

The Child as an Oral Competitor

Women with the smoldering feeling of being left empty-handed, who cannot assert themselves, are prone to develop a specific set of anxieties and conflicts during pregnancy and childbirth.

It is often overlooked that despite all the happiness of a new mother, there is always an inescapable and very real conflict of interests between the mother and the child. The child costs attention, energy, time, and money, so that there is less left over for the mother. The child must be perceived as and actually is an oral competitor. A healthy mother has a realistic appreciation of the extent of the child's demands, and she is able and willing to achieve a compromise, seeing to it that neither party, neither she nor the baby, comes off too badly.

This compromise is not possible for the orally inhibited mother-to-be. In her conscious experience, she does not seem to perceive the child's oral demands, and, simultaneously, she has a subtle and exaggerated notion of the wants and rights of the child, and this subconsciously disturbs her. In her conscious experience, she seems to be an utterly unselfish mother, thinking of nothing but the child's welfare. Subconsciously, she is all the more disturbed by the vision of an all-devouring oral competitor.

Incidentally, this conflict between the interests of the mother and the interests of the child is the reason why contraceptive devices so frequently lead to the fear of carcinoma, to the fear of being devoured from within. The fear of carcinoma is encountered with all sorts of contraceptive devices, not only with the new oral contraceptives; and not a few women even fear that carcinoma can be caused or transmitted by unprotected sexual intercourse.

Symptom Formation in Hyperemesis Gravidarum

The woman who experiences the fetus as an all-devouring oral competitor anticipates a frustration of her own needs. This leads to a stimulation of her own oral needs, far exceeding the activation of oral impulses normally found at the beginning of pregnancy. Such a woman is flooded by oral impulses and their concomitant physiology. But since it is a question of inhibited impulses, neither the experience nor the physiology are carried out to their conclusion. Rather we have the explanation for the numerous oral symptoms in pregnancy: overeating, heartburn, hypersalivation, pregnancy cravings. If the defense exceeds the mobilization of oral impulses, there are symptoms like food aversions or loss of appetite.

The anticipation of oral frustration also results in a generally irritable mood. The transference situation reveals that the vomiting of gastric content is correlated to anger. For, if during the visit to the office, the manifestations of oral impulses exceed the manifestations of residual anger, she is likely to have hypersalivation. If, on the other hand, the manifestations of subdued anger exceed her surreptitious quests and demands, she is likely to vomit gastric content or to feel pressure in the stomach. The question arises whether anger does not lead to a contraction of the stomach and/or duodenum which may be the stimulus that triggers vomiting of gastric content.

To sum up what has been said so far: Hyperemesis gravidarum is characterized by a distinct personality structure; which in pregnancy leads to a specific conflict; which in turn leads to the mobilization of oral and aggressive impulses. The two symptoms of hypersalivation and of vomiting of gastric content are the physiological correlates of oral and aggressive impulses which, although mobilized, are not carried out to their conclusion.

Hyperemesis gravidarum is usually conceived as an essentially hysterical phenomenon, as a somatic expression of the wish to get rid of the fetus by vomiting it out, an expression of the wish to terminate the pregnancy by the same route that, in the woman's imagination, it came about. No dreams or other unconscious material corroborating this concept was observed in this study. Rather, dreams of women with hyperemesis gravidarum typically express feelings of deprivation and the yearning for the good mother.

Anger during Childbirth and Rigidity of the Cervix Uteri

In an initially entirely different project, a study was made of functional disturbances of childbirth.[3] To start with, physically healthy women who had had difficult deliveries were merely subjected to exploration after the event. But it soon appeared advisable to draw conclusions not only from the case histories and retrospective accounts given by the patients themselves, but also from the observation during practical obstetrical work in the delivery room, where it was possible to directly observe the somatic process of childbirth and the accompanying experience.

A moderate amount of anger during childbirth in a mature woman does not lead to rigidity of the cervix and dystocia, but it rather furthers the physiology of childbirth. The anger in a woman who is inhibited in the sphere of aggressive experience, once aroused, cannot develop into full consciousness; hence her anger cannot be acted upon and is not released. Functional rigidity of the cervix is a correlate to such anger that is in operation and that is subdued, both at the same time. In addition to the inhibitions in the sphere of aggressive experience, one subgroup of women with functional rigidity of the cervix is also orally inhibited. This group then is similar in personality structure to the women with hyperemesis gravidarum. In her pregnancy, the woman with hyperemesis gravidarum wishfully thinks of the image of the good mother. But in the delivery room, she feels deserted by this image. Her behavior during labor reveals that she now stays under the influence of the image of the bad mother and she gets angry.

Thus purely psychological observations led to the assumption that both conditions—hyperemesis gravidarum and functional rigidity of the cervix— tend to occur in one and the same individual, an assumption that was statistically confirmed by an evaluation of the hospital charts from former years.[3, 4]

There was no systematic study of the other symptoms mentioned above: overeating and excessive weight gain; cleptomania in pregnancy; food cravings and food aversions; heartburn. But the treatment of many such patients over those years gave the impression that in those symptoms, too, there is a similar pattern of personality structure, conflict and symptom formation. This holds particularly true for a group of severe depressions post partum. The difference between the symptoms can be explained by certain changes of emphasis in what are otherwise similar constellations of personality structure, conflict and inhibited impulse; this was exemplified by the slight difference between the two types of hyperemesis gravidarum— predominant hypersalivation or predominant vomiting of gastric content.

Physiological, Psychological, and Sociocultural Factors in the Causation of Hyperemesis Gravidarum

This concept of hyperemesis gravidarum explains why this disease occurs in some countries much more frequently than in others although the bio- logical basis in the form of predisposing metabolic alterations is the same everywhere. These metabolic changes alone, however, usually do not suffice to bring about actual hyperemesis. Under the living conditions of certain aboriginal cultures where the role, possessions, and opportunities of women are extremely limited, the new baby may be more of an asset rather than an oral competitor. Since her opportunities are restricted anyway, she experiences no further restrictions by a new child. But as soon as she moves from such an environment into town, into the conditions of urban-in- dustrial society, she may well develop hyperemesis gravidarum.

Mirsky[5] has pointed out that peptic ulcer only develops if three sets of factors come together: biological predisposition, personality factors, and certain sociocultural conditions. The same holds true for hyperemesis gravidarum.

In conclusion, it should be mentioned that the uniformity and specificity described in this paper are to be found only if the impulses and their mode of being dealt with are considered, that is, on a level of high abstraction; whereas on the level of the mental derivatives as dealt with in actual psychotherapy, the experience of women with hyperemesis gravidarum shows a wide range of individual differences.

PATHWAYS OF SYMPTOM FORMATION IN PSYCHOSOMATIC SYMPTOMS IN OBSTETRICS AND GYNECOLOGY

From the standpoint of the pathways of symptom formation, psychogenic physical symptoms have long been subdivided into organ neuroses and conversion hysteria. Yet other pathways of psychosomatic symptom formation have to be considered as well.

Organ Neuroses

In organ neuroses, O. Fenichel[6] differentiates three different pathogenic routes. In the case of the *affect equivalent*, the symptom consists of the physiologic correlate of the affect or impulse returning from the repression. The symptoms above during pregnancy and childbirth were explained in this way. Many other psychogenic symptoms in gynecology are similarly manifestations of disturbed motility or secretion. For example, dyspareunia can be due to muscular spasms with or without the full syndrome of vaginism. Other cases of dyspareunia are due to a lack of lubrication, whereas the oversecretion in vaginal discharge can be the physiological correlate of inhibited though operative sexual impulses. Muscular spasms due to fear and, in other cases, due to anger, go by various names such as pelvipathia, spastica, and pseudoadnexitis. Various forms of psychogenic infertility belong here.

To the extent that the impulse, though operative, remains repressed (i.e., insofar as it finds no physical outlet although it is in operation), it leads to a *buildup of excitation*, to neural and chemical alterations. A great many of the more unspecific and vague psychosomatic symptoms that never have found an adequate description seem to belong here. Some aspects of what was formerly called actual neurosis, neurasthenia, and traumatic neurosis, have been attributed to the state of being "dammed-up." Yet there is one more special symptom in obstetrics that needs to be mentioned here. In childbirth, functional rigidity of the cervix uteri develops when anger in a woman with corresponding inhibitions does not find an outlet, while adequate expression of an angry mood rather furthers the softening of the cervix.[3]

The somatic effects of the so-called *unconscious attitudes* form a third subdivision of organ neuroses. An unconscious conflict can lead to habitual innervations of striated or unstriated musculature or to secretions. These functional disturbances alone are directly psychogenic. Morphologic changes which occur as a result can no longer be characterized as directly psychogenic. This is the way in which the classical psychosomatic diseases come about, for example peptic ulcer or bronchial asthma. Based on studies of these illnesses, one spoke earlier of a psychosomatic disease when a morphologic change was present in which psychic factors played a decisive role. Psychosomatic diseases in this sense do not exist in gynecology. Anorexia nervosa and vulvar excema form perhaps an exception.

Conversion Hysteria

In conversion hysteria, too, there are physical symptoms, symptoms at least that the patient takes to be physical. But they come about in an entirely different way. Comparable to the pantomimic expression of an idea, in conversion hysteria the body acts out an idea graphically, the idea being unconscious. For example, the patient who cannot walk or stand may be acting out the idea that she is unable to stand on her own two feet. We know from hypnosis and autogenic training that even the activity of the vasal musculature can be influenced by the ideas which are at work at any given time. While the symptom of organ neurosis is determined by the physiological correlate of the impulse, the symptom in conversion hysteria is determined by the idea connected with the impulse. The conversion symptom thus has a meaning which in the course of psychotherapy can be interpreted. In organ neurosis, by contrast, the symptom as such has no meaning; that is, not the symptom but the underlying conflict alone can be interpreted. The knowledge of the pathogenesis of a psychosomatic symptom thus has practical therapeutic consequences.

In the first decades of psychosomatic research and as some authors still contend today, gynecological symptoms of psychogenic origin were usually considered to be of conversion hysteria nature. Actually, based on my own experience at least, obstetrical and gynecological symptoms are relatively seldom of a hysterical nature. Repressed phantasies seeking expression can of course superimpose themselves on any preexisting physical symptom, regardless whether of somatic or psychogenic origin, thus adding to this physical symptom a certain conversion hysteric component. This should not cause the observer to overlook the altogether different basic pathogenesis of the symptom in question. In gynecology, above all, all sorts of strange sensations, paraesthesias, and psychogenic pains can be, but need not be, a physical representation of unconscious phantasies.

Hypochondriasis and Depressive Symptoms

Hypochondriacal symptoms and complaints are much more frequent in gynecology; as a matter of fact they are rather widespread and constitute a major diagnostic and therapeutic problem. Again these are mainly all sorts of strange or vague sensations and pains, along with worries about health and misgivings. In the patient's view and from the viewpoint of medical practice, it is of little importance that, theoretically speaking, we are not dealing here with true physical symptoms or gynecological disease. As in hysterical symptoms, these women still are gynecological patients, quite simply because they consider themselves such and go to see the gynecologist.

Narcissistic traits are the decisive findings in prehistory and personality structure. To compensate for hurt and wounded self-esteem, they overinvest in and overvalue their body. As in hysteria, in hypochondriases we have a mental rather than a true physical symptom. But unlike hysteria, the salient feature in symptom formation is not the direct return of the repressed impulse but an ego-activity in the service of compensation, namely a shift in the focus of attention.

Finally, many seemingly gynecological patients are cases of masked depressions. Depressive patients quite frequently experience their discomfort physically rather than mentally. In the case of physical symptoms in depression, the course of symptom formation is still quite obscure.

There seem to be two motives why such "nervous" (as they are often called) patients with hysterical, hypochondriacal, or depressive symptoms look up precisely the gynecologist. Behind the conviction that their complaints are of a gynecological nature, they may have the faint awareness of a hidden sexual etiology. In other cases, they view the gynecologist as a lawyer for all female concerns. All too often, the medical profession cannot do justice to the large number of such nervous patients: of their own, they do not go to see the psychiatrist, and the pure somaticist feels that he is not up to coping with them.

Psychosomatic Symptoms as Direct Effects of the Neurotic Conflict

In contrast to the organ neurotic and hysterical symptoms, there are wholly different symptoms which do not originate from the return of the repressed. Rather, these physical symptoms are direct results of the neurotic conflict. They can arise in three different ways.

The *inhibition of a function* as such can amount to a symptom. For example, frigidity, the loss of genital impulses, and anorgasmy are direct results of the neurotic conflict causing the inhibition. This statement of course, refers only to the pathogenesis of the symptoms themselves, and not the whole clinical picture of frigidity.

A *physiological switching* can occur as a different direct effect of the neurotic conflict. For example, if the organism is exposed to greater physical or psychic stress than it can cope with—an energetic consideration—the pituitary can switch from the production of gonadotropin to the predominant production of ACTH. In the ensuing stress amenorrhoea, the function in the service of preserving the life of the individual temporarily takes preference over the functions of propagation. A number of other endocrine disturbances of psychogenic origin are to be explained accordingly. Here the individual symptom no longer represents the return of a specific repressed impulse; it is not a meaningful expression of a repressed phantasy nor is it the physiologic correlate of a repressed impulse. Rather, it is the energetic factor that plays the decisive role in the pathogenesis. Again, the knowledge of the pathogenetic pathway helps us in understanding and treating the individual patient. For we now understand why in endocrine disturbances of psychogenic origin, in contrast to many of the above conditions, no trace of specificity can be found in regard to prehistory, personality structure, underlying conflict, impulse leading to symptom formation.

Similar considerations apply to a *diminishment in the power of resistance*, a further direct result of the neurotic conflict. Any loss of energy can diminish an individual's power of resistance against infection. Psychic conflicts, however, can have an exceptionally exhausting effect, as is easily recognized by observing neurotic patients. This is why even gynecologic infections, among others in the area of the adnexa, have to be considered in discussing psychosomatic symptomatology. As we know from clinical experience, the flaring up of chronic or latent adnexitis often has a relation to traumatic life experiences or neurosis.

To sum up, physical symptoms of psychogenic origin in gynecology are of a conversion hysterical nature in a lesser number of cases. They cannot be compared with those classical psychosomatic diseases characterized by secondary morphological alterations due to unconscious attitudes. In the majority of cases, rather, it is mostly a matter of affect or impulse equivalents or of physical manifestations resulting from stored up excitation. Functional endocrine disturbances and a reduction in the power of resistance to infection can be direct results of the neurotic conflict.

Psychic Effects of Physical Disease

As a further large group of patients in the gynecological hospital, the psychiatrist is confronted with the problem of *psychic effects of physical illness*. When there is a correlation between psychic and somatic findings, the physical symptom is by no means necessarily the result of the somatic alteration. Quite the reverse can be true. This does not only hold true for the manifold clinical manifestations of the chronic or acute brain syndrome. For each somatic alteration can affect the type and degree of the phantasies and impulses operating at a given moment. Such psychic consequences of somatic disease can in a next step lead to a psychoneurotic or organ neurotic symptomatology, namely when the activated ideas are related to repressed conflicts and when the activated impulses are inhibited by fear or guilt feelings. For example, a patient could not make rhyme or reason of her altered self-perception due to an undiagnosed myoma. Phantasies of pregnancy were quickened, and she developed a pseudopregnancy. Psychotherapy produced no result. But the symptomatology disappeared at a moment's notice as soon as the myoma was recognized and removed. In a similar way, protrusion of the small labia or mastitis can result in considerable psychologic complications. Premenstrual, menstrual, or climacteric somatic changes can unleash all sorts of phantasies and impulses and thus, certain conditions given, a symptomatology.

It is only for practical reasons that psychic effects of physical disease are mentioned as a special category. There is no particular route of symptom formation leading from physical disease to psychic effect. The somatic disease simply represents a special type of external event to which the predisposed individual reacts with symptom formation according to the rules described above.

PSYCHOSOMATIC MEDICINE AND CONSULTATION PSYCHIATRY

In the introduction, the question was raised whether psychosomatic medicine can be ordered into the body of conventional medical theory and practice. The list of symptoms enumerated above makes it clear that when it comes to the kind of patients to be treated, the psychosomatic practitioner scarcely differs from other physicians. The discussion of the pathogenesis was intended to show that psychosomatic medicine also in its theoretical concepts does not leave the framework of a conventional medicine. Viewed from these two standpoints, psychosomatic medicine is actually not an independent field, but rather one which can work hand in glove with any other field of medical specialization. The justification for considering psychosomatics as a special branch in medicine derives first and foremost from its special therapeutic instrumentarium, namely in that the medical interview has experienced a specialization in dealing with conflict. The work of the psychiatrist, seemingly so foreign to the conventional hospital for treating somatic disease, is in reality completely fitting for the good of the patient as well as for the good of scientific research.

The scope of psychosomatic medicine has, however, widened beyond the treatment of patients with symptoms of psychogenic origin. While organic disturbances can bring about psychic disturbances, the management of the purely somatically sick patient is being taken up to a growing degree in psychosomatic medicine. It must be understood that in recent years at numerous American hospitals the psychiatric departments have established a so-called extension service in which certain psychiatrists are assigned to certain departments of somatic medicine, for example, the department for heart surgery, for gynecological carcinomas, and so forth, to assist in treating the patients. The medical student is taught by the psychosomaticist how to conduct his relationship to the patient, how to understand the psychologic implications of his diagnostic and therapeutic measures, how the medical practitioner can do his job under psychological aspects. Over and above this, in obstetrics and gynecology, there are many patients to be dealt with who can hardly be called sick in the narrower sense of the word: they have problems connected with fertility and sterility, contraception, sexual adjustment, marriage, and preparation for childbirth.

The question arises whether psychosomatic medicine having widened its scope to such an extent is still the domain of the psychiatrist. Do the terms psychosomatic medicine and consultation psychiatry still refer to one and the same thing? In my view, psychosomatic medicine in the broader sense of the word is the goal and consultation psychiatry is a means toward this end. On the way to psychosomatic medicine, three different stages can be distinguished.

The first stage is the somaticist's recognition that the patient is troubled by something beyond the scope of somatic medicine, and he calls in the psychiatrist. The patient is then simultaneously treated by both: the gynecologist applies the skills of his specialty; the psychiatrist applies his psychological skills. Such an approach is good medicine and already represents progress, but it does not yet fully earn the name psychosomatic medicine. The division between somatic and psychological medicine remains. We merely have psychiatry plus gynecology rather than a comprehensive medical practice. Such a division certainly is inevitable in severe cases but should be reduced as much as possible. The gynecologist should not delude himself into believing psychosomatic medicine is what is done by the psychiatrist.

In a second stage to the eventual development of psychosomatic medicine, things have swung to the opposite extreme. A number of gynecologists have begun to turn into part-time psychiatrists. During most of the day, they conduct a conventional gynecological practice. In the evening, they deal in formal psychotherapy. The same doctor approaches the patient in two distinct roles: first as the gynecologist and then as a psychiatrist. The division between somatic and psychological medicine remains, not in the shape of two different doctors but as one doctor in two different roles. Another problem is the doctor's vacillation between two professional realms, one in which he masters and one in which he imitates mastery.

But Balint's work in England proves the feasibility of an entirely different kind of medical psychotherapy. Psychosomatic medicine in the proper sense of the word is when the expert in somatic medicine applies scientific knowledge and psychological skill at one and the same time. While doing general medicine or while playing the keyboard of his gynecological diagnostic and therapeutic measures, he also helps the patient to unfold, express, and handle his emotional problems. In other words, it is the general practitioner, the gynecologist, who practices psychosomatic medicine, not the psychiatrist.

What then is the psychiatrist's task in psychosomatic medicine? First of all, of course, he takes over the more severe cases, treating them according to the skills of his speciality. Over and above that, he teaches the gynecologist not to become a moonlighting psychiatrist but to develop procedural methods specially adapted to gynecology. Preferably, it is the gynecological resident himself who conducts the treatment of his problem cases. In doing so, he keeps in close consultation with the psychiatrist, discussing with him all the vicissitudes of the case. In addition to the educational benefit of the individual gynecologist, both gynecologist and psychiatrist are thus experimenting on the current task of developing procedural methods specially adapted to gynecology. Here it is above all a matter of changing attitudes and of getting to see things from a different viewpoint and only secondarily a matter of acquiring new knowledge.

It is preferable that the psychiatrist be a fulltime staff member who has his office at the hospital instead of merely coming in every so often. This way, the resident gynecologist can learn from him during daily hospital routines. And it enables the psychiatrist to best do justice to his other essential task in gynecology: psychosomatic research. Being stationed directly at the gynecological hospital gives him access to ample experience with gynecological patients and gives him first-hand insight into the research problems that gynecology expects him to tackle. It also helps him to identify with the gynecologist and thus become more deeply acquainted with the gynecologist's pertinent problems and attitudes.

Yet psychosomatic medicine is not a matter of everyone changing but the psychiatrist. As a result of a feedback from general medicine, psychiatry too is likely to undergo some change, a topic that has received little attention. For one thing, the psychiatrist spending all his working hours in a gynecological setting is likely to relearn to think and feel in the terms of the body and physiology. He learns that more recent developments in psychoanalysis that have proved extremely useful in mental phenomena, that is, in psychiatry proper, are less suited to his special task of dealing with psychosomatic symptoms than the old psychoanalytic id-psychology with its focus on what happens to the impulses.

REFERENCES

1. Alexander, F.: *Psychosomatic Medicine*, Norton, New York, 1950.
2. Schultz-Hencke, H.: *Lehrbuch der analytischen Psychotherapie*, Thieme Verlag, Stuttgart, 1951.
3. Molinski, H.: *Die unbewusste Angst vor dem Kind*, Kindler Verlag, München, 1972.
4. Molinski, H. and Werners, P. H.: Rigidity of the cervix uteri and hyperemesis gravidarum, an obstetrical anger syndrome. *Med. Gynecol. Soc.* 4:118, 1969.
5. Weiner, H., Thaler, M., Reiser, M. F., and Mirsky, I. A.: Etiology of duodenal ulcer. I. Relation of specific psychological characteristics to rate of gastric secretion (serum pepsinogen). *Psychosom. Med.* 19:1, 1957.
6. Fenichel, O.: *The psychoanalytic theory of neurosis*, Norton, New York, 1945.

CHAPTER EIGHTEEN

NONMANIFEST DISORDERS IN CLOSEST RELATIVES OF SCHIZOPHRENIC PATIENTS (A PSYCHOPATHOLOGICAL STUDY OF 818 PERSONS)

I. V. SHAKHMATOVA-PAVLOVA,
I. L. AKOPOVA,
L. I. GOLOVAN,
I. A. KOZLOVA,
L. K. LOBOVA,
V. D. MOSKALENKO,
M. L. ROKHLINA,
G. M. RUDENKO,
T. M. SIRYACHENKO,
and V. L. SHENDEROVA

Genetic studies of schizophrenia have demonstrated that, as compared to the normal population, relatives of schizophrenic patients may develop manifest forms of schizophrenic psychoses and show abnormal personality. The values of schizophrenia morbidity risk obtained by different investigators vary significantly. This may be attributed to the different approaches to schizophrenia diagnostics. Most authors engaged in clinical and genetic investigations of schizophrenia divided the index-cases (probands) into groups on the basis of the static, syndromal qualification of their psychic state; they referred mainly to the primary syndrome at the time of observation and not to the course of the disease as a whole.

Long-term investigations of schizophrenia carried out by the Institute of Psychiatry of the USSR Academy of Medical Sciences have shown that the course of the disease is a parameter very close to its biological essence. The classification of schizophrenia adhered to in the Institute of Psychiatry is based on the forms of the course of the disease. The main principles of this classification have been described in detail by A. V. Snezhnevsky, Director of the Institute[39-41] and other research workers of the Institute.

Three main forms can be discriminated in the course of schizophrenia: continuous, recurrent, or periodic, and attack-like progressive or shift-like schizophrenia. Each form differs substantially in its symptomatology and its development.

Continuous schizophrenia is characterized by a gradual development of a certain set of positive syndromes—pseudoneurotic, paranoial, paranoid, paraphrenic, catatonic, and lack of the tendency toward repeated attacks. The process may be stabilized at a given stage of the course but the intensity of schizophrenic manifestations does not vary significantly. The disease aggravates as the symptoms of this stage are enhanced by the symptoms typical of the next stage. From the very beginning or at different periods of time after the onset of the disease the patient develops negative disorders, such as a decline of psychic activity and emotional bluntness. The level of severity during continuous schizophrenia may vary from a sluggish, very slow course with mild personality changes to rapidly progressive forms, which 1 to 3 years after the manifestation of the disease end in a catastrophic disintegration of personality.

As follows from the very term, the main feature of recurrent or periodic schizophrenia is its recurrent pattern and the development of clear-cut attacks. This feature makes this form of the disease look like manic-depressive psychoses.[18] This appearance is more so because affective disorders are predominant in the attacks whereas personality changes are relatively mild. Attacks may be polymorphic, ranging from purely affective to catatonic, aggravated by changes of consciousness. They may develop in a similar way in the same patient and be entirely different in their structure. Their combination with delusional, hallucinatory, and pseudohallucinatory disturbances delineate distinctly this form of schizophrenia from the typical affective phases of manic-depressive psychoses.

The attack-like progressive or shift-like form of schizophrenia is characterized by a combination of symptoms of the continuous development with acute conditions peculiar to the attacks of recurrent schizophrenia. With respect to the degree of severity, this form also occupies an intermediate position between the two polar courses of schizophrenia. However, clinical manifestations of the disease at all stages (initial period, attacks, intervals between attacks) differ from those occuring in continuous and recurrent schizophrenia. Shift-like schizophrenia has certain features in common with the continuous form: emergence and gradual development of syndromes peculiar to the latter form—pseudoneurotic, paranoial, paranoid, paraphrenic, lucid-catatonic. Shift-like schizophrenia also has some features in common with the recurrent form: occurrence of acute attacks whose clinical picture is characterized by the following syndromes—acute paranoid, depression, or mania; acute paraphrenic; depressive-paranoid; oneiroid-catatonic. The shift-like form of schizophrenia can vary with respect to the degree of severity and may approach either the pole of continuous schizophrenia or the pole of recurrent schizophrenia with regard to the pattern of attacks and the degree of manifestation of negative disturbances in the intervals between the attacks.

The classification of schizophrenia based on the forms of its course is consistent with the classification of endogenous psychoses often used in the pertinent literature (Table 1). The experience has shown that there are no inseparable boundaries between the three forms of schizophrenia described above which arrange a clinicopsychopathological continuum.

Our previous investigation[38] based on clinical and genealogical examinations of 270 patients suffering from the three forms of schizophrenia and of their relatives has indicated a definite relationship between the form of schizophrenia in the index-case (proband) and the general background in the family. Each of the three groups of families (corresponding to the continuous, shift-like, and recurrent course of schizophrenia in the index-case) developed a definite background which manifests itself first of all in the identical form of schizophrenia in the index-case and relatives. The typical nature of the family background finds its expression also in the pattern of distribution of psychoses within the family: predominant susceptibility of the collateral line in the families of patients suffering from continuous schizophrenia and frequent psychoses in the closest relatives in the families of patients suffering from recurrent schizophrenia. The presence of this background, specific for each of the three groups of families, makes it possible to regard the pattern of hereditary susceptibility

TABLE 1. DIFFERENT PRINCIPLES IN THE DIVISION OF ENDOGENOUS PSYCHOSES

Present study	Continuous schizophrenia	Shift-like schizophrenia	Periodical (recurrent) schizophrenia	Manic-depressive psychoses
Kraepelin and Bumke	Schizophrenia		Manic-depressive psychoses	
Mauz	Schizophrenic catastrophe	Shift-like schizophrenia	—	Manic-depressive psychoses
Langfeldt and Rümke	Genuine schizophrenia		Schizophrenoform psychoses, pseudoneurotic schizophrenia	Manic-depressive psychoses
Leonhard	Systematic schizophrenia	Nonsystematic schizophrenia	Degenerative, cycloid psychoses	Manic-depressive psychoses
Mitsuda	Typical schizophrenia	Atypical schizophrenia	Atypical psychoses	Manic-depressive psychoses
Meduna	Fazophrenia		Oneirophrenia	Manic-depressive psychoses

as an important prognostic criterion. In view of the data accumulated it has been suggested that the form of the course of schizophrenia is controlled by constitutional-hereditary mechanisms.

The purpose of the present communication was to describe types of personality which occur most frequently among close relatives of schizophrenics. We attempted to follow thoroughly the life of the people that we examined. We were most interested in the periods of age crises—puberty and involution. We tried to reveal the pattern of responses of these people to various environmental stresses. We also paid particular attention to the dynamics of personality and development of transient psychotic disturbances in personalities of different types.

Regardless of the school and purposes of investigation, all the authors in the world literature have found increased numbers of abnormal personalities in the families of schizophrenics. Clinicians, geneticists, and psychodynamically oriented psychiatrists unanimously agreed that close relatives, particularly parents, of schizophrenics show a striking increase of nonpsychotic or psychotic-like disorders. Kasanin et al.,[17] Levy,[21] Gerard and Siegel,[14] Tietze,[42] Prout and White,[36] Reichard and Tillman,[37] Lidz et al.,[22-32] Hill,[15] Wynne et al.,[43-45] Alanen,[1-5] and Delay et al.[10, 11] gave excellent descriptions of parents of schizophrenics and their relationship with the sick child. According to Delay[10-11] and Planansky,[33-35], abnormal personalities occurring among relatives of the first degree showed a specific state, structurally similar to schizophrenia. Kraepelin,[18] E. Bleuler,[7] Kretschmer,[19] and Planansky[35] regarded abnormalities of this kind as undeveloped, abortive forms of schizophrenia, whereas Berze[6] and Gannushkin[12] described them as schizophrenic constitution. Planansky[35] held the opinion that in schizoid personality the schizophrenic process emerged, developed, and terminated at a level which was clinically unrecognizable.

We know only two papers directly related to the subject of our study. Alanen[2, 3] who examined thoroughly parents and siblings of schizophrenic patients put forth the following classification of disorders: (1) normal, (2) normal or mild disturbances, (3) psychoneurotic disturbances (depression, obsessions, phobia), (4) more serious than psychoneurotic disorders but without psychotic traits (schizoid and paranoid traits within the framework of clear-cut psychopathy), (5) borderline states with psychotic traits, and (6) schizophrenia. The author emphasized that the boundaries within this division were rather vague.

Delay et al.[10, 11] examined close relatives of schizophrenic patients. The authors advanced the following classification of disorders: (1) persons with mental disorders, (2) persons with the "psychotic character," (3) persons with the "neurotic character," and (4) normal. They indicated that the so-called psychotic character was the most common disorder among close relatives of the schizophrenic patient. These are not mentally affected people in the strict sense of the word but, nevertheless, they show disorders very similar to the remissions developing during schizophrenia. Thus the two papers were the first to give a scale of the severity of the disorders which occur in families of schizophrenic patients, although they contained no detailed description of the state. M. Bleuler[8, 9] and Hoffmann[16] confined themselves to a simple enumeration of peculiar traits of the character of relatives of schizophrenic patients: stubborn, obstinate, despotic, reserved, strikingly withdrawn, distrustful, unsociable, pedantic, paranoid, shy, sensitive, dreamers, odd personalities, and fanatics.

This investigation presents the results of studying 346 families of patients suffering from different forms of schizophrenia in the adolescent, adult, and old age. The research method was clinicodescriptive. A detailed case history of phenotypically healthy relatives, in which their whole life was subjected to careful review, was made. They were interviewed many times. Information was also obtained from other relatives. This procedure enabled us to evaluate and compare peculiar features of the character of these people during different periods of their life and to discriminate changes and shifts in its structure. Altogether we examined 818 parents, siblings, and children, we did not include relatives with developed, manifest forms of schizophrenia, those who died or lived separately from the family, or those under seventeen or those who refused to undergo the examination (their number was large). Therefore, our material is to a certain extent incomplete and insufficient for us to speak about the absolute frequency of different disorders; our material is, however, quite reliable for typological purposes.

All relatives with nonpsychotic disturbances were divided into three large categories:

1. Persons with schizoid traits proper.
2. Persons with schizoid traits and predominance of emotional defect.
3. Schizoid persons with phasic affective disorders.

When defining certain types of personality, we referred mainly to similar and common disorders inherent in representatives of different groups, ignoring minor and insignificant differences that certainly took place but did not determine the structure of personality as a whole.

The first group of subjects with schizoid traits proper appeared to be the largest in size—593 persons out of 818; the two other groups were almost equal—the one with phasic affective disorders, 102, and the one with predominance of emotional defect, 82, and the healthy group, 41 persons. As follows from the scheme given in Table 2, these three categories accompany different forms of schizophrenia in a nonuniform manner. Schizoid per-

TABLE 2. FORMS OF SCHIZOPHRENIA IN THE INDEX-CASE

Continuous	Attacklike-progressive (shift-like)	Recurrent (periodic)
Relatives with schizoid traits and predominance of emotional defect (82 persons)	Relatives with phasic affective disorders (102 persons)	
	Relatives with schizoid traits proper (593 persons)	

TABLE 3. "FORMES FRUSTES," ABNORMAL PERSONALITY AND ACCENTUATED PERSONALITIES IN THE CLOSEST RELATIVES OF SCHIZOPHRENIC PATIENTS (IN ABSOLUTE FIGURES)

Relatives with Schizoid Traits Proper (593)	Relatives with Schizoid Traits and Predominance of Emotional Defect (82)	Relatives with Phasic Affective Disorders (102)
(1) *Formes frustes* (46)	(1) *Formes frustes* (0)	(1) Formes frustes of psychosis (15)
(2) Abnormal personality (515)	(2) Abnormal personality (82)	(2) Abnormal personality (77)
Sthenic schizoids (301)		Hyperthymic (37)
Asthenic schizoids (113)		Bipolar (29)
Mixed group (101)		With seasonal changes (11)
(3) Accentuated personalities (32)	(3) Accentuated personalities (0)	(3) Accentuated personalities (10)

sonalities occur in all the three forms of schizophrenia of the index-case though at a different rate. However, personalities with the predominance of emotional defect and phasic affective disorders seem to adhere to the two polar forms—continuous and recurrent practically without overlap.

It appeared then that each of the three main, most common types of personality can be characterized by the different degree of severity. Therefore, we can discriminate: (1) "formes frustes," ambulatory form of psychosis that can be treated in a dispensary; (2) marked abnormal personality; and (3) accentuated personality (Table 3). It should be noted that this division is to a certain extent conditional because it is not always based on clear-cut qualitative differences. We believe it advisable to begin our presentation with the description of abnormal personalities that are most common in the families of schizophrenic patients and then to give a description of personalities with alleviated psychotic forms and accentuated personalities.

PERSONS WITH SCHIZOID TRAITS PROPER

Abnormal Personality (515 Persons)

The typical and common feature of all the people belonging to this group is emotional insufficiency and overt autistic trends; that is, the signs and symptoms on which the concept of schizoid psychopathy is based. At the same time this large group displays significant differences within its subdivisions which concern mainly the "vital tone" in the terminology of Petrilowitsch. This indicates the background which does not depend on the environment and determines the rate and the level of psychic activity. Kretschmer wrote that our attitude to the surrounding world was a play on forces in which our feelings of superiority, strength, and activity alternated with the feelings of diffidence and defeat. The first is usually termed a sthenic and the second—an asthenic life trend. This division of psychopathies into two categories was used by many investigators (Yudin, Kretschmer, Edelstein, Gurewitsch, and Petrilowitsch).

Asthenic Schizoids (113 Persons). From the early childhood they are sensitive, shy, and vulnerable. Some of them show traits of anxious worry about trifles, overestimate "the impending danger," and are said to be panic-mongers. Their sensitivity and susceptibility are combined with properties of egoism and coldness. They rarely have friends and are distant even from their relatives. Sometimes they, however, exhibit an abnormal, infantile affection toward one of the parents. In childhood they display peculiar motor behavior: they are awkward, clumsy, and immobile. They develop sexual feelings and the interest in the opposite sex rather late. They marry in the adult age and occupy a subordinate position in the family; they obey even their growing children. They cannot stand up for themselves and adapt to a new environment with great difficulty. In spite of the fact that they act very slowly, they are very industrious, honest, hard-working, and punctual to the point of being pedantic. Their productivity, often high, in the professional work is combined with utmost helplessness and infantile reactions in everyday life; they are also characterized by general psychic immaturity and frequently by physical infantilism.

Sometimes they are displeased with their position in life but do not do anything to change it. Usually they cannot fight against difficulties and take the line of least resistance. These personalities change very little, if any, with age. Periods of transient decompensation, reactive states which are discussed below, add nothing new to the structure of their personality. Asthenic schizoids occur both among males and females but most frequently they are mothers and sisters of the index-case. Relatives with these traits occur in all the three forms of schizophrenia in the index-case but mainly in its shift-like course.

Sthenic Shizoids (301 Persons). From the early childhood these personalities attract attention by the lack of affection toward closest relatives (even mother). At home they are naughty and willful. They are, however, very good in studies. They are very accurate and diligent and show seriousness and unusual reasonableness. The pubertal period develops smoothly, and they successfully finish secondary school and graduate from an institute. They do not marry until they are independent. Most of them get married because "it should be done," are "the time has come." They seem to be sexually cold. They stick to severe moral principles, and do not drink or smoke. They keep only business relations with other people and can hardly get into more intimate and stable contacts with them. They are cold and indifferent to the worries of their relatives. Having taken offence, they can keep silent and may not be on speaking terms for weeks and months. Throughout their whole life they show hostility which is on the verge of distrust and suspicion toward others.

In adult age they display an excess of energy. Being very active and energetic, they themselves state that they work as machines, sleep not more than 4 to 6 hours, and develop not fatigue. They show extraordinary persistence and perseverance in the field they are interested in and absolute indifference to everything beyond it. When performing their job, they are meticulous and scrupulous. They struggle uncompromisingly against various shortcomings and are ready to defend truth to the detriment of their own interests. They excessively guard their children without allowing them to make a step on their own. At the same time their attitude toward their children lacks cordiality and warmth. They behave strictly and severely, their word is law, and they often punish their children. They believe that their parental duty is only the financial support of the family.

Owing to their pedantic behavior, which sometimes becomes a caricature, and the lack of flexibility in everyday life, these people are rather difficult to live and work with. Their daily schedule is fixed to the minute; they adhere strictly to the established rules. Some of them have overvalued interests such as sports, dieting, flower cultivation, collection-making, studies, excessive affection toward one of the children, and dislike and even hostility toward the other children. As is the case with schizoids in general, the course of time does not leave an imprint on their life curve; they do not change with age. Their relatives think they have strong "steel nerves" and are unaware of the panic reaction. It is difficult or almost impossible to upset their balance. They can pass the difficulties by, ignoring them as if shutting themselves off. Sthenic schizoids are more often males than females. This abnormality is the most common one among relatives of the proband and accompanies all forms of schizophrenia.

Mixed Group (101 Persons). In addition to the abnormalities above, quite a number of the relatives of schizophrenic patients, together with sthenic features, display polarly opposite properties, properties of another "vital tone," namely—touchiness, vulnerability, uncertainty, and susceptibility to remorses ("sthenic with an asthenic sting"). Their sthenic nature manifests itself mainly in their work where they sometimes become obsessed. They exhibit exceptional diligence and honesty in business. They take very seriously all their duties, even minor ones. They are characterized by an enhanced sense of justice and irreconcilability to shortcomings. But beyond their business relations, they are shy and yielding. They can poorly adjust to varying circumstances and cannot show necessary flexibility. In everyday life they are clumsy and, when meeting various difficulties, display hesitating, diffident behavior. This abnormality affects similarly males and females, and occurs mostly in relatives of the patients with shift-like schizophrenia.

It has been already mentioned that personalities with proper schizoid traits belonging to the group above are characterized by a striking invariability of the structure of personality. The personality looks rigid and monotonous in its manifestations. Moreover, some relatives of schizophrenics (113 persons), mostly asthenic schizoids and persons belonging to the mixed group ("sthenic with an asthenic sting"), show distinct reactive depressions. These latter have certain peculiar features. Their mood does not always undergo disturbances immediately after psychogenic trauma. In some cases the disturbance starts at a later moment and develops gradually. It is important that reactive events, the essence of the traumatizing situation, cannot be distinguished throughout the entire disease. Finally, in some cases, the depressive state lasts for a very long time, covering months and years (up to one and a half or two years). In these cases, the traumatizing situation loses its importance for the patient and the depression undergoes increasing endogenization, acquiring a vital shade. We also observed several cases when the same people showed repeated reactive depressions. The patients with reactive depressions varied in their age, but they occurred most often at the age of 20 to 30 and after 45. It should be noted that reactive states occurring at an elderly age are more prolonged. These patients were not hospitalized; few of them were treated in the out-patient clinic. Most of them continued to work, though with great difficulty.

"Formes Frustes," Ambulatory Form of Psychosis

The case histories of some persons[46] belonging to the group with schizoid traits proper contain references to positive (psychotic) disorders that had the form of transitory and often prolonged psychotic episodes of delusional or affective-delusional character or state including obsessions, depersonalization, dysmorphobia, and conversion traits. In spite of this, very few of them consulted the psychiatrist and were treated in the out-patient clinic. Indications of psychotic disturbances were first revealed in the detailed examination of relatives which gave a reliable subjective and objective anamnesis. It is interesting to note that quite frequently psychotic episodes emerged at the same age as psychoses in the proband but developed in a mild form. They occurred most often without any outward cause, but sometimes they followed childbirth, infection, or intoxication.

It seems very difficult to evaluate adequately such cases. It appears incorrect to refer to them as overt, manifest forms because they do not show distinct progressiveness of the process and a decline of psychic activity. Half of the cases displayed clear-cut symptoms of emotional defects prior to the appearance of *formes frustes* disorders, which did not usually increase after positive disturbances. On the other hand, there were cases in which an increase of the traits of emotional defect similar to those described in schizophrenic remissions can be seen following positive disorders. With age these persons became more rude and estranged. They became true despots at home and punished their children cruelly. Women neglected their household duties. Their apartments became untidy and dirty. Because of their suspicions, they constantly were in conflict with their neighbors and relatives; they came to blows and litigation with neighbors and repeatedly exchanged their apartments. Year after year they became more ridiculous. Some of them shared delusional states completely with the proband and refused to send him to the hospital. Many of them avoided consultations with the psychiatrist and prevented his meetings with the healthy siblings. They were alert, behaved pretentiously, and dressed untidily.

It seems inadvisable to study the cases with overt positive and negative disturbances only in terms of psychopathic dynamics. It appears necessary to treat such as *formes frustes*. We believe that they are very similar to schizoid reactions of Gannushkin, schizomania of Claude, and schizophrenic reaction of Popper. Investigations carried out in the Institute of Psychiatry have demonstrated that some patients with delayed manifestation of schizophrenia had in their case history *formes frustes* episodes of the type above which were treated in the out-patient clinic. These forms of the disease occur in persons of the sthenic type, asthenic type, and so-called sthenics with an asthenic sting, being most frequent in the patients of the latter two types.

It should be indicated that all this implies an enhancement and stimulation of the inherent traits, whereas the type of personality and the "vital tone" remain more or less unaltered. In this connection it is very interesting to study formes frustes with a clear-cut change of the "vital tone." We observed the persons in whom the personality changed drastically with age. Most often this took place at the age of 15 to 23 but occasionally this time period ranged up to 40. To describe this change relatives and their close friends used the same words and expressions: "It looks as if he's been changed," or "He has become an adult in age only." The essence of this change is as follows. Being previously shy, timid, and vulnerable, the personality acquires absolutely new traits without an apparent external cause and often after the psychotic events above. He combines energy, persistence, and hypersociability with unusual activity, machine-like performance accompanied by emotional impoverishment, lack of affective resonance, and estrangement. It should be noted that an enhancement of sthenic properties is parallel with an apparent "displacement of the psychesthetic proportion" (Kretschmer) from the pole of hyperesthesia to the pole of anesthesia. We have never observed the reverse change. Thus *formes frustes* are characterized by psychotic disorders in case history and the traits similar to those peculiar to schizophrenic remissions.

Accentuated Personalities

This term has been coined by Leonhard.[44] It implies variants of personality that occupy an intermediate position between healthy and psychopathic persons. Such a personality displays accentuation, that is, a peculiar emphasis of one or several traits. According to the author, each type of the accentuated personality has its own type of psychopathy. They differ only quantitatively. It seems very probable that accentuated personalities of Leonhard are very close to schizothymic persons of Kretschmer.[19] All our cases (32 persons) were undoubtedly schizoids. However, the level of expression of individual traits did not reach that of dysharmony which is typical of abnormal personalities. These people are secretive, selectively sociable, and reluctant in making new acquaintances. They are usually called individualists. They are very fond of books and nature. They have a reputation of good businessmen who take seriously their duties. Some of them are sensitive and vulnerable; others are, on the contrary, energetic, reserved, and dryish. As mentioned above, the discrimination between an abnormal personality and an accentuated personality is rather difficult. However, our studies have shown that this smooth quantitative continuum is very typical of relatives of schizophrenic patients.

PERSONS WITH SCHIZIOD TRAITS AND PREDOMINANCE OF EMOTIONAL DEFECT

Abnormal Personality

All the people referred to in this group (82 persons) are also characterized by schizoid traits. They differ from the group above in a substantially greater expression of emotional impoverishment and personality defect. They display a striking poverty of their psychic constitution. Their life pattern is monotonous. They surprise the observer with an extraordinary conservatism and rigidity of personality. These personality features can be discerned from early childhood through their whole life. The crisis periods of childhood, adolescence, and involution add nothing new. Grave emotional stresses, death of close relatives and friends, complicated situations in the family, and their own diseases cannot upset their balance. They are cool; nothing can alarm or perturb them. They do not see any contradictions in life, and they can easily manage all adversities. They can neither feel compassion nor arouse sympathy.

Taking nothing to heart, they cannot feel happy or sad; they show no affection or warmth toward their relatives and friends. There are no affectionate mothers or careful fathers among them. In their families, disputes develop rarely, and the atmosphere of coolness reigns. They do everything as it should be done; they are exceptionally hard-working, industrious, and punctual. They have a reputation of being model workers, cited as an examples. They have no human weaknesses. It seems that life in its great diversity passes them by. They are not interested in the financial aspect of their life. They feel happy with their life, their social position, and they believe that they can very well analyze and understand everyday life and reality. They reluctantly become intimate with other people and do not feel a need in the social intercourse; however, they do not feel it as a burden and can easily keep friendly and official contacts. They feel a kind of mistrust toward people and prefer to see negative rather than positive traits in them.

They underestimate the real situation, lack a critical attitude toward seriously ill children, and ignore their catastrophic changes. They feel very optimistic about the future of their children and pay particular attention to their daily schedule, food, and rest. They try to treat their children with homemade drugs and means. They distrust the drug treatment in the hospital and, therefore, often prefer to keep defective children at home. They bear patiently aggressive actions on the part of these children. Such abnormal personalities occur primarily among relatives of the probands suffering from malignant continuous schizophrenia and rarely among relatives of the patients with shift-like schizophrenia approaching the continuous pole. The overwhelming majority of them are males.

As mentioned above, all these people show a surprising stability in response to exogenous factors (psychogenic and somatogenic). Therefore, these cases cannot be regarded as *formes frustes* of the disease, that is, as a greater degree of severity. Nevertheless, this very structure of the character with a pronounced emotional poverty resembles very much the remission state after a schizophrenic episode. It can be supposed that such abnormalities, though having indistinct progressive development, are beyond constitutional-psychopathic peculiarities of the personality. It can be suggested that there is a specific type of schizophrenic development with *formes frustes* clinical symptoms in which certain changes in the personality that are usually considered as a result of the schizophrenic process emerge in early childhood or may be almost congenital. It was very difficult to distinguish and describe accentuated personalities among this group.

PERSONS WITH PHASIC AFFECTIVE DISORDERS

Abnormal Personality

This group of subjects (77 persons) is characterized, first of all, by affective disorders. Some of them are constantly in high spirts; others show a distinct bipolar alteration of affective phases or seasonal depression of spirit. All these disturbances pass without specific treatment.

1.   The so-called hyperthymics constitute the largest group (37 persons). All of them display stable, optimistic, elevated spirits which determine the entire constitution of their personality. This feature is inherent and peculiar to them throughout their entire life. It should be noted that an elevated affective background exists in parallel with great monotony and lack of marked modulations. Similar to sthenic schizoids, their work is practically the sole purpose of life. They work productively and advance rapidly. Unlike diverse and easily distracted hyperthymics of the cycloid constitution, their activity is usually unidirectional and devoid of wide and alternating interests. They are always in the midst of people; but in spite of the external sociability, free manners, and seeming frankness, they reluctantly get into close and prolonged contacts with their acquaintances and even relatives. They prefer to be friendly "with everybody and with nobody"; their acquaintances are, in their own terminology, "nodding, imposing no responsibility."

Many of them marry rather late and love only once in their life. When losing husband (or wife), most of them do not marry again. They are cold to their children, prefer not to be engaged in their upbringing, and delegate this to others e.g., (grandmothers and nurses). They confess themselves that their love of children is based on reason rather than on feelings. In the family they occupy the leading position, do not know how and dislike to listen to the others, and cannot endure any objections. They do not go deep into various complications of the famil life, are unaware of concerns and troubles of their close relatives, and usually give general instructions and lectures. They are egoistic and take care of themselves alone. Their relatives characterize them as extremely balanced people. Females, who constitute the majority of this group, have very good health, great physical strength, and exceptional tolerance to starvation and fatigue. As is the case with schizoids proper, they dislike various entertainments and cannot enjoy good rest. Very often they are the last to know about the disease of the son or daughter, and then give a formal consent to send him or her to the hospital. The description above indicates that these people have much more in common with schizoids than with cycloids. There is only one thing that makes them similar to cycloids, that is, an elevated affective background; all other features—lack of sufficient affective resonance and inner warmth, superficial sociability, unidirectional activity, and striking affective monotony—make them look like schizoids.

2.   The next group in size (29 persons) is characterized by a constant change of affective phases. Similar to the proband, this change becomes ob-

vious at the age of 12 to 16 (in girls, with the appearance of menses). Bipolar affective disturbances manifest later in the course of many years, sometimes until 50 or later, having the shape of continuum or a double phase followed by marked periods of even mood. The duration of the phases also varies greatly—from several weeks to several years, those latter occurring though more often. Hypomanias last, as a rule, longer (up to 3 to 5 years) than depressions. It should be stressed that such bipolar phases occur in the families where the proband has similar disorders. Structurally, affective phases are close to cyclothymic ones. The affect alteration exerts an effect on the whole life curve of these persons (contacts, interests, performance, and relationships with the environment). They themselves like hypomanic states when they work very productively, feel more confident in their social intercourse, and become unusually talkative. Many of these people emphasize that during the period of even mood and especially depression, they have to make efforts to keep normal contacts with the people around them.

In view of the fact that they are pedantic, thorough, and overvalue certain ideas, their activity becomes channeled along a very narrow line during the hypomanic state. They become obsessed with one idea; they cannot distract their attention, become engaged in another activity, and alter their interest or occupation. They lack thoughtlessness, diversity, and syntonicity inherent in cycloids. In the family, they are petty, exacting, and fault-finding. They bring up their children following recommendations of the special literature, give them their meals strictly to the schedule, and adhere to a certain diet. They are reserved, show particular care of one of the children, and almost ignore the others. Their cold and egoistic attitude toward their own people becomes very obvious during the hypomanic state. Sometimes parents do not even know what form their children are in. Husbands seem to behave as if they are boarders. They are absolutely indifferent to the disease and the grief of their relatives. Some of them underestimate the severe state of the index-case, even though they understand that he is ill. Others avoid meeting the doctor or try to give him as little information as possible. Sometimes it is very hard to evaluate them properly, since their relatives also have affective disturbances. At early stages of our investigation, we treated the people with the affective disturbances above as cycloids. However, later we understood that there were no genuine cycloids among them. As far as affective phases are concerned, according to Gannushkin,[13] "schizoids are the very people who show susceptibility to their spontaneous emergence."

3. The smallest group (11 persons) includes persons with autochtonic, seasonal depressions. When speaking about the former two groups, it was necessary to differentiate them from other psychopathi · types, particularly

from cycloids. This group involves people with obvious schizoid constitution who developed a clear-cut seasonal (in spring and autumn) decline of spirit at the age of 12 to 25 to continue throughout their life. These periods vary in duration—from a few weeks to a few months. Structurally the depressions can be referred to as cyclothymic, as is the case with the previous group. The personality undergoes no changes with age and displays no signs indicating an increase of the emotional defect or autistic thinking. Periods of temporary decompensation usually leave no traces on them.

A considerable group of people (53 persons) belonging to that with distinct affective disorders exhibited, in addition to the affective phases above that were structurally cyclothymic, delineated reactive states following the termination of which the personality had its former characteristics. They showed the same regularities as the personalities with schizoid traits proper: (1) depressions are long-term and repeat readily, and (2) in an acute stage depressions appear in response to psychic trauma and can be psychologically understood; with time they become more and more vital. In such cases it seems necessary to differentiate these states from endogenous, psychogenically provoked phases. Another peculiar feature of such depressions is that they are rarely accompanied by delusion of personal changes, inferiority, or self-accusation. They may, on the contrary, contain a sort of displeasure with their own people, distrust, and ideas of reference of the sensitive character. Some patients show a pronounced dysphoria, irritability, and malice toward the whole world.

"Formes Frustes"

Similar to the previous group with schizoid traits proper, we refer here to an alleviated form of the disease (15 persons) only in the cases that are not restricted by cyclothymic phases or transitory reactive states. The structure of the attack seems to be more complicated: acute delusional episodes (delusion of persecution, jealousy), prolonged periods of dysmorphobic disturbances with obsession or overvalue symptoms; hypochondrical depressions and atypical hypomanias with sharp psychopathy-like and hebephrenic-like traits that may also have a long-term development; depressions with obsessions; and depressive-paranoid states. Ten out of fifteen cases were mothers of the proband. The psychotic episode followed childbirth in six cases. The described states ranged from several months (delusional and affective-delusional episodes) to 2 to 4 years (hypochondrical depressions, states with dysmorphobic disturbances, and hypomania with hebephrenic-like traits). As mentioned above, these positive psychopathological disorders developed in the same age periods as in the index-case, being, however, alleviated and rudimentary in nature.

Psychotic episodes were followed by personal changes that had much in common with those occurring during an overt schizophrenic process. In some cases such an alleviated event was followed by bipolar phasic affective disturbances that were not observed previously. Other cases displayed a monotonous and stable affective background, resembling structurally chronic hypomania. Still others (mostly after hypochondrical depressions) changed completely their mode of life, enhancing proper schizoid traits, egocentrism, and rigidity. Often the parents who had alleviated psychotic episodes looked much more defective and changed than their children who had several manifest attacks. The persons who developed an alleviated form of psychosis in their youth had both repeated similar attacks and reactive depressions in the involutional period. These abnormalities were not, as a rule, followed by further enhancement of negative disorders.

Accentuated Personalities

We observed accentuated personalities among hyperthymics (10 people) and mainly among the children of the index-case. They are active people but their activity has limited aims. They show certain psychic rigidity, slightly elevated spirits, and great optimism. In spite of their vitality and increased activity, they cannot be referred to as cycloid personalities because they have no lightness and breadth typical of cycloids. From the people with a marked abnormality of the character, they differ in that proper schizoid traits (reticence and lack of emotional resonance) are rather vague. Sometimes we hesitated as to what group—abnormal personalities or accentuated personalities—these people should be referred. This gives evidence that there are no sharp boundaries between these groups, and that the group of accentuated personalities is an intermediate between the group of abnormal personalities and the healthy people. The psychopathic personality has, as a rule, no traits which would not be absolutely inherent in the healthy person but these traits are excessively enhanced, dysharmonically combined. Gannushkin[13] also pointed out that there is no definite boundary between the healthy and affected person, that "in reality there are numerous intermediate stages between the normal and pathological phenomena."

Thus we can see that the scope of personality abnormalities among close relatives of the index-case is rather limited. It involves practically five to six types which occur in them with great constancy and frequency. We did not find the variety of personality types which we had expected and are inclined to conclude that close relatives of the index-case can be referred to the schizoid group in the broad sense of the term. It should be noted that among these people we revealed no psychopaths of other types—epileptoids, conversional characters, or asthenics (psychasthenics). However, it should be indicated that individual epileptoid, conversional, or psychasthenic traits may occur in one of the abnormalities described. But they did not determine the main structure of the personality as a whole and were additions to the clear-cut schizoid abnormality. Thus we can with certainty differentiate these abnormalities from other psychopathic types as well as from cycloids.

It is important to mention that the parents of the proband (as already indicated by Alanen[3]) show much more serious abnormalities than siblings and, especially, than their children. If people with alleviated forms of psychosis and distinct character abnormalities predominate among parents, then accentuated personalities and simply healthy persons occur most of all among siblings and children. It should be also noted that parents do not develop such abnormalities as deep schizoids or "verschroben." Personalities with these abnormalities occur in the relatives of the collateral line. They are, as a rule, spinsters or bachelors who have a reputation of being hermits, odd, and unworldly people. The personalities with such serious deficiency do not usually serve as parents: they do not have either family or progeny.

It seems appropriate to discuss another, very important question that arises from the comparison of our findings with the data obtained in previous investigations. First of all, we would like to explain the reason why we, in our previous publications and in the present study, prefer the term abnormal personality to the term psychopath. Recently other investigators also resorted to the term abnormal instead of psychopathic personalities, because the concept psychopath has lost its clear clinical content. Some authors, especially French investigators, identify "psychopathy" with "sociopathy." This implies that psychopathic personalities exhibit, first of all, a pronounced deterioration of social adaptation (incapacity, frequent hospitalization, and hostility to the society). It can be assumed that these are the cases of the most severe degrees of psychopathy that are on the verge of psychotic forms. Clinical experience indicates, however, that personalities with marked peculiarities of the character, with its distinct abnormalities show, on the contrary, good professional adaptation, and even hypersociability, behaving inadequately in everyday, private life.

Our findings allow the following conclusions to be made:

1. The scope of personality abnormalities among relatives of the first degree is practically limited to schizoid disturbances. We have distinguished three main categories of relatives:

(a) Persons with schizoid traits proper.
(b) Persons with schizoid traits and predominance of emotional defect.
(c) Schizoid persons with phasic affective disorders.

2. It is important to differentiate among nonmanifest disturbances *formes frustes*, abnormal personality, and accentuated personality as manifestation of degree of severity. This is significant for genetic analysis rather than for common purposes.

3. Personalities with schizoid traits, proper constituting the majority of the tested subjects (593 out of 818 persons), occurred in the families of the index-case with different schizophrenic courses, whereas schizoid relatives with predominant emotional defect occurred in families of probands with continuous schizophrenia and those with phasic affective disturbances occurred in relatives of probands with recurrent schizophrenia.

4. Families of schizophrenic patients are characterized by a large number of personalities with disorders of the "schizophrenic spectrum" [manifest forms, *formes frustes* (ambulatory), and pronounced abnormal personality], accentuated personalities, and healthy people. We could not distinguish an apparent subdivision into the normal and manifest forms, which is very typical of monomerically inherited signs. This continuum is consistent with the concept of polymery recognized by the majority of investigators.

In conclusion we would like also to indicate that the data above may well render support to the assumption that the pathogenesis of each clinical form of schizophrenia has one or two elements in common, each of which is characterized by a specific constitutional susceptibility.

REFERENCES

1. Alanen, J. O.: On the personality of the mother and early-child relationship of 100 schizophrenic patients. *Acta Psychiatr. Neurol. Scand.* **1956,** suppl. 106:227–233.

2. Alanen, J. O.: The mother of schizophrenic patients. *Acta Psychiatr. Scand.* **33,** suppl. 124:361, 1958.

3. Alanen, J. O.: The family in the pathogenesis of schizophrenic and neurotic disorders. *Acta Psychiatr. Scand.* **1966,** suppl. 189:654.

4. Alanen, J. O.: From the mothers of schizophrenic patients to interactional family dynamics. In *The Transmission of Schizophrenia,* 1968, pp. 201–212.

5. Alanen, P. J., The families of schizophrenic patients. *Proc. Roy. Soc. Med.* **63**(3):277–231, 1970.

6. Berze, J.: Beitrage zur psychiatrischen Erblichkeits—und Konstitutionsforschung. II. Schizoid, Schizophrenie, Dementia praecox. *Z. Neurol. Psychiatr.* **96**:4–5, 603–652, 1925.

7. Bleuler, E.: Dementia praecox oder Gruppe der Schizophrenien. In *Aschafenburgs Handbuch der Psychiatrie,* Leipzig, 1911, pp. 4, 1.

8. Bleuler, M.: Vererbungsprobleme bei Schizophrenen. *Z. Neurol. Psychiatr.* **127**(3):321–388, 1930.

9. Bleuler, M.: Krankheitsverlauf, personlishkeit und verwantschaft schizophrener und

ihre gegensitigen beziehungen. In *Sammulung psychiatrischer und neurologischer einzeldarstellungen*, Leipzig, 1941, pp. 16, 149.

10. Delay, J., Deniker, P., and Green, A.: Le milieu familial des schizophrenes. *L'Encephale* **49**:1–21, 1960.

11. Delay, J., Deniker, P., and Green, A.: Le mileiu familial des schizophrenes. *L'Encephale* **51**:5–73, 1962.

12. Gannushkin, P. B.: Postanovka voprosa o schizophrenicheskoy konstituzii. *Sovremennaya psychiatr.* **5**:361–378, 1914.

13. Gannushkin, P. B.: *Klinika psychopatii, ich statika, dynamika, systematika*, Moscow, 1933.

14. Gerard, D. and Siegel, J.: Family background of schizophrenia. *Psychiatr. Quart.* **24**:47–73, 1950.

15. Hill, L. B.: *Psychotherapeutic Intervention in Schizophrenia*, Chicago, 1955, p. 121.

16. Hoffmann, H.: *Die Nachkommenschaft bei endogenen Psychosen*, Berlin, 1921, p. 233.

17. Kasanin, J., Knight, E., and Sage, P.: The parent-child relationship in schizophrenia. I. Overprotection—rejection. *J. Nerv. Ment. Dis.* **79**:249–263, 1934.

18. Kraepelin, E.: *Psychiatrie*, 8th ed., Leipzig, 1913, pp. 3, 2, 667–1395.

19. Kretschmer, E.: *Korperbau und Charakter*, Berlin, 1922.

20. Leonhard, K.: *Akzentuirte Personlichkeiten*, Berlin, 1968, 287.

21. Levy, D. M.: Maternal overprotection. *Psychiatry* **1**:561–591, 1938.

22. Lidz, R. W. and Lidz, Th.: The family environment of schizophrenic patients. *Am. J. Psychiatr.* **106**:332–345, 1949.

23. Lidz, Th., Parker, B., and Cornelison, A.: The role of the father in the family environment of the schizophrenic patient. *Am. J. Psychiatr.* **113**:2, 126–132, 1956.

24. Lidz, Th.: The father. *Psychiatry* **20**:329–342, 1957.

25. Lidz, Th., Cornelison, A., Fleck, S., and Terry, D.: The intrafamilial environment of schizophrenic patients. Marital schism and marital skew. *Am. J. Psychiatr.* **114**:241–248, 1957.

26. Lidz, Th., et al.: The intrafamilial environment of the schizophrenic patients. IV. Parental personalities and family interaction. *Am. J. Psychiatr.* **28**:764, 1958.

27. Lidz, Th., Cornelison, A., Terry, D., and Fleck, S.: The intrafamilial environment of the schizophrenic patient. The transmission of irrationality. *AMA. Arch. Neur. Psychiatr.* **79**:305–316, 1958.

28. Lidz, Th.: Schizophrenia and the family. *Psychiatry* **21**:1, 21–27, 1958.

29. Lidz, Th., and Fleck, S.: Schizophrenia, human integration and the role of family. In *Etiology of Schizophrenia*, A. Jackson, (Ed.), New York, 1960, p. 456.

30. Lidz, Th.: Thought disorders in the parents of schizophrenic patients: A study utilizing the object sorting test. *Psychiatr. Res.* **1**:193–200, 1962.

31. Lidz, Th., Fleck, S., and Cornelison, A. R.: *Schizophrenia and the Family*, New York, 1966.

32. Lidz, Th.: The family, language, and the transmission of schizophrenia. In *The Transmission of Schizophrenia*, 1968, pp. 175–184.

33. Planansky, K.: Heredity in schizophrenia. *J. Nerv. Ment. Dis.* **122**:2, 121–142, 1955.

34. Planansky, K.: Schizoidness in twins. *Acta Gen. Med. Gemel-lol.* **15**:2, 151–166, 1966.

35. Planansky, K.: Conceptual boundaries of schizoidness: suggestions for epidemiological and genetic research. *J. Nerv. Ment. Dis.* **142**:4, 318–331, 1966.

36. Prout, C. T. and White, M. A.: A controlled study of personality relationship in mothers of schizophrenic male patients. *Am. J. Psychiatr.* **107**:251–256, 1951.

37. Reichard, S. and Tillman, C.: Patterns of parent-child relationships in schizophrenia. *Psychiatry* **13**:247–257, 1950.

38. Schachmatova-Pawlowa, J. W., Akopowa, I. L., Lobowa, L. K., Sirjatschenko, T. M., and Schenderowa, W. L.: Genealogische Untersuchungen bei Schizophrenie. *Psychiatr. Neurol. Med. Psychol.* **23**:6, 327–334, 1971.

39. Snezhnevsky, A. V.: The symptomatology, clinical forms and nosology of schizophrenia. In *Modern Perspectives in World Psychiatry*, I. G. Howells, (Ed.), London, 1968, Chap. 15.

40. Snezhnevsky, A. V. and Vartanian, M. Ye.: The forms of schizophrenia and their biological correlates. In *Biochemistry, Schizophrenia and Affective Illnesses*, H. Himwich, (Ed.), Baltimore, 1971, pp. 1–28.

41. Snezhnevsky, A. V.: Symptom, syndrome, disease: a clinical method in psychiatry. In *The World Biennial of Psychiatry and Psychotherapy*, S. Arieti, (Ed.), 1971, pp. 1, 151–164.

42. Tietze, T.: A study of mothers of schizophrenic patients. *Psychiatry* **12**:1, 55–65, 1949.

43. Wynne, L. C., Ryckoff, I. M., Day, J., and Hirsch, I.: Pseudomutuality and the family relationships of schizophrenics. *Psychiatry* **21**:205–220, 1958.

44. Wynne, L. C., Day, J., Hirsch, S., and Ryckoff, I.: The family relations of a set of monozygotic quadruple schizophrenics. 2nd International Congress of Psychiatry, Zurich, 1959, pp. 2, 43–49.

45. Wynne, L. C. and Singer, M. T.: Thought disorder and family relations of schizophrenics. *Arch. Gen. Psychiatr.* **9**:3, 191–198, 1963.

CHAPTER NINETEEN

ANTHROPOPHENOMENOLOGICAL
APPROACH TO DYSMORPHOPHOBIA

GIULIA DEL CARLO GIANNINI, M.D., and
ALDO GIANNINI, M.D.*

* Translated by Cherida Lally.

Antonio is a thirteen-and-a-half-year-old boy and the only child of well-to-do parents. Nothing of importance was brought out in the anamnesis, if one excludes a convergent squint in the first months of his life which was resolved spontaneously but still awakened anxiety and preoccupation in his mother, who was unable to accept this "impairment." She maintains, "I was contented only when he was sleeping." Always of a nervous and preoccupied nature, particularly in regard to his school life, Antonio never had friends, says the mother, because, "By nature he doesn't get along with anyone, nobody is to his taste." At the time of puberty phenomena of anxiety with temporary crises of depersonalization appeared, which were subsequently objectified into a dysmorphophobic reality: some months after, in fact, Antonio exhibited crises of violent anger and despair, motivated by "the shame of having freckles." They had not bothered him at all before, but he suddenly saw himself as "ugly, horrendous, disgusting," and was afraid of being with others because, "They will see and touch that face and those hands."

He began to wear his hair falling over his forehead to hide part of his face, and, no matter how hot it was outside, to wear shirts with very long sleeves so that the cuffs would hide the backs of his hands. He avoided going out during the day to prevent being seen and for fear that the sun would worsen his freckles, and only in the late evening would he allow himself a long walk in some obscure part of the city. During the day he repeatedly spent long hours in an anxious and disturbed analysis of his reflection, and, in the face of this repugnant image returned to him by the mirror, he was siezed by fits of anger during which he bit his hands, scratched himself, and broke his nails.

However, Antonio's profound anguish is not restricted to his freckles alone, but to that which they reveal about him to others: "his belonging to another race . . . to an inferior race." There is a juncture of the physiognomical-repulsive connection to his few and rather charming freckles, through which is revealed the secret of his belonging to a race which separates him from the rest of humanity: "Everyone can have defects," says Antonio, "perhaps one is lame or has a bigger nose or a smaller nose, but at least they have a European face and are still normal. It's not that they are different from other people. These here, who has them? Only those who are part of another race . . . an inferior race."

Giovanna, age 29, is a pale young woman who lives in a Tuscan village of 700 people, an extremely traditional place, where everyone knows, talks about, and keeps tabs on everyone else.

She is the only child of parents who are in their 70's. The father, a former workman on a pension had pretended to act as the stern head of the family without actually having those qualities; the mother, a weak figure, pale, fragile and sickly, is a good housewife and has always been close to the daughter in a symbiotic relationship.

As a child, Giovanna was very lively, intelligent, and sweet, appearing relaxed with friends and schoolmates, a little shy and irritable with strangers. She was educated in conformity with the existing norms of a small provincial town, being told to behave properly, and above all, not to make herself talked about and not to expose herself to people's criticism and slander.

Giovanna's drama manifested itself unexpectedly at the age of 13, when a fine down appeared on her face and arms. This initiated long, extended, and fruitless sessions in front of the mirror which revealed more and more a reflection which Giovanna always describes today as "horrifying," grotesque, and obscene. Her father, joking, said to her one day, "You're not turning into a monkey, are you?" Some of her school friends teased her. A consulted doctor, not taking the defect into serious consideration, suggested without much conviction the possibility of depilatory work. No one in the family understood the drama that was taking place. Giovanna left her school, the church, and her friends; she was no longer seen about. She shut herself in her house, acquired a knitting machine, and began using it all day. Only in the evening, after sundown, did she put a timid foot outside of the house, always on her mother's arm; during the day she kept the shades lowered constantly in her workroom.

Why this behavior? Giovanna was "obsessed" with her "down," that fine hair whose existence the mirror reaffirmed, that concealed and hid her slender, agile figure, that flowered like a reproving and monkey-like image under people's eyes. She felt derided, stared at, pointed out, and shunned by everyone else; she could no longer tolerate being in other people's sight, and a feeling of humiliation and unbearable shame posessed her. From that point on, her life was spent shutting herself off, hiding herself so as not to show to others that grotesque, nauseating, and animal-like face; her life became claustral. In the 15 years since, she has left her refuge only twice, and both times were for admission to a psychiatric clinic.

In both of these cases we find ourselves faced with an excessive preoccupation with, and an anguished fear of, partial aspects of bodily "appearance," an appearance which is recognized and experienced as being "deformed, repulsive, unacceptable, and ridiculous." The entire existence is dominated by this preoccupation, and nothing outside of it has any importance. However, these dysmorphophobic portraits and the interest in physical appearance which one finds in various stages of life, particularly adolescence, and which are partially determined by social and cultural codes (and sustained by the cosmetics industry) have little in common. In fact, in dysmorphophobia, the distorted or deformed bodily image relates to a deformity or a distortion in the whole being (to be part of an inferior race for Antonio, to be a monkey for Giovanna). These deformities are not just experienced by the subjects, but are above all recognized in the eyes of others who, acknowledging the deformity, would react with disdain, embarrassment, repulsion, aversion, and disgust.

The dysmorphophobic's difficulty in existing in an interpersonal relationship derives from this fact, as does his conduct of self-isolation, which removes him from the view of others so that they will not remind him of the shame of his body. Because of external appearance, and generally only one aspect of it, the dysmorphophobic rejects his entire being and lives as though he had been rejected and shunned by everyone else.

This crisis of the relationship with one's own body and with other people, which for Antonio and Giovanna manifested itself brusquely and without previous warning at age 13, saw a different evolution and solution in each: in Antonio, an adjustment of his own image took place, as well as a rediscovery of the value and significance of his body, which again became acceptable and presentable to him, and permitted a restoration of relationships with other people; for Giovanna, however, left by herself, her bodily image ultimately worsened so much in its negative bestial capacity that she had no escape in the face of it and had to retire from the world and live in an autistic, closed-off situation.

But which body are Antonio and Giovanna talking about? What is this distorted and deformed image which the mirror reflects back to them, and which they continue to probe anxiously and repeatedly? What is the meaning of this sense of shame or seeing oneself and being seen? How is it possible that a youthful and immature appearance could come to be regarded by the subject as irreparably deformed, ruined, degraded, repugnant, and different?

Only a phenomenologically oriented psychopathology could permit us to "understand" what has been related in all its anthropological significance. What has become a crisis in dysmorphophobia is the possibility of using one's own body as an intermediary in relations with the "other": in the world of coexistence, there is a tendency to pass from subject to object by means of the identification with oneself, with the image gathered from "the-looks-of-others." To make this concept clear, it is necessary to summarize synthetically some of the fundamental phenomena of the body. Husserl teaches that the body can be understood as the intermediary between the sphere of subjectivity and the rest of the world. The phenomenal body (*Leib*) is, originally, a worldly example: It is the body itself, that which is most human—*my, your, his* body; it is through the being, that one reveals oneself, expresses oneself, and experiences and relates to the world. Through it, one is in a double relationship with something other than oneself: something (1) that refers to persons in society and the ambiance in which I live, (the intentionality—"toward the outside"), or (2) that refers to what one finds in oneself in self-experiencing and which then becomes the limits of one's existence (the intentionality—toward the inside"). From this twofold polarity of the being-for-the-inside and the-being-for-the-outside emerges one of the fundamental specifications of the body—that of the contradiction, obscure ambiguity, and problematics of the-body-that-I-am and the-body-that-I-have. If my-body-that-I-am the body becomes obscure, it is transparent and it tends to coincide with the sphere of subjectivity; the-body-that-I-have tends to become a possession, something that is mine, however, without ever having been given solely as an object of nature such as a body (*Korper*) or a corporeal "thing" (the body-object of the anatomists and the physiologists).

The body (*leib*) can then remain either in the undifferentiated sphere of the very existence of the subject (the body lived) or reveal itself in the reflection as a corporeal possession, a "thing" that we have and that appertains to us.

In relationships with others we accede to an analagous experience of our body as an object, which happens when "I," my corporeal being, feels itself the object of the intentionality of "another," subjected to the looks of others, and I in my turn can look at another and make him into an object for me.

Sartre has insisted what a painful experience being observed, being "looked at" by the "other," is for a subject, "the other who disposes me, who violates me, who takes away my subjectivity." The reality in that contact with another presence (in particular, their looking) is often especially painful before one begins to lessen the malaise, the discomfort of being reduced to an "object observed by another."

The phenomenon of massive objectification of one's own body in relationship to another, typical of the dysmorphophobic, can be understood as defining oneself and identifying oneself with one's own corporeal image, and in the assimilation of oneself, however much, into that body-object-image that is reflected by the mirror and in the looks of others.

This identification of oneself through the eyes of others is a contradictory process, destined for failure; it is an identification that takes place through the production of an imaginary object. "This act of imagination, "affirms de Moulin, "is above all a bewitching act, an attempt to identify myself through the glance of the Other in such a way as to 'make me be,' to fill up, finally, that blind spot in my field of perception which is my being." Genetically, we can place this primordial modality of relating oneself to one's bodily image in the first year of life, in that stage which Lacan has called "the mirror stage," which is important because we recognize in it a fundamental moment in the structuralization of relationships with oneself and with others.

Around the age of 6 months, when the psychic life is still based on a fragmented body, the baby placed in front of the mirror shows through his jubilant gesticulation that he comprehends the unity of the human figure as an organized whole. In the form of "enlightened perception," the triumphant acquisition of the image now manifests itself; one perceives oneself as a human form in which one recognizes both oneself and others. Beginning with this mirror image the dismembered body, projected in different segments, substitutes for itself the feeling of being one, affectively and physically, even if the other is constantly changing itself.

This stage is considered by Wallon as a prevalently cognitive phenomenon in the order of the emergence of "recognition of oneself." The recognition of one's own mirror image which follows the recognition of another in the mirror is a complex intellectual operation, in as much as the baby cannot identify himself with an image that never having been "recognized" cannot be "rerecognized." This complex intellectual operation is the acquisition of a "symbolic cognizance of the image."

The first procedure of this consciousness must be the acknowledgment of two spaces; one space "here" where one feels oneself through introspection, and another space "there" where one see oneself or space adherent to the image. The successive identification of these two spaces, notwithstanding their distance, and the turnover of the specular image on the introspective mediating body would be exactly that intellectual synthesis which translates and integrates the model into an image in the redistribution of spatial values.

In the first phase, when the baby shows interest in the mirror image without recognizing it as a reflection of himself, the image represents a "duplicate reality," a "quasi-presence"; the baby plays with it, in fact, looks behind the mirror for the person, or hits his own image. Successively, there is a withdrawal of the value of near reality which had formerly been atributed to the mirror image, and the images more and more assumes its physical significance of a simple apparition without spaciality.

However, the way to this consciousness remains full of gaps, and is imprecise and subject to regression; even when finally arrived at, the concept of physical phenomena dissolves itself. [Not even in adulthood is the image only a simple reflection; it is always an almost-presence (Sartre). Among primitive people, to draw imaginary humans is to deliberately create human beings.]

For Merleau-Ponty, the problem is not as much in understanding that body and image situated in two different points in space are one entity, but in understanding that what the baby is seeing is "what others see when they look at him," *his* image; "To recognize his own image in the mirror signifies to the baby that he has learned that he 'can be visible to himself.' Up to that moment, 'he has never seen himself,' or has only seen parts of his body out of the corner of his eye. Now, using this mirror image, he is in a position to become a viewer of himself. With the acquisition of a mirror image the baby becomes aware of being visible, both to himself and to others."

The coexisting importance of this stage would therefore be the discovery of oneself as an image visible not only to oneself, but to others, and consequently the primordial experience of the objectivization of oneself through the looks of others.

One then acts on the passage from one form or state of existence to another: "The jubilant accession of one's own mirror image," says Lacan, "on the part of a being immobilized by motor impotence and a dependence on being fed, which is the condition of man's young in infancy, there follows, in a model situation, what seems to be the manifestation of a symbolic matrix in which the 'I' manifests itself in a rudimentary form even before it takes concrete shape in the dialectic of identification with another, and its function as a subject has been given into the universal by language." Therefore it is a kind of alienation by which the subject is "watched" (a special monitoring) by his own image, paving the way for the alienation by the "other" (a function unfulfilled by the mirror image). This stage in a still premature phase would then anticipate what will come in "I-other" relationships in socially elaborate situations: the "other" will tend to move away from immediate familiarity and to objectivize that part of oneself that is explorable through looking.

From this dialectic of seeing and being seen, looking at and being looked at, revealing oneself and being discovered, comes, predictably, the phenomenon of shame. (It should be remembered that the baby, indifferent up to now, as he slowly becomes familiar with his own image in the mirror, also becomes timid, shy, and inhibited in front of other people.) Sartre says: from *Being and Nothingness*)

This 'I' which others uncover and that I, without knowing it, am, even though I cannot push it away as an extraneous image, is revealed by 'shame.' And the shame is shame in myself and is recognized by the fact that I am precisely that object which others look at and judge. I cannot be ashamed that my freedom escapes me to become an object given; that 'I' that another knows is beyond every understanding and this 'I' that 'I-am,' I am in a world from which others have expropriated me. Through shame I discover another aspect of my being. Although it appears to be on a reflective level, shame was not originally a phenomenon of reflection . . . shame about one's own structure is above all shame in front of another: I make a vulgar gesture, I neither judge nor censor it, I simply do it . . . but now I raise my eyes, someone was there and has seen me, immediately I realize the vulgarity of my gesture. The Other is the indispensable mediator between 'I' and myself. I am ashamed of myself in relation to others; with the appearance of another I am put in the position of judging myself. I an guilty because shame is, by nature, recognition. Modesty, in particular the fear of being surprised in a state of nakedness, is nothing but the symbolic specification of original sin. Here the body symbolizes an objectivity in demanding the right to see without being seen, namely, to be simply a subject. For this reason, the biblical symbol of the fall after the original sin is the fact that Adam and Eve 'knew that they were naked.'

Shame is a universal condition in adolescence, even if transitory, especially during the times of alienation from one's own body which coincide with identity crises. It is precisely in this period—although, again, it may be temporary—that there is the least possibility of complete mastery and full availability of the body as an instrument; it is in this moment that the body can make the impression that can be fixed and petrified in the looks of others as having attitudes, bearings, and actions that present themselves as awkward, inarticulate, and encumbered. One can pass from normal modesty, through which an adolescent can increase his own sense of value, to normal shame, to that unhealthiness that displays to others exactly that which it would like to hide, and then, into a disgust of oneself, namely, that *Erlebnis* of horror in one's own being that can constitutes the prologue to an existential catastrophe.

The problem of Antonio and Giovanna relates to the bodily image, namely, to being looked at and to shame. Antonio and Giovanna are ashamed of an appearance that they have frozen into a repellent image. They have created a body, and by identifying themselves with this degrading appearance, they lose, in their contempt of it, the possibility of hiding their inner being, and of possibly transcending it. In other words, the appearance has lost its function of hiding or revealing the-being-that-I-am; the being becomes only that which it appears to be. Inside the body (*Korper*), says Cargnello, are only organs, but inside the body (*Leib*) are my most intimate desires and secrets, my secret and private history. Only in the duality of love and friendship, that is, in the sphere of intimacy and reciprocity, do I open my self and reveal my secrets; in plural and social relationships, I keep them tightly hidden. From this aspect, our life can be considered a struggle or conflict between opposing desires—on one hand, the wish to reveal ourselves to others, and, on the other hand, an equally strong wish to hide and conceal ourselves from them. "Everyone of us has had or has the same problem as the sick," Laing affirms, "and each of us has arrived at some more or less satisfactory solution."

This human significance of appearance is also well-defined by Chirpaz:

> I am in the world bodily, and this means that the the being of this man that I am allows itself to be seen and recognized by means of, and at the level of, a corporeal appearance, the appearance being neither an image nor a copy of a pre-existent being (nor a subjugation) . . . this appearance signifies and denotes the being (because my face is not an image of me, it is me). But the appearance can only denote the being within the limits in

which it bases and announces itself in the being that it seems to be, except in the limits of its expression of itself, and on that upon which it bases itself. As a man, I can find a place for myself in the world, or express myself within it, only by means of my appearance, yet, I can never be completely secure that there is total adherence between this appearance, and the being that manifests it.

In a dysmorphophobia, even minimal defects or deformities appearing in some important section of the body surface (areas which are most likely to be either of great significance or of elevated communicative value, such as the eyes, mouth, face, hands, or chest) do not remain localized, but, following a *Gestalt* law, enlarge themselves like an oil-slick, until they encompass the whole of the body surface, so that for other people ones whole body and appearance will come to be involved in this deformity of ones being, and of ones interior life.

This defect that shows itself and makes one transparent, this defect of an alienated body, seen, judged, and possessed by others, this nearly deteriorated object is expropriated in the eyes of all, and is made an object by the world. Antonio and Giovanna could neither rid themselves of it, nor change it. No plastic-aesthetic interventions can be carried out onto this facade built by others, since these interventions only turn one toward the organism, to the-body-in-oneself (*Korper*), and leave the-body-for-oneself and others (*Leib*) unaltered; and it is because of this that the deformity can remain for an entire lifetime, independent of any modifications which occur after the one time that the distorted image emerged and was fixed in, and frozen by other people's looks. It can preserve itself like an anatomical specimen in formalin.

This was the destiny of Giovanna, who for 15 years has not been able to change her way of seeing her own body; nothing is left to her but to break the mirror, and flee from the looks of others, to isolate herself and live in shadows and darkness. Even so, Giovanna's looking at herself (without ever being seen by others) has continued to keep alive in her the grotesque and deformed image of her body-for-others.

Antonio, however, suitably treated, was able to remodel an image of himself and his body that he could accept, and because of this was able to again pick up the threads of his life and reappear in the world and present himself to others. What took place in Antonio that did not in Giovanna? In Antonio, the *Leib* recovered its relativity and ambiguity, that is, its phenomenal essence, that which makes the-being-that-I-am transparent and at the same time, hides me, in general terms of being and having a body.

The accentuation of externalization of the bodily life, the dislocation of the centrality or interior onto the body surface, the being becoming totally an appearance, constitute the model structure of the dysmorphophobic experience. This experience, however much of a misfortune it may be, nonetheless represents an attempt to escape from the threat of annulment and from the unbearable vagueness thematic to anxiety, and of taking refuge in "existingness" and in "resolution" of the repulsive object. This attempt at an existential solution in the face of nothingness and anguish brings great risk with it, since the subject loses an objective view of the world, and being totally externalized, is completely reduced to being seen and thus being an only object in the view of others. We can maintain that a falling into dysmorphophobia depends substantially on the enormous power of the looks of others in the face of the weakness, and the inability to objectivize others with our own eyes. It depends on the inability to look in order to prevent being looked at, to dispossess another to keep from being dispossessed, to objectivize so as not to be objectivized is what Sartre suggests—this is what takes place among most of mankind.

Examined from the angle of corporeity, the dysmorphophobic world offers us the opportunity to recognize those aspects it has in common with, and those that are different from, other psychopathological case studies that occur frequently in adolescence.

First among all of them is mental anorexia, in which, as in dysmorphophobia, the real or apparent attributes of the *Leib* are prevalently or exclusively involved. The anorexic also exists in, and lives with, a body-object-image loaded with negative values and tonalities, but this corporeal experience is not as much a surface deformity through which an internal deformity is revealed as an opacity of the flesh which prevents the transparency of the deepest and most intimate being—that thin, emaciated, intellectual, ascetic, discarnate being that the anorexic would like to be for himself and to others. As in dysmorphophobia, with anorexia one is present at the breaking away from the presence of the body, but in the latter "the shame of the body" (*l'obsession de la houte du corps*) is completely centered on "fat," whose antipathetic qualities are not limited to opacity, heaviness, solidity, and materiality but take symbolic specifications of a fat "thing"— repelling, revolting, obscene, and viscid. The mental anorexic battles strenuously against this fat "thing," and by consistently refusing food, attempts to rid himself of opacity, solidity, and heaviness. From this point of view, the anorexic does not live passively with his fat body, but actively aspires to realize his perverted ideal of a slender, elevated, transparent, light body; and in this sense the German definition of anorexia as a "pubescent desire for thinness" (*pubertat mager sucht*) accurately recognized the active aspects of anorexia.

The dysmorphophobic, on the other hand, suffers, for the most part, without reacting against the deformity (notwithstanding rare and vain attempts at plastic-aesthetic intervention); he surrenders himself to it and is incapable of taking hold of and rescuing himself from his own inferiority.

These are differences which produce two types of profoundly different behavior. After emaciating himself, the mental anorexic is generally no longer ashamed of himself, and returns to a public life, even though his relationships with others remain confined to the shallow and pluralistic, and he maintains only with great difficulty the dual relationships of the reciprocity of friendship and love. But the dysmorphophobic, for whom it becomes extremely difficult to eliminate, reduce, or mask his deformity, almost always drastically avoids contact with others and their looks in the typical conduct of self-isolation comparable to the autistic retirement of the schizophrenic.

Still, in both cases the dimension of coexistence is reduced or constrained; in the dysmorphophobic because he no longer makes any contact with others and avoids them; in the anorexic because contact with others is present but only at a very superficial level, and the other is never addressed in the informal, but always remains an associate or an anonymous. In spite of this, and behind the isolating behavior and retirement from the world, the other is never absent, nor even distant, but is always loomingly present in the form of looks.

A similar problem is found in the case of the sensitive adolescent or in markedly advanced cases of quasi-delusions in sensitive relationships; in this condition it is the other aspect of the *Leib*, its custodial and guardian attributes, which is compromised, because the *Leib* is not just appearance, expression, and revelation of self, but also the guardian of inner being.

Also the sensitive has to shield, cover, and hide himself in front of other people because he feels naked and exposed, and thus becomes reduced to a single dimension of being and having a-body-for-others, an object in a world of objects, a body that is intruded upon, flayed, and violated by being looked at.

There is still the possibility of a modality in life (though it would by necessity be unhappy and forced) even in this sick condition in which the *Leib* is involved in both the aspect that relates to appearance and its aspect as the role as guardian/custodian, because a certain degree of consistency and concreteness is maintained. Only in the experience of the Wahnstimmung and in advanced cases of schizophrenia does every aspect and specification of the *Leib* become dissolved; in these pathological forms one comes to know the very limits of humanity, since here there is a complete disincarnation. The *Leib* is broken into bits, fragmented, and dissolved: the "I" loses every consistency and all adherence to the body, the "I" is now "incorporeal."

CHAPTER TWENTY

TRENDS IN PSYCHIATRY
IN BLACK AFRICA

G. ALLEN GERMAN, M.B.

Over a period of 10 years since the early 1960s, the majority of black African countries have achieved independence. During this period an enormous amount of worldwide attention and interest has been focused on the rapid, frequently traumatic, political and economic changes in these new nations; less attention has been paid to the equally swift and often dramatic changes that have occurred over the same period of time in general standards of health and of health care delivery. For example, smallpox has been totally eradicated from the majority of the areas in question; trypanosomiasis has become increasingly infrequent; the ravages of acute poliomyelitis have been to a large extent controlled and extensive schemes for the rehabilitation of the physically disabled have put into effect in several countries.

During this period also, there has been a considerable increase in the number of medical schools, which, although lacking the benefits of long tradition, seem to be as capable as most in Europe and the United States of turning out large numbers of technically competent young men and women to grapple with the continuing problems of health and health care in their own countries. Thus in the preindependence era, only schools in Dakar (Senegal), Ibadan (Nigeria), and Makerere (Uganda) were well established. At the present time these have been joined by active medical faculties in Accra (Ghana) and Yaounde (Cameroon), and by five new medical schools in Nigeria. Despite setbacks, there are University Faculties of Medicine in Kinshasa (Zaire), Khartoum (Sudan), and Addis Ababa (Ethiopia). In East and Central Africa the old established medical school at Makerere University, Uganda, has played a part in helping establish schools in Nairobi (Kenya), Dar-es-Salaam (Tanzania), and Lusaka (Zambia).

These vital developments in medical education have been brought about by the joint efforts of local governments and assisting governments in developed countries, working in co-operation with international agencies such as the World Health Organization and other groups affiliated to the United Nations Organization. Staffing has, in the first instance, depended on the recruitment of expatriate academics from Europe, North America, and Asia, frequently attracted to Africa by the opportunity to be involved in new developments where planning and achievement can go ahead untrammelled by preexisting systems and structures.

Attention must be directed to the enormous influence these academic medical institutions have had on governmental efforts in the field of health care. Not only have they been influential, but also they have participated directly and to a very considerable extent in the planning and provision of medical services. Academic physicians have been willing to be involved in these activities to a much greater extent than tradition might allow and have seized the opportunity to teach their students and conduct research in the service situation. The need to produce general-purpose doctors, capable of working independently in remote areas and dealing with all aspects of medical care, has led to a blurring of established disciplinary and administrative boundaries, and this in turn has had a great deal of influence on educational practice and on the pattern of health service development.

In the midst of all this, psychiatry has been prominent. The era of African independence has coincided with a period of increased concern about psychiatric needs in more developed parts of the world, and this has been reflected in the important place given to psychiatry in these new African nations in the curricula of their medical schools, in the graduate training of specialists, and in the pattern of development of hospitals and other health facilities.

This chapter is concerned with some aspects of psychiatry in black Africa, particular reference being made to the situation in East Africa where development has been fairly rapid, taking advantage of an excellent climate and the very adequate administrative and communication arrangements developed by colonial regimes. The point has been made that, in writing about Africa in the past, authors have tended to generalize about the African on the basis of particular experience in one geographical area.[20] This is fair criticism, but at the same time it should be pointed out that the problems of the entire black African area tend to be similar, and, although there is diversity, there is also a great deal of homogeneity of tradition, culture, and attitudes, to which must be added the shaping effects of similar colonial systems which have operated throughout the area for nearly a century. The issues and problems of independence have encouraged feelings of common identity among Africans and African states and have led to considerable co-operation, not least in medical and scientific areas with energetic exchange of views. The problems of psychiatric illness throughout the sub-Saharan belt do appear to be very similar.

CLINICAL ASPECTS

Knowledge of the overall clinical situation with regard to psychiatry in black Africa has accrued rapidly in recent years, particularly as a result of increasing research activity based on local university departments of psychiatry. Investigative work has also been carried out in Government establishments by staff working for prolonged periods in various countries. A further stimulus to the collection and integration of information has been the establishment of the Association of Psychiatrists in Africa in 1970. Two publications[3, 24] have already resulted from meetings of this association, quite apart from reports from the three Pan-African conferences of psychiatrists held to date (Abeokuta, 1962; Dakar, 1968; Khartoum, 1972). Obviously problems of staffing, logistic difficulties, poor baseline data, and the sheer size of the issues involved mitigate against the sort of intensive, precise, and sophisticated research that is now characteristic of psychiatry in more developed areas. Also, the analysis of research reports concerning clinical psychiatry in Africa is made difficult by the appearance of such reports in many journals originating in many scattered parts of the world. Attempts have been made to collate this information in recent reviews[6, 8, 9, 11] to which reference should be made.

In his 1972 review Hoorweg[8] states that "the traditional and romantic view that mental illness occurs less in African than in Western societies has not been confirmed by recent investigation." This opinion would be generally supported[6, 7, 14, 21] and is in contrast to earlier views expressed by Carothers[2] and others.[25, 28] Generally these earlier workers confined their attention to mental hospital statistics which were totally unrepresentative of both the prevalence and the morbidity patterns of psychiatric illness in African communities. More recent investigations among the Yoruba,[14] in Ethiopia,[7] and in a Nigerian general practice,[15] indicate that the prevalence of psychiatric disorders and symptoms found in African communities are strikingly similar to prevalence rates reported from Britain and North America. This information forces acceptance of the fact that major mental health problems exist in black Africa and that these will occupy increasing public health attention as the ravages of infectious diseases and malnutrition are reduced.

If there has been general acceptance of the similarity of African societies to more developed societies in terms of prevalence rates for mental disorder, there continues to be controversy as to whether these disorders are the same as those found in Europe and America, and if they can reasonably be fitted into Western nosological categories. Clearly there are differences in the distribution pattern of different types of psychiatric illness. As might be expected, in the African setting, a considerable proportion of acute psychiatric illness is related to physical disease, particularly physical disease involving the central nervous system directly or indirectly. Vitamin deficiency states; encephalopathies of infectious, parasitic, and metabolic origin; toxic states associated with alcohol and other drugs; and the consequences of trauma produce a wide range of acute brain syndromes.[9] On the other hand, African populations have a different age distribution than those of developed countries and the most notable consequence of this is the relative infrequency of psychiatric symptoms associated with aging and degeneration of the brain. Poor maternal nutrition, inadequate antenatal and obstetrical care, and the ravages of encephalitis, malaria, and other brain-damaging infections in childhood produce a large number of children who survive with greater or lesser degrees of brain damage and pose increasing problems for the limited health facilities of developing African nations.

Psychotic conditions such as manic-depressive illness and schizophrenia occur commonly as do a variety of brief lived psychoses, which are usually referred to as acute psychotic episodes (or in French-speaking countries as the "bouffée délirante"). These acute transient psychoses are regularly reported as a special feature of African clinical psychiatry, but it is probable that they were also of widespread occurrence in European clinics and hospitals at the end of the last century.[6] These illnesses characteristically present with acute and disorganized psychotic symptoms and signs; the onset is usually sudden and not infrequently appears to be associated with a significant precipitating event; florid symptoms of confusion, marked, and rapid affective changes, ideational disturbances of delusional intensity, vivid hallucinosis, and dramatic dissociative phenomena are usually seen. The disturbance tends to settle down rapidly, especially with hospital care, and complete recovery is the rule, although further similar attacks are not infrequent. The aetiology appears to include psychic stress (commonly fear of bewitchment) interacting with predisposing physical factors such as toxaemia, malnutrition, exhaustion, and excessive alcohol consumption. Minimal preexisting brain damage may be an important conditioning factor in many cases, and these illnesses are almost certainly related to cultural and environmental factors rather than to race.[6] Early European writers[16, 26, 27] have commented on what are almost certainly identical disorders, relating them to poor conditions of general physical health existing in a cultural setting where there is a high level of superstitious fearfulness on the one hand, and easy acceptance of dramatic and uncontrolled emotional behavior on the other. This culturally determined readiness to accept violent, excited, and agitated behaviors in response to distress, almost certainly helps to colour psychotic states occurring in preliterate Africans. The situation in literate groups is very much more similar to that observed in Europeans and those from other developed countries. In the opinion of this author, there is no evidence to suggest that these acute transient psychoses are qualitatively peculiar to Africa and different in form from those observed elsewhere, although it is clear that there is a great deal of local colour added to the symptomatology which must be taken account of in diagnosis and management.

With regard to states of depression in African subjects, controversy continues as to the precise symptomatology. It is at present generally accepted that depressive illness is of frequent occurrence among Africans, although in view of the youthful age structure of the population, only careful studies of age-specific rates can finally answer questions as to comparative prevalence. Apart from this, the majority of present authors report that ideas of worthlessness, guilt, and sin are not common in the preliterate African.[23] Rather, it is suggested, there is a tendency toward projection as evidenced by the frequency with which persecutory ideas and delusions occur in the depressed African patient. This is an area of considerable interest for further research.

Turning to the schizophrenic syndromes, it is apparent that discussion of this subject in Africa, as elsewhere, is bedevilled by failures to define terms and inconsistencies in the use of diagnostic criteria. In particular, repeated failure to attempt to make a conceptual distinction between process schizophrenia and reactive schizophreniform variants has led to widely differing statements as to the prevalence and prognosis of schizophrenic states in African patients. Thus Lambo[12, 13] appears to consistently include schizophreniform illnesses in his concept of schizophrenia, a procedure which assists considerably toward his conclusion that schizophrenia is of better prognosis in the African, particularly the preliterate African, than it is in the European. This writer shares the view of other workers[1] that process schizophrenia, running a deteriorating course to eventual chronicity, occurs in all groups of Africans and is almost certainly a common disorder.[10] Murphy and Raman,[18] while finding that "mild" forms of schizophrenia appear to have a better prognosis in Mauritius than in England, also conclude that in more serious illnesses, "the proportions remaining seriously disturbed (at long-term follow-up) are virtually the same." These authors, having regard to the apparently better prognosis of "mild" schizophrenia in Mauritius, put forward the hypothesis that this might be so because of more "accepting" social attitudes in the less sophisticated society. Muhangi[17] surveying a rural population in Uganda has also described a group of illiterate chronic schizophrenics. He concludes that the tolerance of their communities has enabled them to remain out of hospital and to occupy a special social niche; however, these people were clearly deteriorated schizophrenics with numerous disabilities in terms of a formal assessment of mental status.

With neurotic disorder in black Africa, the situation is even less clear-cut. In view of the plethora of theories as to the psychopathology of neurotic symptoms and the difficulty in this area of clinical practice of defining cut-off points between illness and health, this is only to be expected. Nevertheless certain generalizations appear to be possible about neurotic disorder in the African.

In the first place neurotic symptomatology is undoubtedly very common. In prefacing his remarks about neurotic conditions among the Buganda of Uganda, Orley[21] states that: "there used to be a myth current in Europe that there were no mental illnesses in Africans, but it has become obvious in medical circles that there are, in fact, plenty of 'mad' people in Africa, so the myth has been changed to suggest that there is no neurosis amongst African subjects." He goes on to point out that the African is surrounded by stresses and worries relating to physical dangers, high infant mortality rates, crop failues, chronic ill health, domestic quarrels, and perhaps most ubiquitous and important of all, the ever-present fear of bewitchment represented by the constant surrounding world of malevolent and hostile spirits. If the core of neurotic disorder be regarded as excessive anxiety, then it is clear to the participant observer (which Orley was) that there is ample stimulus to anxiety in the African's environment and most authors have commented on the frequency with which various forms of anxiety states are found amongst their clinical material. Thus Carothers[2] states that "anxiety is always felt to be an outcome of a bewitchment (and poisoning) which is threatening one's personal or procreative life." Other authors[5, 22] have focused attention on the high prevalence of anxiety symptoms among African students at various levels of the educational system. Diffuse free floating anxiety appears to be relatively uncommon,[10] and Muwazi and Trowell[19] have commented on the frequency with which anxiety states in African patients present with concern about the function of various physical organs. Closely related to neurotic anxiety states are conditions where the impingement of stress leads to an uncontrolled and uninhibited emotional reaction of panic and terror which reaches psychotic intensity with complete disruption of normal mental life. Not only do social and cultural attitudes accept and even encourage the expression of such uninhibited emotional reactions, but also it has to be appreciated that to be "bewitched" is to be suddenly exposed to a life-threatening event with a power to terrify (and even kill) in a way which has long been forgotten in most parts of the developed world. The resultant states, clearly psychogenic, have been referred to as states of "frenzied anxiety" and also as psychogenic psychoses. A variety of hysterical phenomena, usually dissociative, are frequently to be observed in the setting of such acute reactions.

With regard to hysteria, Dembovitz[4] has commented that "hysteria is the hallmark of psychiatry in Africans." Few would go so far as to entirely subscribe to this view, but again, most authors agree that conversion states and dissociative states are very frequently encountered in African patients, often appearing as understandable consequences of the acute and severe anxiety already discussed. Authors such as Carothers[2] and Vyncke[29] emphasise the frequency of aphonia, deafness, motor paresis, blindness, "fits," and other conversion symptoms, together with amnesias and fugues. The conditions are most common in adolescents, but are also encountered in older age groups; precipitants are usually fairly obvious; and, as Kagwa[10] notes, the onset of symptoms often occurs during a febrile episode. Orley comments on the hysterical quality of trances and possession states, and makes the important point that such states are culturally sanctioned, are *expected* of the individual in certain religious rituals, and are often rewarding in that persons who have successfully achieved such states may set up in lucrative practice as a diviner and healer. Generally, hysterical manifestations of the trance type are positively encouraged in many African groups.

These conditions, vaguely referred to as neurotic, cannot be properly evaluated, in Africans as in others, without reference to the complex interplay between individual constitution, intrapsychic mechanisms, present disease and current psychological stress, and lastly but not least, the culturally and socially determined attitude toward which "symptoms" are acceptable and customary and which are not.

As compared with anxiety and hysteria, obsessional-compulsive states seem to be of rare occurrence in the African setting. This is a firm and repeated observation still without satisfactory explanation. Carothers[2] suggests that the infrequency of such disorders in individual Africans is due to the fact that the entire African mode of life is controlled by *group* obsessional rituals. A tendency toward group identification rather than self-identification may be responsible for the frequency of projective, rather than intrajective, mechanisms, and symptoms. The ritual, as a defence against anxiety, may be effectively available for many Africans in ritualistic tribal and religious activities.

Summing this up, it would seem that presently available information suggests that clinical psychiatry in Africa is not very dissimilar to psychiatry in other parts of the world, and that where there are differences, these are comprehensible. The differences that do exist are determined in part by physiological deprivations and physical disease, and in part by differences in cultural values and emphases and by widespread illiteracy. Psychiatric morbidity is certainly just as prevalent as elsewhere; schizophrenia, manic-depressive disorder, and organic psychoses exist in their familiar forms, although in different proportions. Organic psychoses in particular are common, and the presence of background organic factors probably predisposes in part to the high frequency with which primitive, disorganised, and transient psychotic reactions are encountered. Neurotic illness is widespread, and, although this has been little studied, anxiety states presenting as acute frenzies of psychotic intensity, or as various somatic preoccupations, or merging with hysterical phenomena, form the bulk of neurotic case material. Differences between African and European psychiatry are mostly determined by pathoplastic factors and are likely to become less prominent as development accelerates. At the present time the major differences seem to be:

1.   The frequency with which easily precipitated and recurrent transient amorphous psychoses are encountered.
2.   The somewhat better *social* prognosis of process schizophrenia.
3.   The relative absence of self-directed and self-centred symptoms such as notions of worthlessness and guilt, and obsessional-compulsive behaviors.
4.   The widespread use of projective mechanisms manifesting themselves in paranoid thinking of a persecutory type.
5.   The high frequency of hysterical symptoms and states, often in the setting of anxiety reactions of psychotic intensity, which certainly contribute to the problem of "acute transient psychoses."
6.   The widespread tendency, particularly among preliterate patients, to express any state of psychic pain or conflict in somatic terms.

Against this clinical background, African nations are now attempting to develop effective systems of mental health care. If it is accepted that the prevalence of psychiatric disorder is probably as high in Africa as anywhere else, then clearly the psychiatric facilities that have been available in the past must have been totally inadequate to cope with the numbers of people who require help; but at the same time it has to realized that present economic realities make it unlikely that African nations in the foreseeable future could provide for their peoples the same types of expensive psychiatric facilities and services as have been developed in more advanced countries—even if such facilities are desirable or necessary. Mental health service developments and plans for future developments in the African setting, while attempting to provide basic services of as high a quality as possible, have been forced by economic, social, and clinical factors into certain unique and characteristic patterns, which are now considered.

SYSTEMS OF MENTAL HEALTH CARE

At the time of independence, in practically every country in middle Africa, the mental health needs of populations were catered for in two ways. There was, invariably, a central government hospital for the mentally sick, and there was a country wide network of traditional healers.

The mental hospital in colonial African countries, despite the devoted work of individuals, was essentially a custodial institution, usually sited in or near the capital city, and drawing patients from all parts of the country. Conditions were spartan, to say the least, overcrowding was prevalent, and the main criterion determining admission was some form of violent and antisocial behaviour.[21] Patients were taken to hospital, usually by the police, or by relatives, under physical restraint, and once locked up might or might not receive medical or psychiatric help. Many of these institutions were not staffed by medical personnel until the late 1950s. At that same point in time, in other parts of the world, mental hospital psychiatry was becoming increasingly liberalized, and the impact of this trend on African mental hospitals had in some cases appeared before independence. The arrival of independence greatly accelerated it, resulting in rapid and accelerating changes since a point in time approximately 12 to 15 years ago. The attitude of African communities to these hospitals was usually one of some fear and contempt—not dissimilar to community attitudes in other parts of the world. Mental hospitals were places to which Africans were taken because they were "mad," and this madness was recognized by the fact that they were violent and antisocial. They were not expected to be treated, and if they recovered this was a matter of chance; recovery was expected to be transient. Many of the mental health ordinances of this era imply a similarity between the "lunatic" and the criminal.

That these ill-favored mental hospitals should have been regarded as places in which the violent could be kept safely out of the way of society is entirely in keeping with widespread African attitudes to health and disease. Orley[21] has described well this African attitude to disaster—particularly the disaster of physical or mental ill-health. Such unfortunate states or events are not seen as being causally separate categories of human experience but rather the common products of bewitchments and spirit machinations. In this view the individual can only be "protected" "treated," or "cured" by an individual who is expert in matters concerning spirit possession, witchcraft, or sorcery. There is no real conception of an alternative form of treatment, and the proper management of a mentally sick individual would require that he go or be taken to the local expert in these matters—the witchdoctor in popular English usage, but more appropriately described as a priest-healer in view of his social position and function. This procedure, however, might be rendered difficult if violent or agitated behaviour were present, and under these circumstances the afflicted person would be locked up for reasons of control while the priest-healer dealt with matters of therapy. The government mental hospital thus becomes merely a bigger and stronger lock-up and clearly has no therapeutic function since priest-healers do not practice there. No person would be taken there who was "ill" but not violent, and if violence required admission, there would be inevitable attempts by relatives to smuggle in local remedies—or even local traditional practitioners—so that therapy could be undertaken. Well-meaning attempts by authorities to prevent these activities could produce considerable distress among patients and their relatives. Education and the demonstration of effective therapies in psychiatric facilities are now changing many of these attitudes, but they still persist. They were practically universal at the time of independence, and subsequent developments have to be seen against this background.

The presence of a single central custodial mental hospital in a country produces a situation which confers advantages and disadvantages for subsequent psychiatric developments. The major advantage for the psychiatrist in a developing African country is the very paucity of previous provision for the mentally sick. Thus he does not have to expend his energies in frustrating attempts to dismantle an inert and cumbersome administrative structure; nor does he have to concern himself with finding a method of absorbing large numbers of solidly built prison-like mental hospitals into a more efficient and humane psychiatric programme; there is little need for him to struggle with large armies of personnel in various categories, each preoccupied with and defensive about its own status and sacrosanct tradition, and each in varying degrees unwilling to change from the security of well-defined roles to meet the challenge of the present and future. Newly independent African medical services and the few psychiatrists employed by them face enormous problems, but they have at least a fairly clean canvas on which to develop their themes. The only model for progress has been the model of psychiatric care in the more developed countries of the western world, but in view of the emotional aspects of the emergence from colonialism, developing countries have in no way felt themselves bound to copy this model, to say the least.

The disadvantages are equally obvious. One mental hospital of a custodial type is inadequate to meet the requirements of even the violent and more deranged members of a society, quite apart from coping with its nontherapeutic image. Increasing the size of such a hospital, and staffing it with progressive medical and psychiatric staff oriented toward active treatment, and educating the public to accept it are not enough. One central hospital facility means that many patients have to travel or be brought hundreds of miles to reach it; these distances are a considerable barrier in developing countries with poor communications and a population usually too poor to afford mechanical means of travel over long distances. Even if all the patients requiring care can be brought to a central facility, those from more distant parts usually find that the African staff of the unit are unfamiliar with their language and customs. This applies with even more force to non-African staff. Apart from communication problems of this sort, the individual patient is usually unaccompanied by family and relatives, leading to further isolation and lack of support for him and exacerbating the psychiatrist's problem of obtaining relevant and vital information. Discharge from hospital and subsequent rehabilitation in the family and community pose formidable problems in the absence of an opportunity to meet with family members and with employers. Continuing out-patient supervision and treatment is nearly impossible, not the least because of the previous tendency of doctors practicing in up-country hospitals to regard psychiatric patients as being no concern of theirs. Medical officers in general hospitals up and down Africa have, in past years, been products of schools where psychiatry was little taught, and they have practiced in a situation where there was no exposure to the idea that psychiatric disorder could be found in every out-patient clinic and required a serious approach to assessment, management, and continuing care.

In considering developments in psychiatry in black Africa over the past 10 years, one is struck, not only by the common background noted above, but also by the essentially similar solutions that have been arrived at. In almost every country, high priority has been given to the need to *decentralize* services and to bring them close to the communities in villages, towns, and tribal areas which have to be served. However, before decentralization could be achieved, it was obvious that something would have to be developed in the center, and the first step of psychiatric development in these new nations has almost invariably been the development of facilities in the capital cities, usually oriented around the old mental hospital, to a point where these facilities could provide an adequate base for patient care, training, and administrative planning in association with governments and universities. Thus in the four East African countries of Ugana, Kenya, Tanzania, and Zambia, this pattern has been very clearly followed. With the exception of Tanzania, each country has had a large central mental hospital near its capital city (in Tanzania the mental hospital is some hundreds of miles from Dar-es-Salaam, and therefore in Dar-es-Dalaam psychiatric facilities have evolved in the general hospital), and in each case the development of these central facilities has been linked with the presence of psychiatry as a teaching subject in nearby medical schools. The use of the term mental hospital to refer to those central hospitals at the present time conveys a false impression. Although patients are accommodated in a hospital unit separated from the general hospital (with the exception of Tanzania), these old mental hospital units are now functioning very much more like acute units in general hospitals, with a high turnover and short duration of stay. Staff have been recruited in the first instance from more developed countries, and have been joined by increasing numbers of trained African psychiatrists. Staffing levels have been further improved by the development of academic departments of psychiatry whose staff have used the hospital facility as a teaching location, and have been heavily involved in patient care. Thus Butabika mental hospital near Kampala, with a total bed complement of 960 patients, had, in the middle of 1972, six government specialists and six university specialists on its staff, supported by 12 junior doctors with varying degrees of experience of psychiatry. With better treatment services being made available in the central psychiatric facilities of most African countries, the number of patients coming for treatment has increased rapidly. In 1971, Butabika mental hospital admitted and discharged just over 4000 patients, a figure very much higher than equivalent figures from mental hospitals of equal size in Britain, for example. Although large numbers of patients admitted come from central urban areas, it is still the case that many come from considerable distances. Admission to the psychiatric unit usually implies a fairly disturbed psychotic state, although physical violence and aggressivity is no longer the only criterion dictating referral to the psychiatric facility. Pressure of patient numbers, still relatively limited facilities, and a high proportion of organic, manic-depressive, and schizophrenic psychoses in the case material has meant that the therapeutic emphasis in almost every African inpatient facility of this sort has been on intensive psychopharmacological treatment, combined with physical therapies such as ECT. Limited staffing and the need for short periods of admission has meant that individual psychotherapeutic therapies, at least in the hospital setting, have been conspicuous by their absence. On the other hand, within many of these hospital facilities, considerable emphasis has been given to the establishment of therapeutic community systems and social interactional therapies. This has been greatly facilitated by the ease with which the African patient accepts co-operative group activity as a matter of course. The entire sub-Saharan culture is oriented toward therapeutic community techniques, and indeed such techniques are part of the day-to-day life of families, villages, and even larger groups.

Despite development and improvement of central facilities of this sort, it has become increasingly clear to psychiatrists and other personnel practicing in these areas that all they could do was provide an essentially emergency service for the needs of large numbers of people suffering from psychiatric illnesses of some severity. The urban population of capital cities could expect more than this, since their proximity to the psychiatric hospital and its concentration of staff enabled them to be readily admitted if necessary, but equally readily treated intensively and over longer periods of time in an out-patient setting. Busy out-patient departments have therefore developed very rapidly in association with the improving central urban psychiatric facilities. But these outpatient facilities, no more than the urban hospitals, have not been able to meet the needs of the rural African population scattered over wide areas. The necessity to decentralize has led increasingly to the appearance of small psychiatric units located in district and regional general hospitals. The total absence of any custom-built mental hospital or other psychiatric hospital-type units in rural Africa has meant that the appearance of psychiatry in the general hospital setting has been forced more by practical realities than by any particular fashion or theoretical attitude. Throughout East Africa, this pattern is now well-established with small peripheral psychiatric units strategically scattered over Uganda, Kenya, Tanzania, and Zambia. The in-patient component of these units is small, and the bulk of the work is done in out-patient and domiciliary settings. *Decentralization* of this sort has been achieved to greater or lesser degrees all over the black African area.

The main problem in developing such extended services has been the provision of professional staff. The need to upgrade mental hospital facilities in capital cities and in association with university departments of psychiatry has led to a concentration of the very few psychiatrists at the center. The desire to provide psychiatric skills peripherally appears to have had practical consequences for planners which, very broadly, have led to the planning and steady implementation of the decentralization of skills in three phases.

The first phase has been based on the concept of *delegation* of the traditional psychiatric-medical role to ancillary personnel. There is nothing new about this in the African situation, where for many years now a category of paramedical staff—medical assistants—has provided basic medical care in a variety of areas. Such people have been recruited from high schools and given a 3 or sometimes 4-year training programme in practical diagnosis and treatment. The reality of limited resources, both financial and medical, has led to such delegation of traditional medical skills being accepted without rancour and without much argument. However, like their more highly qualified medical colleagues, the medical assistants have been given little training in psychiatry. Recognizing these needs, most African countries have developed various programs of giving additional training in clinical psychiatry to various categories of nonmedical staff. In Zambia, this training has focused on the development of "psychiatric assistants"— mostly young men trained entirely in psychiatry (with some relevant physical medicine) over a period of 3 years. In Uganda, the emphasis has been on upgrading psychiatric nursing staff to the point where they have been able to take limited clinical responsibility for the diagnosis and treatment of patients with psychiatric disorders. In most African countries, until the arrival of medical staff in the 1950s and 1960s, mental hospitals were largely run by nursing staff and other paramedical staff, and these groups have had a long tradition of taking very much more responsibility for clinical care than their opposite numbers in more developed countries. Generally, they have proved exceedingly competent in so doing and have developed qualities of responsibility and initiative in a most striking way. Such personnel have proved to be the backbone of the new decentralized general hospital psychiatric units. In Uganda, these units are each headed by an upgraded psychiatrically qualified nurse who has had some years of experience in the central mental hospital facilities. Apart from routine administrative work, this nurse is responsible for the initial assessment and diagnosis of patients admitted to his unit, whether as in-patients or as out-patients. He also takes responsibility for initiating treatment, and is helped in doing this where necessary by the general duty medical officers working in other parts of the general hospital. Mature nurses and psychiatric assistants in this sort of setting have proved capable of responsible diagnosis and therapy with major psychopharmacological agents, and have also proved able, with some support from the general hospital medical facilities, of giving ECT. However, in most cases, it has been the practice to further support them by a system of visits undertaken by senior psychiatrists from the urban centres. Such visits, on a weekly or monthly basis, not only enable the clinical work of the preceding period to be reviewed and difficult clinical problems to be dealt with, but also provide for the continuing education of peripheral unit staff and the maintenance of high levels of morale. From the peripheral unit, it has become increasingly customary for a series of services to extend outward into the region and district. In Uganda, these forays have been made on bicycle by nurses-in-charge and their juniors, enabling small out-patient sessions to be held in remote dispensaries and a good deal of home visiting to be undertaken. In Zambia, mobile teams in four-wheel drive vehicles have undertaken this task. The rear compartment of these vehicles has been fitted up as a consulting room in which the records of patients can be kept. Such mobile clinics conduct roadside outpatient sessions, where new cases are seen and assessed, and where follow-up cases are given continuing care. In this way, practically the entire country has been covered by regular psychiatric services.

The second phase of this program involves the equipping of all medical graduates with considerably increased sophistication about psychiatry. The expanding medical schools noted in the introduction to this chapter have, over the past 10 to 12 years, developed intensive and extensive programs of undergraduate training in psychiatry which have been clearly influenced by the more sophisticated and imaginative curricula appearing in old-established medical schools in developed parts of the world. At the universities in Dakar, Ibadan, Kampala, Nairobi, Dar-es-Salaam, and Lusaka, the undergraduate medical student is now likely to spend between 300 and 400 hours in clinical psychiatry, with considerable emphasis on practical clinical experience and on taking responsibility for patient care under supervision. In most of these universities, psychiatry has become an examinable subject before the medical qualification is granted. Thus, in the last 3 or 4 years of the decade just ended, a quiet revolution has taken place in terms of the psychiatric knowledge and skills of general duty medical officers working in district and regional general hospitals and in smaller units, often in remote areas. The increasing availability of such well-trained medical men and women has meant that the paramedical auxiliary, running decentralized units, has found himself increasingly able to call on doctors in general hospitals without encountering hostility, which was the previous usual consequence of ignorance and anxiety. As new peripheral units are developed, it has proved increasingly possible to place these in the overall charge of a medical officer who can thus undertake psychiatric work as part of his general duties. Apart from anything else, these intensive undergraduate programs appear to have led to increasing recruitment of doctors into the postgraduate study of psychiatry.

The third phase of development is just commencing and this is the effort to train African psychiatrists in their own countries through local postgraduate residency programs. Such programs leading to local qualifications in psychiatry have been introduced recently in Nigeria and in Uganda, and not only enable African doctors to learn psychiatry in their own cultures and communities, but also prevent the loss of these doctors' services to their own countries while undertaking lengthy courses overseas. However, there are also considerable numbers of African doctors training in other countries, and most of these are likely to return in due course to take up positions as specialist psychiatrists in various areas. The need for expatriate personnel continues, especially in academic psychiatry, where the training of indigenous counterparts is exceedingly lengthy and time consuming.

Eventually, given a continuing supply of trained indigenous psychiatrists and the continuing economic and political development necessary to support them, one can foresee the spread of specialist psychiatric skills outside the main urban centers to the peripheral units where the specialist psychiatrist will become responsible for district or regional psychiatric services. When this occurs (and it has already started to occur in Zambia, Nigeria and certain other countries) one might envisage the district psychiatric services becoming fairly autonomous, staffed by African personnel with special and intimate knowledge of the language and culture of the district, and utilizing mobile teams of social workers and nurses to provide education and various forms of continuing care throughout extensive rural areas. As in the Western world,* traditional healers, formally or infor-

---

* By this is meant that the healing and caring role of priests, ministers-of-religion, and faith-healers in the Western world appears similar if not identical (at a higher level of sophistication) to that of the African traditional healer.

mally, will be increasingly associated with these services as their vital function "within-the-culture" of dealing with anxiety and other causes of crisis is recognized. The central urban facility will continue to exist, probably in increasingly close association with university departments of psychiatry, and, in addition to meeting the needs of the metropolis, will function as a reference facility for the rest of the country.

In addition to this basic development of services, various other systems of care have grown up in different African countries in response to insights about local needs and conditions. Thus the famous Aro Village complex in Nigeria is a traditional Yoruba village to which patients requiring psychiatric treatment come, and in which they lodge with villagers willing to earn some additional income from this source. Patients are accompanied by relatives, and during their stay in the village attend a village day hospital where various forms of therapy are available. The involvement of the relative in this process ensures that following discharge the family of the patient is well-informed as to the nature of his illness, and can be expected to continue to co-operate in follow-up. The village setting reduces the stigma of mental hospitalization, and maintains the patient in a community setting where normal interpersonal relationships can be fostered and developed. Attempts have been made to imitate this system in other parts of Africa with varying degrees of success. Generally, the tight village structure of Aro has been found difficult to replicate, and in many African countries the decision has been taken to construct villages specifically for psychiatric patients. In Tanzania, Dr. Charles Swift and his colleagues have developed several such villages, many of them built in previously unpopulated areas, providing village type accommodation for chronic patients and other patients where the patient can live with his family (and with nursing staff and their families), enjoying a fairly normal existence in a community where continuing psychiatric treatment is available. These villages in Tanzania have been greatly facilitated in their development by the Tanzanian concept of self-reliance and by the Government-sponsored programme of "Ujaama" villages, a term referring to the basic concept of communal self-help. Similar efforts are being made in Uganda and in other African countries, the emphasis being on treating acute patients or maintaining chronic patients in a life situation which is more realistic than a formal mental hospital. In the African setting, the extended family is still the most common form of familial organization, communal activities are highly valued, and decision-making by group consent is the rule. Thus village groups, whether they are diluted by nonpatient residents or not, seem to form viable entities in which the nature of the organization makes a major contribution to the social setting in which good mental health is likely to be fostered. Cultural factors have promoted this development, but also of importance is the availability of land and the fact that most Africans still live on the basis of a subsistence economy and are therefore able to produce their own food and other requirements from village lands. There are obvious economic advantages in this sort of organization, and another advantage is that the community can see that psychiatric patients are capable of self-support and of making a contribution toward the total society in a way which is not possible if psychiatric patients are routinely hidden away behind the walls of mental hospitals.

A great deal of development has yet to occur in Africa. There are pressures within the continent to imitate the developmental patterns of the West. At the same time Africans are increasingly aware of and proud of their culture, and Europeans working in Africa have come to recognise the enormous value of African social and community skills. With care and concern for local values, it seems more than possible that a psychiatry will develop in Africa which will have much to teach a world struggling to reassert the importance of the individual and the relationship between individuals.

REFERENCES

1. Boroffka, A.: Psychiatrie in nigeria. *Z. Neur. Psychiatr.* **176**:103–104, 1964.

2. Carothers, J. C.: *The African Mind in Health and Disease: A Study of Ethnopsychiatry*, Monograph series, World Health Organisation, Geneva, No. 17, 1953.

3. Commonwealth Foundation Occasional Paper No. IV: *The Delivery of Mental Health Care*, G. A. German and W. Kiernan, (Eds.), Commonwealth Foundation, London, 1969.

4. Dembovitz, N.: Psychiatry amongst West African troops. *J. Roy Army Med. Corps* **84**:70–74, 1945.

5. German, G. A. and Assael, M.: Achievement stress and psychiatric disorder amongst students in Uganda. *Israel Ann. Psychiatr.* **9**:30–38, 1971.

6. German, G. A.: Aspects of clinical psychiatry in sub-Saharan Africa. *Brit. J. Psychiatr.* **121**:461–479, 1972.

7. Giel, R. and Van Luijk, J. N.: Psychiatric morbidity in a small Ethiopian town. *Brit. J. Psychiatr.* **115**:149–162, 1969.

8. Hoorweg, J.: Africa (south of the Sahara). In *Psychology Around the World Today*, V. S. Sexton, and H. Misiak, (Eds.), Brooks/Cole Publishing Co., Monterey, 1973.

9. Jilek, W. G. and Jilek-Aall, L.: Transient psychoses in Africans. *Psychiatr. Clin.* **3**:337–364, 1970.

10. Kagwa, B. H.: Observations on the prevalence and types of mental diseases in East Africa. *E. Afr. Med. J.* **42**:673–682, 1965.

11. Kiev, A.: *Transcultural Psychiatry*, Free Press, New York, 1972.

12. Lambo, T. A.: Schizophrenia and borderline states. In *Transcultural Psychiatry, Ciba Foundation Symposium*, De Reuck and Porter, (Eds.), London, 1965.

13. Lambo, T. A.: Schizophrenia, its features and prognosis in the African. In *Deuxième Colloque Africain de Psychiatrie*, Paris, 1968.

14. Leighton, A. M., Lambo, T. A., Hughes, C. C., Leighton, D. C., Murphy, J. M., and Macklin, D. B.: *Psychiatric Disorder Amongst the Yoruba,* New York, 1963.

15. Mbanefo, S. E.: The general practitioner and psychiatry. In *Psychiatry and Mental Health Care in General Practice*, University of Ibadan, Department of Psychiatry and Neurology, 1971.

16. Meynert, T.: Amentia, die Verwirrtheit. *J. Psychiatr.* **9**:1–112, 1889.

17. Muhangi, J.: The nature and prevalence of psychotic states in elderly people in a rural area in Uganda. Paper read to Third Pan-African Psychiatric Workshop. Proceedings to be published. Mimeograph available from Department of Psychiatry, Makerere University, Kampala, 1971.

18. Murphy, H. B. M. and Raman, A. C.: The chronicity of schizophrenia in indigenous tropical peoples: Results of a twelve-year follow-up survey. *Brit. J. Psychiatr.* **118**:489–497, 1971.

19. Muwazi, E. M. and Trowell, H. C.: Neurological disease among African natives of Uganda: A review of 269 cases. *E. Afr. Med. J.* **21**:2–19, 1944.

20. Orley, J. H.: Cultural correlates of mental illness amongst the Baganda. Mimeograph, Department of Psychiatry, Makerere University, Kampala, 1968.

21. Orley, J. H.: *Culture and Mental Illness*, East African Publishing House, Nairobi, 1970, p. 24.

22. Prince, R.: The "Brain-fag" syndrome in Nigerian students. *J. Men. Sci.* **106**:559–570, 1960.

23. Prince, R.: The changing picture of depressive syndromes in Africa. Is it fact or diagnostic fashion? *Can. J. Afr. Stud.* **1**:177–192, 1968.

24. Proceedings of 2nd Pan-African Psychiatric Workshop: *Mental Health of Children in Developing Countries*, A. C. Raman, (Ed.), Association of Psychiatrists in Africa, Mauritius, 1970.

25. Shelley, H. M. and Watson, W. H.: An investigation concerning mental disorder in the Nyasaland natives. *J. Men. Sci.* **82**:701–730, 1936.

26. Stransky, E.: Zur Lehre von der Dementia praecox. *Cbl. Nervenheilk. Psychiatr.* **15**:1–19, 1904.

27. Stransky, E.: Zur Amentiafrage. *Cbl. Nervenheilk. Psychiatr.* **18**:809–816, 1907.

28. Tooth, G.: *Studies in Mental Illness in the Gold Coast*, London, 1950.

29. Vyncke, J. C.: *Psychoses et Nevroses en Afrique Centrale*, Académie royale des sciences coloniales, classe des sciences naturelles et médicales, Brussels, 1957.

NAME INDEX

Numbers in parentheses are reference numbers and show that an author's work is referred to although his name is not mentioned in the text.
Numbers in *italics* indicate the pages on which the full references appear.